HITLER'S
HOLOCAUST

GUIDO KNOPP

This documentary record is the legacy
of millions of victims
Simon Wiesenthal

First published in 2000 by C. Bertelsmann Verlag GmbH, Munich
under the title *Holokaust*.
This English translation first published in 2001 by
Sutton Publishing Limited · Phoenix Mill
Thrupp · Stroud · Gloucestershire · GL5 2BU

This paperback edition first published in 2004

Reprinted 2005, 2007

Research: Alexander Berkel, Silke Gampper, Christine Kisler
Translation: Angus McGeoch

British Library Cataloguing in Publication Data
A catalogue record for this book is available from the British
Library

ISBN 978-0-7509-3782-5

Typeset in 10/12.5 Galliard.
Typesetting and origination by
Sutton Publishing Limited.
Printed and bound in England by
J.H. Haynes & Co. Ltd, Sparkford.

HITLER'S
HOLOCAUST

GUIDO KNOPP

Translated by Angus McGeoch

SUTTON PUBLISHING

CONTENTS

PICTURE CREDITS

LIST OF ILLUSTRATONS

FOREWORD

I warmly welcome the publication in English of Guido Knopp's new book *Hitler's Holocaust*. As Guido Knopp himself points out, the book arises from an acclaimed television series recently shown in Germany and soon to be available to viewers in many other countries. I had the privilege of being part of an international team of advisers – including such prominent experts as Yehuda Bauer (Israel), Christopher Browning (USA), Eberhard Jäckel (Germany), Peter Longerich (Germany/Great Britain), and Peter Witte (Germany) – who helped to shape the series. The very first discussion I had in Munich with the producer, Maurice Philip Remy, convinced me of the seriousness and thoroughness with which he and his researchers, who were by then already scouring archives throughout the world (especially in the recently opened documentary collections in eastern Europe), were undertaking the task. And when I learnt that Guido Knopp, winner of numerous awards for earlier outstanding TV documentaries, would direct the production for ZDF (the German equivalent of BBC2) I had no doubt that the series would be a major success.

This book is able to draw upon the extensive research of the team of researchers working for the television series as well as the notable advances in international scholarship made in recent years by historians of the Holocaust. Since the opening of the archives in eastern Europe following the collapse of the Soviet bloc, research on the Holocaust has been transformed in scope, leading to a great extension of knowledge. Important new monographs have been written, some of the most significant by younger German scholars, casting new light on the emergence of the 'Final Solution' (as the Nazis called the murder of the Jews). Much of this new research is only available in detailed studies whose readership is largely confined to specialists. It is among the great merits of Guido Knopp's book that it is able, not least through the vivid and readable style he deploys, to make the findings of this extremely valuable scholarly research accessible to a wide readership.

In any historical field where issues of great complexity are concerned, differences in interpretation are inevitable. Leading historians of the Holocaust have, in fact, reached wide agreement on many significant points of interpretation. But the character and limitations of the archival remnants of this mega-crime against humanity mean that views will continue to vary on some important issues – such as the nature and timing of the decision (or decisions) to implement the Final Solution. There was disagreement on this and some other still open questions even among the group of expert consultants on the television series; on some points Guido Knopp and I would see things differently. Nonetheless, I admire the way his book shows excellent command of the latest scholarship which is presented to a wider public in a fair, balanced, and accessible way. The author skilfully weaves often highly complex and detailed academic findings into a lucidly written account which is horrifying, dramatic, and moving while remaining free of pathos. The many eye-witness accounts of victims presented are intensely harrowing. The photographic material is gripping in its horrific depictions. And the assembled testimony of perpetrators alongside the almost unbelievably inhumane documentary extracts cited from Nazi leaders and bureaucratic 'desk-top murderers' offer insights into warped mentalities which sometimes seem to come from a strange world and a bygone age – but in fact existed in a highly modern state and society not far away and not long ago.

To read Guido Knopp's book poses the question with renewed sharpness: what motive could anyone possibly have for wishing to deny that such terrible events happened? The precision with which the author has pieced together the evidence in constructing such a compelling picture of this total collapse of civilisation highlights once more not only the historical absurdity but also the unstated prejudice that lie behind Holocaust denial. Only the wilfully perverse could refuse to accept that which the book so excellently portrays: the enormity of this crime against humanity, the magnitude of the disaster suffered by the Jews of Europe.

Beyond the strictly historical questions, the moral dimension of the Holocaust remains inescapable. And here it is, perhaps, of significance that the book and the television series from which it emanated are German products. No country has explored more thoroughly than has Germany the most painful and distressing parts of its recent history. Guido Knopp and his co-authors are of a German generation to which can be attributed no culpability for what took place under Hitler. But the book testifies to the honesty and openness with which they approach this darkest episode in their country's history, and the responsibility they feel in facing up to that history. That way has led to, and will continue to lead to, positive shifts in mentalities and a heightened sense of public morality. In bringing a deepened awareness of the Holocaust to a wider public, this book is making its own contribution to such advances, both within Germany and elsewhere.

Hitler's Holocaust is a well-researched and graphically written account of how the people of a civilised and cultured country could become involved in the perpetration of inhumanity on a gross scale. It deserves the widest possible readership. I am grateful for the opportunity to add this foreword to the English edition, and wish Guido Knopp's book every success.

Ian Kershaw
2001

INTRODUCTION

This book came into being as a result of the research for a
television series which is being broadcast all over the world:
Hitler's Holocaust – probably the most comprehensive attempt so
far to present this crime against humanity through the medium of
documentary film. For two years researchers working on the
project looked for new material in over fifty archives, from
Washington to Moscow, viewed millions of feet of film, and
examined and evaluated thousands of original documents. In this
process they came upon new sources which had not hitherto been
available to researchers. Often they are only fragments – but even
the smallest find can help to fill in the famous blank areas in the
story. There is little that is more revealing, for example, than
scenes filmed in secret by an amateur cameraman, of the ghetto, of
pogroms and the public harassing of Jews, of transportation to the
extermination camps. And many of these newly discovered sources
are sometimes like pieces of mosaic which help academics to fill
gaps in the documentary record.

The present book has also benefited from this preliminary work.
Like the television series, it is divided into six chapters: from
Hitler's assault on the Soviet Union, which marks the beginning
of the Holocaust, up to the liberation of the concentration camps
in 1945. We were able to make use of interviews with over 500
contemporary eye-witnesses – often Jewish survivors who, in the
last years of their lives, have found the strength to testify for the
first time – people who now live in many different countries: in
Russia, Germany, Lithuania, Latvia, Denmark, Poland, Israel,
South Africa, Canada, Hungary, Austria, the Netherlands, Slovakia
and the United States. They are still alive, they can still be
questioned. In ten more years this last chance will have gone for
ever. And this is also true of the dozen or so perpetrators who
agreed to be interviewed.

That is why this project comes at an opportune moment. It is only in the last few years that we have had free access to archives in Eastern Europe, where the Holocaust took place. It has at last been possible not only to examine previously unpublished documents but also to look at film never shown before.

What the television series attempts to achieve is also reflected to an equal extent in the book: a concern for authenticity. It was important to place every foot of film, every newly found document and every eye-witness account in its precise historical context – in its correct period in time and its exact location.

No crime in the long history of humankind has so appalled us, none so stubbornly resists to this day all attempts at explanation. Why it could all happen remains an open question. If, however, we try to show *what* happened and by what means it was done, then this will actually help to answer the question about the reasons. It is in this sense that the film series and the book both represent an attempt at a historical summing-up – one which we want to bring to the attention of as many people as possible.

Manhunt

It started with the manhunt. In the early hours of 22 June 1941, while Hitler's mouthpiece, Goebbels, tried to sell the invasion of Stalin's empire as a preventive war, the Wehrmacht's divisions were thrusting deep into the interior of the Soviet Union. In their wake came the so-called *Einsatzgruppen* or 'action squads': 3,000 men who carried out their murderous assignment to the rear of the front line. Their primary objective was the extermination of the 'Jewish-Bolshevist intelligentsia'. Their orders were unambiguous and applied chiefly to 'Jews in party or government positions'. Hitler had repeatedly hammered home to his henchmen that 'Bolshevism' and 'Jewry' were synonymous. In the very first days of the war against Russia thousands of Jews had been shot by the *Einsatzgruppen*; furthermore, these were predominantly men of military age.

For Hitler, this was the war he had long dreamed of: a war of annihilation aimed at gaining 'living-space in the east', the spawn of his deluded notion of a great Germanic empire stretching from the Atlantic to the Urals. The indigenous population was to be expelled, dispersed, 'racially drained', 'scrapped' – to use the sinister vocabulary of Himmler's 'General Plan East'.

While German armoured divisions were encircling entire Soviet armies, Himmler's murder squads followed in the bloody tracks of the NKVD. The Soviet secret service headed by Lavrenti Beria had killed tens of thousands of people, most of them belonging to non-Russian nationalities. Now, in the Ukraine, Lithuania and Latvia, where pogroms had not been uncommon in the past, the German occupiers kindled the hatred of the local populations and watched them commit appalling massacres of the Jewish population, who for no reason were made the all-purpose scapegoats.

By mid-June the Germans had penetrated so deep into Russian territory that in the Führer's eastern headquarters the mistaken impression arose that the war was already won. In the 'Wolf's Lair', as it was known, the spoils were divided. Himmler was to maintain civil order. More than 30,000 men, battalions of the *Ordnungspolizei* (Order Police) and selected formations of the *Waffen-SS* (Military SS), were on hand for the 'pacification' of the region, as it was cynically termed. As Hitler saw it, the partisan war proclaimed by Stalin actually benefited them: 'It gives us the opportunity to wipe out anyone who opposes us.' Those receiving the orders knew who the principal targets were.

Yet the Nazi dictator had underestimated the Soviets' capacity for waging war. It was in the Pripyet Marshes that the first noteworthy actions were carried out behind the lines. With the deployment of the SS on the spot the manhunt gained a new dimension. For the first time large numbers of Jewish women were among the victims. A report at the end of July noted drily: '800 Jews and Jewesses shot, aged from 16 to 60.'

From mid-August onward, for the first time, even children were being killed, as they were in the Ukrainian town of Byelaya-Tserkov, on the instructions of Field-Marshal von Reichenau. This is the devastating report by SS-*Obersturmführer* August Häfner, who was in charge of the shooting: 'The children were lifted down from the convoy trucks. They were made to stand above the pit and then shot. If we hit them, we hit them.'

It was not only in Byelaya-Tserkov that units of the Wehrmacht were brought in to assist with mass shootings, at other places soldiers were witnesses – and more. Not all of them were guilty of these crimes, not a great many even, but too many – especially in the towns. Some reacted with horror, others with disgust. Only a few protested. Hardly anyone enquired about the reasons. Quite a number never heard anything about the crimes, being exclusively occupied with their own survival. Then again there were others who applauded the murderous activities of the *Einsatzgruppen*, urged the perpetrators on and humiliated the victims at the very moment of their death. Sometimes regular soldiers committed murder themselves – often, though not always, on orders from above. In letters to relatives and friends at home there is comparatively little to be found about this first phase of the murder of Jews. But when the soldiers came home on leave they told of what they had seen, often whispering behind their hands. In this way news of the mass shootings in the east gradually trickled through.

Decision

It was probably in September 1941 that Hitler made his decision to murder every Jew in Europe. The dictator was the driving force in setting the machinery in motion towards industrialised mass killing; he was the central authority. In matters relating to the Jews he made all the important decisions, but always remained dependent on executives like Himmler and Heydrich – men with a fatal eagerness to obey, and with the ability to get inside the mind of the tyrant, to penetrate his criminal psyche, to divine his presumed wishes and to fulfil them.

The deportation of Jews from Germany or occupied Poland to the conquered lands to the east was not actually meant to begin until after the Soviet Union had been defeated. Hitler wanted to achieve his victory over Stalin by autumn 1941 at the latest.

At first his gamble in the east seemed to have paid off. The war against Russia was going according to plan, and the opposition appeared to have little to put up against the whole weight of the German onslaught, while the death-squads of the SS and the police went on with their killing behind the lines. But only a few weeks later the certainty of victory evaporated. The strength of Soviet resistance had been underestimated. The war would last longer than expected. Hitler's hatred of the Jews became more intense. He held them solely responsible for his own crimes: the war and the thousands of deaths at the Front.

His obsessive vision of confronting an 'international Jewish conspiracy' was reinforced when Great Britain and the USA formulated the common objective of putting an end to the Nazi tyranny once and for all. The dictator now agreed with the wish of his henchmen Heydrich and Goebbels, to begin the deportation of Jews from Germany, Austria and the 'Protectorate of Bohemia and Moravia', as the occupied region of Czechoslovakia was called. They were to be 'resettled' in areas where at that very moment the Jewish population – men, women and children – was being annihilated without distinction. Deportation amounted to a death-sentence. At the same time work started on building the death camps.

Ghetto

What did this mean for the Jews in Germany? Sometimes the horror came to them with correct and cultivated manners. For example, the Gestapo officials whose job was to fetch seven families from what was designated a 'Jewish dwelling' on Berlin's elegant Kurfürstendamm, introduced themselves politely, requested them to bring their luggage and accompanied them to a waiting furniture-van. It was a journey that would end in death.

Other Jewish families received a letter couched in fine language, addressed to the local branch of the Reich Jewish Association, asking them on a certain day to 'make themselves available for emigration transport'. Either on foot or in the last compartment of the tram (still accessible to them) they made their own way to the nominated collection point – often in broad daylight, under the eyes of all. There was an eerie normality about the exodus of the German Jews from Hitler's Reich, organised by officialdom and accompanied by bureaucratic formalities. From the autumn of 1941 onward more than 130,000 German Jews were forced to begin the journey which, for the overwhelming majority of them, had no return. Millions of victims from the occupied or allied countries followed their fated path. Very few of them had any idea what unspeakable misery would await them. To calm their fears they were told about labour camps or agricultural estates, and were tricked with forged greetings cards from fellow-victims who had already been dragged off. Instead, the deportees found themselves to begin with in the ghettos of cities like Łódz or Riga. They were waiting-rooms of death. Even someone who survived the misery, hunger and cold, slave labour in the ghetto factories, random shootings and deadly epidemics in the overcrowded slums, was destined for death. With grim regularity human transports arrived in newly constructed extermination sites not far from the ghettos, where murder was being committed with industrial efficiency. From 1942 onward countless deportation trains ran non-stop directly into the unloading bays of the death camps.

Death-factory

Death from overwork, cold, hunger or shooting – in the long run all these methods of killing appeared too troublesome to the perpetrators. So it was that on 5 September 1941, in Block 11 at Auschwitz, a test was set up: on that day for the first time the SS used a preparation of hydrocyanic acid called 'Zyklon B', on human beings – 'successfully', as *Hauptsturmführer* Rudolf Höss noted with satisfaction. Later he remarked: 'I must say frankly, the gassing had a reassuring effect on me, since of course in the foreseeable future a start would have to be made on the mass extermination of the Jews. I always dreaded the shootings. Now I was reassured that we would all be spared these blood-baths.' Nearly 400 Soviet soldiers and around 300 sick Polish prisoners met their death in the first experimental gassings at Auschwitz. The method for the impending industrialised killing had been discovered – faster, cheaper and quieter than the originator of the racial mania himself could ever have dreamed.

While the German advance on the eastern front had come to a standstill, while Rommel in North Africa had captured Tobruk but was driven back at El Alamein, the decision on the 'Final Solution of the Jewish Question' was put into effect. On 26 March 1942 the first trainload of Jewish women from Slovakia, organised by Adolf Eichmann, arrived at Auschwitz. Their death-sentence had been passed; only the execution was – for the moment – postponed. There was still insufficient capacity in the human slaughterhouse. Three months later this 'bottleneck' had also been overcome. The new camp complex of Auschwitz–Birkenau with its underground gas-chambers I and II was 'ready for operation'.

On 14 July 1942 Himmler was summoned to the Führer's headquarters. Hitler put pressure on his henchman: the 'Final Solution' must be completed by the end of the year! The *Reichsführer-SS* then proceeded to carry out an inspection of Auschwitz. The 'visitors' programme' included the selection and gassing of a trainload of Jews from Holland. The process of extermination was followed with close attention by Himmler. To the very last moment the murderers tried to lull their victims into a false sense of security. The undressing-rooms adjacent to the gas-chambers had signs on them like 'Shower' and 'For Disinfecting'. It was recommended to the victims that they should hang up their clothes and remember the number of the hook – so that they could find their things again later. Then an SS man chivvied them along: 'Hurry up, the food and coffee are getting cold.'

The presence of prisoners in the *Sonderkommando* or 'special detachment' helping the camp staff, provided the victims with further comfort – they were Jews like themselves. 'The people had been washed and were still smiling. We had to keep quiet about what was going to happen to them', recalls Jehoshua Rosenblum, a survivor of the *Sonderkommando*: '. . . and when the last one had gone into the gas-chamber, the door was closed and immediately two SS men threw in the Zyklon B through an opening in the roof.' The amount needed for a killing operation: 5 kilograms – for 1,500 people. 'After a while I heard piercing screams from inside, people banging on the door, wails and groans . . . The noise, which to start with grew louder and more unmistakable, died down minute by minute and soon changed into a gasping death-rattle from hundreds of throats. The gas had penetrated their lungs and caused a paralysis of the respiratory system', reports Filip Müller, another prisoner in the *Sonderkommando*.

After 15 or 20 minutes the killing-operation was over. With their bare hands the members of the *Sonderkommando* dragged the dead bodies from the gas-chamber and took them to the cremation area. Before they were thrown into the fire, specialist 'work-groups' went into action. The gold fillings were removed from the teeth of the dead, and the women's hair was cut off. The gold fillings were melted down and sent to the Reichsbank in the form of gold ingots.

Himmler was satisfied with the whole operation. Before he left an informal party was held, at which Himmler must obviously have spoken about the reality of Auschwitz. Shortly afterwards, the Breslau industrialist, Eduard Schulte, got to hear of this conversation by roundabout means. He was a man with a conscience. Without delay he boarded a train bound for Switzerland. In Geneva he secretly passed the information on to two contacts in the Jewish community. Through them the horrifying news reached the World Jewish Congress. 'We discussed it for over six hours. Is it possible that millions of Jews are being put to death? And it was another two days before we became convinced that it was not only possible but even probable', we are told by Gerhart Riegner, at that time head of the Swiss section of the Congress. For a long time the mass murder had been bitter reality: not only in Auschwitz, but in Chelmno, Belzec, Sobibor, Treblinka and Maly Trostinets near Minsk, Jews were being systematically gassed. It was only in 1943 that Auschwitz–Birkenau became the central human abattoir of the regime – and thus the symbol for the entire Holocaust.

Those human beings who, after an agonising train journey, were selected for labour on arrival in the sidings of a concentration camp, were for the most part condemned to a wretched and protracted death. Shipped to the camp like cattle, the prisoners were first registered and marked with a tattoo. 'From then on we were just numbers', recalls Helena Gombosovà, from Slovakia. What followed was weeks of pointlessly excruciating physical exercises, ruthless drilling and beatings – endless beatings. In primitive wooden barracks, originally intended to house 52 horses each, 800 people were now crammed. The huts were so infested with rats and lice that diseases quickly developed, especially typhus. This meant that time and again the occupants of entire blocks were wiped out, from one day to the next. After a few hours of fitful semi-sleep, the daily routine began before dawn with a head-count. The bodies of those who had died during the night were thrown out of the huts. Those prisoners fit for work headed off for gravel-pits, quarries, farms and arms factories in the vicinity. The annihilation of the Jews through labour was an extremely profitable business for the SS. The average life expectancy was nine months, the proceeds from 'hiring out' was 6 marks per day, less costs of feeding and accommodation – 6 pfennigs per day. Net profit 1,631 Reichsmarks per labour-slave!

By the middle of 1943 the eventual defeat of the Third Reich had become inevitable – yet in Auschwitz the everyday killing routine continued unchanged. The military setbacks only increased Hitler's determination to annihilate every Jew in Europe. The German armed forces were ordered by the dictator no longer to fight exclusively for the 'final victory', but also – largely without their knowledge – for another reason: in order to cover up the Holocaust. This second war within a war was one Hitler wanted to win at all costs.

Resistance

Why was Auschwitz repeatedly photographed by the Allies, but never bombed? On 20 August 1944 three prisoners looked up into the sky above Auschwitz, full of hope. From the south a deep drone could be heard – planes of the US 15th Bomber Squadron. But once again the bombs dropped elsewhere, this time on the fuel refineries of Monowitz, only 5 miles from the death-camp. 'I simply cannot understand why they didn't help us', complains ex-prisoner Andras Lorenczi. He and many of his fellow-victims had no greater desire than to be bombed by the Americans. 'At least they could have hit the crematoria', says Lorenczi, 'then maybe a few thousand would have had to die. But we were so familiar with death, anyway.' Bombs on Auschwitz? The destruction of the scene of the crime as a protest against the crime?

By October 1944 still no bombs had been dropped on Auschwitz, and Nahum Goldmann of the World Jewish Congress made a last attempt to change the minds of the military. After the deputy US Secretary of Defence, John McLoy, had fobbed him off with the misleading information that it was the British who made the decisions about bombing-targets in Europe, Goldmann turned to the British Air-Marshal Dill, who stated bluntly that 'the British had to conserve their bombs for military targets, and that the only salvation for the Jews lay in the Allies winning the war'.

There were other forms of resistance – even in Germany. Despite all the attempts to keep it secret, the mass murder provoked courageous and desperate opposition. The people who deserve to be rescued from oblivion are the courageous men and women who put their own lives in danger to save their Jewish fellow-citizens: from officers in military counter-intelligence (the Abwehr), who smuggled Jews into Switzerland in the guise of agents, through to all those who provided food and hiding-places for the more than 6,000 Berlin Jews who went underground. 'He who saves but one life saves the whole world' – this wise saying from the Talmud is true of others besides Oscar Schindler.

From the study of letters and Wehrmacht orders it can be proved today that even some members of the circle who plotted to kill Hitler on 20 June 1944 were involved in the Holocaust – as accessories and, regrettably, as perpetrators. The case of General von Stülpnagel, for example, who in 1941 advocated the war of annihilation and also played an active part in the attempted coup in 1944, shows the gaping gulf that can sometimes exist between reality and the idealised view of it.

Most dramatic of all was the resistance by the Jews themselves. It began belatedly. 'People simply didn't want to believe it', recalls Marek Edelmann, one of the leaders of the Jewish uprising in Warsaw. Not until orders were given for the final 'clearing' of the ghetto did the victims make a stand. They fought bravely and desperately and forced the SS to keep calling in reinforcements and heavy weapons. The unequal battle lasted three weeks. In the end the former ghetto was left a smoking ruin. The superior arms of the German culprits had won – as they did in all other rebellions in ghettos and camps, in Warsaw or Sobibor. Yet the message from the victims, that they would not be led like lambs to the slaughter, remains with us.

The history of resistance against the Holocaust also throws up the pressing question as to why, in the face of the monstrosity of this crime, there was no massive protest within Germany. Only on one isolated occasion was there any kind of public demonstration. In February 1943, when the last Berlin Jews were being deported, their non-Jewish friends and relatives protested for several days outside the collection point in Rosenstrasse and forced the regime to release 1,500 men and women from 'mixed marriages'. This 'rebellion of the heart' was successful. But it remained an exception.

Liberation

In the spring of 1945, when Allied troops reached the concentration camps, the martyrdom which had lasted for years came to an end. From camps within Germany the Allies were able to release hardly more than 50,000 Jewish survivors. Almost six million people had lost their lives. What the soldiers saw in the camps was beyond all imagining: heaps of corpses the height of a man lined the roads. Draped in rags, the few survivors gazed at their liberators with expressionless eyes.

'They just lay there and stared at us. And we stared back', remembers the British colonel, William Roach, whose unit occupied the concentration camp at Bergen–Belsen in north-west Germany. A horrified outcry went around the world, when pictures from the camps showed inconceivable horrors. Yet these were 'only' concentration camps. There were no pictures from the extermination camps, which lay far to the east, mainly in Poland.

In the last twelve months of the war Hitler's henchmen, of greater or lesser importance, had staged the final act of this horrific drama, in which they tried to drag their victims to destruction with them. In the spring of 1944 the long arm of the Holocaust reached Hungary, the only country in Europe in which the Jewish population had so far remained spared. In just twelve weeks 437,000 Hungarian Jews were deported to Auschwitz. Most of them were murdered immediately. By 1944 Auschwitz was no longer a secret; the Hungarian tragedy was played out in the full light of day. Even now the feeling has never left the survivors that the world abandoned them to their fate.

When the Allied armies reached German territory, Heinrich Himmler issued the order that the inmates of the camps located in the east were to be marched back into Germany. Not one must fall into Soviet hands alive. Tens of thousands of half-dead people dragged themselves westwards on these death-marches. They were heading for German or Austrian camps: Mauthausen, Flossenbürg, Dachau, Buchenwald, Sachsenhausen, Dora-Mittelbau, Neuengamme and Bergen–Belsen – which turned into ante-rooms of hell. Crammed into the smallest of spaces, the victims spent the final hours of the regime in a race between death and liberation. The guards watched the prisoners dying from hunger and disease. When the Allies reached the concentration camps, they were dumbfounded at the scale of the horror. It was something which – despite knowledge of the camps' existence – no-one had thought possible.

Many victims remained silent, often for decades. Sometimes not even their children knew what sufferings a father or mother had been through. Not until today, at the end of their lives, have many found the courage to talk about their torment, and to provide a testimony for posterity. The way back to the past is painful, yet there are some for whom it is bound up with the hope that by taking it they can contribute to ensuring that what once happened is never repeated. To this day the survivors bear the scars of the Holocaust on their bodies and in their souls. Their liberation has not been able to free them from that.

Consequences

Today, when we put the question of guilt for all this to a representative sample of Germans (and Austrians), the majority of those questioned reply that 'Hitler', 'his henchmen' or 'the SS' were responsible for the mass murder. Only a minority place the blame with 'the Germans as a whole'.

However, everyone *did* contribute their part of it. There is no doubt that Hitler was the prime mover. Without Hitler there would probably have been no invasion of the Soviet Union, without Hitler there would have been no Holocaust. This does not mean that the guilt can be shifted on to one individual. Yet it was only Hitler's criminal energy that released the criminal energy of others. Hitler had an iron grip on his henchmen. They carried out what the dictator ordained – or what in their view the Führer had in mind. The murder of the Jews did not result from a sequence of uncoordinated bureaucratic measures within the dictatorship, but was a state-organised crime deliberately staged by Hitler. Hitler not only set the killing in motion, he also managed it, through his delegate Heinrich Himmler.

This does not mean the accomplices are acquitted – quite the contrary. Hitler's Holocaust was carried out by many little Hitlers – hundreds of thousands of willing executioners, who later pleaded that they were under orders – as a rule they were not psychopaths, but perfectly normal, 'ordinary' men. What the latest detailed research reveals is terrifying. It shows how thin is the veneer which separates human beings from the inhuman beings who are prepared, apparently without a second thought, to slaughter their fellow creatures. For what motivated them was not only and not exclusively a murderous anti-Semitism. Rather, it was the opportunity, which a satanic regime had offered them, of indulging their basest and most repulsive instincts. Millions of people, not only in Germany, looked on and looked away. Millions certainly knew enough to understand quite clearly that they did not want to know any more.

This was possible in Germany – and if there, then it is possible anywhere. Genocide in the twentieth century has not been restricted to Germany: the murder of millions was committed in Stalin's gulag, in Cambodia and in China. What makes the Jewish Holocaust so unparalleled in history is the industrialised manner in which the deed was carried out. Those of us Germans who were born after the war cannot be held responsible for the Holocaust. But we are all the more responsible for the memory of it. Responsibility means making oneself fully open to history.

My thanks are due to Eberhard Jäckel for casting a critical eye over the whole book. My thanks also go to Ian Kershaw for his many excellent suggestions. I thank my co-authors Vanessa von

Bassewitz, Jörg Müllner, Peter Hartl, Michaela Liechtenstein, Christian Deick and Friederike Dreykluft, who provided me with superb drafts – and above all Maurice Philip Remy who, as producer and originator of the television series, did invaluable preparatory work.

CHAPTER ONE

MANHUNT

KNOPP/VON BASSEWITZ

> Anti-Semitism on purely emotional grounds will find its final expression in the form of pogroms. However, rational anti-Semitism must lead to a carefully planned legal curbing and eradication of Jewish privilege . . . though its final, unalterable objective must be the removal of the Jews altogether.
>
> *Hitler in a letter, 1919*

The rattle of rifle salvoes was swallowed up in the wide expanse of the dunes. On the white sands south of the lighthouse at Liepaja in Latvia (then known by the Germans as Libau) hundreds of people were gathered – German occupation troops, and Latvians as well. What had drawn them there was certainly not the beauty of the Baltic Sea, sparkling in the evening sun. On the grass-covered dunes there was a bustle of activity. The crowd of rubbernecks watched as grey Wehrmacht trucks struggled with engines howling, through deep sand on the track across the dunes. On their open platforms, crammed tightly together, stood men on whose jackets were patches of bright yellow fabric. When the vehicles halted, an order rang out causing a stir on the truck platforms. Hurriedly but awkwardly, the men jumped down off the trucks. These civilians seemed strangely bemused as they staggered, wordless and uncomplaining, through the dunes – forced to hurry along by the guards with kicks and blows from their rifle-butts. '*Achtung!* The next two groups!' a businesslike German voice ordered. In groups of five the prisoners were driven to the edge of a deep pit and then forced to jump down into it. There they stood side by side, motionless. No-one put up a fight, there were no despairing cries. Above them, at the edge of the pit, militiamen of Latvia's 'self-defence force' raised their carbines to their right shoulder. A few seconds to aim, then the crack of a salvo, felling the men in the pit. Only a few yards away, the next group of five had watched it all – there can be no doubt at all that these men, too, knew what was about to happen to them.

In Libau, in July 1941, the shooting of hostages was a daily occurrence. Since 29 June the town with its naval harbour had been in German hands – following the Wehrmacht's invasion of the Soviet Union, it had only taken a week to defeat the town's defenders – Soviet sailors and the militia formed from workers in the Torsmare dockyard. But there were still exchanges of fire between German occupiers and scattered defenders. Reason enough for the men of *Einsatzkommando 2* to 'pacify' the town of Libau with 'the most ruthless of methods', as the orders put it. A call for assistance had come from the town commandant, a lieutenant-commander in the German navy. It was he in fact who had announced the draconian reprisals: 'For each individual attempted assault, act of sabotage or looting, ten of the hostages in German hands are to be shot.' The first 'hostages' were shot on 4 July with the assistance of the SS component of *Einsatzgruppe 2* – they were 47 Jews and five Latvian communists. Three days later the local commandant raised the number of hostages to be shot in reprisal to 100 for each German soldier wounded.

The German *Einsatzkommandos* – Hitler's willing executioners in the struggle against the 'international Jewish–Bolshevist enemy' – knew exactly who were to be selected as hostages: the Jews of the town that had just been captured. So far, their victims were still Jewish men 'capable of bearing arms' – those were the orders they had received. As yet, women, children and the old were spared.

In the night of 17–18 June Russian patrols again made probes into German Reich territory and could only be driven back after a prolonged exchange of fire. This means that the time has now come when it is necessary to take action against this plot by the Jewish and Anglo-Saxon warmongers, and those, also Jewish, who hold power in the central Bolshevist government in Moscow.

Adolf Hitler, 22 June 1941

I remember the Germans marching in, in the summer of 1941. We fled to a village and hid there. Then the Lithuanians with white armbands – they were the ones who killed Jews – immediately began to torment us, to take everything from us, to beat us up and kill our children. They thought that all Jews were communists and had to be stamped out.

Rozèle Goldenstein, Lithuanian Jew

My father went down the street to find out whether there was still some way to escape, and he disappeared. We never saw him again and I presume he was dragged off somewhere by the Lithuanians or was shot. No-one saw him again and no-one knows what became of him.

Zvi Katz, Lithuanian Jew

Teams of thugs combed the houses in search of hostages; young Jewish men were picked up on the streets without warning – they were easy prey for their pursuers, because a decree by the local commandant on 5 July obliged Jews to wear a patch of yellow cloth on their chest and back. It was around this time that Fanny Segal, then a sixteen-year-old high-school girl, lost her father – he had suspected that terrible things were in store for the Jews of Libau. 'One day he came home and told my mother that they were digging graves by the sea. "I think those graves are for us", he said.' His fears were realised on 8 July, as Fanny Segal recalls: 'We were working in an army camp outside Libau. At five o'clock the Germans took us back to Libau where we were told we had to apply for work permits. We went to the centre of town. There was a big hall in a big building there. There were several hundred of us, and suddenly an order came: 'All the men outside!' My father began to cry; he kissed me and gave me his watch. He knew it was the end.' A total of 1,000 Jewish men were executed in Libau in the first month of German occupation, by *Einsatzgruppen* and the Latvian 'self-defence force'.

There were other Libaus everywhere behind the German front line in that summer of 1941. Only a few days after the invasion of the Soviet Union on 22 June 1941 Hitler's Wehrmacht had rolled across the western border region of the vast Red empire, and countless Jews were suddenly confronted with a German occupation which they could not yet assess, but which they would soon come to know in all its horror. In the summer of 1941 it looked as though nothing could halt the German war-machine that had become so accustomed to victory. Virtually everything was going as planned. Armoured columns had pushed across the River Bug on five undamaged bridges and, along the entire front, crushed the Soviet troops stationed in the border region. The swift armoured advance was followed up by the infantry divisions. Within two days the Army Group North reached the Lithuanian city of Vilnius. Units of the Army Group Centre also advanced at breakneck speed. The 3rd Panzer Division under General Model only took six days to cover the 265 miles from Brest-Litovsk, near the Polish border, to Bobruysk in Byelorussia; on 27 June they set a record of 69 miles in one day. The Blitzkrieg strategy perfected in Poland and in the French campaign seemed to be bringing success even in the wide open spaces of Russia. For one thing was clear to everyone involved: a swift advance was necessary if the war objectives were to be achieved before the onset of the Russian winter – the Germans only had two months left before the annual autumn rains turned the Russian soil into an endless morass, and mud would hamper the progress of the tanks.

The army which marched into Russia on 22 June 1941 was the largest force in history to be assembled for a single campaign: almost 3.2 million soldiers, divided into seven armies, four armoured groups with 3,580 tanks, 7,184 artillery pieces, 600,000 trucks, 750,000 horses, and three *Luftflotten* comprising more than 2,000 aircraft. At 3.15 a.m. on the morning of 22 June 1941, this mighty war-machine attacked along a front 960 miles in length – from the Memel estuary on the Baltic to the Black Sea.

There is probably not a German soldier left who doubts that in the event of a successful Bolshevist invasion of Europe, the Jews would have wiped out absolutely everything German. It is all the more incomprehensible, then, that in a detachment which shot 7 Jews on a patrol, men still asked why they were shot. . . . If a patrol finds out that in a village the mood among the population is expectant and anxious, and in that village you wipe out the Jews and their Bolshevist supporters, then in a very short time you will sense a sigh of relief in the village. . . . There are no compromises in this, only a very clear and unambiguous solution, and that is, especially here in the east, the complete annihilation of our enemies. These enemies are, however, no longer human beings in the European cultural sense, but animals who from an early age have been brought up and trained as criminals. And as such they must be eradicated.

Situation report by Generalmajor von Bechtolsheim,
commandant in Ruthenia, 10 October 1941

The twenty-year-old Polish Jew, Arnold Arluk, still felt secure in his little home town of Lida in northern Poland, for Lida lay in the Soviet-occupied part of the country. Arluk knew nothing of the plans and strength of the Wehrmacht, which stood at the ready on the other side of the demarcation line. But what he saw of the Red Army in Lida impressed him: heavy tanks and artillery reinforced the Soviet garrison which had been stationed there since September 1939. The whole town was completely moulded by the military presence. By night trains loaded with military equipment rumbled westward. 'We knew something was up'. Arluk remembers. He had learned from broadcasts by Britain's BBC that German troops were massing behind the River Bug, which formed the frontier. Yet when the Germans did indeed strike out on Sunday 22 June 1941, he was taken completely by surprise. It was only some hours after the attack that he – like the rest of the Soviet population – heard that the war had begun. The 6 a.m. news from Radio Moscow still made no announcement about the attack on Russia which had already taken place. It was not until nearly midday that the invasion by Hitler's troops was revealed on Radio Moscow to the Soviet population, and then it was not done by Stalin himself but by the Soviet Foreign Minister, Molotov, in the General Secretary's name: 'At 4 a.m. today German troops attacked our country without the slightest warning and without a formal declaration of war. Our cause is just. The enemy will be defeated. Victory will be ours.'

The second surprise for Arnold Arluk was the speed of the German advance. The fighting did not last long. Arluk was amazed to see how the Wehrmacht moved from Bialystok towards Minsk 'as though out for a stroll'. In his home town the Soviet army was in disarray – and suddenly the garrison that had impressed him so much was gone. In spite of all this, he could not make up his mind to flee. 'We knew there would be anti-Semitism; we knew there would be reprisals against Jews, but that outright murder would take place, that a race would be wiped out – we never suspected that.'

As a precaution he went underground for a few days. When he ventured out from his hiding-place again, he could tell that for him, as for all Jews, a new and cold wind was blowing in Lida. The German occupiers went down the streets with lists and fetched Jewish men from their houses. 'It was a list of intellectuals, of people in the public eye, doctors, lawyers, a number of factory managers – they were dragged out of their homes, but without their wives or children.' Arluk immediately assumed that Polish fellow-citizens had helped the Germans draw up the lists. He felt helpless, just as helpless as the townspeople who stood at doors and windows for hours, watching this activity. At first he thought that the men were merely being arrested. They were assembled in the town's market square and then taken away in trucks. But before long Arluk and all the other silent observers knew what was happening to the men – they heard shots coming from the forest beyond the barracks. As Arnold Arluk explains: 'It was a small town and soon people came along who had been on the spot and told us that men were being shot and buried.'

He and his fellow-Jews suspected that the German occupation heralded the start of a time of terror. From now on, one predominant feeling gripped him: 'Fear. Fear, because for the first time we had seen killing, not just persecution. A fear about what do I do now? There was nothing I *could* do.' The action was all on the part of the occupiers. The field commander of the Wehrmacht decreed that the Jews had to be made recognisable. 'To begin with we didn't wear stars, just a white armband with a Star of David marked on it and the word "Jew" written inside the star'. Arluk explains. The young man made a decision that saved his life: he went into the forests and joined the partisans.

> The Germans came to our town but only stayed for a short while, about a week. In the course of that week we certainly got a foretaste of what was awaiting us. Many of our men were arrested and locked in the synagogues without food or drink. In a nearby town they even set fire to synagogues, with people in them.
>
> *Irene Horovitz, Ukrainian Jew from Borislav*
>
> It was 5 o'clock in the morning when we suddenly heard bombs exploding. Window-panes shattered and everyone panicked. Of course, we didn't know what was happening. We believed the Red Army was strong enough to teach the Wehrmacht a lesson. About ten days later German troops marched into our town and the disaster we'd been warned of began. We were now in the same situation as those refugees from Germany and western Poland who had told us horrific stories, which we didn't want to believe.
>
> *Samuel Pisar, Jew from Bialystok, north-east Poland*

The war which had descended on the Soviet Union and its people was different from anything that had been known before – as Fanný Segal, Arnold Arluk and many of their Jewish fellow-sufferers quickly came to realise. But the other Soviet citizens – civilians and Red Army alike – were to experience this as well. The German soldiers were not only equipped with weapons of

steel and the latest military technology. Their Führer, Adolf
Hitler, had provided those who believed in him with the
ideological armament needed to wage this war with utter
ruthlessness. For Hitler, 22 June saw the beginning of the war he
had always longed for. On 3 March 1941 the war leader had
issued instructions to Alfred Jodl, chief of operations of the
armed forces high command (OKW), which amounted to an
order to murder – and indeed it was clear enough who the
perpetrators were to be and who the victims: 'This coming
campaign is more than just a clash of arms; it will lead to a
conflict between two ideologies', we read in the OKW war-diary.
'The Jewish-Bolshevist intelligentsia that has hitherto oppressed
the people must be removed. . . . Whether it might be necessary
to deploy elements of the SS alongside the secret field police was
something which would have to be examined with the
Reichsführer-SS. The need to put all Bolshevist bosses and
commissars out of action immediately would indicate its
necessity.' At a conference on 30 March 1941, which brought
the top brass of the Wehrmacht together in the Reich
Chancellery, the dictator spoke quite openly about how this war
was to be waged: 'The conflict will be very different from the one
in the west. We have to abandon the attitude of soldierly
comradeship. The communist never has been any comrade of
ours and never will be.' The chief of the general staff, Franz
Halder, dutifully noted in his diary: 'We are involved in a war of
annihilation.'

Finally, we read in the *Guidelines for the conduct of troops in
Russia*, issued on 19 May 1941 by Wilhelm Keitel, the OKW
chief-of-staff: 'Bolshevism is the deadly enemy of the National
Socialist German people. It is against this subversive ideology and
its proponents that Germany is fighting. This struggle requires
ruthless and energetic measures against Bolshevist agitators,
partisans, saboteurs and Jews, and the total stamping out of all
active or passive resistance.' In this decree borderlines were
deliberately blurred rather than clearly drawn, and Jews were
mentioned in the same breath as 'Bolshevist agitators'.

In the Ninth Fort in Kaunas Jews were locked up – three or four hundred of them. Holes were dug in the ground – graves – where they were required. We were then taken to the Ninth Fort. There were a number of Germans there, SS troops. They had set up machine-guns and used us to escort the Jews, twenty or thirty at a time, to the graves. After a head-count the order came: 'Ready – forward.' Straight into the graves. There they had to lie down and these SS men shot them where they lay. They were lying face down. The Germans fired their machine-guns – raking them over and over again. Anyone still moving was finished off by the Germans. The victims went to the graves calmly, with bowed heads. They made no fuss – it was a tragic thing to see. It was a thoroughly unpleasant business to be involved in. But we were given as much to drink as we wanted. And after that, when the schnapps began to work, we all had the courage to take part in the operation. As the last men were brought forward, I fired as well. I can't understand why our officers agreed to such a thing. I hated the whole affair. But when you're in the army you get given orders. And an order has to be carried out.

Petras Zelionka, former Lithuanian auxiliary gendarme

The essential objective of the campaign against the Jewish-Bolshevist system is the complete smashing of its power-structure and the eradication of Asiatic influence in the European cultural domain. . . . The soldier must fully understand the necessity of hard but justified retribution against Jewish sub-humanity. . . . Only in this way will we do justice to our historic task of freeing the German people once and for all from the Asiatic–Jewish peril.

Generalfeldmarschall *Walter von Reichenau, commander of the 6th Army, in an order of 10 October 1941*

The arbitrary linking of Bolshevism with Jewry was an *idée fixe* of which the dictator never let go. Now, in the summer of 1941, at the zenith of his power, Hitler wanted 'Operation Barbarossa' to bring the achievement of his long-cherished goal: the destruction of 'Jewish Bolshevism'. In this way the Soviet threat which – as Hitler and a good many Germans saw it – was a combination of Jewry and Bolshevism, had to be removed. The concept of Bolshevism as domination by the Jews over the Slavic masses in Soviet Russia was part of the original ideological repertoire of the National Socialist movement. In *Mein Kampf* Hitler got carried away by his abstruse assertion that pre-revolutionary Russia thrived from the 'Germanic core of its upper ruling classes'. However, this old Russia had been wiped out by the Bolshevik revolution of 1917. After the revolution the place of the old Germanic governing class had been taken by 'the Jew'. In his polemic, Hitler evoked the alleged reign of terror by the Jews in Russia: 'In seizing political power, the Jew casts off his last remaining veils. The Jew of popular democracy becomes the Jew of blood and the tyrant of nations. . . . The most fearful example of this is offered by Russia, where with truly fanatical savagery, and often with inhuman torture, he has killed – or allowed to starve – close on 30 million people, in order to secure the domination of a great nation by a bunch of Jewish scribblers and stock-exchange gangsters.' Hitler saw the empire in the east as a threat. 'In Russian Bolshevism we are seeing the attempt of Jewry to achieve world domination in the twentieth century.'

Paradoxically, however, he also made it known that he considered the Soviet empire to be weak: 'Just as it is impossible for the Russian, by his own efforts, to shake off the yoke of the Jews, so it is equally impossible for the Jew to maintain that vast empire in the long term. . . . The giant empire in the east is ripe for collapse. And the end of Jewish domination in Russia will also be the end of Russia as a state.' For the Germans, therefore, undreamed-of opportunities presented themselves. In *Mein Kampf* Hitler announced a completely new and expansionist foreign policy: 'With this, we National Socialists are deliberately drawing a line under the direction of Germany's pre-war foreign policy. We are beginning again where we left off six centuries ago. We are calling a halt to the eternal Germanic drift towards the south and west of Europe and turning our eyes to the land in the east. We are finally putting an end to the colonial and mercantile policy of the pre-war era and switching to the policy of the future, the policy of soil and territory.' For Germany, he claimed, was a nation without space, which had to acquire room for itself if it was to have a future at all. Thus one of the key phrases in *Mein Kampf* runs: 'The right to soil and territory may become an obligation if, without an enlargement of its territory, a great nation appears doomed.'

In this country they [the Jews] are and remain chiefly responsible for the subversion and existing mess in every respect. Isolating them from the rest of the population seems imperative. . . . Complete command of this long-standing communal conflict combined with the elimination of the Jews is at the same time the key to the total political and economic pacification of the region.

Oberleutnant *Helmut Mann, counter-intelligence officer of 221 Security Division, in a handover report for the civil administration of Erich Koch, 28 July 1941*

'Operation Barbarossa' bundled together all the ideological and strategic elements of Hitler's thinking in one practical solution. His belief in the superiority of the 'Aryan German' over the 'subhuman Slav', his anti-Semitism and anti-Marxism were combined with the well-advertised intention to free Europe from the scourge of 'Jewish Bolshevism'. At the same time he wanted to destroy its power centre in Moscow in order to secure the future of the German master race in its new *Lebensraum*. All these points could be linked with a further strategic objective in the Russian campaign: the shattering of the military strength of the Soviet Union in order to guarantee Germany's position of supremacy in Europe.

I was not the first one to come across a German soldier. It was the woman living next door to us, who was escorted home by a soldier. He was very nice and she was full of praise for all the Germans she met. This made a good impression on me. All right, they were soldiers, but we didn't find anything wrong with them.

Alex Faitelson, Lithuanian Jew

The Ukrainians welcomed the arrival of the Germans, since they got the impression that the Germans wanted to give them a state of their own. And the Germans gave the Ukrainians a free hand to do whatever they wanted with the Jews.

Irene Horovitz, Ukrainian Jew

The ideological war was also always to be a war of the races. How natural it seemed for Hitler to equate the Soviet leadership with Jewry. In order to bring about the collapse of the Soviet state and to destroy it irreversibly, it was therefore necessary to eradicate the communist officials, the state and party functionaries, just as much as the members of the intelligentsia: 'The intelligentsia who serve Stalin must be annihilated. The governmental machinery of the Russian empire must be smashed. In the empire of Greater Russia it is necessary to apply the most brutal force.' This task, Hitler said, was 'so difficult that the army could not be expected to handle it alone'. The army, he claimed, lacked the fanatical determination which distinguished his 'Black Guard' – the ideal force for murderous 'special assignments'. He knew that he could depend on the *Reichsführer-SS*, Heinrich Himmler, just as he could on Himmler's right-hand man, the head of the Central Office of Reich Security, Reinhard Heydrich. In the spring of 1941 they jointly set up the so-called 'action squads' (*Einsatzgruppen*), specifically for the coming war against the Soviet Union.

The *Einsatzgruppen* were nothing less than mobile death-squads. It is true that in addition to executions they had a wide range of other tasks to perform: such as the confiscation of documents in the conquered areas, hunting down prominent Soviet figures, building up a network of informers, recruiting auxiliaries from the local population, the establishment and training of militias. But the principal task of this 'Central Security Office on wheels' was unambiguously defined as the 'combating of all elements hostile to the Reich and to Germans in enemy territory behind the fighting troops'. In concrete terms that meant they were to follow in the wake of the Wehrmacht, systematically comb the already occupied areas for actual and potential enemies of the Third Reich, and murder them. It is true that the shootings were mainly carried out by assigned detachments of the *Waffen-SS* and the *Ordnungspolizei*, and later increasingly by Lithuanian, Latvian and Ukrainian auxiliaries – but they were always commanded by an officer from the *Einsatzgruppen*. Wilhelm Höttl, a former SS *Sturmbannführer* and leading member of the foreign secret service of the Central Office of Reich Security, remembers, in the spring of 1941, how the tasks were formulated in bureaucratic language. 'Take the Jews out of circulation? We knew straight away that meant physical annihilation.'

> In the event of a unit remaining in one place for an extended time, Jewish quarters or ghettos are to be closed off without delay, if they cannot be immediately cleared out. Obviously, when doing this, care must be taken to keep back the skilled workers.
>
> *Brigade order No. 8 to the SS Cavalry Brigade, 28 September 1941*

In spring 1941 four *Einsatzgruppen* were assembled and given military training in the frontier-police school at Pretzsch, near Wittenberg. The personnel of the special mobile units were recruited from among officials or trainees in the Gestapo, the Criminal Police and the Security Service. They were joined by three companies of the *Waffen-SS*. In addition, some 500 men from the 9th battalion of the *Ordnungspolizei* were allocated in companies to the four *Einsatzgruppen*.

These were each divided into two *Sonderkommandos* (special commandos) and two or three *Einsatzkommandos* (action commandos) – in total the four *Einsatzgruppen* comprised about 3,000 officers and men, including close on 1,000 soldiers of the *Waffen-SS* and police reservists. For the purposes of provisions and military support, *Einsatzgruppen* A, B and C were assigned to Army Groups North, Centre and South respectively. *Einsatzgruppe* D was under the command of the 11th Army, which moved out from Roumania into the Soviet Union.

On 17 June their commanding officers were personally briefed by Reinhard Heydrich about their impending duties, and the murderous objectives were revealed to them. The security boss left them in no doubt about the 'toughness and difficulty' of the task ahead of them. The conflict between the two ideologies would have to be conducted with all 'ruthlessness'. In the first weeks of action Heydrich's instructions were easy to interpret – the murder assignment was aimed at a vaguely defined 'Jewish-Bolshevist ruling class': state and party functionaries of any kind, but especially 'Jews in party and government positions' as well as 'other radical elements (saboteurs, propagandists, snipers, assassins, agitators etc.)' This applied principally to men of military age. It was left to the discretion of the individual *Kommandos* to define these target groups more precisely. It should be noted that no unambiguous order for the murder of the entire Jewish population of the Soviet Union had been issued to the *Einsatzgruppen* before the start of the Russian campaign – that came later. Within a few weeks the mass killing of Jews developed from the murder of communists, which had been considered a priority.

After the invasion of the Soviet Union, the fighting troops were followed by the *Einsatzkommandos* on every sector of the Front. Johann Adolf, Count von Kielmansegg, then a staff officer in the 6th Panzer Division, recalls the beginning of the war in Russia in 1941: 'On 17 March we received the order to advance, followed by the appropriate instructions, then suddenly we were told: there are *Einsatzgruppen* of the SS coming, who have special duties. You must integrate them in your columns. They were not under our command, but merely seconded to us for transport and supply purposes. We were told to get them across the frontier and then they had their own job to do.'

> Germany has never attempted to carry its National Socialist ideology into Russia, but it was the Jewish–Bolshevist holders of power in Moscow who tried ceaselessly to impose their domination on us and other European nations, not only intellectually but above all through military might.
>
> *Hitler, 22 June 1941*
>
> The dejudification of the region allocated to the unit included, in particular, the towns of Chomsk, Motol, Telechany, Svieta Volka and Hancewicze. The villages located near the military roadway were, after checking with HQ, initially excluded because at the time the Jews had to be brought in for labour service on the road. The dejudification will probably be carried out later by the police.
>
> *Gustav Lombard, head of the mounted unit of the 1st SS Cavalry Regiment, in a report dated 11 August 1941*
>
> The housing of Jews in ghettos appears to be a priority task and a difficult one, in view of the large numbers. This is in the process of being carried out. In collaboration with the field and local commands, suitable districts are already being sought in all the towns.
>
> *Report from Minsk by the SD (Security Service), 23 July 1941*

The infantrymen and tank-crews who were fighting on the front line in the summer of 1941 took no interest in these new troops – in this phase of the war the Wehrmacht had other things to worry about: they were pursuing the enemy, swallowing the dust from the hastily built military road; they suffered losses whenever the Soviet army made a stand and fought. In these days of constant tension they gave little thought to the ideological background to their conflict which Hitler had constructed, nor to the 'necessary retribution against the subhuman Jew'. Ulrich Gunzert, then an

Oberleutnant in the Pioneers, describes the everyday experience of the front line soldier in this way: 'At the Front, as a battalion commander, I was concerned with the Russians. I had absolutely nothing to do with the shooting of Jews. I didn't even think about it. When you're in action, real action, everything else is unimportant. Only what the enemy is doing, how you deal with the enemy, how you finish him off, how you survive – those are the only things that completely occupy you.' That is confirmed by Baron Philipp von Boeselager, formerly an *Oberleutnant* in the 86th Infantry Division: 'I was in the reconnaissance section. So we were way out in front. There was fighting every day, and we advanced every day. We didn't bother about the Jews; we had no idea whether there were Jews in a village or not. It was of no interest to us; what interested us was our task – we had to occupy this or that line and see whether it was clear of enemy.'

I'd like to stress this again clearly: most of the men knew nothing about the Nazis' crimes, to the extent that I personally knew. The senior staff officers had to know and were in a position to know, but not the soldiers. I don't even think the divisional commanders knew – one or two perhaps – but not the bulk of the divisional commanders. But the generals certainly did know. Manstein knew, and the field marshals knew what disgusting things were going on.

Baron Philipp von Boeselager, former Wehrmacht officer and member of the 20 July plot against Hitler

These are political disputes which don't interest us, or rather, they are of interest, but we're not allowed to do anything about them. These things aren't our concern.

Generaloberst *Busch, commander of the 16th Army, having witnessed the shooting of Jews in Kovno in autumn 1941*

In the first weeks of the campaign most of the soldiers hoped for a quick victory, which would shatter the communist empire, at least west of the Urals. The fear of Bolshevism haunted many minds – it was not only the population at home in Germany, but also the soldiers at the Front who believed the Soviets capable of any evil, which certainly included an assault on Western Europe. That is why Goebbels' 'Ministry of National Enlightenment' heaped the Germans with propaganda about the 'necessity' of the attack on the Soviet Union. The words that boomed out from the 'People's Receivers' and appeared in the newspapers encouraged many to interpret the German invasion as a 'preventive war'. 'Soviet army shattered – the Führer saves Europe from Bolshevist invasion!' was, for example, the headline in the *Völkischer Beobachter* on 30 June. Hans-Günther Stark, then a *Leutnant* in the 93rd Infantry Division, recalls how the troops felt about the Soviet empire they were confronting: 'The British in North Africa were opponents, the French, too, had been our opponents; we didn't regard them as *enemies*. But the Soviets were our enemies, and bitter, ideological enemies at that.'

> I don't think anyone can dispute the fact that the officer corps, even the senior officers, had the same fundamental core of anti-Semitism as did the majority of the German people, and incidentally the majority of most other European nations.
>
> *Ulrich de Maizière, Wehrmacht officer in 1941*

From the start, the Wehrmacht was also drawn into the ideological war against 'Jewish Bolshevism'. Naturally, the tasks which the generals, officers and men set themselves were at the outset purely military: it was a matter of delivering a crushing blow to the Red Army in a Blitzkrieg. Yet in addition to the military conquest of the eastern territories, the Wehrmacht was also to have the task of liquidating all the political commissars within the Red Army, and to hand over all Jews among their prisoners-of-war to be murdered by the *Einsatzkommandos* – which took place on a large scale. Thus the senior officers of the Wehrmacht became inextricably implicated in the criminal policy of the Nazi regime. Orders were issued to the armies of the east which were intended to remove any scruple from the conduct of the soldiers.

The opposition were deliberately branded as 'criminals': the prime targets were the political commissars in the Red Army. 'The commissars represent an ideology that is totally opposed to National Socialism. Therefore the commissars are to be liquidated. Commissars and GPU men are criminals and must be treated as such'. Hitler had proclaimed. The so-called 'commissar order' issued by the army high command on 6 June 1941 stated that commissars were 'on principle to be disposed of immediately by shooting'. The only senior officer to voice even the mildest concern about this was *Feldmarschall* von Brauchitsch, commander-in-chief of the army, who insisted that the commissar order was only to be carried out in secret – not out of sympathy for the potential victims, but from a worry about the 'discipline and self-control' of the German soldiers. In fact he added: 'The disposal of commissars must take place inconspicuously, after their removal from the actual battle-area, and under the orders of an officer.' In the following weeks, however, it turned out that not all the commanders who were aware of the commissar order were prepared to apply it or to pass it on to their subordinates. Yet those were the exceptions. In the zone covered by Army Group Centre alone, the Wehrmacht shot 3,000 to 5,000 commissars, and *Einsatzgruppe* B some 10,000.

However, another order was to have fatal consequences for the way the population – and especially the Jews – were treated in Russia. This significantly increased the freedom of action of the Wehrmacht and of all other elements deployed: 'Actions committed by members of the Wehrmacht and its supporting personnel against enemy civilians cannot be a matter for prosecution, even when the action constitutes a military crime or offence', ran an order concerning the 'exercise of martial law in the "Barbarossa" zone' issued by *Generalfeldmarschall* Keitel on 13 May 1941. In order to give even a rough cloak of legality to the involvement of the Wehrmacht in an ideological war of annihilation, these order laid down that population of the occupied country was no longer protected by the internationally recognised laws governing the conduct of war. Furthermore, a wider definition was given to the term 'partisan', against whom the decree was directed: it now applied not only armed civilians, but also unarmed persons such as 'agitators, distributors of leaflets, arsonists' and those who were merely suspected of such activities. Where it was not possible to identify individual perpetrators, violent collective measures were to be taken, such as the shooting of hostages or the burning down of whole villages. Decisions on such matters lay with officers on the spot. This judicial decree from now on gave officers the freedom to arrest and order the shooting of individuals without any formal charge. The ultimate consequence of this decree was that Wehrmacht soldiers – on orders from an officer – could massacre civilians without having to answer to a German court martial.

There were 500 of us Jews; we were all rounded up. In Vyshniniai they shot my father. He was still a good-looking young man of 41. They took them all away, 23 men, and shot them all. The Fascists were there already. They were Germans. They raped our girls, robbed us all, tore our clothes off, stole our gold. We weren't well off, but we still had something. Then the troops drove off leaving instructions about what was to be done with the Jews: and the Lithuanians did their bit – adolescents, men, the old, were all shot. The woman with little children weren't yet being shot. Then they started to shoot all the little boys. Then the boys put on little dresses, so people wouldn't notice that they were boys. They were still not shooting girls. Then, in Giruliai they weeded us out one morning. They divided us up; the holes in the ground had already been dug in Giruliai. And my mother and little brother were shot there. My little brother was ten years old. He was born in 1930. What do I have left of him? Some photos from America. I take these photos and talk to them, I kiss them. My relatives in America sent them to me.

Rozèle Goldenstein, Lithuanian Jew

It is probably superfluous to say any more about the Jews. One can perhaps debate about the most suitable measures for removing the Jew from the regions placed under our authority. But it is quite clear he must be removed, for the Jew is a partisan!

SS-Standartenführer *Hermann Fegelein at a conference in Mogilev, 24–6 September 1941*

We knew that the Nazis wanted to rid Germany of Jews. They were to be resettled somewhere in the east or in Palestine. . . . The fact that they now wanted to kill them all straight away only gradually sank in.

Dr Gerhard von Jordan, then deputy district captain in Zloczow

I was forced to watch a Ukrainian volunteer throw a young woman and her child to the ground and then place them in such a way that the child's head was under the mother, so he could kill both of them with one shot.

Hubert Pfoch, former soldier in the Wehrmacht

Through instructions such as the commissar order and the judicial decree the Nazi leadership could look forward to a radicalising and brutalising of the fighting, by which even traditionally minded Wehrmacht soldiers were to be locked into the war of annihilation. This was the war that Hitler wanted: free of any consideration of the bonds of civilisation. In this war of his, no rules were to apply which might have guaranteed a minimum of humanity.

The Russians – in the verdict of propaganda – were *Untermenschen*, subhuman beings, an 'inferior racial mix' of Jews and 'Asiatic hordes', who were being given fancy ideas by the commissars. The troops generally provided fruitful soil for this kind of manipulative hype. An underlying tendency towards feelings of superiority, contempt and a sense of mission, was certainly there already. The former fighter-pilot, Count Heinrich Einsiedel, recalls: 'Even before the Russian campaign there had been orders telling us the opposition was not human, they were subhumans, Slavs and Jews, who had to be exterminated so that we could have living-space. There were men I admired greatly as officers, but they had the notion that after the war they would have aristocratic estates on the Black Sea near Odessa and would whip their Russian serfs.' Einsiedel also remembers tangible anti-Semitic attitudes: 'Sometimes one actually heard people saying that the Jews had to be destroyed. It soon became an accepted principle. The Jews, the Jewish Bolshevists and international Jewish communism – they are our enemy and against them anything is legal.'

> The drunken SS officers told us how they had been treating the Jews. And that's how I knew that ghastly things had been done to them. That those were crimes and that they were out to exterminate the Jews.
>
> *Ulrich Gunzert, former Wehrmacht officer*

Yet despite the continual equating of the 'deadly enemy of Bolshevism' with Jewry many German soldiers kept their distance from anti-Semitic measures. In many places they witnessed reprisals against the civilian Jewish population, saw executions outside villages, watched the murder of innocent people committed by Germans in uniform. But they also noticed that the perpetrators wore uniforms and insignia which differed from the Wehrmacht. 'They weren't part of the Wehrmacht, but special units, mainly SS', says the former officer Peter von der Osten-Sacken, describing his first encounter with the *Einsatzgruppen* death-squads. 'Shortly after the occupation of the town in question by the Wehrmacht the Jews were rounded up in the market square. A horrifying sight. And many of the infantrymen who happened to be looking on, couldn't understand it. They said: what's going on? What kind of measures *are* these? We can't go along with this! You noticed this opposition even among the ordinary soldiers. But not all of them of course. Many were indifferent.'

Leutnant Stark was not one of the indifferent ones, although on 26 June 1941, four days after the start of the campaign, he was in a hurry. He and his battery were needed up at the Front – he knew that perfectly well. The Russians were fleeing. Now they must be pursued, pushed back beyond the River Dvina. The German armoured spearheads were already far advanced here in Lithuania, continually driving the Russians before them. Compared with the armour, units like the horse-drawn artillery to which Stark belonged, moved at a snail's pace through the recently conquered territory. But at least there was no more fighting here.

So the twenty-year-old lieutenant was all the more surprised on that afternoon to hear shots from carbines – pistol-shots were also audible. Stark had an inkling that something was wrong, but he could see nothing. 'Bols, go and take a look. There's something going on a few hundred metres to our right', he ordered his sergeant. 'Bols grabbed two NCOs and went off to recce – a little later *Leutnant* Stark saw Bols waving. '*Herr Leutnant*, come here!' Stark reacted immediately – when he reached Bols he saw they were standing at the edge of a steep-sided gravel-pit. And in the pit there was shooting – people were being executed, slowly but methodically, always three at a time – their executioners were Lithuanians and an SS man. Stark saw about 300 civilians in the pit. 'Stop that!' he yelled, and the next moment he was sliding down the slope on the leather-reinforced seat of his breeches. Down below the shooting stopped simultaneously – the murderers looked up at the edge of the pit and saw three men with machine-pistols levelled at them, while a Wehrmacht officer was charging towards them shouting. 'What's going on here? Where are the orders from my divisional commander telling you to carry out these shootings? Have you got a written order?'

His determined military demeanour had an immediate effect – the Lithuanians were impressed. Even before their SS leader could react, Stark ordered them with all the authority of a Prussian officer: 'Chuck your carbines into the pit! You're under arrest!' The Lithuanians did as they were told. When the SS man hesitated, *Oberwachtmeister* Bols cut in from the edge of the pit: 'You try anything, son, and I'll drill you full of holes!' More and more soldiers from Stark's battery gathered by the pit; soon afterwards the divisional field police arrived and took the murderers, who had killed nearly twenty people, away with them.

For Hans-Günther Stark the matter ended there. 'What happened to them was no longer of interest to me. Wasn't my job. I'd put a stop to an obvious wrong there. It was a pure reflex action; I couldn't have acted any other way, ' Stark remembers. His intervention had no adverse consequences for him: 'At first I heard nothing for quite a while. Then my CO told my I had acted quite correctly, exactly as he would have done. I had done the right thing. Case dismissed.'

> In all my longer discussions with officers I was questioned about the shooting of Jews, without having alluded to it. I gained the impression that the shooting of Jews, prisoners and commissars was almost universally disapproved of in the officer corps. . . . The shootings were regarded as damaging to the honour of the German army, something foreign to the German officer corps.
>
> *Major Rudolf-Christoph, Baron von Gersdorff, in the war-diary of the Supreme Command of Army Group Centre, 9 December 1941*
>
> But then we gradually got to hear what the Army Group already knew. What Gersdorff, the CO and Tresckow knew. In fact Tresckow came over every day to discuss the front line situation with the Field-Marshal. Then gradually we got a few answers to our questions and began to see where they stood. That increased one's unease and gradually one had to admit: this is a criminal regime. For a long time you wouldn't accept it, and didn't even know for certain, but now you knew it.
>
> *Baron Philipp von Boeselager, former Wehrmacht officer and member of the 20 July plot*

It was not often that courageous Wehrmacht soldiers took such decisive action. On the contrary, the remoteness which many individual soldiers felt towards the *Einsatzgruppen* and their crimes had little to do with the discussions which had been held at the highest levels. In principal, what had been agreed to was logistical cooperation. An agreement between Heydrich and the Quarter-master-General of the Army, *Generalmajor* Eduard Wagner, obliged the armies to provision the *Kommandos*, in other words to supply them with food, fuel and ammunition.

Yet there were many other forms of support. Cases are known where the Wehrmacht introduced measures in occupied territory, without which it would have been impossible for many of the SS *Kommandos* to carry out the murder of the Jews. Thus, after the arrival of the Wehrmacht in captured villages, the field or town commanders usually ordered the identification and registration of the Jewish population. In many places large posters ordered the resident Jews to 'identify themselves by wearing white armbands with a Star of David on both arms'. The posters also announced: 'The free movement of Jews is suspended with immediate effect.' This meant in practice that from then on the Jews were restricted to their home town, virtual prisoners already, and escape was next to impossible. Thanks to this 'preparatory work' by the regular army, the conditions were already created whereby the *Einsatz*- and *Sonderkommandos* only had to round up their identified and registered victims before liquidating them.

There are also proven cases of Wehrmacht trucks being made available to transport the victims, or personnel provided to cordon off the execution areas. There is no disputing the fact that, especially in the rearward areas, quite a number of Wehrmacht units were directly confronted with the crimes of the *Einsatzgruppen* against Jews. Many reacted to them with horror and disgust. Yet in only a few cases did soldiers intervene – as *Leutnant* Stark did – or protest against the death-squads. Scarcely anyone enquired as to the reasons for the killing. Without a word, the majority of them accepted it as 'the order of the day'. Most wrote nothing about it in letters from the Front to their families, but when home on leave many poured their hearts out. Spectators became accessories – which, objectively speaking, made them share the guilt. Others never learned anything of the crimes, but were preoccupied with their own survival at the Front. And there were soldiers who applauded the murderous activities of the

Einsatzgruppen, urged the perpetrators on and humiliated the victims even as they faced death.

In addition, the Jewish leaders and intelligentsia, with the exception of essential specialists such as doctors, have largely been liquidated by the German Security Police, in accordance with their instructions.

Situation report of the field command in Minsk province,
14 August 1941

Women were screaming, flinging their hands up, tearing at their clothes, just to get some pity. And the children began to scream. They suddenly saw their mothers lying dead beside them. Then they themselves were killed. And then you could still see SS men going through the rows, shooting those still alive in the head with a pistol.

Ulrich Gunzert, former Wehrmacht officer, witness to a mass
shooting in the Ukraine

The Lithuanians wanted to get rid of the Jews themselves. They'd waited a long time for this and now they could do it. They knew they wouldn't be punished for these crimes. And what's more, they were out to get hold of the Jews' wealth.

Rozèle Goldenstein, Lithuanian Jew

There are quite a number of cases to prove that soldiers themselves committed murder – often, though not always, under orders. A lieutenant in the Pioneers, Wolfgang Schöler, who was then twenty years old, witnessed a murder in a village that lay a good way behind the front line. 'A *Hauptmann* was shooting looters, or men he took to be looters. He left them lying where they had fallen. One of them was a Jew. He was still alive, but in a coma. The Jew was lying near a fence, in his kaftan, and when he somehow recognised me, he screamed "oy-oy-oy" and uttered other such sounds of pain. I was at a loss, what should I do? My helplessness was probably mixed with a certain cowardice. If I had carried him away, then someone, maybe the *Hauptmann*, would have come along and asked: "Who's taken my Jew away?" Then a little later I went back to him and by then he was dead. No-one is born a martyr and in a way I was glad that he died afterwards, because it took the decision away from me.' Schöler knew there was little he could do about it, but young as he was he realised that something very wrong had happened. 'That arrogance, playing judge and executioner at the same time; that really had nothing to do with the code of honour of the Wehrmacht or at least of an officer.' The twenty-year-old drew his own conclusions: 'I promised myself that if, in my own sphere of command, I could prevent such things, then I would do so. Everyone, in their own job, must do what is humane.' Admittedly this was not the general rule. 'Glad to report Wehrmacht has right attitude towards Jews.' From the 'Incident report USSR No. 14', this refers to the pogrom against the Jews of Tarnopol on 6 July 1941, covertly incited by *Sonderkommando* 4b, in which Wehrmacht soldiers, Wehrmacht members of the SS 'Viking' Division and Ukrainian militiamen bestially murdered about 600 people. And the 'Incident report USSR No. 119' from *Einsatzkommando* 5, dated 20 October 1941, concludes as follows: 'Contrary to plan, in Uman as early as 21.9.1941, violence was committed against the Jews by members of the militia, with the involvement of numerous members of the German Wehrmacht. During these events, the Jewish homes were all demolished and robbed of all articles of use or value. This action was also almost exclusively carried out by members of the Wehrmacht.'

The Jewish population of the conquered territories were not prepared for the brutality of the death-squads. Abiding by the terms of the Hitler–Stalin Pact the Soviet press had, prior to 22 June 1941, scarcely reported on the anti-Jewish measures and acts of violence in Hitler's 'Thousand Year Reich', and the *Einsatzgruppen* ruthlessly exploited the widely prevailing naivety. Many East European Jews had only the vaguest notion about the Germans; the educated classes tended to regard the German people as respectable, civilised and cultured – the nation of 'poets and thinkers' that had produced Goethe and Schiller. Why then should they expect racially motivated killings carried out by death-squads specially assembled for the purpose?

The victims, several hundred of them – there may even have been nearly 1,000 men and women – were brought in by truck. For the moment I don't recall any children. The people brought in had to lie down or kneel in a hollow washed out by the rain, about 100 yards from the well. There they had to take off their outer clothing. About ten people at a time were made to stand at the edge of the well and were shot from behind by a firing-squad, also about ten strong, of whom I was one. After the salvo they fell head first into the well. Out of fear, some of them jumped into the well while still alive. The firing-squad was changed several times.

On account of the mental stress that I too was exposed to in this shooting, I cannot in all honesty remember how often I stood by the hole and how often I was allowed to stand down.

As you can imagine, this shooting did not take place in the calm with which it is now being discussed. The women screamed and cried, and the men as well. Some attempted to escape. The soldiers rounding them up shouted just as loud. If the victims didn't do as they were told, they were beaten. In this connection a red-haired SS man particularly comes to mind, who always had a length of cable with him, and when things weren't going as he wanted, he laid into people with it. So they had no other choice. . . . Until the last victim fell into the well, the shooting lasted barely one afternoon. Something I well remember about this execution was that afterwards the SD men were drunk and later got a special ration of schnapps. We in the civil police didn't get any and I remember we were very upset about it.

Richard Tögel, policeman, member of Einsatzkommando *10a,*
in a court statement

Zvi Katz, a Jew from Lithuania, recalls the days before the Germans marched into his homeland. The possibility of fleeing was discussed among his family. But his grandfather calmed their fears: 'If the Germans do come, what of it? I still remember them from the time of the First World War; they're all very cultivated people. What higher thing can there be than German culture?' But in Hitler's Reich, German culture lay prostrate.

> . . . A *Sonderkommando* was detailed off to round up all the Jews. They were told they were going to Minsk. But they were going into a big, deep hole in a big, deep forest, and they all had to stand on a big heap of sand, then rat-a-tat, and in one day 9,500 of these nasty elements were gone, every last one. . . . We even fetched ourselves a little Christmas-tree from the forest, and tomorrow evening it will be shining out in our cosy little home here in the distant east, as a silent reminder of our beautiful German homeland . . .
>
> *From a letter by a soldier, Heinrich Schumacher,*
> *23 December 1941*

> So I was actually present at the great mass-death the day before yesterday. With the first truckload my hand trembled a bit as I fired, but you get used to it. By the tenth truckload I was aiming calmly and fired straight at many women, children and babies.
>
> *Walter Mattner, police secretary, in a letter from Mogilev*
> *to his wife in Vienna, 5 October 1941*

> The solving of the Jewish problem . . . was tackled energetically on the part of the *Einsatzgruppen*, particularly in the area east of the Dnepr river.
>
> *Report No. 6 of the Einsatzgruppen for the period*
> *1–31 October 1941*

From the first day of the Russian campaign the *Einsatzgruppen* murdered communists, intellectuals and especially – in accordance with Heydrich's orders – 'Jews in party and government positions' as potential 'troublemakers'. Soon they developed a cynical routine. For example, in July 1941 SS *Hauptscharführer* Felix Landau confided to his diary: 'At 6 a.m. I was suddenly awoken from a deep sleep. Report for an execution. OK, do I just have to

play the part of executioner and afterwards gravedigger? Why not?
I am detailed to the firing-squad and will probably have to shoot
men cursing as they die. We drive a few kilometres along a
highway, then turn off to the right into a wood. At present there
are just six of us and we look for a suitable spot for shooting and
burial. After a few minutes we have found the sort of thing. The
candidates for death arrive with shovels to dig their own graves.
Only two of them are weeping. The others certainly have amazing
courage. What on earth can be going through their minds at this
precise moment? I believe each of them has a small hope that
somehow he won't be shot. The candidates are arranged into
three shifts, as there aren't that many shovels. Strangely, I feel no
emotion. No pity, nothing. It just happens, and then it's done
with. Slowly the hole gets bigger, two of them are crying non-
stop. I make them dig more and more, so they won't think so
much. During the work they do in fact calm down.'

After the Second World War, Felix Landau was tried as a
'perpetrator of excesses' and condemned to life imprisonment.

In order to impose the desired morgue-like calm on the
conquered regions of the Soviet Union, the death-squads were
supported by eleven battalions of 'Order Police' (*Ordnungspolizei*
or ORPO). These units of militarised emergency police consisted
partly of men in older age-groups who could no longer be called
up for service in the Wehrmacht, but partly also of volunteers
recruited in 1939, who, faced with an imminent war, had joined
the police in order to evade military service. The officers and
NCOs were experienced ORPO personnel. All these policemen,
'perfectly ordinary men', as the American historian Christopher
Browning calls them, received no more than two months special
training in preparation for their new assignments in Russia. When
they decided on a career in the police, none of them could have
guessed that one day they would become the executives of a
murderous occupation policy. Nevertheless they fitted perfectly
into the system of planned liquidation of 'enemies of the state'.
And in the end many not only carried out the orders they were
given, but allowed themselves to be drawn into atrocities.

On 27 June 1941 Pipo Schneider, company sergeant-major of
the 3rd Company of 309 Police Battalion was, with his motorised

column, rumbling towards Bialystok. When he and several other police officers discovered some vodka shops in the town, they didn't wait to be invited – they looted the stocks and helped themselves generously. Then they returned dutifully to their assignments. The same day, the battalion CO, Major Ernst Weis, gave orders for the town of 80,000 inhabitants to be combed and all Jewish men to be rounded up – no more, no less. The rest he left to the initiative of his junior officers. Pipo Schneider had a clear idea of what he had to do now. Among his men he was already well known as a fanatical racist, who 'saw red at the mere mention of a Jew', so people said. His anti-Semitism, combined with the effect of the alcohol, rose to a murderous rage. In a hunt for male Jews he shot at least five; other members of the battalion followed his lead and killed equally indiscriminately, finally murdering several of their prisoners.

I remember a young girl turned up in the office and said she had witnessed her parents, brothers and sisters being shot. She herself had been able to stay hidden; she said she was Jewish herself and could she please be shot. That shocked us all so much, we didn't know what to say. To begin with we just didn't believe such a thing could be possible. But it soon turned out to be true. And it wasn't an isolated case. It often happened that individual Jews who had stayed hidden, and hadn't had a chance to disappear into the forest somehow, saw no other way out but to report to the German authorities and say: yes, I'm a Jew too. I suppose they may have still believed there was some humanity in the Germans and hoped to escape with their life. It was quite dreadful.

Peter von der Osten-Sacken, former interpreter and special officer in the Von der Groeben Infantry battalion

What began as a pogrom ended in systematic shootings. In a park Jews were liquidated in groups; rifle salvoes echoed through the streets late into the night. The survivors were driven by policemen into Bialystok's chief synagogue – people were forced in with blows from rifle-butts until there was no room to fit in any more. The terrified Jews began to sing and pray aloud. Then Pipo Schneider began one of the most brutal massacres of those weeks: he posted guards all round the synagogue, now crammed with 700 people, and bolted the doors. The building was set on fire with petrol. Hand-grenades were flung through the windows to increase the effect of the fire. Already caught by the flames, the few who tried to flee from the synagogue were mown down by machine-gun fire. Those who died were mainly men, but some women and children had also been driven into the Bialystok synagogue – although they were not officially included in the German murder programme.

The Bialystok Jew, Samuel Pisar, was eleven when he lived through that night of terror: 'I woke up and saw flames leaping up over part of the town. It wasn't in our district, but when we looked out of the window, the sky was glowing red. We didn't yet know what it meant, but we knew that the big synagogue stood in that part of town. We suspected the worst.' Pisar was proved right. 'When we found out what had happened, we didn't take long to realise what Hitler was planning – we knew from that moment on that a dreadful fate awaited us.'

The 'action' in Bialystok, in which at least 700 Jews were burnt to death in the synagogue and a total of around 2,000 people died, was not the result of unambiguous orders, but arose from the personal initiative of a number of fanatical ORPO men. The other members of that police battalion allowed themselves to be carried along with it, or 'instinctively' fulfilled the expectations placed on them. Their commanding officer, Major Weis, was found drunk by Wehrmacht soldiers of the 221st Security Division. When asked to explain himself he took refuge behind the assertion that he had no idea what had been happening.

The personnel of Police Battalion 309, who predominantly came from the eastern Rhineland, had with over-hasty obedience turned into murderers. Not all were trigger-happy sadists, or fanatical anti-Semites like Pipo Schneider. Many policemen acted under peer pressure: to them, keeping the respect of their colleagues was more important than any feeling of human solidarity with the victims. For them the Jews were outside the

sphere in which they felt any obligation or responsibility towards
their fellow human beings. Added to this the war conditions
created a typical polarisation between 'us' and 'them'. The
increasingly long spells of action against defenceless civilians finally
had the effect of habituating them to it. Many of the men who
had difficulty in getting used to the murderous work increasingly
numbed their souls with alcohol when off duty. Only a few
withdrew from group pressure and refused to carry out shootings
in person. Though despised by their 'comrades', there is no
proven case of such refusal leading to any serious disciplinary
measure.

Killing – whether systematically or through bloodlust – was not a
speciality of the Germans in the first weeks of the war in Russia.
Stalin's secret police, the NKVD, also knew a thing or two about
this bloody work – and the German soldiers now saw them with
new eyes. For example, in the town of Tsortkov which, since the
Russian invasion of eastern Poland, now belonged to the Ukraine:
here the men of the 101st Jäger Division could indeed feel like
liberators as they entered the town – liberators from the terror of
the NKVD, whose legacy the then *Unteroffizier*, Baron Meinrad
von Ow, was among the first to discover: 'We came to a gloomy
building; the door was open and we went in to see if any Russians
were still there. We recoiled in horror; the sight that met us in the
courtyard was appalling. Half-decayed corpses everywhere, and by
the wall lay more dead, some of whom had been horribly
massacred.'

What the Germans saw here, and also in Tarnopol, Riga and
Zloczov, was the result of Soviet occupation policy. Since
September 1939, when Stalin had made common cause with Hitler
against Poland, the eastern part of Poland had been under Soviet
occupation. For two years the Soviets had tried rigorously to
impose their system on those regions occupied by Ukrainians, Poles
and Jews. What followed were dismissals from jobs, appropriation
of property, persecution and deportation to Siberia. These affected
everyone who was considered politically 'unreliable' or who refused
to accept the new nationality – Poles, Ukrainians and Jews in equal
measure. The most vicious persecution was by the NKVD, backed

by a dense network of informers. Their objective was the suppression and if necessary the 'elimination' of all opposition forces – politicians, civil servants, intellectuals, teachers, Ukrainian and Polish nationalists, and Jews.

> Jewish houses were looted and many people were killed in their own homes, usually by Ukrainians, and the Poles looked on.
> *Irene Horovitz, Ukrainian Jew, who witnessed pogroms in Borislav*

Before the arrival of the Germans in Lvov, 5,000 prisoners were incarcerated in the city's three gaols. Following the invasion by the Wehrmacht, from 24 to 28 June, there were atrocities there too. At first Stalin's political police murdered methodically – the Soviet secret police chief, Beria, had ordered the shooting of all 'counter-revolutionary elements' whom it was no longer possible to deport. Hundreds of inmates were shot in the neck in their cells, other prisoners had their skulls smashed with sledge-hammers. When, in the chaos before the Germans marched in, there was an attempt at a mass breakout, the Soviet warders fired at the escapers with machine-guns and ended by throwing grenades into the still over-crowded cells.

On 29 June German troops were outside Lvov; the Russians had withdrawn from the city the previous day. The people of the city began searching for friends and relatives among the rotting corpses which the Soviets had left behind. And they vowed to take their revenge. The real culprits had fled, but scapegoats were quickly found. Quite a number of their Jewish fellow-citizens were considered – in most cases wrongly – to be supporters of the communist system. Added to that was a long-standing and deeply rooted anti-Semitism. The rapidly established Ukrainian militia began rounding up Jews from all over the city. The German soldiers had no intention of preventing them, least of all those members of the *Einsatzgruppen* who were present – since it was part of their job to 'instigate' pogroms as 'inconspicuously as possible'.

A Polish woman, Jaroslawa Woloszanska, was twenty-two when she saw what happened to the Jews of Lvov, where they made up nearly a third of the city's 340,000 population: 'They rounded up Jews in Janowska Street. They got the Jews to carry the corpses out of the prison. They were beaten up on the street. I saw it myself. There was a terrible pogrom against the Jews. They came at dawn and dragged people out of their houses. Worst of all, they even killed children. It was all quite dreadful! The whole city stank of death and decay. I can remember I kept on washing my hands. Everybody was shocked by what the Russians had left behind. You heard the crying of the people being dragged along the street. Where I lived, they took a Jewish family away. You heard the children crying and the screams of the women. I didn't see anything, I just heard the screams. It was terrible.'

Irene Horowitz, also Jewish, experienced at first hand how neighbours suddenly became deadly enemies. She saw people she knew well dragging Jews from their homes and chasing them through the city with kicks and blows. Local collaborators and auxiliary police acted with monstrous brutality, spurred on and inflamed by the populace. It was all too easy to load blame on to the Jews. More and more Jews, including women and children, were corralled in the prisons under the eyes of the occupying Germans. The half-decayed corpses of the victims of Stalin's secret police had to be recovered and washed. The Jews were forced with truncheon blows to carry out this work.

For Irene Horowitz the worst thing was the fact that no-one stood up for their Jewish fellow-citizens: 'I was one of *them*. I had the same blood in my veins. I went to the same schools as Poles and Ukrainians We were friends, we had fun, we danced and sang together. And suddenly we were no longer human beings to them. We were just Jews.'

The housing shortage, which affected Kiev in particular because of the extensive fires and shelling, was relieved after the liquidation of the Jews by the reallocation of released Jewish homes

Situation report by the Einsatzgruppen, *31 October 1941*

In Riga there is general talk of mass-shootings of the Jews previously housed in the ghetto. The great majority of the citizens of Riga talk about it with satisfaction and are hoping for the total removal of the Jews and thus the release of the ghetto for housing purposes.

Report of the head of the SS and police in Latvia and commanding officer of the Ordnungspolizei, *23 December 1941*

Members of the *Einsatzgruppen* watched the murderous activity – and many took part in the orgy of violence, on their own initiative. SS *Hauptscharführer* Felix Landau willingly obeyed Heydrich's orders not to stand in the way of 'efforts by anti-communist or anti-Jewish circles to clean up their own back-yard'. In his diary he wrote this about a day in Lvov: 'Hundreds of Jews run along the streets, their faces covered in blood, gashes in their heads, fingers broken and eyes hanging out. Some blood-spattered Jews carry others who have collapsed. At the entrance to the citadel soldiers stand with truncheons as thick as your fist, hitting out at anyone they see. At the entrance the Jews are pushing their way out, so rows of Jews are piling on top of each other like pigs, and whimpering like you never heard, and more and more of these cocky Jews trot off covered in blood. We stand there and wait to see who will take charge. No-one. Someone has released the Jews. Anger and hatred are being let loose on the Jews. Nothing against that, only they shouldn't allow the Jews to run around in that condition. . . . Anyway – like many of my colleagues – I'm disappointed with this operation. Not enough fighting, in my opinion, hence my lousy mood.'

In three days 4,000 Jews were beaten to death on the streets – by the local militia and by sections of the population. Lvov was not an isolated case. In an October 1941 report by the head of *Einsatzgruppe* A, SS *Brigadeführer* Dr Franz Stahlecker, we read: 'In the very first hours after we marched in, albeit under considerable difficulties, local anti-Semitic forces were induced to mount pogroms against the Jews. In accordance with orders, the Security Police were determined to solve the Jewish problem with all means and with complete decisiveness. . . . It had to be shown to the outside world that the indigenous population took the first measures of their own accord, as a natural reaction against decades of suppression by the Jews and against terrorisation by the communists in former times.'

The pogroms which, on Heydrich's orders, the *Einsatzgruppen* were to instigate 'without leaving traces', were welcome if only because it was hoped that the excesses of the local population would reduce the scruples and resistance of the Wehrmacht. Furthermore, the brutal reaction of the population provided the German perpetrators with a useful yardstick for their own crimes.

Away to the left we saw trucks arriving, from which poured people who then stripped naked and stood in a queue, as though they were waiting for a bus. The queue was 600, 800, maybe 1,000 metres long. And to the right, where I had seen those graves, I heard shots every 20 seconds or so. Then this chain of naked people – men, women, children, old people – moved forward a few metres, and paused. Now and then, someone broke away from the queue and tried to escape – then collapsed under the fire from the Ukrainian militia.

The really Christian reaction would have been to get undressed on the spot and join the queue. . . . Those trained firing-squads, extermination squads, would probably have arrested me as a lunatic and sent me to some kind of therapeutic or psychoanalytical clinic. . . . Perhaps they would even have shot me. But I don't think so. I believe they were trained only to fire at the objects of their murder operation.

Baron Axel von dem Bussche, Wehrmacht officer, witness to a killing operation against Jews in Russia

In order to increase acceptance of the pitiless persecution of the Jews, Propaganda Minister Goebbels greedily seized on the horrific reports coming from the eastern front, about 'Jewish massacres and acts of vengeance against innocent pro-German Ukrainians'. After nearly two years of reticence towards the Soviet

Union, imposed by the Hitler–Stalin Pact, the Propaganda Minister needed material to stir up the fears of the German people and at the same time build up the bogey of the 'deadly Jewish-Bolshevist enemy'. Film of the discovery and exhuming of corpses in the NKVD prison in Lvov gave both Goebbels and Hitler their cue: 'The Führer now wants us to rev up the big anti-Bolshevist campaign'. Goebbels dictated for his diary on 6 July.

According to statements made after the war by former army commanders, Hitler is said to have ordered that all reported Soviet crimes 'must be punished with great severity by the execution of everyone connected with them, even if only remotely'. Wolfgang Schöler, a lieutenant in the railway pioneers, saw for himself the horrors in Lvov: 'At that moment I felt that the war against the Soviet Union was not completely unfounded after all. You said to yourself, people like that must be prevented from doing such things.'

Throughout July 1941 the German newsreels reported on the alleged massacre by the Jews of Lvov and gave ideological guidance: 'No mercy for the culprits, the Jews.' In the Reich, the films with appropriate commentary achieved their purpose. On 7 July the Security Service, reporting on the mood among cinema-goers, stated that 'the great majority expressed the conviction that today precisely these kind of images of the true nature of Bolshevism and Jewry in their terrible reality must be shown again and again'.

In mid-July 1941 Hitler believed that victory in the east was imminent. The warlord was more than ever convinced of his own 'genius'. He referred to himself in the same breath as Frederick the Great, Napoleon and Bismarck. He spoke of them as he might of close acquaintances. What linked him with these historic figures, he claimed, was the knowledge of what 'cyclopean labour it meant for him, as one man alone, to build a state anew'. Hitler discussed with his satraps how his new Reich would look. On 16 July 1941 Göring, Rosenberg, Keitel and Hans Lammers (head of the Reich Chancellery) met in the Führer's headquarters in the forests of East Prussia, to divide the spoils. The occupied regions were to be placed under a German civil administration and the 'General

Commissionerships' of Ostland, White Ruthenia and the Ukraine were formed. Hitler made no secret of the future he planned for the newly occupied areas in the east. The new eastern frontier was to follow roughly the line of the Ural mountains. Germany would have to secure this frontier for all time and could not allow any other military power to arise west of the frontier. 'It must be possible for us to control this eastern territory with 250,000 men and some good administrators. Look at the British, who with a total of 250,000 – of which about 50,000 are military – rule 400 million Indians. Our conquered lands must be dependent on German rulers for ever.' The successes of the advancing German troops and the statistics delivered by the *Einsatzgruppen* put Hitler in high spirits. He was deluded into believing that anything was possible.

In the bottom drawers of his academically educated planners there already lay a fully formulated concept for the future: the 'General Plan East'. A swift victory over the Soviet Union and the total economic plundering of the conquered territories would bring a decisive improvement to German raw material and food resources. This colonial exploitation was only possible through subjugation, the rapid Germanisation of the conquered eastern territories only possible though the expulsion and decimation of the 'Slavic masses'.

With the conquest of the vast Soviet empire the long-term war objective, the creation of a self-sufficient, blockade-proof Greater Germany was to be realised. In order to carry through this 'policy of conquest' the 'contributing regions' within the USSR were to be systematically sealed off. The economic exploitation of the food-growing capacity of the Soviet regions was in the hands of the Economic Staff East. Under Herbert Backe, permanent secretary in the Reich Ministry of Food and Agriculture, the so-called 'Starvation Plan' was developed, which was to be applied in the eastern territories: 'Umpteen million people in this region will become superfluous and will either die or be forced to emigrate to Siberia.' The German leadership predicted that as a result of this starvation policy some 30 million people in the conquered territories would die. Yet the objective of conquest and exploitation was a longer-term plan of the Nazi leaders, which in essence could only be tackled after the defeat of the Soviet Union.

> . . . I have reported for a special operation tomorrow. . . .
> Tomorrow, for the first time, I will have a chance to use my
> pistol. . . . Who cares about twelve hundred Jews who are not
> needed in a town and have to be bumped off? By the time I
> come home, I'll have a lot of fine stories to tell. But enough of
> that for today, otherwise you'll think I'm bloodthirsty.
>
> *Walter Mattner, police secretary, in a letter from Mogilev*
> *to his wife in Vienna, 2 October 1941*

While the top men of the Third Reich forged their megalomaniac
killing plans, their opposite numbers in the Kremlin were trying to
ride out the crisis. Stalin knew that this war was a matter of the
very survival of his empire. On 3 July 1941 he addressed the
Soviet people in a broadcast speech: 'Comrades! Citizen! Fighting
men of our army and our navy! Brothers and sisters! Our country
is in grave danger! In the occupied regions conditions must be
made intolerable for the enemy and all his accomplices. They must
be pursued wherever they go and destroyed, and all their measures
must be foiled.'

To Hitler, the partisan war called for by Stalin did not seem any
cause for concern. On the contrary, the warlord was positively
exultant: 'The Russians have now given orders for a partisan war
to be fought behind our lines. There is actually an advantage in
this: it gives us the opportunity to exterminate whoever and
whatever opposes us. . . . This vast area must of course be pacified
as speedily as possible; the best way to do this is to shoot dead
anyone who looks the least suspicious.'

Meanwhile, far away from the Führer's headquarters,
hundreds of thousands of German soldiers were attempting to
survive – in a war where all rules were set aside. In the months
that followed, fear of partisans made it ever harder for reasonable
Wehrmacht men to draw a line between the necessities of war
and unbridled, murderous repression. Former *Oberleutnant*
Ulrich Gunzert describes how the fear of partisans inflamed an
already tense atmosphere: 'The partisans, of course, made us
react in a way that was perfectly understandable, and there was

no way I could prevent it, even among my own men. When they caught a partisan, they simply bumped him off. Why? Because our wounded were being set upon and inhumanly massacred. Their penises were cut off, they were slowly hacked to death, limb by limb. We knew it was happening.' This led to hatred. 'At best we showed pity towards women and children. Children were not killed. But men were – whenever we caught them, they were killed. That was quite clear.' In explaining the mood of the Germans, he admits: 'I dare say we were sometimes perhaps too tough in the way we dealt with the partisans. I wouldn't dispute that. But on the other hand the behaviour of those partisans towards our men, especially the wounded, was so inhuman that even I myself felt one had to take revenge.'

Who was a partisan, and who merely supported them? This was often a hard question for the occupying troops to answer. The leadership further blurred the boundaries by equating Jews with partisans – an unjustified connection. Hitler was delighted with an order issued by the commander-in-chief of the 6th Army, von Reichenau, to all army groups: 'The soldier must fully appreciate the necessity for the harsh but just retribution against the Jewish *Untermensch*. It has the further purpose of nipping in the bud any uprisings to the rear of the Wehrmacht, which in our experience are always fomented by Jews. Should the use of weapons by individual partisans be discovered to the rear of the army, then the most draconian measures are to be taken. These are to extend to the male population who would have been in a position to prevent or warn of attacks.' Once again it was mainly the Jews who were being targeted. 'Where there's a Jew, there's a partisan. Where there's a partisan, there's a Jew', went the slogan.

Hitler himself demanded implacability on the part of his troops. On 22 July he announced: 'Given the large expanse of territory, the troops available to secure the conquered eastern regions are insufficient, unless not merely is all resistance subject to the judicial punishment of the guilty, but the occupying power spreads the kind of terror which alone is capable of removing from the population any tendency to rebelliousness!'

At the end of July the German armies had to stop and draw breath, to regroup and make good the losses of men and equipment. For the first time Stalin could take new hope that the Front would be stabilised, and called for increased resistance against the German troops. Despite its high losses the strength of the Red Army to fight back was not exhausted. At this time German intelligence officers were amazed to discover that Soviet units continued to fight bitterly, even when their communication lines were cut off, that fresh divisions from the rearward area were constantly being thrown into the battle, and that civil resistance was growing in strength. For the first time Hitler had to acknowledge that he had greatly underestimated the Soviet war potential.

> During the war one could at least try to be transferred out of an *Einsatzgruppe*. I myself tried it successfully. . . . After being sent back to my unit I was not demoted or disadvantaged in any way, except that I had a personal rift with Heydrich until the day he died. I dare say there were cases where being transferred out of an *Einsatzgruppe* was detrimental. But I can't recall any particular instance. Anyway, no-one was shot for it, as far as I know. In the Central Office of Reich Security there was also the possibility of volunteering for front-line service, or being released for other duties.
>
> *Franz Six*, SS-Oberführer, Einsatzgruppe *B*,
> *in a statement to the court*

At the beginning of August 1941 it was clear that the Blitzkrieg strategy was not succeeding in the Soviet Union, as it had in Poland and France. A violent dispute now arose between Hitler and the army commanders. The warlord halted the advance on Moscow and ordered that the strategy he had favoured in 1940 be put into effect: to reach Kiev and the Donets Basin in the south, and deprive the Soviets of their agricultural and industrial resources there. Also, Hitler's principal objective had always been to get free access to the oilfields of the Caucasus. *Generaloberst*

Alfred Jodl, head of operations in the Wehrmacht High Command, did not contradict him, but noted in a private comment that this was perhaps a development that would determine the outcome of the war: 'Hitler instinctively shrinks from following the same route as Napoleon. To him there is something uncanny about Moscow. He is afraid of a struggle to the death there against Bolshevism.'

This battle was no longer only being fought between regular armies over great strategic objectives, but also behind the lines in rearward areas whose security was vital for the supply of the fighting troops. Here was the fighting ground of the partisans. In 1941 their activity was still limited to fairly isolated acts of sabotage which had little military effect. But they created insecurity – for instance in the Pripyet Marshes of White Russia (Byelorussia). This vast area was traversed by rivers and streams, which flowed into the River Pripyet. This kind of terrain was scarcely accessible to vehicles. Between large stretches of boggy ground and forest there were a few islands of cultivable land. On these islands were numerous little villages, with a high proportion of Jews in their population.

At the outbreak of war a number of Soviet units, who had been overrun by the Germans, had retreated into the Pripyet region. North and south of the marshes the Wehrmacht had advanced a long way, but the Pripyet and its marshes remained a thorn in the German flesh. The southern and central parts of the marshes were not yet under their control and it was feared that the partisans could threaten the Wehrmacht's long supply-lines. As yet the partisan operations called for by Stalin were uncoordinated, but the Wehrmacht leadership saw the danger that in the long run large German forces would be tied down.

On 17 July 1941 Hitler gave his henchman Himmler the authority to issue instructions on policing to the Reich Commissioners Lohse and Koch. Himmler now saw that the time had come to deploy the police battalions and SS brigades under his command, in addition to the Security Service's *Einsatzgruppen*, in order to bring to reality the obsession for living-space in the east. The war on partisans was a welcome excuse to intensify the fight against the Jews.

Two days later Himmler ordered the transfer of two mounted SS regiments to the crisis zone on the Pripyet. The *Reichsführer* got his men in the right mood with 'guidelines for search and patrol of marsh areas': 'Where the population are, from a National Socialist standpoint, hostile, inferior racially and as human beings, or even, as is very often the case in marshy areas, comprised of locally based criminals, then everyone suspected of helping the partisans is to be shot, and the women and children are to be deported, livestock and food are to be confiscated and taken to a secure location. The villages are to be burned to the ground.' On 27 July SS *Standartenführer* Hermann Fegelein passed on to his units a crucial order from Himmler: 'Jews are generally to be treated as looters.' Those in charge did not hesitate to equate partisans with Jews – for them combating potential partisans was equal in importance to killing the Jews who were found in the villages.

> Entire divisions were bottled up and some surrendered to the Germans. But there were people who could see what the Germans were after. There were a lot of Jews among them, who then fled into the forests and built up partisan units. Later they were supplied from the air. I myself came across a woman lieutenant in the Soviet forces, who had been dropped by parachute with the task of organising the partisans. And that must have been as early as the first months of the Russian campaign.
>
> *Peter von der Osten-Sacken, former interpreter and special officer in the Von der Groeben infantry battalion*

At 7 a.m. on 30 July the mounted sections of the two SS cavalry regiments set off on the first 'cleaning-up operation' in the marshes. A day later, Himmler added teeth to his operational orders in a private conversation with Erich von dem Bach-Zelewski, as 'Senior SS and Police officer' the responsible commander in that region. A radio message to the sections said: 'Express orders of the *Reichsführer-SS*. All Jewish males must be shot. Drive the women into the bogs.'

The mounted SS men of the 1st Cavalry Regiment acted with the utmost brutality – in the villages they passed through they killed all Jews, even women and children. And they used machine-guns to mow the people down swiftly and indiscriminately.

The 2nd Regiment restricted itself to shooting men between the ages of eighteen and sixty. Jewish women and children were driven into the bogs, as ordered. But Himmler's executioners reported with disappointment: 'Driving women and children into the bogs was not the success it should have been, because the bogs were not deep enough for them to sink in. In most cases, at a depth of about three feet you come to firm ground, so that complete submersion was not possible.'

By 13 August Bach-Zelewski's thugs had murdered 13,788 'looters'. Of their victims 90 per cent were Jews, the rest were stray Red Army soldiers and supposed communists. This activity by the SS cavalrymen in the Pripyet Marshes had brought a new dimension to the mass murder of Jews in the occupied eastern territories. From now on, not only were men murdered, but women too.

> Of course, I didn't know the exact figures, but I'd heard that 250,000 Jews had been killed in the area of Army Group South alone. . . . So we knew that hundreds of thousands of people had been killed because they were Jews. It was so appalling that it made one's heart ache to think about it. But I also knew that 100,000 Germans had been put to death by euthanasia. The contempt of the regime for human life – that was the appalling thing, the fact that people were robbed of all their rights.
>
> *Baron Philipp von Boeselager, former Wehrmacht officer and member of the 20 July plot*

While the killing operation was being carried out over a period of many weeks, fathers and mothers were separated from their children. There were ghastly scenes in the villages that had been 'cleansed' by the *Einsatzgruppen*. Mothers were beaten and their children torn from them, babies were left to their fate in the houses. 'We children were separated from our parents; I was only just eleven. My mother wanted us to stay together and die together. But we were torn away from each other. I wasn't allowed to stay with my mother. All the time I only wanted to be killed along with her and my brother', Rozèle Goldenstein tells us. As a child she witnessed the liquidation of her own family: however she herself was not yet destined for death. No more thought was given to her future as an orphan than to the killing of her parents. As yet there had been no general order that Jewish children should also be killed. This was soon to change. From mid-August onward, throughout the occupied territories, the *Einsatzgruppen* crossed the boundaries of a killing operation which up to that point had been directed primarily against Jewish men of military age, and then also against women, and pursued the policy of indiscriminate slaughter of the Jewish population. Now even the children had to die.

For the time being a select few professionals, doctors, key skilled workers and other specialists were spared, along with their families, in order to work for the occupiers. Later, when the Germans retreated, even they were, for the most part, murdered.

The men of the 295th Infantry Division had many weeks of hard fighting behind them when, in the middle of August, they entered the town of Byelaya-Tserkov – to 'freshen up', as they were told. The exhausted infantrymen wanted nothing but peace and quiet. But in Byelaya-Tserkov there was no question of that. In this town with a large Jewish community, 40 miles south of Kiev, the soldiers heard shooting. Franz Kohler, a radio operator with the division, wanted to see for himself what was going on in the nearby woods. When he arrived at the shooting range of the local barracks, he could not believe his eyes. 'There's a row of people standing there, all doing somersaults at the same time. What the hell's this, I thought. I went closer and saw that they were all being shot. They all fell into the ditch.' Part of *Sonderkommando* 4a, a platoon of *Waffen-SS* and the Ukrainian militia, were in the process of murdering several hundred Jewish men and women. Kohler saw dreadful things. 'There was an elderly man with two women, they must have been his daughters; they were the last three. He took the women in his arms, then an SS man came along and shot them in the neck with a pistol.' When the appalled Franz Kohler asked what would happen to the children, one of the riflemen replied: 'Nothing to do with us. We're only shooting from age fourteen to granddads. We don't bother with the children.'

It was not until several days later that the men of the 295th Division learned what had been done to the children of Byelaya-Tserkov. The SS had locked them up in a building on the edge of town, without food or water. A week later trucks came to take the first children away – to be shot. Some ninety children were left. In a pitiful state they just vegetated, under the guard of Ukrainian militia. Their whimpering and crying could be heard all over the neighbourhood. Before long, word of the children's plight got around among the soldiers stationed in the town. On the afternoon of 20 August a Catholic chaplain, Ernst Tewes, and his Evangelical colleague Gerhard Wilczek were having lunch in the officers' mess. An NCO, in great distress, told the two clergymen about the plight of the Jewish children and asked them for help. The building in question was checked and the Catholic chaplain sent the following report through official channels: 'We found about ninety children in two rooms . . . children aged from a few months up to five, six or seven years old. . . . The two rooms in which the children were held were in a filthy condition. The children were lying or sitting on the floor, which was covered with their excrement. Most of them had flies on their legs and their half-clothed bodies. Some of the bigger children (aged two, three or four) were scratching the mortar from the walls and eating it. The air was disgustingly polluted; the small children, especially those who were only a few months old, cried and whimpered continually.' He had been told that these were the children of Jewish men and women who had already been shot, and that they were simply waiting to be shot themselves.

Appalled by the fact that children were to be murdered, the senior officer of the general staff, *Oberstleutnant* Helmuth Groscurth, seized the initiative and immediately went to see his commanding officer, *Feldmarschall* von Reichenau. This man, the field commander responsible for Byelaya-Tserkov, had previously stated that he considered the 'extermination of Jewish women and children to be an urgent necessity, regardless of what form it takes'. Groscurth's hope of rescuing the children was quickly dashed. In reply Reichenau, a careerist in the Third Reich, decreed: 'I have decided in principle that, once begun, this operation is to be carried through in an appropriate manner.' Then the field marshal angrily denounced the *Oberstleutnant* for having written that 'these measures against women and children' were no different from the 'enemy atrocities' which were 'continually being announced to the troops': 'I have to say that your statement is incorrect and extremely inappropriate and unhelpful. Furthermore it is contained in an open document that has passed through many hands. The report would have been better suppressed altogether.' So much for the morality of *Feldmarschall* von Reichenau. The commander-in-chief of the 6th Army approved and ordered the murdering of Jewish children.

August Häfner, SS *Obersturmbannführer* in *Sonderkommando* 4a, recalls the discussion about who should undertake the shooting of the children of Byelaya-Tserkov. From the start, Häfner had great misgivings about detailing members of his *Waffen-SS* for it, since they were all young men, many of whom had children of their own at home. When Häfner proposed that the local Ukrainian militia should take over the task 'no objection was raised to the suggestion from any side'. In such cases the Germans settled for the duty of cordoning off the area – and many actually deluded themselves that in this way they could not personally be held guilty for the death of the children, since only the local collaborators were responsible for it.

The operation carried out by the SD on 13.11 rid me of useless mouths to feed; and the 7,000 or so Jews remaining in the town are all harnessed to the labour process; they work with a will on account of their permanent fear of death, and in the spring they will be carefully examined and weeded out for a further reduction of their number.

Gerhard Erren, Commissioner for the Slonim region,
in a situation report, 25 January 1942

From a moral standpoint there was apparently a distinction between shooting adults and shooting innocent children and the aged. Jouzas Maleksanas, an officer in a Lithuanian volunteer police battalion, can recall this 'operation' almost 60 years after the event: 'Cry? No, we didn't cry; we didn't shed any tears over it. We felt guilty, but in the end we had to do what we were told. Not one of us refused to obey the order, not one of us put up a fight against the "operation". We simply weren't able to.' In 1941 Maleksanas could not afford to display any emotion to his German superiors, nor towards his victims – for him, obedience was the prime consideration.

Rozèle Goldenstein experienced the brutality of the death-squads at first hand: 'They rounded us up, in order to shoot us. Some tried to escape. But they were shot on the spot.' Rozèle presumed the last moments of her life had come. For her the walk towards the freshly dug pit was almost a relief after days and weeks of waiting alone: 'They had shot my mother, but allowed me to live. I wanted to be dead as well, and now the time had finally come. I knew I would see my mother again. I was certainly very frightened, but one thing was sure, I would rather die than go on living like that!' As if by a miracle, the young Jewish woman survived the shooting. As the first shots were fired she dropped into the pit, bodies fell on top of her and covered her as she lay motionless. Rozèle was now convinced that her end had come. Only after some minutes did she realise she was still alive. When she heard the murderers leave the clearing in the forest, drunk and singing loudly, she crept out of the pit and hid.

Usually the riflemen tried to make sure that those they had executed really were all dead. As Maleksanas explains: 'Parents often tried to shield their children from death by putting their arms round them. They didn't realise that the children suffered even more that way. Because if they couldn't be shot, they suffocated under their parents in the pit. I always tried to aim straight at the heart, where the yellow star was. So as to be sure they were really dead.' If the Germans noticed, when filling in the pit, that 'something was still moving' they delivered a *coup de grâce*.

I saw people laying into the Jews, but I reckon, if there are men standing around who outrank you – would you go up and say 'Come on now, don't do that'? When one thinks back on it today, of course it all seems very easy.

Wolfgang Schöler, former Wehrmacht soldier

The prime mover behind all these events, Adolf Hitler, was kept extremely well informed about every detail. Since 1 August the order had been in force: 'Reports on the work of the *Einsatzgruppen* in the east are to be presented to the Führer as they come in.' The instruction from the Gestapo chief, Heinrich Müller, was followed to the letter. It may seem an absurdity that on the one hand these barbaric operations still had to be carried out in complete secrecy, while on the other the need was felt to document the crimes in the smallest detail. From August onward, the 'activity and situation reports of the *Einsatzgruppen*' were radioed to Berlin by the group commanders on a daily basis. In the so-called incident reports the 'performance' of the *Sonder-* and *Einsatzkommandos* was itemised in detail.

That day the whole squad, except for the sentries, was sent out at about 6 a.m. for this shooting. Everyone who was available had to go. . . . We halted on a surfaced road, where it came to an end in open country. A huge number of Jews had been assembled there and a place set up where they had to put down their clothes and their luggage. Half a mile away I saw a big natural ravine. It was sandy terrain. The ravine was about 30 feet deep and 400 yards long. At the top it was about 80 yards wide and at the bottom about 10 yards wide.

As soon as I arrived at the execution area, I and some other fellows had to go down into this hollow. It wasn't long before the first Jews were led into the ravine. The Jews had to lie down near the sides of the ravine with their faces to the ground. There were twelve riflemen in all, in three groups. Jews were led down to each firing-squad simultaneously.

> The Jews who came after had to lie on the bodies of those who had been shot previously. The riflemen stood behind the Jews and shot them in the neck. I can still remember to this day the horror that overcame the Jews, who could look down from the edge on to the corpses in the pit. Many of them cried out in terror. You just can't imagine what strength of nerve it took to carry out that filthy business. It was horrible.
>
> *Kurt Werner, member of* Sonderkommando *4a, in a statement to the court about the massacre on Babi Yar on 29 and 30 September 1941*

In addition to the daily reports, *Einsatzgruppe* A submitted an overall report listing the activities of the unit up to mid-October. In it we read: 'It was always to be expected that the Jewish problem in the east would not be solved by pogroms alone. On the other hand, the cleansing operations by the security police in accordance with basic orders was aimed at removing the Jews as comprehensively as possible. For this reason extensive executions have been carried out by *Sonderkommandos* in the towns and countryside.' Attached to the report was a 'summary of the number of persons executed'. According to this, by 15 October 1941 *Einsatzgruppe* A had already murdered 118,430 Jews and 3,387 'communists'. A further 5,500 Jews had fallen victim to the pogroms instigated in Lithuania and Latvia. The commanding officer of *Einsatzkommando* 3, SS *Standartenführer* Karl Jäger, also submitted his account. In his report dated 1 December 1941 he talked of 137,346 Jews being liquidated. In August the numbers leapt up. Even the number of children murdered in the various executions was now indicated separately. Thus, for example, we read in the report for 19 August 1941: 'In Ukmerge: 298 Jews, 255 Jewesses, 88 Jew children.' On 2 September he states: 'Janova: 112 Jews, 1,200 Jewesses, 244 J-children.' Then for 9 October: 'Svenciany: 1,169 Jews, 1,840 Jewesses, 717 J-children.'

The list could be continued endlessly. At the end Jäger wrote: 'I can state today that the objective of solving the Jewish problem for Lithuania has been achieved by *Einsatzkommando* 3. In Lithuania there are no longer any Jews, except those on forced labour plus their families. I wanted to get rid of these working Jews and the families as well; however, this provoked a sharp challenge from the civil administration (the Reich Commissioner) and from the Wehrmacht.' In addition, Jäger's report contained some practical hints for future mass murders: 'The carrying out of such operations is principally a question of organisation. The decision to systematically rid every district of Jews required thorough preparation of each operation and the reconnaissance of local conditions in the district in question. The Jews had to be assembled in one place or several places. Depending on the number, space for the required pits had to be found and the pits dug. The length of the route from the assembly-point to the pits was on average 4 to 5 kilometres. The Jews were transported to the execution area in batches of 500, with gaps of 2 kilometres between each.'

In accordance with basic orders, the systematic cleansing operations in the eastern territories encompassed as complete a removal of Jewry as possible. With the exception of Ruthenia, this objective has been essentially achieved through the execution to date of 229,052 Jews.

Secret activity report of Einsatzgruppe *A for the period from*
16 October 1941 to 31 January 1942

The death we gave them was a nice quick death, compared with the hellish torment of thousands upon thousands in the dungeons of the GPU. Babies flew in a big arc through the air and we picked them off them in mid-flight before they landed in the pit or in the water.

Walter Mattner, police secretary, in a letter from Mogilev
to his wife in Vienna, 5 October 1941

Reports arrived from death-squads in other regions. *Einsatzgruppe* B reported 45,467 shootings up to 31 October, In the same period *Einsatzgruppe* C accounted for a far larger number of liquidated Jews: with 75,000 executions this group took second place in the 'success ratings'. In the incident report we read: 'Several reprisals were carried out in the framework of the major operation. The biggest of these took place immediately after the capture of Kiev; for this, Jews and their entire families were used exclusively.' The 'major operation' near Kiev, mentioned here, is today still a synonym for Nazi crimes in the Soviet Union: on 29 and 30 September 1941 33,771 Jews were shot by *Einsatzkommando* 4a of *Einsatzgruppe* C in the ravine of Babi Yar. In the operational area of *Einsatzgruppe* D, up to December 1941, a total of 54,696 people were murdered; 90 per cent of those killed were Jews. The number of Soviet Jews who fell victim to the *Einsatzgruppen* in the first five months of the eastern campaign exceeded half a million.

In the reports, the shootings of Jews were usually described as 'reprisal measures'. Other code-words in the incident reports, such as 'punishment measures', 'sedition' or 'communist agitation' were intended to conceal the crimes which began on Soviet territory in the summer of 1941.

> Then the SS and the SD arrived and it was a very different story. They began organising the killing. The SS carried out their operations with the help of the Lithuanians. The ones who did the shooting were Lithuanians under the supervision of the SS. I would say there were ten SS men and eighty Lithuanians in the groups that organised things there.
>
> *Alex Faitelson, Lithuanian Jew*

The perpetrators were SS men, convinced Nazis and fanatical racists, but there were also members of police battalions, who scarcely seemed destined to become murderers. Their officers demanded dreadful things of them, and their employer, the *Reichsführer-SS* Heinrich Himmler, knew that very well. He worried about his executioners. And so, in an order dated 12 December 1941, to the 'senior SS and police officers', he drew attention to the 'duty of care' of the superiors for their men: 'It is a sacred duty of the senior and commanding officers, personally to ensure that none of our men, who have this difficult duty to perform, are ever coarsened or suffer any harm to their nature or character. This task will be carried out through the sternest discipline in the performance of their duties, and through a companionable get-together at the end of a day that has brought with it difficult tasks of this nature. However, these companionable get-togethers must not end in alcoholic abuse. They should be evenings when – circumstances allowing – people sit down to eat the best of German home cooking, and the time should be filled with music and lectures introducing our men to the finer spheres of German intellectual life and sensibility.'

We knew that in those little towns of 5,000 or 6,000 people, many Jews were shot and buried there. The rest came into the cities, so that the surrounding countryside was 'Jew-free'.

Arnold Arluk, partisan

I was so bitterly disappointed that the German Wehrmacht, or Germans in general, could do such a thing. At first I thought: look, in the First World War they claimed that the Germans had hacked children's hands off and things like that. Then again, I said: we're not hacking anyone's hands off. What can I say now? It was something wicked. A wicked thing happened there.

Franz Kohler, radio-operator with the 295th Infantry Division and witness of shooting of civilians by Germans

However, this sort of diversion did not help all the perpetrators. As a prisoner in a concentration camp, Simon Wiesenthal worked in an SS field-hospital in Lvov. 'Are you a Jew?' he was asked one day by a nurse there. When he said he was, she asked him to follow her. On the first floor of the building she took him to a door. 'Go in there.' Wiesenthal did as he was bid.

'I went in. And then I heard a voice: "Come closer." I go closer and suddenly I see a head, bandaged, with holes cut for the nose and mouth, and where the eyes should be there are stains. The man says: "Sit down." Then he says: "You were surprised to be summoned to me. I know I'm in a room for the dying. And when the nurse told me there were Jews working outside, I asked her to bring a Jew up to me. She didn't ask me why. You see, I've had terrible experiences, and have done terrible things myself."' He told Wiesenthal that, a few months before, in Dnepropetrovsk, he and his unit had locked a group of Jewish prisoners in a house. They each had to take a can of petrol with them. '"And then we machine-gunned the building until the whole thing caught fire. People jumped out of the windows. We saw a man with his child . . . he held his hand over the child's eyes before jumping. And we were given the order to fire. The next day we advanced further; on the other side were the Russians and we were supposed to launch an attack. All at once I saw them again before my eyes – the family burning, and I just stood still. Then a grenade exploded in front of us. I got splinters in my face. I don't have eyes any more and that's why I'm here."' While the dying SS man was telling Wiesenthal this, he beckoned him to sit by his bed. 'He made room for me, and I had my hands on the bed', Wiesenthal relates. There in front of him lay one of the perpetrators, an SS man, who knew he was laden with guilt and now sought forgiveness. Wiesenthal continues: 'Yet while he was talking, I withdrew my hands. I was hearing the confession of a perpetrator. It was not really a confession in the sense that he regretted anything. But he had asked for a Jew and now expected something from me which I was not empowered to give. I stood up and, without saying a word, left the room.'

CHAPTER TWO

DECISION

KNOPP/MÜLLNER

They were having a high old time in the Chantilly night-club in Paris. The establishment in the rue Fontaine offered everything that German gentlemen in Paris understood by *savoir vivre*: subdued lighting, beautiful dancing-girls and unlimited red wine. This is where the occupiers came to relax from their duties, well away from home. On the evening of 3 October 1941 the atmosphere was exuberant, as usual. It was already well past midnight when a naval officer, *Korvettenkapitän* Neurer, suddenly succumbed to the effects of alcohol. One of his chums took him by the arm and dragged him outside to a waiting car. The others at the table looked at each other. 'The skipper's had enough', they agreed.

A conspiratorial group had gathered in the Chantilly that evening. SS-*Obersturmführer* Sommer from the *Einsatzkommando* of the security police and SD, a contact called 'Stephan', an agent by the name of 'Dr Keller', *Kapitän* Neurer and a Frenchman who was to be recruited as a new spy within the French underground. Throughout the evening there had been a great deal of coming and going at their table. Six or eight men, apparently French, joined them but after some time left the club in small groups, only to return a little later. Something seemed to be going on. But no-one at the table wanted to talk about it. Not until the following morning did *Obersturmführer* Sommer claim: 'We certainly had a brilliant alibi for last night', and added with a smile, 'It worked really well again!'

Indeed, everything had gone according to plan. While Sommer and his colleagues were enjoying themselves in the Chantilly, explosive charges were being placed in seven Paris synagogues. At

2.05 a.m. a bomb detonated at the synagogue in the Avenue Montespan. Flying debris damaged houses within a 50-yard radius. At 2.45 a.m. another charge went off in front of the synagogue in the rue des Tournelles. At 3.30 a.m. the synagogue in the rue St-Issure was hit. Even the largest synagogue in Paris, in the rue de la Victoire, was targeted. Window-panes shattered, neighbouring buildings were severely damaged and two Wehrmacht soldiers slightly injured. Throughout the city, Parisians were woken by explosions. Rumours quickly began circulating that the British had been bombing the city. As day broke and it was revealed that only synagogues had been affected, suspicion fell on the Germans. Had they not set fire to synagogues in Germany as well?

> From 1942 onwards we had big problems. We had to wear yellow stars, we were no longer allowed into cinemas, swimming-baths or theatres. There were signs up saying: 'No admittance for dogs or Jews.'
>
> *Denise Holstein, French Jew*

German sources in Paris immediately denied any involvement. Those responsible, asserted *SS-Obersturmbanführer* Dr Helmut Knochen, were 'French anti-Jewish extremists', the incident was 'a purely French matter the investigation of which lay with the French police'. Knochen, the head of the Security Police and the SD (Security Service) was Heydrich's man in Paris, and was eager to dispel any suspicion that Germans might be behind the attacks. As was customary in SS circles, he attributed the blame to the victims: 'The opinion most frequently heard is that the attacks were fomented by Jews themselves, in order to generate a mood of sympathy among the broad mass of the population.' Many French would even regard the French police as the instigators and would assume that the *chef de cabinet* of the Paris Prefecture of Police, Dallier, was a key contact between 'Jewish capital' and the executive authorities. The latter view was apparently prevalent among journalists.

There is no doubt that the correspondent of the Nazi Party newspaper, *Völkischer Beobachter*, was part of this group. 'These incidents', it reported, 'show clearly that certain French circles are placing the blame for the tension of the last few weeks not only on communists but also on the intellectual inspirers of the acts of terrorism, namely the Jews.' Knochen of the SS was delighted to see what attention the attacks attracted in Paris. 'Young people in particular have warmly welcomed the fact that at last some visible action is being taken against the Jewish community', he reported to Berlin. 'Among members of the Anti-Jewish Institute the view is taken that it is a good thing the Jews were being publicly taught a lesson.' The prevailing opinion, he said, was that the blame fell on the Jews.

> The situation got steadily worse; one ban followed another. You were no longer allowed to sit on a park bench, no longer allowed on the streets after six or eight o'clock in the evening, no longer allowed on trams. You could only travel by train with special permission, you needed a special travel permit. We could only go shopping between three and four in the afternoon. And we were banned from going to any public place of entertainment, cinema, theatre, opera – even parks. New prohibitions kept coming. At quite an early stage we had to hand in our cars, then later even our bicycles, typewriters, radios, cameras. Then the Jews had special work duties on Sundays, in addition to their job during the week.
>
> *Erza Jurman, German Jew*

Knochen was satisfied. The deception seemed to be working. For the truth was that the French police were not behind the outrages, nor were Jews responsible. Knochen himself had made them possible. The explosives came from the Central Office of Reich Security in Berlin. Knochen's immediate superior, Reinhard Heydrich, had been in on it from the start. Very soon, however, the SS's cover was blown in Paris: a French anti-Semite named Eugène Deloncle, who was collaborating with the Germans, had asked the security service in Paris for help – and received from Berlin twelve canisters of fluid explosive for the strike against the synagogues.

> The world war has come, and the necessary consequence must be the annihilation of the Jews. This question is to be considered without sentimentality.
> *Joseph Goebbels, diary entry for 13 December 1941*
>
> The Führer has taught us all not to seek solutions for today but for centuries hence.
> *Heinrich Himmler in a speech on 2 March 1941, in Breslau*
>
> Under all possible circumstances we must as quickly as possible see to it that we remove the Jews from the *Generalgouvernement* (occupied Poland).
> *Hans Frank, entry in his official diary for 22 July 1941*

For the commander-in-chief of the German forces in France this was nothing less than a scandal. After the Paris attacks a new wave of acts of sabotage on Wehrmacht installations was to be expected. However, Reinhard Heydrich refused to show any remorse. The head of the security police and security service within the SS assumed full responsibility. The attacks, Heydrich said, were intended to show everyone in France 'that Jewry can no longer feel secure in what was once their principal power-centre in Europe'. He said he had 'for years been occupied with preparing the Final Solution of the Jewish question in Europe. I carry full responsibility for this also.'

Clearly Heydrich had just been waiting for the right moment. Deloncle's proposals, he admitted, 'were only taken up by me at a moment when, from the highest quarter, Jewry was being identified in the severest terms as Europe's troublemakers, who ultimately had to disappear from Europe'. By 'highest quarter' he meant Hitler. The 'moment' was September 1941. One or two weeks were all he needed to prepare the Paris bomb attacks. The explosions were to serve as a declaration of war on all European Jews – a portent of their coming destruction. It was at about that time that Hitler had finally decided that all Jews had to disappear. They were to be deported to the east, where death awaited them, where they were to be shot, or murdered in gas-trucks and soon in gas-chambers. Something had changed fundamentally. Hitler's determination to destroy had become more extreme. In August and September 1941 the dictator was on course towards mass murder on an industrial scale.

In fact, the deportation of Jews from German territory and from occupied Poland to the conquered territories of the east was not supposed to begin until after the victory over the Soviet Union. By autumn 1941 at the latest Hitler wanted to have defeated Stalin and then, from a position of strength, to have fulfilled one of his greatest wishes – an alliance with the British Empire, whose favour he had so long courted in vain; and to whom, after Stalin's defeat, there would remain no choice but to sue for peace with the Reich, or so the dictator believed. Europe would then be 'pacified' in the way he wanted it, both Moscow and Leningrad would be razed to the ground, a continent would be subjugated – and the way open, with Britain's support, to challenge the next enemy, the United States, in a struggle for world domination. The European war would have become a world war for which Hitler, in his racial and ideological madness, held not himself but Jewry responsible – moreover, a world war which, as Hitler had pronounced at an early date, would mean the end of the Jews in Europe. On 30 January 1939 he 'prophesied' something which no-one at the time was prepared to take seriously: 'If the Jews of international finance inside and outside Europe succeed once again in plunging the nations into a world war, then the result will not be the Bolshevisation of the earth and thus the victory of Jewry, but the annihilation of the Jewish race in Europe.'

Since the invasion of the Soviet Union the mass killing had escalated. One of many apocalyptic scenarios foresaw every Jew in Europe being sent to a remote reservation beyond the Urals – which meant in effect condemning them to death by starvation. The overcrowded ghettos in the *Generalgouvernement* (German-occupied Poland), where hunger and disease created a living hell, were to be, as

Hitler put it, 'only transit-camps, as it were'. In the east, the future 'living-space' of the 'Aryan race', nothing would remain the same. The plans for the monstrous programme of murder had already been worked out in detail. According to the 'General Plan East' produced by Himmler's Reich Commission for the Conservation of the German National Character, the whole of Poland, the Baltic countries, White Ruthenia and parts of western Ukraine, were, within 30 years, to be settled by ten million 'ethnic Germans'. Fourteen million people of 'good racial stock' were to be 'Germanised' and 31 million to be 'junked' beyond the Urals. In the planning documents death was a substantial factor. 'Umpteen million' dead by starvation were allowed for. Most of those would be Jews.

My prophecy will find its fulfilment in the fact that Aryan humanity will not be destroyed by this war, but the Jew will be exterminated. No matter what the struggle may bring, or how long it may last, that will be the ultimate result.

Adolf Hitler in a message to Nazi Party members,
24 February 1942

The Germans proceeded in a very systematic way. They had precise information, they knew exactly where most of the Jews lived. First, we had to go around wearing the Star of David. Then we had to hand in all musical instruments and radios. Of course we couldn't go the cinema any more. In trams we could only travel in the rear compartment. The only place we could go as kids and teenagers in Prague was the Hagibau, a football ground with a small park next to it. That was the only place we could enjoy a bit of greenery. Obviously, we were thrown out of school, out of high school. I then started an apprenticeship as an electrician. That only lasted for three or four months, then that was banned as well.

Chanan Bachrich, Czech Jew

All that was supposed to happen after the defeat of the Soviet Union. It was therefore all the more surprising when, in

September 1941, the timetable for the Holocaust was changed fundamentally. Hitler had suddenly decided to 'solve' the 'Jewish Problem' sooner than planned, and Reinhard Heydrich, officially entrusted with the preparations for the 'Final Solution', was fully in the picture. The ambitious manager of the killing operations only gave his approval to the Paris terrorism when he had received the crucial signal from 'on high'. He did not assume responsibility and risk conflict with the Wehrmacht until he could be sure of Hitler's protecting hand. On the other hand, why would Heydrich have to have recourse to the 'highest quarter', if the term 'disappearance' had meant some harmless process? Heydrich knew that the killing had taken on a new dimension. The most extreme phase of the Final Solution was about to commence. The war of annihilation was intensifying, and the crimes at the Front, where Jews were being shot in hundreds of thousands, were developing into the murder of the century.

Since the beginning of the Russian campaign, the death-squads of the SS and the police had been murdering behind the lines of the swiftly advancing Wehrmacht. Heydrich had instructed them to execute all communist career politicians, party officials, Jews in party or government positions, as well as 'other extremist elements (saboteurs, propagandists, snipers, terrorists, agitators, etc.)', to shoot 'inferior Asiatic commissars' and 'gypsies', and pre-emptively destroy the 'Jewish-Bolshevist intelligentsia'. From the first day of the invasion of the USSR the killing programme proceeded with merciless efficiency. It was in Garsden, a Lithuanian border town, on 24 June 1941, that a squad of state police from Tilsit in East Prussia, and Protection Police from Memel, murdered the first Jews: two hundred men and one woman, who was married to a commissar. By December of that year the number of those shot by the *Einsatzgruppen* would rise to over half a million.

At the Front as well, Hitler's calculated gamble was paying off. The Blitzkrieg concept, which had been perfected in Poland and France, seemed to be effective once again. The three German Army groups completely overran the Red Army. With apparent ease the armoured spearheads plunged deep into Russian territory. Their opponents were clearly unable to resist the weight of the onslaught. Within only four days the two Panzer armies of Army Group Centre closed the ring behind the Russian forces, who were fighting between Minsk and Bialystok. Four Soviet armies totalling forty-three divisions were surrounded. The first battle of encirclement in 'Operation Barbarossa' began. Not long afterwards the German High Command reported the capture of 323, 898 Red Army prisoners.

Winning seemed so easy that the normally sober Chief of the Army General Staff, Franz Halder, noted in his diary on 3 July 1941: 'It is probably no exaggeration to say that the campaign against Russia was won in 14 days.' A euphoria, like that in June 1940 when France was triumphantly defeated, swept through the Führer's headquarters. 'I keep trying to put myself in the enemy's position', Hitler mused on 4 July. 'For all practical purposes he has already lost the war.' The situation on the fronts, combined with Hitler's pathological hatred of the Jews, dictated the timetable for decision in the weeks to come.

Seldom had Hitler been so sure of victory as during those first weeks of July. By the middle of the month Army Group Centre was only 150 miles from Moscow and its advance seemed unstoppable. In the south the Ukrainian front had been breached. Now the Reich was already preparing for the end of the fighting. From July onwards newly manufactured tanks were no longer despatched to the Russian Front but were held in reserve for new battles in the Middle East. It seemed that 'Barbarossa' really was the 'game of sand-castles' that Hitler had expected it to be. 'You only have to kick the door in and then the whole rotten building will collapse', he had declared to the commander-in-chief of Army Group South. Now reports from the Front seemed to exceed his optimistic expectations. The rapid advance increased Hitler's confidence to ecstatic heights of victorious euphoria. He told the Japanese ambassador, Oshima, that he believed the fighting would be over by the middle of September.

The goal seemed within his grasp and the further the Wehrmacht advanced towards Moscow, the better Hitler saw the chances of his genocidal vision being realised. Moscow and Leningrad he planned to 'raze to the ground', so there would be no need to feed their populations; he predicted a 'national catastrophe' for the Soviet Union. As he explained on 16 July: 'Basically what we have to do is break up this gigantic cake into manageable pieces, so that we can firstly dominate, secondly administer and thirdly exploit it.'

Time and again the triumphant Hitler allowed his thoughts to roam ahead to the period after 'Barbarossa'. He wanted to turn the conquered territories in the east, the Crimea, the Baltic countries, Galicia and the Caucasus as far east as Baku into a German 'Garden of Eden'. To achieve this, 'all necessary measures' would have to be taken, which meant, in concrete terms, an ethnic cleansing through 'shooting, resettlement, etc.' The German 'paradise' had to be 'pacified as quickly as possible'. On the following day, 17 July 1941, Hitler now officially assigned to the *Reichsführer-SS*, Heinrich Himmler, the new area of activity of which *de facto* notice had been given some time ago: 'using police authority to secure the newly occupied eastern territories.'

> But what is to be done with the Jews? Do you think they will be accommodated in village settlements in the *Ostland*? In Berlin they said to us: What's all the fuss about? There's nothing we can do with them in the *Ostland* or in the Reich Commissionership; liquidate them yourselves. But there are 3.5 million Jews; we can't shoot them, we can't poison them; nevertheless we can begin operations which will in a way lead to successful extermination. This of course will be in conjunction with the major measures that are being discussed in the Reich.
>
> *Hans Frank, to members of the administration of the* Generalgouvernement *in Poland, 16 December 1941*

Himmler exploited his new authority without delay. Within days he doubled the number of SS killers behind the front line. He impressed upon the commanders of the death-squads that they were carrying out a 'historic task'. From now on the *Reichsführer* paid more frequent visits to his officers in the east, in order to motivate them to kill more and faster. The war would not last much longer, that was certain. And in the meantime those who could be killed, he calculated cynically, would not have to be deported later. The death-squads were still shooting exclusively men, mainly commissars, party officials and 'other extremist elements'. In the war of annihilation against the Soviet Union, their job was still to kill the 'Jewish-Bolshevist intelligentsia'. As yet Hitler had not finally made his mind up about the fate of Europe's Jews.

The phrases that still applied were that they should be deported, 'resettled', removed from Europe in whatever way possible. 'The Jews are the scourge of humanity', Hitler told the Croatian leader, Marshal Kvaternik, on 21 July 1941. Where they were sent, be it to Siberia or Madagascar, was immaterial.

My father always said: 'Am I supposed to leave my German fatherland, just because some jumped-up criminal is in power? If that's so then millions of decent Germans would have to emigrate.'

Then, after the night of the pogroms in 1938, he must have got the feeling that there was no future in Germany and Hitler would win out. So he tried to arrange emigration but there wasn't a country in the world that would accept an ordinary Jew.

Hans-Oskar Löwenstein de Witt, a partly Jewish German,
classified by the Nazis as a 'full Jew'

The Poles were divided into various groups. In those days there were anti-Semitic groups, but there were also some who helped the Jews. They were known as 'Benefactors of humanity'. They risked their own lives. If it was found out that a Polish family had hidden Jews in their house, every member of the family was killed by the SS.

Stefan Grayek, Polish Jew

While the Wehrmacht advanced seemingly unhindered and the death-squads continued their bloody work, the question which had been discussed for years, as to how the 'Final Solution' was to be effected in practical terms, still remained unanswered. Many possible ways were sounded out. Yet with every day that passed a decision became more urgent. The situation in the ghettos of Poland's *Generalgouvernement* was worsening dramatically. 'There is a danger this winter that not all the Jews will be able to be fed', wrote *SS-Sturmbannführer* Rolf-Heinz Höppner, head of the SD's Posen (Poznan) section, in a letter dated 16 July 1941, to Adolf Eichmann who ran the Jewish desk at the Central Office of Reich Security. He was referring to the ghetto in Łódz, which now lay within Reich territory. 'We should seriously consider whether the most humane solution might not be for those Jews who are no longer fit for work to be finished off with some kind of fast-acting agent. At all events that would be pleasanter than letting them starve to death.' Meanwhile, the *Generalgouverneur*, Hans Frank, refused to establish new ghettos in Poland, 'since, according to an express declaration by the Führer on 19 June this year, in the foreseeable future the Jews will be removed from the *Generalgouvernement*, which is intended only to be a kind of transit-camp' for the Jews en route to 'reservations' beyond the Urals.

Since the beginning of 1941 Reinhard Heydrich had been working on a comprehensive programme for deporting all Jews from Europe to the east. Now, with victory apparently so near, the day was approaching when Hitler would order the last and most radical phase of the Final Solution. Heydrich wanted to be ready for the decision on what Hitler called 'the Final Solution of the Jewish question, which is without doubt going to come'.

Of all the henchmen who assisted Hitler in his crimes, the head of the Central Office of Reich Security, the only central authority dedicated to carrying out the 'will of the Führer', was certainly the most ambitious. At the peak of his treacherous triumph he had a document drafted by the 'adviser on Jewish matters', Eichmann, which was signed by Hermann Göring on 31 July 1941. With this document, Göring, who had been charged with the 'overall solution of the Jewish problem' in 1938, authorised Heydrich 'to make all necessary preparations for an overall solution of the Jewish problem in the German sphere of influence in Europe'. The Holocaust, which had begun with the murders by the *Einsatzgruppen* in the east, was now to reach over the whole of western Europe as well, and even into French North Africa. With these 'discretionary powers' Heydrich had secured his position. They promoted him to the position of supreme 'Commissioner for Jews' for the whole of Europe – responsible for one of the things most important to Hitler. Göring, Heydrich stated in January 1942, had given him the job 'on the instructions of the Führer'. He had signed the authorisation in the sure knowledge of the Führer's will.

To introduce the project, Heydrich gave a private presentation to senior echelons of the military in the Hotel Majestic, the HQ of the military administration. In it he called for cooperation between the military command and the new head of the SS and police, and at the same time – almost as a little present to his hosts – he let out a few secrets about the Wannsee Conference, including the trial killing of deported Jews by driving them around in a sealed van and feeding in the exhaust gases.

This was on 7 May 1942. Up until then we had assumed, based on reports on Kiev and other mass slaughters, that the destruction of the Jews in the east was probably restricted to a number of specific incidents and locations. And now for the first time we heard the word 'gassing' used and found out that completely new methods of exterminating Jews were being considered.

Walter Bargatzky, former major in the Wehrmacht and lawyer with the Paris commandant's office; member of the assassination plot of 20 July 1944

For the first time it will not be others who will bleed to death; this time, for the first time, the good old Jewish law will be applied: an eye for an eye, a tooth for a tooth.

Hitler in a speech in the Berlin Sports Palace, 30 January 1942

> We should seriously consider whether the most humane solution might not be for those Jews who are no longer fit for work to be finished off with some kind of fast-acting agent.
>
> *Rolf-Heinz Hoppner, head of the Resettlement Office in the Reich city authority, Posen (Poznan), in a letter to Eichmann, 16 July 1941*

Even though in many places the Holocaust developed its own internal dynamic, Hitler remained the driving force behind the mass killing. To his executioners, whether Himmler, Heydrich or Göring, he made it clear what they had to do, by a verbal order, by a hint or merely by an approving nod. No document was to prove his personal responsibility for the Holocaust, no suggestion should sully the myth of the just and upright Führer. Yet despite all the camouflage, the evidence for Hitler's guilt is overwhelming. On four occasions Himmler referred to a 'Führer Order' for the so-called Final Solution, not without craving sympathy for how hard it was for him to carry out Hitler's instructions. 'It was the most terrible task that any organisation could be given: the task of resolving the Jewish question.' Telling the Reich Commissioner for *Ostland*, Hinrich Lohse, about the shootings, he said: 'My command is whatever the Führer wishes.' Again and again we find things in the documents which point to Hitler as the driving force of the Holocaust. In late 1941, when the Adviser on Jewish Questions in the Ministry of the Interior, Bernhard Loesener, told the permanent secretary, Stuckart, that he could longer remain in his post, Stuckart reacted with amazement and indignation: 'Don't you know that these things are being done on the highest orders?'

Hitler was the highest authority; in the 'Jewish question' he made all the important decisions, but remained dependent on executives like Himmler and Heydrich – men with the fatal 'virtue' of over-eager obedience and the ability to get inside the mind of the tyrant, to penetrate his criminal psyche, to divine his presumed wishes and to fulfil them. Hitler had precise information about what his instructions led to. On 1 August 1941, the day when Heydrich assumed full authority, the Gestapo chief, Heinrich Müller, told the heads of the four *Einsatzgruppen* that Hitler wished to be kept fully updated on their work. From then on, the Führer's HQ was regularly supplied with details of the mass killing in the east. On 31 December 1942 his personal adjutant, *Sturmbannführer* Pfeiffer, presented him with Activity Report No. 51 'to the Führer', about the Jews shot by the *Einsatzgruppen* between August and November. Hitler noted the figure: 363, 211 dead.

However the dictator never personally witnessed a shooting. 'Where would I be', Hitler explained in October 1941, 'if I couldn't find men I trust to handle the jobs that I can't do myself; tough men, who I know will take drastic measures, just as I would.'

At the head of those perpetrators who willingly helped Hitler with the annihilation stood Heinrich Himmler. In the summer of 1941 the *Reichsführer-SS* wanted to get an on-the-spot picture of the murderous activity and capabilities of the mobile slaughterhouses. At 11.30 a.m. on 14 August he took off in a special aircraft from Lötzen airfield in East Prussia. He was bound for Minsk in Byelorussia, a city which in the weeks to come would, like Riga, be the destination for Jews dragged off from the Reich. Two cameramen filmed the visit. The newsreel shots have been preserved, but one of his stopovers is missing. On the morning of 15 August 1941 Hitler's hangman, Himmler, wanted to attend an execution himself. Arthur Nebe, head of *Einsatzgruppe* B, had ordered 100 Jews and alleged partisans to be fetched from Minsk prison. One of those destined for death had fair hair and blue eyes.

> Himmler asked: 'Are you a Jew?'
> 'Yes.'
> 'Are both your parents Jews?'
> 'Yes.'
> 'Have you any forebears who weren't Jews?'
> 'No.'
> 'Then I really can't help you.'

The execution began. Himmler did not want to miss anything and stood at the edge of the pit. The victims were instructed to lie with their faces to the ground. Himmler betrayed no emotion –

even when, in the heap of bodies, two women were still moving. 'Look at the men's eyes', the 'Senior SS and Police Officer for Russia Central', Erich von dem Bach-Zelewski, is reported to have said to Himmler at that moment. 'Those men will have no nerves for the rest of the their lives. We're breeding neurotics and savages here!'

Himmler showed some 'understanding', nevertheless he persuaded the riflemen that their task was necessary, that they should free themselves from moral reservations, and that he and Hitler took the responsibility. Battles would be fought here, he claimed, from which coming generations would be spared.

After Himmler's visit *Einsatzgruppen* and regiments of the Order Police began, throughout the occupied regions of the Soviet Union, to murder Jewish women and children as well. Since the latter could not be considered as potential workers, they were called 'useless mouths'. But food was scarce, even for the German conquerors. Hundreds of thousands of Soviet prisoners-of-war died an agonising death by starvation in German camps. Women and children were shot, so that they no longer had to be fed. But principally they were shot so as to extinguish all trace of Jewish life in the Soviet Union. Hitler and Himmler radicalised their policy of annihilation when things were no longer going 'according to plan' on the fronts, and the euphoria of victory veered into crisis.

Then what were called racial-genetic investigations were carried out on me: my nose was measured, and the lobes of my ears. I was a boy of eleven or twelve years old. The length of my penis was measured. Frightful. Then a sample of my blood was taken and it was discovered that I had pure Nordic-Germanic ancestry. Admittedly there was one condition: my mother just had to sign a little piece of paper to say that my Jewish father was not my real father, and that I was descended from an Aryan. That was a wonderful scientific explanation, wasn't it?

Hans-Oskar Löwenstein de Witt, classed by the Nazis as a 'full Jew'

By the middle of July the end of the Soviet Union seemed only a matter of a few weeks away. At the beginning of the invasion Hitler had prophesied that the Wehrmacht would be in Moscow by 15 August and on 1 October Stalin would surrender. Yet Soviet resistance could by no means be broken as swiftly as the warlord was accustomed to from his previous Blitzkrieg successes. The massacres by the death-squads stirred up hatred against the conquerors. Stalin threw more and more divisions against the advancing Wehrmacht. Each passing day showed how seriously the Red Army's strength and fighting spirit had been underestimated. At the end of July 1941 the German advance in the central sector of the front around Smolensk came to an unexpected halt, and remained stuck for almost ten weeks. German losses increased dramatically; the situation reports became visibly more apprehensive. Hitler soon sensed that he had been working on assumptions that were too optimistic, indeed plain wrong.

At the height of summer it was already clear that the war could no longer be won by the end of the year. The Russians were fighting 'like wild animals', and had 'gigantic' resources to draw on, as Hitler complained to the Japanese ambassador, Hiroshi Oshima. The following year he freely admitted to the Finnish head of state, Marshal Mannerheim, how seriously he had underestimated the Soviets: 'They had the most massive armaments imaginable. If anyone had told me that a nation could take the field with 35,000 tanks I would have said, you're insane. I would have said: "My dear sir, you are seeing everything double, tenfold. You are mad. You are seeing ghosts." I didn't think it possible.'

The more time went by, and the more slowly the troops advanced, the more nervous Hitler became. 'How much time have I left to finish Russia off, and how much time do I still need?' he wondered at the end of July 1941. Admittedly the Red Army's fighting strength had dwindled, but even the Wehrmacht commanders had to concede that they were far from having destroyed their opponent. Walther von Brauchitsch, commander-in-chief of the army, called Stalin's army 'the first serious opposition'; and the length of the war was telling on their nerves. Hitler looked particularly worn out, and for a time he even toyed with the idea of accepting a reasonable offer of peace from Stalin, provided Germany could notch up the largest possible territorial gains. Only a few weeks earlier Hitler would not have wasted a second on such thoughts.

We knew what was happening in Germany. There was a widely read Polish-Jewish press. We were always up to date on things in Germany. But there was a huge difference between what we read and heard, and what took place from the first day the Germans marched into Warsaw.

From the moment the Germans arrived in Poland the Jews were no longer human beings. The Germans began to hunt us and pull us in for various kinds of work; they humiliated us, beat us up for no reason and distributed food to everyone except Jews. They began by confiscating the Jews' assets in various ways, starting with their homes, then the stock in their shops and their personal possessions at home. Not all, but most Jews – I can't give an exact percentage – were left without a job or a home. Jewish society was pauperised.

Professor Israel Gutman, Polish Jew

The unshakeable certainty of victory had evaporated. 'The Führer', Goebbels confided to his diary on 19 August 1941, ' is very annoyed with himself for letting himself be so deceived by the reports from the Soviet Union about the Bolshevist potential. It is particularly his underestimate of enemy armour and air power that has given us a lot to cope with in our military operations. He has taken this very hard. We are now in a severe crisis.'

The ambitious target of beating Stalin by 1 October now seemed unachievable. True, Hitler's armies continued to advance towards Moscow and Leningrad on a broad front, but progress was much slower than expected. Time was working against the dictator. Soon the muddy season would begin.

The higher the German losses rose, the more frequently Hitler turned in his nightly monologues to the 'Jewish question'. And there was another theme which the dictator broached surprisingly often in the midst of the crisis of August 1941: November 1918,

Germany's defeat – the most traumatic incident in his life, for which, with pathological obstinacy, he claimed the Jews were responsible. Once again, the disgrace of Versailles, seldom mentioned during the Blitzkrieg days, had forced its way into Hitler's thinking. In 1925 he had written in *Mein Kampf*: 'If at the beginning of the war and during it, just twelve or fifteen thousand of those Hebrew race-defilers had been subjected to the same poison gas that hundreds of thousands of the finest Germans, from all classes and callings, were forced to endure in the field, then the millions who died at the Front would not have been sacrificed in vain.' Now, in 1941, hundreds of thousands were again dying at the front – as they once had in Flanders, where Corporal Hitler had himself been exposed to a gas-attack. Back then, he convinced himself that 'Jewish–Bolshevist agitators' had engineered Germany's defeat by their revolution – and made his own sacrifice pointless. Willi Schneider of Hitler's personal escort squad remembers hearing the Führer declare: 'As long as tens of thousands of German men daily shed their blood and give their lives so that the Bolshevist plague does not overwhelm our European culture, then that criminal race of Jews will certainly not have a very nice life.'

In the east it is the Jews who will have to pick up the bill. In Germany they have already paid part of it and in future will have to pay a lot more.

Joseph Goebbels, diary entry, 19 August 1941

Later on there was an order from the military that even in winter, if you were wearing a hat and met a German soldier, you had to remove it in salute. I never wore a hat, even when it was cold and snowing, so as not to show any respect to those murderous Nazi soldiers.

Stefan Grayek, Polish Jew

It was not only the underestimated military potential of the enemy that had infuriated Hitler that August. Another event preoccupied him and once again whipped up the obsessive fear that he was confronted by an 'international Jewish conspiracy'. On 12 August 1941, after the long but eventually victorious battle for Smolensk, hopes of a swift victory were raised once again. Hitler was convinced that he would soon be marching side by side with Britain and the United States. However, only two days later this confused dream had burst like a bubble. Great Britain and the USA had reaffirmed their old friendship. What was worse, President Franklin D. Roosevelt and Prime Minister Winston Churchill announced in the Atlantic Charter an objective which struck a chill in Hitler's bones, namely the 'final destruction of Nazi tyranny'.

The Charter, signed on 14 August, came as a shock to Hitler. His plan to gain a swift victory over the Soviet Union and then force Britain to make peace was retreating into the distance. Even if Stalin's empire did collapse, Britain certainly did not stand alone and had no reason to seek an alliance with Germany, as Hitler had calculated. Furthermore, from as early as 1 July 1941 the USA had been on course for war. Britain and the USA were bound to do everything possible jointly to support the Soviet Union in its struggle against the Nazi dictatorship. Hitler's nightmare had become a reality: he believed he was encircled by Britain, Russia and the USA – a 'Jewish conspiracy'.

To Hitler, Jews had always been the ones 'pulling the strings', manipulating every nation. 'Behind Britain stands Israel, and behind France and behind the USA', he convinced himself. 'We know the power behind Roosevelt: it is the Eternal Jew.' Hitler seized on the Atlantic Charter as the latest proof for his crudely racist ideological theories. So seriously did the warlord take the Charter that he forbade an astonished Goebbels to publish its full text. Not until weeks later, on 3 September, did the magazine *Weltdienst* write about the 'Jewish background to the Churchill–Roosevelt meeting'; 'Through the meeting in mid-Atlantic the triumvirate of Churchill, Roosevelt and Stalin has become a reality. Jewish-British plutocracy, Jewish-American high finance and Jewish Bolshevism in the Soviet Union have shown conclusively that they form a single, solid unit.' That is how Hitler actually saw it.

The crucial point was that the Charter bore witness to America's readiness for war. World war was an immediate threat and in Hitler, as we have seen, that inevitably awoke memories of the First World War. There were astonishing parallels to be drawn: the Russian campaign had long since ceased to be a Blitzkrieg, but threatened to become a war of attrition as in 1914–18. In the fourth year of that war Russia had collapsed and had been forced to sign the peace treaty of Brest–Litovsk. Germany seemed bound to win – yet lost the war nonetheless, because America had intervened. Now a repetition of the same scenario was looming with America's probable entry into this war. However, if it were to come to another world war, the conditions for Hitler's 'prophecy' of January 1939 would be fulfilled: the consequence would be the 'annihilation of the Jewish race in Europe'.

On the very day after the announcement of the Atlantic Charter Heydrich sent telegrams to the heads of the *Einsatzgruppen*, instructing them either to burn all their orders in the presence of a witness, or else to return them immediately to Berlin by courier. Shortly afterwards the COs of four *Einsatzkommandos* were relieved of their duties at their own request. After the war they would say that the new orders were no longer identical with those under which they had been appointed. It now became normal practice to shoot even women and children. The killing took on a new dimension.

At that time my father was very seriously ill. I went with him to Professor Eicke at the charity hospital, and he told us he was sorry but he would not treat Jews.

Werner Goldberg, a 'Jewish half-caste' under the Nazi definition, and former Wehrmacht soldier

According to German propaganda Jews were not human beings; they were considered lice, rats, spiders.

Marek Edelmann, member of the Jewish resistance in the Warsaw ghetto

> To express outrage about something, one does of course need
> a modicum of freedom. And we no longer had that.
>
> *Ulrich de Maizière, at that time an officer on*
> *the Wehrmacht general staff*

Did this sentence of death on the Soviet Jews also decide the fate
of every Jew in Europe?

On the day when the annihilation of all Soviet Jews began, a
group of forty high-ranking officials from ministries and Party
offices discussed 'immediate measures' against the 70,000 Jews in
Berlin. When they reached the item on the agenda about 'the
reduction of the meat rations for non-working Jews', the
permanent secretary in the Ministry of Propaganda, Leopold
Gutterer, threw in the suggestion that they be 'carted off to
Russia', but added 'the best thing would be to kill these people off
altogether'. In the end Gutterer went along with his colleagues'
wish: identification of the Jews.

As *Gauleiter* of Berlin Goebbels was driven by a fanatical
determination to make the capital of the Reich 'Jew-free'. 'The
Jewish problem', he wrote in his diary on 12 August 1941, 'has
become acute, and once again especially in the capital.' They
lived in large apartments with 'Aryan servants' while 'German
families, the wives and children of soldiers at the Front, are
sitting in damp basements or cramped attics'. The Jews, he
claimed, were 'whingers and wet-blankets' and for that reason
had to be given identification marks. Goebbels was familiar with
Hitler's obsessive idea that in the First World War Jews on the
home front had seized the 'dagger' and plunged it into the back
of the supposedly victorious German army. On 18 August he
made his way to the Führer's HQ in East Prussia to get Hitler's
approval for the introduction of the Star of David.

Four days after the publication of the Atlantic Charter Hitler
was looking, as Goebbels wrote, 'somewhat strained and sickly'.
An attack of dysentery was the official explanation. But the
trembling hands and the nervous wagging of the head pointed to
a damaged nervous system. Had Hitler been affected to such an

extent by the Anglo-American alliance? It was probably also due to the unstable situation on the Eastern Front.

> We know the power behind Roosevelt. It is that Eternal Jew, who considers the moment has come for him, when he will condemn us as well to that horror which we have all had to see and experience in Soviet Russia. We have seen the Jewish paradise. Millions of German soldiers have been able to gain a first-hand insight into a country in which that international Jew has been destroying and wiping out people and property. The President of the United States may perhaps not comprehend this himself. That merely demonstrates his intellectual limitations.
>
> *Hitler in a speech to Reichstag deputies on 11 December 1941,*
> *on his declaration of war against the USA*

In conversation however, the dictator certainly seemed very much his old self. He immediately got around to his 'prophecy'. Goebbels wrote in his diary: 'We discuss the Jewish problem. The Führer is convinced that his prophecy in the Reichstag, that if Jewry were to succeed in provoking another world war, it would end in the annihilation of the Jews, is being proved correct. It has been coming true in recent weeks and months with almost uncanny accuracy. In the east it is the Jews who will have to pick up the bill; in Germany they have already paid part of it and in future will have to pay a lot more.'

Goebbels did not need long to persuade Hitler that Jews should be identified by a yellow star and the word 'Jew'. He agreed immediately. From 15 September every Jew in the Reich from the age of six upwards had to wear the yellow Star of David. The victims were being branded and discrimination against them reached a new high: they were not permitted to travel on public transport, nor to own a telephone, nor to buy newspapers, and they could not leave their homes without special permission. Even their food rations were cut back.

As recently as August 1941 Hitler had refused to approve Heydrich's 'evacuation plans'. Jews were not to be deported from the 'Old Reich' until after the 'final victory'. Heydrich now changed down a gear and worked out a proposal for the 'partial evacuation of larger cities'. Goebbels also tried unsuccessfully to get Hitler to agree now to the deportation of Jews from the Reich, especially from Berlin. The Führer put his propaganda minister off until 'after the end of the eastern campaign'. As late as 13 September 1941, Adolf Eichmann, who had overall responsibility for deportations, instructed the 'advisers on Jewish matters' in the Foreign Office that the removal of 8,000 Serbian Jews to Russia, or to the *Generalgouvernement* of Poland, could not be considered under any circumstances. Not even Jews from Germany could be transported there. The Jews, Eichmann suggested, should be shot locally.

Only a few days later, however, Hitler had changed his mind. On 17 September 1941 the warlord expressed a more extreme view. The German Reich and the Czech 'Protectorate' of Bohemia and Moravia, he informed Himmler in the Führer HQ, must 'as soon as possible' be 'cleared and freed' of all Jews. But where should they be sent? The *Reichsführer-SS* gave orders that 60,000 Jews were to be temporarily accommodated in the Łódz ghetto, so that they could be 'shipped further eastward next spring'. With this he was pronouncing a death sentence on those to be deported. For what awaited them in Łódz was death through starvation or disease. What had prompted Hitler to make this decision?

Meanwhile the situation at the Front was looking brighter. The depression caused by the August crisis had vanished. Once more a triumphant euphoria was welling up. On 8 September Petrokrepost fell and with it Leningrad's last link with the interior; soon afterwards, on the south-western front, the ring round the Soviet troops was closed near Kiev. One report of success followed another. In this phase of the war, news reached Hitler from the Soviet Union which must have increased his bitterness towards the Russians. The Soviet state president, Kalinin, had ordered the deportation of 400,000 Volga Germans to Siberia. These were ethnic Germans who had settled in the region in the nineteenth century. In fact the number was probably 600,000. It was clear that most of them would not survive transportation and exile. As a countermeasure, Alfred Rosenberg, the minister for the occupied eastern territories, wanted to expel 'all Jews in central Europe, likewise in the most easterly areas under German administration'.

Rosenberg despatched one of his officials, Otto Bräutigam, to the Führer's East Prussian headquarters with this proposal. There a report about the forced resettlement of the Volga Germans had already been received. *Oberst* Schmundt, Hitler's chief Wehrmacht adjutant, nevertheless received Bräutigam immediately. Rosenberg's proposals were an important and pressing matter, which the Führer would be most interested in, he informed Bräutigam. That was on 14 September 1941.

Two days later, on the night of 16 September, Allied aircraft once again flew a sortie against a major German city, this time Hamburg. Fifty-six British bombers dropped their deadly cargo on the Hanseatic city, damaging shipyards, factories – and homes. The raid left some 600 Hamburg inhabitants without a roof over their heads. In view of the housing shortage throughout the Reich, it seemed virtually impossible to find new homes for them. But *Gauleiter* Kaufmann had an idea for which the time seemed ripe. He asked Hitler 'to have the Jews evacuated, in order to make it possible for at least a small number of the bombed-out citizens to be allocated new homes'. Kaufmann got what he wanted: 'The Führer agreed to my proposal without delay and issued the necessary orders for the deportation of the Jews.'

Around this time a succession of events heightened Hitler's hatred of 'the Jews' as being the people supposedly to blame for everything. Among these was an incident in the Atlantic, which would have grave consequences, and which clearly showed that the defiant words of the Atlantic Charter would be followed by deeds.

On 4 September 1941 the American destroyer *Greer* had located the German submarine, U-652, given chase and dropped three depth-charges on it. The U-652 retaliated with two torpedoes which both missed their target. President Roosevelt used the incident as a reason for abandoning United States neutrality, which in any case had only been a formality. On 11 September he announced in a radio broadcast his 'shoot on sight' order: in other words to attack without warning any warships of the Axis powers found in American territorial waters. With this an undeclared war began between the American navy and German U-boats. All this fitted only too well into Hitler's fantasy of an 'international Jewish conspiracy' aimed at provoking a world war. In prison after the war, one of Hitler's secretaries told the BDM leader, Jutta Rüdiger, of the ideas that were going round in Hitler's mind at the time: 'If the Jews succeed in driving America and Germany into war with each other, then I will no longer show any mercy. Many people are dying on both sides, good, worthwhile people, whether in Britain, in Germany or in France. But the Jews never make any sacrifices; they always stand in the background holding the strings. And for that I will show no mercy.'

Only Japan's entry into the war on Germany's side might still prevent the USA's complete involvement in Europe. Japan would be in a position to tie down American troops. But even Japan, in this phase before Pearl Harbor, was attempting a *rapprochement* with the USA. Hitler was threatened with complete isolation. In those few days Hitler ceased to believe that he could conquer the world in a series of Blitzkriegs. He now devoted most of his attention to the battle for 'Fortress Europe' – and to the murder of the Jews.

'The Führer is of the view', Goebbels noted on 24 September 1941, after a discussion with Himmler and Heydrich in Hitler's presence, 'that the Jews must gradually be removed from the whole of Germany. The first cities to be made Jew-free are Berlin, Vienna and Prague.' It would begin with Berlin. 'It will be possible for this to proceed as soon as we have managed to resolve the military problems in the east.'

It was now that Heydrich gave his approval for the blowing-up of the Paris synagogues. The 'highest quarter' had decided that the Jews must 'disappear' from Europe.

It is forbidden for Jews who have completed their sixth year to appear in public without displaying the Jewish star. Anyone infringing this ban either deliberately or through negligence will be punished by a fine of up to 153 Reichsmarks or imprisonment for up to 6 weeks.
Police regulation on the identification of Jews, 1 September 1941

> Regarding the Jewish question the Führer is determined to make a clean sweep.
>
> *Joseph Goebbels, diary entry, 13 December 1941*

Two weeks later, on 6 October 1941, Hitler stressed once more, 'all Jews must be removed from the Protectorate, and not just to the *Generalgouvernement*, but further east straight away.' They were to be deported to regions where at that moment the Jewish population was being murdered indiscriminately. To 'resettle' them there during the war has to be seen as a death sentence. At the scene of the crimes, in the east, there had long ceased to be any doubt as to what 'resettlement' actually meant. Hans-Adolf Prützmann, Senior SS and Police Officer in Riga, put one of his men right on this: 'No, it's not what you think – they're to be despatched into the Hereafter.'

However, for one last time Hitler hesitated to give the priority requested for the deportations, and once again he blamed the course of the war for this. 'At this moment it is not feasible, only because of the great pressure on transport resources', he said on 6 October.

Apparently the dictator wanted to await the outcome of one of the 'decisive battles' in the east. By the end of September Kiev was in German hands. On 7 October Vyazma and Bryansk were encircled, and 637,000 men of the Red Army became prisoners-of-war. The fortunes of war seemed again to be favouring Hitler. 'Full of a mood of victory', transport problems no longer interested him. The enemy in the east, he announced to the Germans, had been beaten once and for all. Hitler now considered the moment had come finally to get rid of the 'fire-raisers' who, in his deluded mind, he held responsible for his war.

'The Führer wishes that if possible by the end of the year the Jews should be removed from German territory', Heydrich decreed on 10 October 1941, in Prague. On 15 October the first wave of deportations began. By 4 November. 19,827 Jews and 5,000 Romany and Sinti gypsies had been transported on twenty-five trains to Łódz from the Reich. They came from Vienna, Prague, Berlin, Cologne, Frankfurt-am-Main, Hamburg and Düsseldorf. On their arrival in the Łódz ghetto deathly conditions awaited them. Starvation and disease decimated the inhabitants. In each month of 1941 between 1,700 and 1,800 were dying in the ghetto. What was to be done with all the new arrivals? Were they all to be shot?

During his visit to Minsk, Heinrich Himmler had seen what continuous killing meant for the men who were doing it. The suffering of the victims left the SS chief cold. He was only interested in the wellbeing of the killers. While some of the perpetrators shot their helpless victims with growing enthusiasm, others had difficulty coming to terms with the orders to murder. This was true not only in Russia and not only for Himmler's SS men. 'The shooting of Jews is easier than that of gypsies', we read in an activity report from 704th Infantry Division, which was carrying out an order in Serbia to shoot 100 Serbian prisoners for every German soldier killed. 'One has to admit', the report goes on, 'that the Jews are very composed as they go to their death – they stand very calmly – whereas the gypsies howl, scream and move around all the time even when they are in the execution area. Some even jumped into the pit before the salvo was fired and tried to play dead. At first my soldiers were not affected. But on the second day it was already noticeable that one or two did not have the nerve to carry out shootings over an extended period. My personal impression is that during the shooting one has no psychological inhibitions. These only begin the day after, when you are quietly reflecting on it in the evening.'

Heinrich Himmler was determined to alter the conditions at the scene of the shootings and to make killing easier for the perpetrators. He gave Arthur Nebe, the head of the *Einsatzgruppen*, the task of finding alternative methods of killing people efficiently while sparing the nerves of those doing the killing. For, as he pointed out to Nebe, the Final Solution would never be achieved by shooting alone. This view rapidly became accepted in most of the *Einsatzgruppen*. After one of the worst massacres, the slaughter of over 33,000 Jews in the Babi Yar ravine near Kiev, the writer of the death-squad's report came to this sober conclusion:

'Even if, by this means, as many as 75,000 Jews are liquidated at one time, it is nevertheless clear today that it will not be possible to solve the Jewish problem in this way.'

Nebe seemed to Himmler to be the right man to find a new 'more humane' way of killing, since he was an expert in this field. He was in charge of the Institute of Criminology in the Central Office of Reich Security, which had already shown inventiveness in developing new methods of killing as part of the 'euthanasia' programme. Nebe got down to work straight away. In Minsk he had two dozen mentally ill people locked in a bunker so that they could be killed by explosives. The first test failed. A larger explosive charge was detonated. This time the killing worked. No-one survived. 'In the surrounding area', one eye-witness described the hideous scene, 'parts of bodies were lying on the ground and hanging from trees.'

Nebe continued with his experiments. He had metal hoses sent from Berlin for his next trial in an institution for the mentally ill in Mogilev. 'Nebe had the window bricked up and left two openings for the gas pipes', recalled one of his staff after the war. 'When we arrived, firstly one of the hoses I had brought with me in the truck was connected up. One end was connected to a car's exhaust-pipe. In the wall there were lengths of piping into which the hoses fitted snugly. . . . After five minutes Nebe came out and said there was no noticeable effect. Even after eight minutes he could still see no effect and asked what should be done now. Nebe and I came to the conclusion that the car's engine was too small. So then Nebe had the second hose connected to a personnel-carrier belonging to the Order Police. Then it only took a few minutes before the people lost consciousness. We let both engines run for maybe another ten minutes.' Hundreds of people were gassed by this method in Mogilev.

The Jewish people were terrorised by the Germans, the SS. The SS men were like robots, they did everything that Hitler ordered. Every Jew was very wary of the SS, because there wasn't a decent person among them.

Morris Venezia, Greek Jew

No-one ever asked after me, no-one ever sent me a postcard or asked my parents where I was and if they could have my address. The cowardice of the German intellectuals was indescribable. That was one of the worst experiences for me.
Gerhart Riegner, German Jew, emigrant to Switzerland in 1933, and senior official of the World Jewish Congress

At roughly the same time as Himmler was returning from Minsk to his headquarters, Adolf Eichmann, 'adviser on Jewish affairs' in the Central Office of Reich Security, was setting off on an official trip to Auschwitz. He wanted to discuss important 'details' on the spot with the commandant of the concentration camp, Rudolf Höss. As Höss recalled after the war in a conversation in a Polish prison: 'Eichmann acquainted me with the killing by exhaust gases from trucks. However, this would be "out of the question for the mass deportations expected in Auschwitz"'. Killing Jews with carbon monoxide gas as was done in the 'euthanasia' centres in Germany, 'would require too many buildings, and the procurement of enough gas for mass numbers would be a problem'. The 'specialists', Eichmann and Höss, discussed the organisational 'problems' of the Final Solution for a while longer but came to no conclusion. On leaving, Eichmann promised to make enquiries about a gas that was 'easy to obtain' and which did not require 'any special installations'.

Although the perpetrators did not know it, the killing agent was already in the camp. But it was only a chance experiment that brought it to light. In June 1941, when the Auschwitz concentration camp was stricken by an epidemic of typhoid, the Hamburg pest-control firm of Tesch & Stabenow attacked the lice with a material called Zyklon B. Later, the experts instructed ten to fifteen SS men on how to use Zyklon B. At the same time, engineers working on the expansion of Auschwitz were taking an interest in a 'gassing chamber' in which the inmates' clothing was to be disinfected and the lice rendered harmless. At the end of August the first 'provisional de-lousing facility' in Auschwitz was ready for service. It had ventilators with which the chambers could be filled with or emptied of air. This means that even at this early stage the Auschwitz camp already possessed the theoretical know-how for killing people with gas. In September this was put into practice for the first time.

Up till now the Soviet prisoners-of-war who were brought to Auschwitz had been shot. However, on 5 September 1941 a new method of killing was tested. In the original Auschwitz camp, a former Polish army barracks, nearly 600 Russian prisoners and about 300 seriously ill Polish prisoners were locked in the cellar of Block 11. The windows and doors were sealed. SS men opened the containers of Zyklon B. Within seconds the pea-sized blue pellets dissolved into a deadly cloud of poison gas in which a few of the victims nonetheless survived the night. Clearly the concentration of gas was too weak. The SS men began a second trial, and filled up with more Zyklon B. This time no-one survived. The method for killing millions had been discovered.

A few days after the murder operation in Block 11 some more PoWs arrived in Auschwitz. This time, however, the gassing did not take place in the cellar but in the morgue of the crematorium – in a room which had facilities for pumping air in and out. It is probable that from September 1941 onwards the first gas-chamber was operating in Auschwitz, and being used for the murder of prisoners-of-war.

At the same time Heinrich Himmler was negotiating with the Wehrmacht High Command about taking over 100,000 PoWs for forced labour in the concentration camps – that is to say, they would simply be worked to death. In great haste plans were drawn up for a PoW camp at Auschwitz–Birkenau. The first plans that are known about were produced on 7 October 1941, and a revised version of these was drawn up seven days later. The plans did not yet provide for a crematorium. However, on 11 October the chief designer at the firm of Topf & Sons, market leader in Germany in the construction of crematoria, was summoned by telegram to Auschwitz 'in connection with the building of a new crematorium'. On 21 and 22 October detailed discussions were held on site between the camp management and the chief designer. According to the plans a crematorium was to be constructed with the capacity to reduce 1,440 bodies per day to ashes. This meant that the entire occupancy of the camp, which was designed to hold 125,000 prisoners, could be burned in just 87 days. In October the Construction Office of the SS started work on the site of the camp at Birkenau. In November 1941 Tesch & Stabenow received an order for nearly half a ton of Zyklon B.

As long as the death-factories were still under construction, the perpetrators in the east went on looking for ways of making the killing less painful to themselves. On 25 October 1941 a civil court judge named Wetzel, one-time head of the Nazi Party's Racial Policy Office and now a close colleague of Alfred Rosenberg, the Reich minister for the occupied territories, dictated a secret memorandum on the 'Solution of the Jewish Problem'. It was addressed to *Gauleiter* Hinrich Lohse, 'Reich Commissioner for *Ostland*'. The contents of the document left no room for misunderstanding: 'In the current situation there are no doubts about the removal of those Jews who are unfit for work, using the Brack method.' The 'Brack method' was the term used to denote the carbon monoxide trucks employed in the 'euthanasia' operation, and 'the current situation' meant what Wetzel had found out the day before, from SS *Oberführer* Victor Brack, head of Hitler's private office, 'on instructions from the Führer'.

The method applied in the 'euthanasia' operation, that of murdering people in mobile gassing trucks, appeared to the perpetrators at first to be a thoroughly practicable alternative to shooting. But the small number of murder trucks available would not be sufficient to kill the millions who were targeted. Even the killing-centres, in which tens of thousands of mentally and physically handicapped people had been put to death in the 'euthanasia' operation, could not be considered for this purpose. They were located in Germany. To murder people there would have attracted too much attention. However, the staff of the gassing establishments had been available since 24 August 1941, when Hitler ordered that an end be put to the 'euthanasia' operation. These men could still be used. It was their 'specialist knowledge' that finally made the industrialised mass murder possible.

Since early 1940 these 'experts' had been carrying out Hitler's intentions, according to which those of 'inferior race' whose existence was simply 'dead weight' possessed no right to life. Only in a war, Hitler calculated, could mass murder be concealed. For this reason, war and annihilation remained inseparably linked as his core objectives. It was therefore no coincidence that in later speeches he consistently but falsely dated his 'prophecy' in January 1939 to the first day of the war. Nor was it a mere slip of the pen that made him retrospectively put the date of 1 September 1939 on his written authorisation for the first systematic mass killing in the Third Reich, the 'euthanasia' programme – that, of course, was the date when Hitler's Wehrmacht swept into Poland and unleashed the Second World War. In reality it was not until late October of that year that Hitler empowered his head of Chancellery, Philipp Bouhler, and his staff physician, Dr Karl Brandt, so to widen 'the powers of doctors, to be specified by name', that they may administer a 'mercy-death' to 'incurably sick' people.

As the pretext for mass murder in gas-trucks and gas-chambers, Hitler resorted to an opinion survey carried out in Saxony in the 1920s, which had been 'evaluated' by his personal doctor, Theo Morell. A number of parents of severely handicapped children had given an affirmative answer to the hypothetical question as to whether they would 'agree to the painless termination of their child's life', but had stressed that they would not want to make this decision themselves. 'One ought not to imagine', Morell commented obsequiously, 'that no beneficial measures might be carried out without the fiat of the sovereign people.' Around this time, the dictator received a timely petition from a young father for his baby son, born blind and severely malformed, to be granted a 'mercy-death'. Hitler needed little persuasion and despatched Dr Brandt to see the family in Leipzig in order to comply with their request. It was the first 'euthanasia' murder and at the same time the launch of a large-scale killing programme that was to become the forerunner of the Holocaust.

It seemed very odd to me that the girls I had been good friends with since I was small – where we lived was just a little village – suddenly wouldn't play with me or speak to me any more. They had joined an organisation where they sang all sorts of anti-Semitic songs.

Helena Gombosova, Slovakian Jew

You can scarcely imagine the fear which the sight of a uniform suddenly triggered. Once I saw German soldiers – they'd got hold of a bearded Jew, who had the long hair and black clothing that religious Jews wore. The soldiers asked the neighbours if anyone had a pair of scissors. It really upset me that day to see some people actually open their window and throw out a pair of scissors – Polish neighbours! And the soldiers gleefully cut the man's beard off.

Tobi Biber, Jewish woman from Cracow, Poland

In the following two years more than 70,000 inmates of mental institutions were murdered in the gas-chambers of six killing-centres, in the name of 'the nation's health'. The perpetrators named this 'Operation T4', after the address of the head office at Tiergartenstrasse 4, in Berlin. The locations where these crimes took place were Grafeneck in Württemberg, Hadamar in Hessen, Brandenburg and Bernburg in Prussia, Sonnenstein in Silesia, and Hartheim, near Linz in Austria. The weak and the sick, according to Hitler's hideous concept of 'racial hygiene', had to be 'culled' so that a 'biologically pure' nation might develop to a higher level.

In Germany the tracts written by pseudo-scientists in genetics and ethnology in the 1920s and 1930s had prepared the ground for the widespread opinion that a 'valueless life' had no right to protection. But what this theory called for became in practice a murderous nightmare. Things went embarrassingly wrong: one family was presented with not one but two urns for burial; another was informed by the hospital that their relative had died of an 'infection of the appendix', when in fact this had been removed years previously. Horrified citizens compared death certificates which had the same date and in which the supposed cause of death given was identical.

A dreadful suspicion about what went on in these hermetically closed-off killing-centres began to haunt the minds of the victims' relatives. Unrest was smouldering in the Reich. Even Party members were incensed by the horrifying procedures in these institutions of death. The offices of the Nazi Party were swamped with enquiries. 'When the matter becomes as public as it clearly now is', warned the *Reichsführer-SS*, Heinrich Himmler, 'it means there are faults in the way it is carried out.'

The nation was greatly alarmed, especially when individual clerics raised their voices in protest. Theodor Wurm, the Evangelical bishop of Württemberg province, was one of these. Pastor Friedrich von Bodelschwingh wrote on the matter to the Ministry of the Interior. But the clearest and most telling objection was voiced by the Bishop of Münster, Count Clemens August von Galen. It had come to his attention that mentally ill patients at Marienthal, near Münster, were being shipped off, and that in hospitals and nursing-homes all over the province of Westphalia lists existed of patients who were to have their lives terminated, as being 'unproductive national partners'. Von Galen made representations to the relevant authorities but received no word of reply.

After a week in which still no statement was forthcoming, von Galen went on to the offensive. On 3 August 1941 he stood up before his congregation in St Lambert's Church in Münster and denounced the murder of those 'unworthy of life' with scathing words: 'The verdict is passed: they can no longer produce goods, they are like an old machine that no longer works, like an old horse that is incurably lame, like a cow that no longer gives milk. What happens to an old machine like that? It gets scrapped! And what happens to a lame horse or an unproductive piece of livestock? . . . No, I will not pursue this comparison to its conclusion, terrifyingly accurate though it is.'

The bishop, who soon earned the respectful title, 'The Lion of Münster', had accurate information about the institutional murders. In order to present his congregation with a concrete example, he described from the pulpit the case of a 55-year-old farmer from a country village near Münster, who had been mentally disturbed for some years and had been taken into the Marienthal hospital. 'He was not totally insane. He could receive visitors and was always happy whenever his relatives came to see him', von Galen recounted. One of his sons, who had been fighting at the Front, had visited his sick father only a short time before. It had been hard for him to say goodbye, for the son had been very fond of his father. Then von Galen came to the point: 'His son, the soldier, will almost certainly never see his father again on this earth, for since then the old man has been put on the "unproductive" list.' At the hospital a relative was fobbed off with the information that he had been removed to another place and his family would receive news in the near future. 'What will this news say?' asked von Galen. 'The same as it does in other cases? That the man has died, the body has been cremated and the ashes can be sent to them on payment of a fee. In that case the son, who is serving in the field and risking his life for his German compatriots, will never see his father again on this earth, because his German compatriots at home have put an end to the man's life.'

No doubt every one of those men and women in St Lambert's Church had a relative, friend or acquaintance who was fighting on the Eastern Front at that very moment. The bishop was well aware of that. His words struck a chord in the hearts of the churchgoers: 'If it is permissible to do away violently with unproductive human beings, then woe betide our brave soldiers who return home with serious injuries, as cripples or invalids.'

Such unambiguous words encouraged other clergy, both Protestant and Catholic, to publicise the crime. The murders were no longer a secret. Von Galen's message spread like wildfire throughout the Reich. Britain's Royal Air Force dropped leaflets containing the sermon over German cities – and the regime reacted nervously. A man in Aachen, who had passed on one of these leaflets, spent several months in a Gestapo gaol. It was not long before top Party officials began to think about hanging the bishop. But a martyr was the last thing the regime needed. The 'problem' had to be solved in a less conspicuous manner. At the very moment when the 'Charitable Foundation for Institutional Care' was preparing to 'disinfect' patients from Westphalian institutions, as the murderers referred to the gassing, Hitler gave verbal instructions on 24 August 1941 for the programme to be called off. In a critical period, when the advance on the Eastern Front was stalled, this was the only possible way of avoiding greater unrest, perhaps even open protest by Christian believers.

This was the only occasion on which institutional pressure put Hitler's destructive drive on hold. At least that was how it appeared. In reality the 'mercy-death' operation continued. To the very end, mentally ill concentration camp inmates were murdered under the bureaucratic code '14f13'. The 'euthanasia' powers are the only known example of Hitler's signature being appended to an authorisation of mass murder. It removed from bureaucrats, doctors and nursing staff all moral and judicial scruples about killing helpless human beings. Henceforth Hitler held strictly to his pronouncement, in a secret speech to Party officials, of the principle on which he acted: 'Information that can be given verbally shall not be put in writing – ever!'

For those involved in the 'euthanasia' murders, the termination of the programme by no means meant they were out of a job. The staff of the killing-centres were given a new assignment: the 'Final Solution of the Jewish Problem' in the east. Thus it was that the 'gassing specialist' Christian Wirth was transferred by the 'Office of the Führer' from the Brandenburg killing-centre to an institution in the Lublin district of Poland, where he was to assist the SS and police chief, Odilo Globocnik, in carrying out a 'special assignment from the Führer'.

Christian Wirth, in fact a commissioner in the crime police, had built up three euthanasia establishments and was present at the first trial gassing in December 1939 in Brandenburg. In the early autumn of 1941 Wirth and other 'specialists' from 'T4' travelled to the Lublin district in order to set the machinery of annihilation in motion. Before this they had been made by Himmler to take an oath of secrecy. He sent the perpetrators on their way by saying that he expected things of them that were both superhuman and inhuman. But those were 'the Führer's orders'.

The circle of those initiated into the crime of the century grew wider. Adolf Eichmann, the 'adviser on Jewish matters' in the Central Office of Reich Security, was one of those who learned that a new dimension in murder was approaching. It was probably in September 1941 that Heydrich summoned his transport boss. As Eichmann recalled after the war, his superior 'informed me in his characteristically clipped manner of speech: "The Führer has ordered the physical destruction of the Jews in the German sphere of influence. This is a war that was forced on the German people by international Jewry."' There followed a few sentences on other matters, Eichmann remembered, then Heydrich instructed him abruptly: 'Go and see Globocnik in Lublin. The *Reichsführer*

[Himmler] has ordered him to kill the Jews in the anti-tank ditches that have been dug there. Go and take a look and tell me how far he has got.' Globocnik, formerly the *Gauleiter* of Vienna, was the chief of police in Lublin, and the anti-tank ditches in question formed the northern boundary of what was later to become the Belzec extermination camp. On 13 October 1941 Himmler had given him the job of establishing a site for killing Jews in the *Generalgouvernement*. There were still two million Jews living there under German occupation.

Eichmann made his way to Lublin via Prague. He knew what was going on 'in the east'. At his desk in Department IV B 4 in the Central Office of Reich Security he had, since 24 July 1941, been reading the daily 'USSR incident reports', which detailed the mass murder of Soviet Jews by the firing-squads. On his arrival in Lublin he was taken by an SS *Sturmbannführer* into a forest. Eichmann finally found himself in front of several wooden huts, and the SS man explained to him that they needed to be sealed up, 'as a Russian submarine engine was going to be installed, from which the exhaust gases would be piped into the rooms', as Eichmann wrote in his memoirs. He immediately returned to Berlin and made his report. From then on Eichmann travelled east several times, so that he could report on how the work of the death-factories was progressing.

I would like to ask you, before I continue, to agree with me firstly on the formula: in principle we only feel compassion for the German people, and with no-one else in the world.

Hans Frank, addressing officials of the Generalgouvernement, *16 December 1941*

That creation of nature, apparently quite indistinguishable biologically from a human being, with hands, feet, a sort of brain, with eyes and a mouth, is, however, something quite different: a fearful creature, a mere approximation to humanity, with humanoid facial features – yet mentally and spiritually of a lower order than any animal.

Heinrich Himmler, 1942

Construction was proceeding apace. Near Lublin, Globocnik got Soviet PoWs to build the barrack-huts for a gigantic camp – later to become the Majdanek extermination camp. Preparations also began at Sobibor, in eastern Poland, in autumn 1941. A Polish railway worker recalls German officers visiting the station at Sobibor three times. 'While they were there they took measurements, the loading platform was measured and the length of the siding which led away from the platform. . . . A bit later trains arrived at the station carrying thick doors which had rubber seals.' Jews dug pits and put up a fence around the site. A woman asked Richard Thomalla, a site manager with the SS Border Security Squad, what all this was intended for. 'You'll see soon enough', he replied. 'There'll be plenty to laugh about.'

Also in early October 1941, the *Sonderkommando* of Crime Commissioner Herbert Lange, who in June and July had murdered over 7,000 people in gas-trucks in Poland, combed the Warthegau district in search of a suitable site for an extermination camp. In Chelmno, 30 miles north of Łódz, they found what they were looking for. An abandoned country house seemed to Lange like the ideal location. In its park those 'unfit for work' from the Łódz ghetto were to be murdered to make room for new deportees from the Reich. The Chelmno death-trucks, box-vans in whose zinc-lined interiors about fifty people could be killed within 15 minutes, had long ago completed their first deadly journeys. In the Polish transit camp of Soldau, during the 'mercy-death' operation, 1,558 patients from East Prussian mental hospitals had been 'evacuated', as it was termed, with diesel exhaust-fumes.

Soon people were being murdered throughout the east using the 'T4' method. One of the perpetrators, who did his murderous work firstly in the T4 killing-centre at Hartheim and later in the extermination camps of Belzec and Sobibor, summed things up like this: 'In the camps, the same things were carried out as in Hartheim, except that in the camps those killed were exclusively Jews.' The principle was the same, but the number of victims was on quite a different scale.

At the same time as Lange was fitting out a death-camp in Chelmno, SS *Brigadeführer* Friedrich Uebelhoer, the governor of nearby Łódz, was observing events in the ghetto which made him suspicious. The local Gestapo, he reported in a letter to Berlin on 9 October, had for the last few days been reorganising the ghetto. Forty thousand Jews, he said, had been moved to a 'labour ghetto', while over 100,000 Jews unfit for work were to be resettled in a 'maintenance ghetto'. This was unworkable, the SS man warned, because the area set aside for it was far too small. As early as 16 July SS *Sturmbannführer* Rolf-Heinz Höppner, head of the SD's Posen (Poznan) section, had reported to Eichmann on the appalling conditions in the Łódz ghetto and suggested, 'sterilising all Jewish women who could still produce children, so that with this generation the Jewish problem really will be solved once and for all. These things may sound somewhat fantastic', Höppner wrote, 'but in my view they are entirely feasible.'

This view began to gain acceptance. In mid-October 1941 the first death-trains arrived in Łódz from Germany. The fate of the men, women and children in the trains was sealed. The extermination camps in Belzec, Chelmno, Majdanek, Sobibor and Auschwitz–Birkenau were under construction and the Jews were forbidden to leave the ghettos on pain of death. They were sitting in a deadly trap.

Meanwhile, Reinhard Heydrich was pressing for a meeting with Himmler at Hitler's headquarters. On 25 October this was arranged. The triumvirate of destruction sat facing each other. Heydrich wanted to discuss 'a series of fundamental questions and various details', and it was not long before Hitler took up the key theme of his policy: the 'criminal Jewish race' whom he insanely held guilty for the German war dead. Once again he returned to his 'prophecy', that if the 'the Jews' once more plunged the nations into a world war, the consequence would be the destruction of the Jewish race in Europe. 'These criminals', he raged, 'have the two million dead in the Great War on their conscience, and now there are hundreds of thousands more. Let no-one tell me we can't send them into the mire! Who is caring for *our* people? It's a good thing that the terror is spreading, terror that we shall exterminate Jewry.'

Even at this early stage word was indeed spreading that in the east something terrible was starting to happen. On 23 October 1941 the editor of the hate-sheet *Der Stürmer*, Paul Wurm, wrote to Franz Rademacher, an 'expert on Jewish matters' in the Foreign Office: 'On my journey back from Berlin I met an old Party colleague, who is dealing with the Jewish question in the east. In the near future a good number of the Jewish vermin will be wiped out by special measures.' Goebbels, too, had long since become used to thinking of Jews no longer as human beings. On 1 November he visited the ghetto in Vilnius, and wrote about the deadly conditions which the German perpetrators had themselves created: 'Even a short tour of the ghetto gives a horrifying picture. The Jews are crouching on top of each other, figures too repulsive to look at, let alone touch. . . . Hanging around in the streets are terrifying figures that I wouldn't want to meet on a dark night. The Jews are the lice of civilised humanity. Somehow they must be eradicated, otherwise they will continue to play their role as troublesome tormentors.'

I myself had the clearly defined job of supervising the work of the *Einstazgruppen* using gas-trucks in the east. That is to say, I had to ensure that the mass killings carried out in the gas-trucks proceeded in an orderly manner, and that meant paying special attention to the technical operation of the trucks. I would like to mention here that two types of gas-truck were in use: the Opel Blitz, a 3.5 tonner, and the big Saurer truck which, as far as I recall, was 7 tons. Because I had been given this assignment by Rauff, I travelled east in mid-December 1941, with the object of reaching *Einsatzgruppe* A (Riga) to do a spot-check on the gas-trucks. . . . In Riga I learned from Standartenführer Potzelt, deputy commander of the Security Police and SD in Riga, that Einsatzkommando Minsk could not manage with the three trucks available there and further trucks were needed. I was also told by Potzelt that what they had in Minsk was an extermination camp. I flew to Minsk in the *Einsatzgruppe*'s Fieseler Storch. In the plane with me was

> Hauptsturmführer Rühl, the head of the Minsk extermination camp, with whom I had been negotiating in Riga. Rühl put the request to me, to obtain additional trucks, as he was not keeping up the required rate of exterminations.
>
> *August Becker, 'specialist' in euthanasia, gassing and 'inspector of gas-trucks', in a court statement*

The death-factories were not yet ready for use. The mass murder was still carried out by firing-squads, here and there supported by the Wehrmacht, and assisted by the pogrom-minded section of the Baltic population. Soon the overcrowded trains were rolling out from the Reich, along hundreds of miles of track and straight into the hands of the death-squads in the Baltic countries. On 25 November 1941, in the Ninth Fort in Kaunas, an old Tsarist stronghold in Lithuania, *Einsatzkommando* 3 of *Einsatzgruppe* A shot the first 2,934 German Jews, from Berlin, Munich and Frankfurt-am-Main.

> We knew about *Kristallnacht*, but we thought it was like one of the pogroms in the Soviet Union or Poland, which lasted a few days, and then the Jews could get back to a normal life.
>
> *Renée Firestone, Jewish woman from the Hungarian-occupied zone of Slovakia*
>
> The *Volksdeutsche* [ethnic Germans] in Łódz behaved appallingly. They looted, terrorised, beat people up, and took away the homes of the Łódz Jews. At that point in time they were our most dangerous enemy, the *Volksdeutsche* living in Łódz.
>
> *Arnold Mostowicz, Polish Jew*

As early as 12 November Himmler, certainly with Hitler's knowledge and approval, gave the order for the destruction of the Riga ghetto – with the object of making room for new transports of Jews from Berlin, the Rhineland and Westphalia. In preparation for this day pits were dug in a thickly wooded area 5 miles outside the Latvian capital. All day long, under the pretext that they were being resettled, Jews dressed only in their underclothes were forced by men of *Einsatzgruppe* A to walk to the pits in temperatures around freezing-point. It was now 29 November and a transport of 1,000 Jews had just arrived from Berlin. At the pits SS men forced the victims to undress completely and lie face down on the ground, side by side. The soldiers, using machine-guns set for single shots, fired into the back of their necks. Then more victims had to lie on top of those just shot, and so on until the pits were filled with bodies. In just two days, in the Rumbula forest, 16,000 Jews from Riga and Berlin died as victims of Hitler's racial mania. A few days later, the massacre was repeated. This time 8,000 Jews died.

By a coincidence the massacre of 30 November was witnessed by Otto Schulz-DuBois, a reservist *Hauptmann* with the Pioneers. Apart from the sight of the murders themselves, the most shocking thing was the coarse laughter of the SD men in their bloody frenzy. Schulz-DuBois was determined to report the crime. By a devious route his report finally reached Hitler's headquarters, where it was read by Admiral Canaris, the chief of the *Abwehr* [military counter-intelligence]. He drew the Führer's attention to the atrocities and their consequences for the morale of the troops. As Schulz-DuBois wrote to his wife, Hitler is said to have replied: 'I think you're getting soft, *mein Herr!* I have to do this, because after me I'm sure no-one else will do it!'

DuBois also described to his wife the ghastly conditions in which the Jews deported from the Reich to Riga had to live: 'In one farmyard 4,000 people from Württemberg are living; housed in barns and with little to eat and drink, they are, of course, dying like flies. It's odd suddenly to hear nothing but Swabian accents. A lot of the children are dressed in nice ski-clothes, and everyone gave a great impression of courage. In the old ghetto here, on the other hand, you hear Berlin voices; the other day I saw a lot of well-dressed children standing by the barbed wire; they were begging from Jews who work in the town: "Hey, Uncle, give us a bit of bread, Uncle!" That has since been banned. How long will it be before they too are "resettled" to the pine-forests, where I recently saw, in the snowy landscape, mounds of earth over five large pits.

The mounds had subsided badly in the middle, and despite the cold, there was a sickeningly sweet smell!' *Hauptmann* Schulz-DuBois was told by the SS commandant in Riga: 'There were 50,000 Jews living in Riga. We have already liquidated half of them. The other half will have to work for us for a while, but will then be liquidated as well.' Otto Schulz-DuBois did not survive the war. He died of heart failure in February 1945.

Hitler's dark threat was taking on a real form. 'At this moment we are seeing the fulfilment of that prophecy', Joseph Goebbels wrote on 16 November 1941 in the glossy weekly magazine *Das Reich*, 'and a fate is being dealt to Jewry which, though harsh, is richly deserved. Compassion or even regret is entirely inappropriate.' On 18 November 1941 Alfred Rosenberg, minister for the occupied eastern territories, gave German journalists an off-the-record background briefing in which he made it clear that the Final Solution had started. 'There are still some six million Jews living in the east, and this problem can only be solved through a biological eradication of the whole of European Jewry.' Either all Jews would be forcibly moved beyond the Urals, or they would be exterminated, on which point the gentlemen of the press were kindly requested not to report in concrete terms. Rosenberg recommended that they should not write the harsh truth about the murders, but of the 'total solution of the Jewish problem'.

Reinhard Heydrich who, as head of the Central Office of Reich Security, had been charged with the Final Solution, also wanted to discuss this with senior civil servants. Since early November Heydrich's transport chief, Adolf Eichmann, had been preparing an interministerial conference on the 'Jewish question', which was to be held on 9 December 1941 at a lakeside villa outside Berlin, 56–8 Am Grossen Wannsee. But the date had to be scrubbed. On 7 December Japan attacked the American Pacific fleet at Pearl Harbor, and on 11 December Hitler declared war on the United States. 'Due to the events suddenly announced', the participants were told, the Wannsee Conference had to be postponed at short notice. The sole purpose of the talks was to bring the bureaucracy in on Hitler's decision to murder the Jews, and to discuss how the crime of the century might be organised. A week or two here or there would make no difference.

Every time, someone else was missing; Every time, another of the girls I worked with, or of my friends, had been taken away. There were fewer and fewer of us. No-one stopped to wonder whether we would ever see them again. I expect every person keeps a little bit of hope.

Miriam Rosenberg from Berlin, a 'half-Jewess' under the Nazi definition, forced to work in the Siemens factory

In a manner of speaking, the Jews were actually 'confined to barracks'. Their homes had been taken away and they were crammed into single apartments, so that the deportations could be arranged with relatively little effort.

Dr Albert Massiczek, until 1938 a member of the illegal Austrian SS, later in the resistance

We lived in a predominantly Christian district and only heard from friends and acquaintances about the German atrocities against Jewish people. My schoolfriend told me that he and 3,000 other Jews were taken to a place outside the town, called 'Devil's Rock'. There the Jews had to run round in a circle, each laden with heavy stones. Anyone whose strength gave out was immediately killed. Then they were ordered to lie down and not raise their heads. Anyone who *did* raise his head was also shot immediately. At the end of that day only 300 of the 3,000 returned.

Karl Horowitz, Polish Jew

By now all four *Einsatzgruppen* had their own gas-trucks. In Chelmno, the first extermination camp, industrialised killing began on 8 December 1941. Jews were forced into the airtight vehicles. The deception system functioned right to the end: SS men explained to the Jews that they had to have a shower and then they would be taken to Germany to work. After they had handed in their clothes for 'disinfecting' and their valuables for 'safe keeping', they were driven with whips and cudgels down a dark underground passage. It appeared to lead into the open air, but in fact ended at a wooden ramp which led to a large black hole

– the load compartment of the gas-truck. 'Here the Jews, completely naked, were loaded into sealed trucks for the purpose of "de-lousing" or other such hygienic measures', Eichmann reported in his memoirs. In them he describes, full of self-pity, how the murder proceeded. 'Then the doors were suddenly shut. A doctor asked me to look inside through a small round spy-hole, but I could not do it. It finished me. Because inside the truck, once it moved off, the exhaust fumes from the engine were released. I then drove to a spot some distance from Chelmno, and there I saw a pit about 5 metres by 20 or 30 metres in size, filled with corpses, and when the truck arrived at about the same time, the doors were flung open and dead Jews fell out. . . . A Polish civilian pulled the gold teeth from the bodies with a pair of pliers.'

As it turned out – contrary to what was intended – the gas-trucks made life no easier for the murderers. During the journey the exhaust fumes in the load compartment only gradually reached the fatal concentration. The death agony of the victims lasted 15 minutes. Heart-rending screams could be heard in the driver's cab of the gas-truck. With this method, Himmler's desire to make the killing easier on his men could only be met to a limited extent.

On 1 December 1941, Hitler addressed one of his monologues to a small circle of confidants: 'Many Jews have not even been aware of the destructive nature of their presence. But those who destroy life, expose themselves to death, and not even they can escape that. When the cat eats the mouse, who is to blame? The cat, or the mouse? The mouse, who has never done any harm to a cat?'

While industrialised mass murder was beginning in Chelmno, on the Eastern Front the Wehrmacht was caught in a serious crisis. The hard Russian winter was sapping the strength of the inadequately equipped troops. The Red Army began a major offensive, and the German front caved in just short of Moscow. The German armies' aura of invincibility faded away. The Reich was taken by surprise and lost the military initiative. Furthermore, Hitler's declaration of war on the USA opened up new fronts. Here now was the world war in which Hitler had always seen an 'international Jewish conspiracy'.

On 12 December 1941 the dictator summoned all the Nazi *Reichsleiter* and *Gauleiter* to the Reich Chancellery, to inform them, too, of his decision to destroy the Jews of Europe. Goebbels noted in his diary: 'Regarding the Jewish question, the Führer is determined to make a clean sweep. He has predicted to the Jews that if they once again bring about a world war, they will see their own destruction in the process. That was no empty phrase. The world war is here, and the annihilation of the Jews must be the necessary consequence. This question is to be considered without any sentimentality. We are not here to feel pity for the Jews, but only for our own German people. If the German people has once more sacrificed nearly 160,000 dead in the eastern campaign, then the instigators of this bloody conflict will have to pay for it.'

Among the listeners was Hans Frank, head of the *Generalgouvernement*, the principal location of the murder of the Jews. Back at his administrative capital of Cracow, and inspired by Hitler's speech, he addressed his staff in clear terms about the 'Jewish question'. Frank appeared to know precisely that the hour had struck. There would be a 'great Jewish migration'. 'Gentlemen, I must ask you to arm yourselves against all compassionate considerations. We must annihilate the Jews, wherever we find them and wherever it is at all possible, in order to maintain the overall structure of the Reich. . . . The *Generalgouvernement* must become just as free of Jews as the Reich is. Where and how that is done is a matter for the authorities which we must create and put to work here.'

A few days later, on 18 December 1941, Hitler again raised the topic of the 'Jewish question' with Himmler in his 'Wolf's Lair' headquarters. The outcome of this conversation can be read in the official diary of the *Reichsführer-SS*. The Jews are to be 'stamped out as partisans', it says. This certainly did not mean only the Soviet Jews. The matter of their murder had been settled long ago. By now every Jew in Europe was a potential candidate for death.

On 25 December 1941 Streicher's anti-Semitic rag, *Der Stürmer*, wrote: 'If the danger of the procreation of that curse of God in Jewish blood is finally to be brought to an end, then there is only one way to do it: the extermination of that people that is born of the Devil.' Hitler was one of those who read Streicher's pamphlet. On 28 December 1941 he annotated the text with words which allow us to look deep into that mind, warped by a pathological hatred. 'What Streicher has done in the *Stürmer*: he has drawn an artistically idealised Jew; the Jew is far nastier, far bloodier, more satanic, than Streicher depicted him.'

On the same day, 28 December 1941, the mayor of Poddembice, near Łódz, writing his *Wartheland Diary* under the pseudonym of Alexander Hohenstein, quoted the dark forebodings of a Jewish woman dentist: 'I feel we are heading for an evil and irrevocable fate, a terrible end. . . . The rumours and fears, I am sure, have a very real basis. None other than Hitler himself said years ago, clearly and unmistakably: "If America enters the war, that means the end of Jewry in Europe."' Hitler did not use those precise words. But that is what he meant.

The gassings of Jews in the Belzec camp up to 1 August 1942 can be divided into two categories. In the first series of trials we were dealing with two or three convoys each of four to six trucks, each of which held 20 to 40 persons. On average 150 Jews were delivered by each convoy and were killed. These gassings were not yet part of a systematic extermination operation, but at first we wanted to test and check the capacity of the camp, to see how gassing could be carried out technically. . . . For the next 6 weeks Belzec camp was quiet. Then suddenly in early May *SS-Oberführer* Brack arrived in Lublin from the Führer's office. He negotiated with Globocnik about the further annihilation of the Jews. Globocnik said he had too few men to carry out this programme. Brack stated that the euthanasia was being run down and that he would now be regularly allocated the T4 people, so that the decisions of the Wannsee Conference could be put into effect. . . . Then, up until 1 August 1942 we ran a second series of trials. In this period a total of five or six transports came to Belzec (as far as I know) each with five to seven railway wagons holding 30 to 40 persons each. Jews from two of these transports were gassed in the small chamber, then Wirth had the gassing shed torn down and erected a massive new building, whose capacity was considerably greater. In this new gassing building Jews from the remaining transports were then gassed.

Josef Oberhauser, SS-Obersturmführer, *statement to the court*

At that time even men like *Generalgouverneur* Hans Frank did not know exactly how the mass murder would be put into effect, a fact which Frank openly addressed in his Cracow speech: 'One way or another we have to make an end of the Jews.' They would have to disappear. But how, when and where? Frank left the questions unanswered. 'In January', he declared, 'a major discussion is to be held on this question in Berlin, to which I will send our permanent secretary, Dr Bühler. This meeting will be called by *SS-Obergruppenführer* Heydrich.'

The venue for the meeting, 'followed by breakfast' as the invitation said, was the SS hospitality house in Berlin, at 56–58 Am Grossen Wannsee. On 20 January 1942, when the Chelmno death-factory had been operational for many weeks, Heydrich welcomed eight ministerial permanent secretaries, six police and security experts and a ministerial director to the Wannsee Conference to discuss what had already been decided by Hitler: the murder of every Jew in Europe. Minutes of the meeting were taken by the 'adviser on Jewish matters', Eichmann. It was he who produced the facts and figures for Heydrich's opening speech, in which the security chief emphasised that Göring had appointed him on 31 July 1941 to be 'the executive responsible for preparing the Final Solution of the Jewish problem in Europe'.

Six months after obtaining Göring's signature, Heydrich was spelling out the details at the Wannsee villa: 'In the context of this Final Solution of the European Jewish problem, around eleven million Jews have to be taken into account.' In the east they would 'be engaged in forced labour', in which 'doubtless the majority will drop out through natural wastage'. 'The few who will inevitably be left', Heydrich explained to the gentlemen around the conference table, 'will no doubt be those with the greatest stamina, and will have to be treated appropriately since, representing a natural selection, they must be seen as capable, upon their release, of forming the nucleus of a new Jewish revival.' They would firstly be taken to a 'transit ghetto' then transported eastward – to their death.

Being 'treated appropriately' is a turn of phrase from the dictionary of inhumanity. It was coined by Eichmann, the minute-taker. He 'translated' what was said openly around the conference table into the coded language of the murderers. In reality, as

Eichmann admitted during his trial in Jerusalem, the participants talked in 'very blunt terms' about 'killing, eliminating and annihilation'. In late January 1942 Eichmann informed all police stations in the 'Old Reich' and all 'central offices' that the deportations since October 1941 were 'the beginning of the Final Solution of the Jewish problem in the Old Reich, the eastern territories and in the Protectorate of Bohemia and Moravia'.

By the end of the Wannsee Conference, if not before, all the senior decision makers in the Reich were acquainted with and jointly responsible for the murder of the century. All were agreed that the shipping-off of the Jews should be forced ahead as rapidly as possible. 'We have to do it quickly', Hitler said. 'It is no better if I have a tooth drawn out by one centimetre every three months. Once it is out, the pain is over. The Jew must be taken out of Europe. Otherwise we will never get a European settlement. . . . I'm just saying the Jew has to go. If he dies in the process, I can't help that. If they don't go voluntarily, I can only see one thing – absolute extermination.' For a long time now there had been no question of voluntary emigration. Hitler wanted a final reckoning – and was firmly fixed in his delusion that the Jews were to blame for everything, for the losses at the Front, even for the hundreds of thousands of dead Russian prisoners-of-war. Why, he asked in all seriousness, 'why did the Jews instigate the war?'

Again he cited his 'prophecy' of annihilation, this time on 30 January 1942, before a packed audience of arms workers, field nurses and wounded soldiers, in Berlin's Sportpalast. 'For the first time', he shouted to the crowd, 'it will not just be others who bleed to death, but this time, for the first time, the good old Jewish law will apply: an eye for an eye, a tooth for a tooth. The hour will come when the most evil international enemy of all time will have spoken his last lines for at least a thousand years to come.' He repeated, on the anniversary of the founding of the Nazi Party in late February, that his prediction would be fulfilled, 'the Jew' would be exterminated: 'Whatever the struggle may bring with it, or however long it may last, this will be the ultimate result.' The longer the war lasted, the greater the losses became and the more Hitler's hopes of victory dwindled, the more terrible became the situation of the Jews in Europe.

In place of emigration, a further possible solution, that of evacuation of the Jews eastward, has now emerged following the relevant prior discussions with the Führer. . . . In the context of this Final Solution, around eleven million Jews have to be taken into account.
From the minutes of the Wannsee Conference, 20 January 1942

People talked about killing and elimination and annihilation . . .
Adolf Eichmann on trial in Jerusalem, 24 July 1961,
when questioned about the subject under discussion
at the Wannsee Conference

Why should I look on a Jew with different eyes than on a Russian prisoner? Many are dying in prison-camps because we have been driven into this situation by Jews. But what can I do about it? Why did the Jews instigate the war?
Hitler's table talk in the 'Wolf's Lair', 25 January 1942

In the spring of 1942 there began what Hitler called the 'reckoning' – the murder of the Jews in the ghettos of the *Generalgouvernement* in Poland. The death camps of Belzec, Sobibor and Treblinka went into operation in what was named 'Operation Reinhard' after Reinhard Heydrich, who by this time had been assassinated by Czech partisans in Prague. Between 16 March and 20 April 30,000 people were taken from the Lublin ghetto to Belzec and there murdered in the gas-chambers. Joseph Goebbels knew about this. On 27 March 1942 he confided to his diary: 'Starting with Lublin, Jews from the *Generalgouvernement* are being shipped eastward. The procedure to be adopted is pretty barbaric and not to be described in more detail. Not many of the Jews themselves will be left. In broad terms it can be stated that 60 per cent of them will have to be liquidated, while only 40 per cent can be put to work. The former *Gauleiter* of Vienna [Odilo Globocnik], who is carrying out this operation, is doing so with circumspection, using a method that does not attract too much attention. A sentence is being carried out on the Jews which is admittedly barbaric, but which they fully deserve'. Once again, Goebbels emphasised, Hitler was the 'persistent pioneer and advocate of a radical solution'.

It was Hitler alone who, in August and September 1941, as the highest authority, had set the process in motion which led to mass murder in the factories of death. The decision was his alone. He willed the 'disappearance' of the Jews from Europe. At the earliest stage of his political life, on 16 September 1919, he had declared in a letter that the 'removal of the Jews altogether' was the 'immovable goal' of anti-Semitism. In the second volume of *Mein Kampf* he wrote that this removal was only possible by the sword. As early as the 1920s he was repeatedly speaking of 'extermination'. At that time his ideas of annihilation were still vague and ill-defined, but they developed a power that never let go of him. Annihilation in the sense of murder had not been Hitler's firm purpose at the outset, but the idea of murder fermented in him until, in the late summer of 1941, he gave expression to it and turned his 'prophecy' of annihilation into deadly reality. Military setbacks, his delusion about an 'international Jewish conspiracy' and his obsessive idea that the Jews were to blame for the death of German soldiers, and were responsible for the war which he alone had fomented – this confused mixture of groundless and deluded notions, coupled with the premonition that the war could not now be won, formed the fertile ground from which Hitler's decision grew.

The blowing-up of the Paris synagogues in early October 1941 thus seemed like a signal announcing the beginning of the annihilation. At this point, most of the victims seemed unwilling to believe anything so inconceivable. Yet the death sentence on the Jews had been pronounced. From the spring of 1942 onwards, Eichmann's death-trains were on the move from every part of Europe – first to the ghettos, then into the death camps.

CHAPTER THREE

GHETTO

KNOPP/HARTL

The professor of Romance Languages had called in at the little dairy shop on Dresden's Chemnitzer Platz countless times. But it was a long time since he had been given a friendly welcome there, and lately they had only served him grudgingly. Yet on that autumn day things were even worse. A small crowd of junior Hitler Youth cadets in their black uniforms rushed towards the shop yelling, as the old man went in. ''E's a Je-ew! 'E's a Je-ew!' the boys mocked cruelly, while Victor Klemperer exchanged his food-coupons, stamped with a 'J', for a meagre ration. 'Je-ew!' they shouted after the sixty-year-old man who fled with head bowed, as fast as his legs would carry him, away from this public humiliation.

> Even in Germany the Jews once laughed at my prophecy. I don't know whether they're still laughing today, or whether the laughter has already faded. But I can now assure them that the laughter will fade everywhere.
> *Hitler in a speech in the Sportpalast, Berlin, on 30 September 1942*

Since 19 September 1941 Klemperer had finally ceased to be counted either as a citizen of Dresden, or a Protestant Christian, or even as a retired university professor. Since that day small children had been free to make fun of him in public. And there was nothing the old man could do about it. From that day on Victor Klemperer was obliged to wear a patch of yellow material on the left breast of his coat, on which the word *Jude* was written in mock-Hebrew lettering. 'Am seized by a despairing rage', Klemperer wrote in his diary, when he heard about the decree. It was small consolation that his gardener whispered to him cheeringly: 'Don't you worry about the star. We're all human beings, and I know a few good Jews', or when the woman with the vegetable-stall surreptitiously slipped him some tomatoes or onions – 'forbidden fruit'.

From then on he could not take a single step without the painful feeling of being stared at on every side. Wherever he stopped he was pilloried as a 'traitor', a 'sponger' or whatever other hostile imagery the propaganda of the day had dreamed up. His fellow human beings had turned into an auxiliary police force. Branded with the star, everything he did aroused the suspicion of passers-by. Filled with shame Klemperer hid within his four walls, and only ventured out on the streets, if at all, under cover of darkness. For a long time he had been disenfranchised, despised and ostracised. Now he was isolated – a stranger in the city he knew so well.

> This is our tragic dilemma. Jews have the right to live only if they work to meet the needs of the German military. It is like that in Vilnius, in Rovno and in dozens of other towns where mass slaughter has been instituted against the Jewish population. Only those who work directly or indirectly for the Germans, stay alive. There is no precedent in history for such a tragedy befalling a people. A people the Germans hate with every fibre of their being, can only purchase their reprieve from death at the price of helping their enemy to victory. And this victory means the total destruction of the Jews throughout Europe and perhaps the world.
>
> *Dr Emanuel Ringelblum, Jewish resistance leader (1900–44)*
> *in notes written on 8 May 1942*

As it was for Klemperer, so was it for over 200,000 people living in Hitler's Reich, who were now compelled to display their

Jewish origins – even if unimportant to them – as a mark of anathema. The suicide-rate soared among the persecuted minority, because they could not bear the disgrace and the street violence.

Yet in many places the yellow star produced precisely the opposite effect to that which was intended. There were instances of courageous individuals pointedly offering cigarettes or a seat on the bus to Jews, or slipping food to them or sweets to their children. Those who were opposed to the identification-mark secretly called it the 'Yellow Star of Honour' or '*Pour le Sémite*', in joking reference to the *Pour le Mérite* decoration for bravery. These occasional demonstrations of sympathy were enough to trigger a propaganda offensive by the regime. 'Whenever Herr Busybody or Frau Bleeding-Heart sees an old woman wearing a Jewish star and feels a twinge of pity', warned Goebbels in the weekly magazine *Das Reich*, 'would they kindly not forget that . . . the Jews are our ruination. . . . If someone is wearing a Jewish star, it means they are identified as an enemy of the people. Anyone who has any private social contact with them, is one of them, and must immediately be assessed and treated as a Jew.' These warnings were followed by drastic action: Goebbels did a deal with the Gestapo, whereby 'non-Jews' who 'showed themselves in public with Jews', were immediately to be 'consigned to a concentration camp'.

---

1. Jews who have completed their sixth year are forbidden to appear in public without a Jewish star.

2. The Jewish star consists of a piece of yellow cloth, palm-of-hand sized, with the six-pointed star drawn on it in black and the word *Jude* [Jew] written in black. It is to be sewn on firmly and worn visibly on the left breast of the clothing.

*Section 1 of the police regulation on the
identification of Jews in Germany,
1 September 1941*

Around that time the famous article appeared in the Jewish newspaper, in which it said: 'Wear your Jewish star with pride'. When I saw it I underwent a sort of mood-change: Now I am a Jew, I am identified and I will wear this mark of distinction accordingly. My inner development was the opposite of what they actually wanted from us. Instead of being oppressed, inwardly I walked tall from then on.

Gad Beck, classed by the Nazis
as 'Half-Jew'

On the first day I wore the yellow star I went into the street and one of my non-Jewish friends came towards me. I hoped she would come up to me and say how sorry she was about it all. But when she saw me, she crossed to the other side of the street and passed me by. I realised then that something dreadful was happening and we were completely on our own.

Renée Firestone, a Jewish woman from the Hungarian-occupied
zone of Slovakia

A decree of 24 October 1941 threatened anyone openly displaying sympathy towards the branded minority with three months in concentration camp. Compassion had become a criminal act. In Berlin, as Miriam Rosenberg tells us, the police arrested a Christian mother, simply because she had kissed her daughter, who was wearing a star. In Vienna a wounded Jewish First World War veteran, with an artificial leg, fell on an icy pavement; he lay there for three hours, vainly asking passers-by for assistance. No-one dared stop to help him up.

A woman in Stuttgart described in her diary how she unleashed an absolute storm of popular fury, simply because she offered her seat on a tram to an elderly Jewish woman with swollen legs. 'Jew-lover!' 'You're a disgrace!' and other insults were hurled at her by the passengers, until the tram stopped on an open stretch of track and the conductor forced the two to get off.

> It is recommended that, prior to deportation, the Jews to be evacuated are concentrated in one place. Shipments of at least 1,000 Jews each will be carried out according to the timetable established in agreement with the Reich Ministry of Transport, which is distributed to the offices involved.
>
> *From the 'Guidelines for the technical procedures for the evacuation of Jews to the east (Auschwitz KL)', issued by the Reich Central Security Office on 20 February 1943*

Indifference and habit ensured that in the long run the decree of ostracism succeeded in its purpose. At that time, most people were too preoccupied with the impact of the war to show any concern for the fate of those being persecuted. Within a short time the yellow star had become part of the scenery on the streets of every German town and village. And soon it became a rarer and rarer sight. 'Once this sign is worn by every Jew', Propaganda Minister Goebbels noted triumphantly in his diary, 'the Jews will very soon cease to show themselves in our city centres. They will be driven out of public life.'

Yet, for all that, this stigma, reminiscent of the Middle Ages, was only the outward symbol. A flood of regulations had already reduced life for those Jews who remained in the Reich to a wretched, marginalised existence: very few still lived in their original apartments and houses; their tenancies were terminated, properties were compulsorily purchased at much less than their true value. Instead, they were moved to what were defined as 'Jew-houses', in which whole families were crammed into one room. Eerily, this uprooting took place 'in accordance with regulations', organised by the local government 'Jewish resettlement departments' issuing officially stamped documents. Systematically the expellees were torn from established relationships, cut off from their familiar surroundings, robbed of their life histories. Anyone who has anonymity forced upon them can be deprived of their rights all the more discreetly. It was internment, but without exclusion-zones, walls or barbed wire. 'In police terms, the ghetto is impossible to keep under surveillance', was the devious logic of

Gestapo chief Reinhard Heydrich. 'The way we do it today is that we don't even allow the Jews to stay in the same house – the German occupants of the block or building force the Jews to collect together. Controlling the Jews through the watchful eye of the entire population is better than having thousands or tens of thousands of Jews in one district of the city, where I cannot provide surveillance by uniformed officers on a day-to-day basis.'

The Jewish residential district is sealed off from the rest of the city by fire-breaks and separating walls, and by the walling-up of blocks, windows, doors and other apertures. The walls are 3 metres in height, with the addition of a further metre of barbed wire. In addition, motorised and mounted police patrols provide surveillance.

Waldemar Schön, head of the Resettlement Office, in a lecture on the Warsaw ghetto, 20 January 1941

The Jews feel happy in their own residential area; they are glad to have been generously allowed their own way of life.

From an article: 'The Jews at Home', in the magazine Berliner Illustrierte *of 24 July 1941*

The Jews were prisoners among their countrymen, who gave no indication as to whether they were well disposed towards the outcasts, whether they would stand aside in indifference or deliver them up to their executioners. The terror reached its peak of effectiveness, largely thanks to the countless accomplices who considered these judicial wrongs to be just and proper.

Statutory regulations legalised the creeping destruction of Jewish life with ever more harassing restrictions. Even before the beginning of the Second World War most Jews in Germany had been deprived of their profession, their property and their rights; intimacy with non-Jews and even staying at holiday resorts or spas were punishable crimes. Bit by bit they had to hand over their jewellery, furs, woollens and radio-sets. Their telephones were cut off. They had to move out of their apartments. On trains and buses they were obliged to give up their seats to other passengers and strict curfews had to be observed. They were not allowed hot water, or an elevator, and could not even use balconies. They could only obtain a limited amount of food and no clothing at all. From 1940 onwards they were called up for compulsory labour and in October 1941 lost every vestige of employee protection. They were not allowed to leave their home town without a permit and from 1941 onwards they could only use public transport for longer journeys and then only with a worker's pass. During the war they were deprived of everything that makes human life worth living: schooling, cinema, theatre, hairdressing, pets, newspapers, cigarettes, electrical appliances, bicycles, typewriters, books. A decade was all it took to reduce respected individuals to objects of derision and contempt, with scarcely an existence worthy of the name.

On 26 May 1943 the so-called Jewish quarter was sealed off – it wasn't a ghetto as such, but the streets in Amsterdam where most of the Jews lived. A car drove through the streets with a loudspeaker, saying: 'Attention, attention. This is the German police. You are to be collected from your houses. Bring rucksacks and lunch-boxes with you, as well as blankets. Nothing will happen to you. You are going to work in Germany.' That was all.

Jules Schelvis, Dutch Jew, deported to Westerbork

This very existence was now under threat. The yellow star was a signal for the systematic expulsion of the Jewish population from Hitler's Reich. 'The Führer wishes', as his executioners put it, to see 'the Old Reich and the [Czech] Protectorate, from west to east, cleared and made free of Jews.' That was the message passed on by Himmler on 18 September 1941, to the Reich governor in the Warthegau district of Poland, Arthur Greiser. In compliance with his orders, the SS chief authorised the initial removal of 60,000 Jews. The terminal destination of these transports was to be the ghetto of Łódz – known as Litzmannstadt in Nazi-speak – which came under Greiser's jurisdiction.

The officials on the spot were not best pleased about the imminent arrival of tens of thousands of expellees. In the Łódz ghetto, with an average of five people per room, there was already serious overcrowding and supplies of food and drink were threatening to dry up. The local government chief, Uebelhoer, raised objections to the human transport, 'both on grounds of public health and police security, and of economic and nutritional policy, as well as lack of accommodation'. After negotiating over further destinations in the former Soviet zone of occupation, Eichmann's department reduced the first wave of deportations, planned for October and November, to 25,000 people.

> When removing the names of Jews from the registers in local registry-offices, the destination should not be entered, but simply the words 'gone away, address unknown'.
> *From the 'Guidelines for the technical procedures for the evacuation of Jews to the east', 20 February 1943*
>
> It was a shock. We didn't think we would be sent a transport docket. We had to be ready in three or four days. So we began to think about what we should take with us, and what we should leave behind. . . . It was terrible, packing that little suitcase: what to put in? Winter things, summer things, a book, something to eat? And Father was ill – tuberculosis. We had no medicines. It was terrible.
> *Ruth Elias, Czech Jew*

In Berlin the deportation officials remained unmoved by the predictable fate of their victims. They had their instructions and a quota to fulfil: 20,000 Jews – 5,000 from Vienna, 5,000 from Prague, 4,200 from Berlin, and the rest from Cologne, Frankfurt, Hamburg, Düsseldorf and Luxembourg. In addition there were 5,000 Romany from Austria – 25,000 human lives, 25,000 individual tragedies.

'They pulled bedridden women from the hospitals, old men from the old people's homes. The sick, the lame, the blind and the dying, all arrived', as Oskar Rosenfeld described the scene in his diary. As one of the victims, he could keep a daily record of the fateful progress of the Prague Jews to the Łódz ghetto and of the effect the sudden expulsion had on them. 'Our homes were abandoned, with all their furniture and possessions. The beds were still warm, the tables laid, crockery and books were still on the shelves, in the hall and bedrooms there were still clothes and blankets . . . carpets, pictures – and the hyenas, both foreign and native, having heard about the departure of the Jews, were already waiting to get their hands on their possessions.'

> At one point the average number of people to a room reached between six and eight. And remember, only a proportion of the tenements had any sanitation. All the garbage-pits and garbage-trucks were full to overflowing. These conditions, which the population were living under right from the start, can scarcely be compared to anything known in Europe at that time.
>
> *Arnold Mostowicz, Polish Jew,*
> *occupant of the Łódz ghetto*

From official reports and private notes we learn how unscrupulously Party members and private citizens jostled each other to get a share of the booty that had been left behind. Bad feeling was rife toward Nazi Party functionaries who kept the best items for themselves and made the apartments of deported Jews available to their own clients instead of to needy 'national partners'. Public auctions of the belongings left behind were extremely well attended.

On the other hand, the shipping-off of ostracised neighbours sometimes provoked revulsion and sympathy. It was among churchgoers, especially, that critical voices were raised about the undignified treatment of fellow human beings. In Bremen four members of the Confessional Church were imprisoned for showing solidarity with the deportees. Many people feared Allied air raids or that there would later be reprisals in response to the deportation of the Jewish minority. Ludwig Haydn from Vienna noted uneasily in his diary that 'they were shoving Jews into open trucks, like cattle for slaughter. The old people, who couldn't walk, were lifted on to the trucks sitting on chairs. The way people reacted to the expulsion was that most of them looked away ashamed, but others laughed and were delighted by the sight.'

This time, too, public reaction was divided, according to people's attitude to the regime. The fact was that no attempt was made to conceal the deportations. Anyone who cared to look could see it on the open streets in broad daylight. 'It was no longer anything unusual', Rosenfeld wrote in his diary, 'to see Jews with rucksacks, suitcases, bags, bundles and bedclothes, jostling at the tram-stop to climb into the last car – Jews were forbidden to travel in the other cars – and how they often had to be pushed off the platform of the last, usually overfilled, car. There were people among them who had already emigrated three times – from Berlin to Vienna, from Vienna to the Sudetenland, from the Sudetenland to Prague – and each time they had begun a new life, quietly hoping they would finally find peace, and satisfied with even a modest little corner.'

The Jews designated for transportation are to be collected from their homes on 30.3.42. . . . Before the Jews' departure an official will collect all cash and valuables (jewellery, gold and silver items, gold clocks) with the exception of wedding-rings. The official will then make out one of the enclosed receipt-forms at the home of the Jew in question. . . . On arrival at the reception-camp the Jews must only be in possession of their identity-cards. . . . Ration-cards are to be collected up and handed over to the responsible economic office.

From the guidelines of the Münster Gestapo
for the deportation of Jews from Bielefeld,
30 March 1942

> The Jewish Council in the person of its chairman or his
> deputy is obliged to accept the orders of the German
> authorities. The council is liable for their complete and
> conscientious performance. The instructions which the
> Council issues for the execution of the German directives are
> to be obeyed by all Jews, male and female.
>
> *Hans Frank, in a decree on the setting up of Jewish Councils,*
> *28 November 1939*

Yet there was no peace. The hunting-down and persecution was
merciless. The bureaucracy of deportation functioned with extreme
efficiency. The instruments used with utter cynicism were the
victims' own representatives. In every town the Jewish Councils
had supplied the authorities at an early stage with the necessary
demographic data, had effected the concentration of the
persecuted in 'Jew-houses' and had kept them informed about
every new harassment. Now, under pressure from officialdom, the
Jewish community leaders helped in the deportation of their
people, with circulars and office premises, supplies and staff. The
bureaucrats of death compelled their victims to assist in the
perpetration of the crimes against them – one of the most
infamous characteristics of the annihilation policy.

In Berlin in early October 1941, for example, *Oberinspektor* of
Gestapo Franz Prüfer summoned three council members of the
Jewish community. After swearing them to secrecy he informed
them about the imminent 'resettlement' of the Berlin Jews. The
Jewish leaders were to take part in the operation, otherwise it would
be carried out by the SA and SS and they knew 'what would happen
then'. The Jewish leaders had to supply a list of several thousand
names and gather all important data about these people by means of
questionnaires. The Gestapo would then select 1,000 members of
the Jewish community for transportation to the Litzmannstadt
(Łódz) ghetto. The community leaders were responsible for seeing
that these candidates were ready and appropriately equipped for the
journey. For the benefit of the Jewish population the transportation
was declared to be a 'home clearance operation'.

The chairman of the Jewish Council, Moritz Henschel, complied with these demands in the hope that in this way he might retain at least some influence over the treatment of the victims. To ensure the smooth functioning of the process, the Cultural Association of Berlin provided secretaries, office staff, porters, nurses and transport marshals, who were to look after and supervise the deportees at the assembly-points.

'One felt that something never conceived of, something radical and far-reaching, was in progress', Oskar Rosenfeld wrote in his diary of his premonition. 'A new epoch in catering for the Jews, in the resolving of the Jewish question, has begun.'

> I believe my father realised exactly what was happening, when my parents were taken away. . . . The Gestapo came into the house and said, in 24 hours you have to be at the Schiesswerder, that was an assembly-point in Breslau. But only my parents, not my sister and me. And of course our first instinct is, we want to go with our parents. And so my father said, I'll go to the Gestapo and ask for permission for you to come with us. And he came back and said: No, you're not allowed to come with us, because, where we're going, people go soon enough. When I think back, I believe my father knew where he was going and what would happen, and he thought, where we're going, people go soon enough. So, stay where you are; maybe you'll survive.
>
> *Anita Lasker Walfisch, Jew from Breslau*

The Final Solution began with bureaucratic formalities. Under orders from the Gestapo, the relevant local branch of the Reich Jewish Association informed those affected, in the bleakest terms, that they were to 'make themselves available' on certain days for 'migration transport' – no reason, no explanation. Instead there followed a 'declaration of assets' in which the addressees had six pages on which to note down laboriously their entire possessions, from bank deposits to neckties. In other words they had to provide a catalogue for their own looting. As if that were not enough, the deportees were asked to hand over personally the portable items listed, such as typewriters, bicycles, or binoculars, as well as any remaining valuables, before leaving on the transport. Furthermore, they had to make a 'donation' from their bank account, which was 'expected from you on the occasion of your migration'. The injustice was dispensed with meticulous care, as though this shameless robbery was nothing more than the settlement of an outstanding income tax demand.

> The disgraceful thing was that it was actually the Jewish community who assembled these transports and selected the people to go on them. The Germans were only in the background. One hardly saw them really.
>
> And at night there were even Jewish messengers who came to tell us that we weren't allowed on the streets after 8 p.m. And they brought these deportation-papers.
>
> *Dr Jan Osers, Czech Jew, then living in the Prague ghetto*

Those who did not follow the instructions faithfully found they were dealing with the full force of state violence. Accompanied by vigilantes from the Jewish community, the police conducted house-searches among the deportees who did not obey the directives. They searched for family members who had gone underground, checked the financial circumstances of those they had pounced on, or escorted them to the assembly-points, where they sometimes had to wait several days for their transport. In other cases the manhunt followed a deceptive routine, as Hans Oskar Löwenstein learned to his cost in Berlin: 'A scruffy furniture-van drove up. Then a man in uniform came and said politely: "You must be Fräulein So-and-so, Herr and Frau So-and-so, Please bring your luggage!" A woman living with us had even packed her evening dress, because she had heard there were night-clubs in the east. Then we went off quite calmly to the reception-point.'

In these waiting-halls – often empty exhibition halls or ware-houses were used – it was officials of the Jewish communities who kept the deportation lists, carefully registered the items of luggage that had been brought along, and authorised the handing over of assets left behind. Name after name was crossed off on the transport lists – the last vestige of an individual personality. Names were replaced by numbers, which were displayed on a placard hung around the neck.

Then the new arrivals had to hand in the keys to their apartments, so that the authorities could remove the plundered furniture and belongings without delay. Even this looting was subject to bureaucratic regulation. The first in the queue were the tax authorities, who confiscated anything in the apartment that appeared useful for internal purposes, especially tables, bookshelves, carpets, chairs, paintings and typewriters, even bed-linen and musical instruments. Articles of lesser value were passed on to the *Nationalsozialistische Volkswohlfart* (NSV, the Nazi welfare organisation) which was allowed to put these goods to charitable use, or else sold to junk-dealers. Jewellery and stamp collections were sent to the Pawnbroking Institution in Berlin, securities to the main branch of the Reichsbank, sewing-machines were sent to the ghetto administration in Łódz for the manufacture of uniforms, and printing-machines were sent to the *Reichspressekammer*, which controlled the press in Germany. Jewish literature was sent to Rosenberg's staff for study. That at least was what was laid down officially. In reality, more often than not, the taxmen found nothing left in the flat except discarded goods. Most of what was of any value the Gestapo had already 'secured' for their own use. In consequence there was a constant tug-of-war between ministries and offices over the share-out of the spoils.

Finally, on arrival at the assembly-points, having been robbed of everything else, the victims even had to hand over their personal documents, deeds, powers-of-attorney, identity papers and any cash they had on them. No receipt was given. A signature made under duress empowered the Jewish council, and thus their German oppressors, to dispose of the abandoned assets at their discretion. To give a veneer of legality to this pillage, the police had previously issued a blanket statement that 'the ambitions of those Jews who are to be deported to the Litzmannstadt ghetto are hostile to the state and the nation' and thus the confiscation of their assets was justified.

A short time later, on 25 November 1941, the looting was placed on an 'orderly' legal basis. Statute 11 of the Reich Civil Code laid down that a Jew 'who has his normal domicile abroad', in other words 'stays there under circumstances which lead to the presumption that his residence there is not purely temporary', cannot have German Reich nationality and his assets thereby revert to the Reich. The 'normal domicile abroad' was in most cases a ghetto or concentration camp in the east.

Reports are being received from various provincial municipalities of suicide by Jews. Apart from friends from mixed marriages, the population has been taking no interest in the transport of Jews and appears to have come to terms with it.

Consul-General Otto Bene, representative of the German Foreign Office in the Netherlands, in a report of 30 April 1943

We knew, we heard rumours, that one day we would be deported. But we couldn't visualise what was meant by that or what would happen.

Tobi Biber, Jewish woman from Poland

At the end of the humiliating proceedings, a heterogeneous crowd of lawyers, doctors, engineers, professors, authors, actors, musicians, businessmen, craftsmen, labourers, and homeless – Czechs, Austrians, Germans, emigrants, orthodox Jews or atheists with no affinity to the Jewish faith – had become a single column of prisoners, who possessed nothing more than a rucksack or a suitcase, and often not even that, with enough food and drink for three days and only the clothes they stood up in.

One of the Jewish 'helpers' at the time, Helmut Lohn, described the depressing scene in the Cologne suburb of Deutz: 'Towards evening they have all been checked. The exhibition hall is now full of people who are sitting on their luggage or trying to sleep on the cold stone floor. Departure will not be for another 24 hours. At four in the morning we are given permission to bring them some coffee. We are glad to be able to hand round hot drinks. Already the first death is being mourned: a little baby of a few months old who had to be brought along despite being ill. It was feverish and died in its sleep from the sudden change in temperature. It did not even have to make the journey, and we could bury it here.

'Shortly before dawn we hear the sound of marching feet and a company of SS comes into the hall singing the song '*Kameraden, Soldaten, stellt die Juden, diese Lumpen, an die Wand*' [Comrades, soldiers, line these Jewish scoundrels up against the wall]. Their weapons are cocked and the SS are permanently assigned as an escort for these people.'

With relentless insistence the thugs hustled the waiting crowd towards the railway station. In the haste and the crush, the few helpers who were approved by the Gestapo had difficult in getting the frail, the lame and their luggage on to the trains.

Oskar Rosenfeld describes his experiences in Prague: 'Young, old, ancient, ill, lame, blind, the dying and children, were marched to a station somewhere. Along the way there we could see the faces of the Czechs at their windows; all were serious, some faces were sad, pensive, distraught. A train was standing waiting. We scattered and climbed aboard the coaches according to the number which everyone had to have visibly marked on their luggage. It all happened quickly, the men in field-grey pushed us, their bayonets glinting. There was a lot of shoving and pushing but not a voice was to be heard. The compartment doors were slammed shut and the windows closed. No-one was allowed to show themselves at the windows. A shipment of shorn and intimidated sheep – that was the "evacuation" of the Jews from Prague.'

We had no idea where the train was taking us. We only knew we were being deported to another place. We even thought that nowhere could be worse than the ghetto in Łódz, that the war would soon be over and things would get better for us.
Ester Brunstein, Polish Jew, deported from Łódz ghetto to Auschwitz

I was unaware of what was awaiting us, although transports had gone to Theresienstadt before us. All I kept thinking was: what can happen to us anyway? I'll be able to work somehow. Then we were told that Theresienstadt had its own Jewish administration and I believed it.

Chana Bachrich, Czech Jew, deported from Prague, March 1942

During those weeks this kind of exodus was taking place in most of the big cities of Hitler's Reich – just as public, just as noiseless and just as well organised. The elaborate logistical procedure was controlled by a complex administrative structure from a multiplicity of central and local offices, both civil and military. But all the threads led back to Department IV-B-4 in the headquarters of terror, the Central Office of Reich Security (RHSA). The man who managed this relatively inconspicuous department, responsible for all deportations in the territory under German control, with the exception of the Polish *Generalgouvernement* and the occupied areas of the Soviet Union, was SS *Obersturmbannführer* Adolf Eichmann. He could show relevant experience for the job: in 1938, in Vienna, he had developed a system based on threats and blackmail, whereby more than 150,000 Austrian Jews were forced to emigrate.

In the course of the Second World War emigration was replaced by deportation, but nothing much had changed in the arrangements leading up to it. Eichmann's specialist knowledge was in great demand – it qualified the 35-year-old for this desk job in which he administered the transportation of millions of human beings to their death. In most of the countries occupied by the Wehrmacht his emissaries prepared the registration, plundering and forcible removal of the Jewish population. His staff ordered up transport trains and planned the logistical follow-through. The Ministry of Transport was responsible for the rail traffic and established timetables for the deportations. Once the departure times were fixed, Eichmann's office issued instructions to the police and SS authorities giving departure-points and destinations. The Reichsbahn (state railways) then took over the transports, officially known as 'special trains'. Though the deportees were crammed into goods-wagons, the railway authorities charged passenger fares: 4 pfennigs per person per kilometre, half-fare for children under ten years, infants free of charge. For train-loads of 400 or more they even offered a 'group rate'. The RHSA booked one-way tickets for the deportees, return tickets for their escorts. In many cases the arrangements were made by the 'Central European Travel Agency'. Cynicism could scarcely be taken further.

In order to make best use of the limited rail capacity at the height of the war, it was necessary to obtain the agreement of the military authorities and the department controlling the economy. Sometimes the railwaymen simply declared deportation trains to be military trains in order to get priority to pass through some bottleneck. They appeared to realise what expectations the Nazi state placed on them. Or else it was made clear to them in no uncertain terms. In his deportation report, one Gestapo official from Düsseldorf expressed indignation about a stationmaster: 'It seems necessary for a senior authority to make it clear to this railway employee that he has to treat members of the German police in a different way than he does Jews. I got the impression that he was one of those *Volksgenossen* [national partners] who still likes to talk about the "poor Jew" and to whom the concept of "Jew" is completely alien.'

As a rule, the people crammed into the wagons had no idea of the fate they were travelling towards. Many cherished the absurd hope that they might exchange their pitiful, marginalised existence in bomb-threatened German cities for a tough but regulated life in an eastern labour camp. Others had volunteered to go, so as not to abandon others in their family to an unknown fate. Most saw their deportation as a further fateful blow in a continual struggle for survival, which daily brought new suffering.

We were afraid of the unknown. We only thought we would have to work in factories, in the arms industry, in road-building, mining, etc. But perhaps we didn't want to think about what the sick would do in the east, and what would the frail ones have to do? So we thought, well, maybe there are old people's homes and maybe they'll have to peel potatoes and work in the kitchen; that was the sort of thing we imagined. But we didn't want to think beyond that.

Jules Schelvis, Dutch Jew, deported to Westerbork

> My objective is to get the Jews out as quickly as possible. This is not a pleasant task, it's a dirty job. But it is a measure which, seen in the context of history, will be of great significance. I will gladly atone in Heaven with my soul for what I have done here to the Jews.
>
> *Hans A. Rauter, Himmler's representative, in a speech to his*
> *subordinates, 22 March 1943*

'It was getting dark', noted Oskar Rosenfeld, 'and we were thirsty. When the train stopped somewhere in the middle of the night and one of the Jewish transport marshals tried to fetch some water, the men in field-grey laid into him, shouting and swearing. There was no water . . . it was a long night. Suddenly one of the steel-helmets went along the coaches flinging open the compartment doors and giving a menacing order: all the men have to shave and polish their shoes. . . . So we had to arrive in Łódz looking nice and smart, well turned-out, not to say dapper. Well, we finally knew where we were heading.'

> The Jews were not allowed to read newspapers or listen to the radio. They had no contact with people who knew what was happening. By contrast, the underground movements had a radio transmitter, and could listen in to various stations. So they could tell us what was happening at the Front. That was very important because, from the point of view of morale, knowing what was really happening meant a kind of hope, a faith in the future. That was a very important spiritual prop.
>
> *Prof. Israel Gutman, Polish Jew, former occupant*
> *of the Warsaw ghetto*

But like most of the 20,000 Jews who were dragged off between 16 October and 4 November 1941, they arrived at the little station of Radegast near Łódz, not knowing what awaited them. Like many phases of the crime, the arrival of the 'special trains' was also the subject of meticulous record-keeping. 'The unloading was done in such a way that batches of Jews from six railway carriages at a time were assembled into a column and escorted by two police officers to the gates of the ghetto', according to the 'debriefing report' by the deputy section commander of Litzmannstadt. 'The Jewish marshalling service had to lead the individual columns to the reception camps in the ghetto. The luggage was unloaded by the Jewish labour service and taken to the ghetto on vehicles belonging to the ghetto administration. Horse-drawn carts were on hand to transport the old, sick and weak Jews. Those Jews were taken into the care of Jewish doctors. Despite unfavourable weather and the difficulties created by the fact that a large number of the railway carriages only had one door at each end and the corridors and exits were very often obstructed by pieces of luggage, the unloading and the transporting of the Jews to the ghetto was completed smoothly in a very short time.'

To the perpetrators it may have been 'smooth', but to those on the receiving end it was a pitiless experience. 'The train stopped in open country', wrote Oskar Rosenfeld, 'and the doors were flung open. Tired out, at the end of their tether, with suitcases in their hands, more than a thousand people stepped down from the footboards. Deep mire, mud, water wherever they stepped. It was autumn. A Polish-Russian autumn. Gestapo in field-grey herded them along. "Get a move on! Run!" shouted the fair-haired, well-fed young men. One I'll never forget – with a reddish, bushy beard, reddish eyebrows, a piercing gaze and snarling voice. He shouted at the "new settlers": "Run, you Jewish sows!" and pushed the women who did not know where to turn. Where on earth were we? Who did we belong to? Where was the helping hand, reaching out to us? Who was taking over the 1,000 who had been flung into the desolation of Łódz? No-one. Nothing. You could not think. Your brain was empty. You even forgot that you had eaten nothing for a day and a night.'

We cannot allow ourselves to believe that the ones who were taken from us are still alive, that the trains only deported them. . . . The killing of thousands was only a prelude to the liquidation of millions. . . . What we are faced with is a fully and cleverly worked out system, which for the moment is still hidden from us.

*Abba Kovner, Jewish youth-leader in Vilnius
and later Hebrew poet,
in late 1941*

The ghetto was set up in the most run-down part of Łódz. In my opinion, there wasn't a more primitive area in the whole of Poland, and I imagine in the whole of Europe even – it made a mockery of any public sanitation regulations, a mockery of any kind of healthy living conditions.

*Arnold Mostowicz, Polish Jew, then an occupant
of the Łódz ghetto*

In the ghetto, school continued for a while longer, and that part of our lives was always very important. We refused to be demoralised by the conditions, we wanted to be on a par with other children, and the political and social life of the ghetto had to be maintained.

*Ester Brunstein, Polish Jew,
then an occupant of the Łódz ghetto*

To the Jews coming from major German cities, the deportation to Łódz must have seemed like a journey back in time, back to the Jewish world of the Middle Ages. And yet, apart from its name, the 'ghetto' that awaited them had nothing in common with the well-established Jewish quarters of the past. The 'Jewish residential districts' set up in the cities of occupied Poland were nothing more than prison-camps, ante-rooms of death.

In February 1940 the German police chief in Łódz had decreed that the districts of Stare Miasto, Baluty and Marysin,

which were in a particularly dilapidated state, be declared a
ghetto area. Of the houses, mostly primitive wooden shacks, 95
per cent were without running water or main drainage. All non-
Jewish occupants of the designated streets were forced to leave
their homes by 30 April. In their place, in addition to the 60,000
Jews already living there, 100,000 Jews from other districts and
outer suburbs were moved in. Anyone who did not comply was
threatened with death. On the night of 6 March 1940 two
hundred Jews were shot in their homes or on the street, as a
reprisal for attempted escapes and delaying tactics in the move. 'It
was forcible resettlement', recalls Arnold Mostowicz who, as a
doctor in the Jewish rescue service, accompanied the evacuees.
'Whole streets, entire districts were cleared with unprecedented
brutality. There were large numbers of dead and injured. I could
scarcely keep up, rushing from one dead or wounded person to
the next, as thousands of Jews were forcibly cleared from the so-
called Jewish quarter. After that, the rest went voluntarily. That
meant that they could take more with them and prepare
somewhat more calmly for this migration to the ghetto.'

   In order to create some separation from the adjacent
residential areas, the German authorities unceremoniously
ordered whole blocks to be torn down and in their place set up a
no-man's-land with barbed wire, watch-towers and checkpoints.
From now on it was a punishable offence for Jews to leave the
ghetto – and those living in the rest of the city could no longer
enter it without a special permit. Anyone caught crossing the line
without a permit, or smuggling goods, or even going too near
the perimeter, risked being shot without warning by the German
police. Even the Jewish marshals, whose job it was to supervise
the ghetto, had to maintain a distance of 15 metres from the
perimeter.

   The fundamental reason for establishing the ghetto was
isolation. Personal relationships with the outside world were cut
off from one day to the next. Brick walls and barbed wire were
visible wherever one looked. Night curfews reinforced the feeling
of imprisonment.

We had to carry big, heavy oxygen-flasks on our own. That
was very dangerous, of course. One day they asked for a sign-
painter, so I volunteered. Once, in winter, I was standing
outside by a captured Soviet locomotive which was being
painted with German insignia, numbers, the Nazi eagle, etc.
There was a Pole standing there and he said: 'That man's an
engineer.' The German supervisor called me into his office
and asked: 'Why did you lie to me? I'm an engineer too.' He
gave me a rather stern look and I replied: 'I can do one of
two things; either I tell the truth, or I go on lying.' But
he wanted to know the truth, so I said: 'The truth is that
people with qualifications, like me, are killed straight away.'
The next day I was told to go to the drawing-office. There
were Poles and ethnic Germans working there. I was given
a drawing-table. My 'colleagues' sent a delegation to the
boss of the drawing-office and told him they didn't want to
work alongside a Jew. Believe it or not, the drawing-office
manager was furious. He said: 'I suppose you think you're
better than him!' In the end I was assigned to the office of a
construction company. It was thanks to that man that
I survived.

*Simon Wiesenthal, Austrian-Israeli, head of the Holocaust
Documentation Centre since 1967*

This loss of liberty went hand in hand with a large-scale process
of expropriation. In the course of being rehoused, the Polish Jews
had to leave behind most of their possessions. These 'unclaimed'
assets were confiscated without delay. Whatever the internees were
able to take with them to the ghetto by way of money or valuables
was commandeered in a blanket operation or taken in payment for
food supplies. This enforced exchange into a specially introduced
ghetto 'currency' was designed to collect up every last Reichsmark
or foreign banknote as well as gold and silver items. In this way,
the section of the population which had made its mark on the
cultural and economic life of the Polish city, was uprooted and
despoiled in a few short months.

All the Jews were left with was their ability to work. And that was mercilessly exploited in the ghetto. As the war went on, the eastern ghettos were turned into workshops supplying uniforms, boots, ammunition-cases and weapon components to the Wehrmacht, the very organisation which was threatening to destroy them. And yet the Jewish labourers hoped to escape death by carrying out 'important war work'. For their clients the ghetto represented an important source of income. In Łódz over 70,000 people were engaged in slave labour. Each one of them generated a profit of 5 Reichsmarks per day for their employers while costing a mere 30 pfennigs in upkeep.

However, since a large part of the confiscated assets and earnings flowed directly back to the Reich, at no time did the ghetto administration have adequate resources to provide basic subsistence – even though, as deputy governor Moser stated, foodstuffs preferably of 'inferior quality' should be supplied. In order to reduce costs, the German authorities reacted with further drastic cutbacks in food rations and a strictly utilitarian level of upkeep. 'Further savings and food-rationing within the ghetto', we read in a memorandum from the Senior City Inspector of Łódz dated 2 December 1940, 'are to be achieved through the setting up of communal kitchens and mass catering for the Jews. Nutrition is to be comparable with that of prison food, and so designed that working Jews are on one diet, while inactive Jews are on an inferior diet.' The justification which follows could scarcely be surpassed in its cynical inhumanity: 'The working Jew who – from an ideological standpoint – represents an exploitable asset to us, is in organised mass production comparable to a machine which can only be run at maximum revolutions if it is kept properly oiled. . . . The immediate installation of communal kitchens to provide prison-style food with an extra portion for those engaged in very heavy work . . . is an urgent necessity, in view of the high drop-out rate of skilled Jewish workers, because it is only their full-time employment that can guarantee the self-sufficiency of all the Jews and can, as far as possible, protect the state from unprofitably subsidising the upkeep of Jews who are in any case seen as a national plague.'

The workers cost nothing, they belonged to the SS, they were its 'property'. To begin with they told us that, like any other company, we could charge a certain amount to the SS. But I never saw any money change hands.

Ludwig Wolf, former manager of a mattress factory in the Warsaw ghetto

Among the Jews I came across when I was in the Többens offices, I never saw any fear, only a will to work. They worked in order to survive.

Gisela Birmes, non-Jewish employee of the Többens company in the Warsaw Ghetto

Hunger was the ghastly scourge of the ghetto inhabitants. It defined their existence and blocked out all other thoughts. The quantity of food delivered was never enough to allay their hunger, and for many was not even sufficient to live. Time and again people at the end of their strength collapsed in the open street. Emaciated, dull-eyed children squatted on the ground and begged passers-by for a piece of bread. The struggle for survival had robbed them of all the joy of a child's life and made them look prematurely old. Everyone's thoughts were directed towards somehow getting hold of a food coupon, exchanging their last pitiful belongings on the black market for anything edible, or perhaps sneaking into the soup queue for a second time. Starvation brought death to the ghetto. The appallingly low level of nutrition gave rise to widespread disease. Large parts of the ghetto population suffered from acute tuberculosis; in May 1941 the public health authorities officially registered 20,000 cases. Epidemics raged in repeated waves. 'The ghetto was hit by one of the biggest outbreaks of dysentery in history', the ghetto doctor, Arnold Mostowicz, tells us. 'Out of 170,000 people, around 50,000 to 60,000 fell ill and mortality was very high. Acute tuberculosis was also very common and took a high toll. An epidemic of typhoid fever swept through the ghetto – I caught it myself – and there was a flood of typhus infection.' A

total of 43,000 people died in the catastrophic conditions of the
Łódz ghetto.

There is often something lying on the pavement, covered
with newspapers. Sticking out from underneath there are
usually dreadfully emaciated or unhealthily swollen legs. They
are the corpses of people who have died of typhus, and have
simply been thrown out by their fellow-occupants in order to
save the cost of burial. Or else they are homeless people who
have collapsed in the street.

In front of every gap in the wall stands a guard. A few of
them are Germans who look at the crowd with contempt, the
rest are Polish police or Jewish marshals who get a clip round
the ear if they don't carry out their orders impeccably.

The hordes of children are really the ones who keep the
ghetto fed. If a German looks away for only a second, they
nip across to the 'Aryan' side. There they buy bread, potatoes
and other things, which they hide under their ragged clothes
and then have to sneak back the same way. . . . Not all the
German sentries are murderers and hangmen but I'm afraid
many of them quickly go for their guns and fire at the
children. Every day – though it's scarcely credible – children
are taken to hospital with gunshot wounds.

Ludwik Hirszfeld, from notes made while living
in the Warsaw ghetto

In order to numb the pangs of hunger they seized in desperation
upon every imaginable substitute for proper food. They literally
scrabbled at kitchen waste, until the authorities decreed that
potato-peelings could only be distributed to the needy on
presentation of a medical certificate. Radish-leaves or the grounds
of 'coffee' made from barley also served as nourishment of a sort.

Those most affected by the hardship were the weakest
occupants of the ghetto: the sick, the old and the very young.
Almost a third of all babies born died within twelve months. In
the first half of 1941 a fifth of all deaths were among children aged

fourteen or under. Parents were forced to look on helplessly as starvation sapped the health of their sons and daughters. Since fathers frequently shared their rations with their children, thus damaging their own ability to work, the ghetto administration finally gave orders that workers should be fed on site in the factories. These lines, written by a desperate father to a friend outside the ghetto walls, sound like a hopeless cry for help. The letter, which never reached its addressee, was discovered after the war, buried in the grounds of the Auschwitz death-camp: 'My daughter said to me, "I want to go on living". I am prepared to sell everything, to give up the last thing I possess, but please save my child! I do not know if I will manage to keep her alive. This morning I did everything possible. She was given four different injections, which at least helped to the extent that she did not fade away as we watched. I am now going to her again. But what can anyone do to help when the only medicine that works – food – is lacking? And who has enough money to buy anything from others? The greatest fortunes are not enough for that! The prices are astronomical: bread 600 . . . flour 300, potatoes . . . margarine 900, saccharine . . . in short, it is literally impossible to save anyone's life.'

Approximately 500,000 people lived in ghettos and died of starvation. Only human solidarity helped us to keep going through those two years.

Martin Gray, Polish Jew, occupant of the Warsaw ghetto

No-one – no artist, writer or painter – has the imaginative power to convey what we experienced during those 365 days. We don't believe it ourselves – and I doubt if even in the future anyone will believe – what happened in that period. It is fortunate that we don't have the ability to look into the future, because if we did, we would not have lived to see the present.

Ephraim Barasch, member of the Jewish Council of the Bialystok ghetto, on 29 June 1942

The desperate struggle against starvation often had a fatal outcome. From the report to his superior office by police constable Naumann, who was on duty with Ghetto-patrol 6 in Litzmannstadt on 1 December 1941: 'At 15.00 I saw a Jewish woman climbing the ghetto fence. She poked her head through and attempted to steal turnips from a passing cart. I availed myself of my firearm. The woman was fatally hit by two shots.' The report went on to say that two cartridges had been expended. The report was a routine administrative formality, for the shooting of a starving sixty-year-old woman trying to steal a turnip was permitted under German law.

For the new arrivals from Germany, Austria, Luxembourg and the Czech 'Protectorate', who up to that point had still contrived a meagre existence, this was a new and shocking revelation. 'A slight feeling of discomfort afflicts the body', observed Oskar Rosenfeld after his first few days in the ghetto. 'My stomach loosens and gradually sags. Hesitantly, almost fearfully, I run my hand over my twitching body; it comes up against bones and ribs, and discovers its own boniness. I suddenly sense that only a short while ago I was fatter, fleshier, and am amazed at how quickly the body deteriorates. One evening a man collapsed on the pavement. A man of sixty-eight, an eminent professor of medicine from Germany. He was carried to his hut. The doctor arrived and felt his heart and pulse, then shrugged his shoulders and went away, came back and gave the sick man an injection. It did no good. The professor died. His legs were swollen, scabs were visible on his arms and thighs. The usual name for this is starvation oedema. Here it is called exhaustion.'

Some children had made holes in the wall and gone over to the Aryan side to buy two kilos of potatoes. As they came back to the ghetto the Germans killed them. It was frightful.
Mark Edelmann, former Jewish resistance fighter
in the Warsaw ghetto

There were whole families living on the pavements. People became numbed, inured to it, because they knew that what happened to those people, namely that they died, in due course could and would happen to them too.

Prof. Israel Gutmann, Polish Jew, former occupant of the Warsaw ghetto

We were afraid, and never went near the barbed wire which was very close to the street. Sometimes people were shot if they went into the street. This tended to happen whenever the guards felt like it. They weren't given orders or anything. If they wanted to they just did it.

Ester Brunstein, Polish Jew, former occupant of the Łódz ghetto

In the hopelessly overcrowded Łódz ghetto the 25,000 who arrived in late 1941 were hardly welcome guests, especially since most of the expellees were elderly and very few were suitable for the workforce. Compared with the impoverished and emaciated occupants of the ghetto, who had already suffered two years of appalling hardship, the newcomers looked like prosperous citizens. With the few possessions they had managed to salvage in their suitcases, for a while they still had something to exchange on the black market. This forced the prices up even higher and aggravated the plight of the existing inhabitants. To make matters worse, the old and new occupants generally came from totally different worlds. Academics, doctors and musicians from Frankfurt, Cologne or Berlin had little in common with Polish-Jewish craftsmen and market traders and often had no way of making themselves mutually understood. 'It was incredible', remembers Ester Brunstein, who was condemned to a ghetto existence from the start. 'They arrived, very well dressed, nice-looking, neat, but with very few possessions. Over time we had found ways of coping with the shortages. But they were totally unprepared for the hunger, the overcrowding and the filthy water. They were used to a very different standard of living and so they died in larger numbers than the "old inhabitants".'

Behind the wall which separates the Warsaw ghetto from the outside world, several hundred thousand condemned people await their death. . . . The prescribed daily number of victims is 8,000 to 10,000. . . . Railway wagons wait in a loading-bay. The executioners push as many as 150 people into each one. . . . The doors are sealed. Sometimes the train leaves as soon as it is loaded, sometimes it stands for days in some siding. That no longer matters to anyone. None of these people . . . will be left alive . . .

Illegal leaflet from the Catholic 'Front for the Renewal of Poland', printed in 1943

The unheralded wave of deportations intensified the already rampant supply shortage in the ghetto. For lack of domestic fuel the inhabitants had already begun ripping out and burning doors, windows and floorboards. Even before the transports arrived from the west, there were only 25,000 rooms available for a ghetto population of 144,000 in Łódz. Now outsiders were being crammed into the overcrowded quarters. Schools had to close to provide the newcomers with at least a roof over their heads. Even more people had to eke out their existence in the smallest of spaces. 'We squeeze together as close as ever we can. Children are gurgling, crying, grizzling; the sick are making the noises of their illnesses, coughing, wheezing, snoring, scratching, grunting, groaning, sobbing, tossing one way then the other; the creaking of floorboards and animal noises fill the emptiness of the night.' Such is Oskar Rosenfeld's vivid description of his first nights in the slums of Łódz.

Behind the ghetto walls a hopeless battle for space and survival was being fought out. Since every job in a ghetto factory, and every loaf of bread, assumed an existential value in the daily life-and-death struggle, the atmosphere of competition was palpable, even though the chronicles of the ghetto also contain countless stories of unstinting self-sacrifice. Under inhuman conditions, it often required superhuman efforts to maintain any human dignity.

'One washroom for a thousand people', commented the Prague-born author, Oskar Singer, bitterly, on the dehumanising process in Łódź. 'Under such conditions, how long does it take Europeans to lose their veneer of civilisation? Is it possible to maintain one's culture in the face of draconian punishments such as being deprived of soup or of a plank-bed? How can people avoid being eaten by lice if they have no way of washing, changing or airing their bedding, or their underwear? What use is culture then? If only one of those responsible had spent a single night in that hell-hole! . . . My pen shrinks from describing the horrors there, with people sleeping and living for months on end on bare boards, and this in the heart of Europe! What is asked of these people? How can anyone even dare to criticise their behaviour? Is it not rather the case that the responsible authorities should apologise to those newly banished there for ever being placed in such a condition? . . . What were these people meant to become? Certainly not a Jewish nobility. Wretched figures skulking in the shadows, robbed of all self-respect, whose one wish was to get out of that hell!'

Thus many saw that the only way out was somehow to escape from the ghetto. Anywhere else seemed to offer more hope than this walled-up death-camp, from which almost one-fifth of those deported there from the west during the winter of 1941 would not get out alive. Their decease, if one can ascribe such a word to this planned morbidity, was part of the calculations for this 'decimation-ghetto' as the German governor, Uebelhoer, once had the frankness to call it.

In the transports sick and frail people were seen more and more often. And it also happened that there were people with injuries among the arrivals, because the transport escorts – SS men, police, Latvian irregulars – used to fire at random into the crowds. The sick, frail and wounded were taken to the field-hospital by a special labour detachment. In the hospital area the arrivals were made to stand or lie beside the grave. When no more sick or wounded were expected, it was my job to shoot those people. This I did by shooting them in the neck with a 9 millimetre pistol. They then collapsed or fell to one side and were carried down into the grave by the two Jewish hospital workers. Quicklime was scattered over the bodies. Later, on Wirth's orders, they were burnt in the grave itself.

The number of people shot by me, after the arrival of a transport, would vary. Sometimes it was two or three, but sometimes as many as twenty, or maybe even more. There were men and women, old and young, and sometimes even children involved.

Willi Mentz, SS guard in Treblinka, known as
'the Shooter', in a court statement

'As you will already know, my dear friend, from my previous letters, they have set up what are known as *Sammelwohngemein-schaften* (communal residences), in which the newly resettled Jews from the Old Reich are included.' The writer describes the mass slum existence in a draft letter to a friend outside the ghetto. 'In the last few months all these "communities" have been nests of misery and countless diseases. The death-rate reached such a dangerous level that it felt as though everyone was waiting for their turn to come. Then suddenly there was a big change: quite unexpectedly the communities were broken up. Their members were evacuated to an unknown destination.'

We were given no comprehensible explanation as to why these ghettos had to exist. It was terrible; those barbed-wire fences and armed sentries every few metres. Any escape was absolutely impossible.

Ester Brunstein, Polish Jew, occupant of the Łódz ghetto

That is why, when the first call for 'resettlement' went out, hundreds came forward voluntarily, driven by despair, and because they were promised an occasional loaf of bread or a few ounces of wurst. 'It can't be any worse . . . "there"', is how Oskar Rosenfeld described the motives of the volunteers in his diary. 'There might even be more bread and potatoes if we get farm work. Potatoes here cost 35–60 marks per kilo, one cigarette costs 3 marks. People from Vienna, Berlin and Cologne are the first victims. The transports are moving off.'

They started in December 1941 with the removal of 5,000 Romany from Austria, not one of whom ever came back. From 1942 onwards trains overloaded with human cargo shuttled endlessly towards unspecified destinations and came back empty. 'The word went round', Rosenfeld noted, 'that the evacuees were going to work on the land in Polish villages, but that was pure rumour. The only thing the ghetto inmates saw and knew was 700 to 800 Jews being driven out of their shacks, rooms and holes every day. The temperature had dropped to minus 15°C. Jews were even picked up on the streets and taken to the railway station.'

They told us we would be put to work in the east. And that we would be better off, and everyone who worked would be able to earn their daily bread.

Chanan Bachrich, Czech Jew, deported from Prague in March 1942

We got a postcard from my younger sister:

'Don't write to us any more. We're being sent off and we don't know where to.'

And that was the last I ever heard of my parents and my younger sister.

Tobi Biber, Jewish woman from Poland, occupant of the Cracow ghetto

---

Gradually the suspicion seeped through that the terminus of the deportations held a horror that exceeded anything suffered hitherto. It is true that greetings cards from the 'emigrants' were received by relatives in the ghetto, intended to reassure them of their wellbeing. On 12 April 1942 an SS officer brought word of a well-appointed labour camp near Kolo on the River Varta, where the deportees would now cultivate the land and build roads. Yet not much more than a month later considerable quantities of second-hand clothing arrived in the ghetto warehouses: prayer-shawls, skirts, trousers, underwear, jackets and overcoats, which were wrapped in blankets and sheets. While they were being sorted, letters and identity documents fell out from burst seams. It was quite evident that these belongings had not been packed by the people who had once owned them.

In the weeks that followed, the German inhabitants of the Warthegau were able to acquire large quantities of clothing at knock-down prices. However, traces of their origin were not always entirely obliterated, as one of the largest recipients, the German Winter Aid Charity (WHW) complained in an indignant letter: 'A large proportion of the clothing items are heavily stained and some even covered with patches of dirt and bloodstains.' Many of the articles still had the Jewish star attached to them. 'There is a danger that returnees who are placed in the care of the WHW will discover the origin of these clothes and that this will bring discredit on the WHW.'

Despite all attempts at secrecy, in a relatively small area such as occupied Poland, it was not possible to conceal the fact that hundreds of thousands of 'resettled persons' soon disappeared without trace. Investigations by the Polish underground and statements by railway workers yielded indications that, not far from the ghettos, camps had been built, behind whose barricades more deportees disappeared than there could possibly be room for. Ben Helfgott who, as a slave labourer in the Łódz glass-factory, was initially exempt from deportation, could observe the daily transports going along a nearby stretch of track: 'The people in the trains were screaming, and I remember the Poles, who we worked with, making jokes about it. More and more Jews were being taken away to be made into soap. Of course, we laughed about it. How on earth do you make soap out of human bodies?' No amount of cynicism was adequate to grasp the reality of the annihilation industry, which far exceeded the wildest imaginings of people alive at the time.

The Germans insisted that a doctor be on hand at the deportations from the ghetto. The presence of a doctor examining everyone, prior to deportation, gave deportees the hope that they were bound for some kind of work, not their death. And the Germans wanted to maintain calm during the journey. They didn't want any escapes, they didn't want any mutiny.

Arnold Mostowicz, Polish Jew, doctor in the Łódz ghetto

For me the most important thing is still, as always, the removal to the east of as many Jews as is humanly possible. In the brief monthly reports from the security police all I want to know is the volume of deportations and the number of Jews left at that point in time.

Heinrich Himmler in a letter to the head of the security police and the SD, 19 April 1943

In the autumn of 1941 a *Sonderkommando*, led by the crime commissioner and SS *Hauptsturmführer* Herbert Lange, arrived in the little Polish town of Chelmno (known to the Germans as Kulmhof), some 36 miles north-west of Łódz. It was the first of the towns which the executives of the annihilation policy had selected as the location for a type of death-factory that had never been seen in history. Lange's experts already possessed relevant experience. In East Prussia in May and June 1940 they had supervised the murder of over 1,500 mentally ill patients in converted trucks, with the exhaust fumes from powerful petrol engines. Now the Nazi leadership had given them the task of developing this process to carry out mass killings in a stationary plant. Chelmno/Kulmhof was the first camp designed exclusively for mass extermination. The commencement of operations there marked the transition from the creeping death of the ghettos to planned annihilation.

With 10 to 15 members of the security police and 70 or 80 civil police as guards the unit began its work on 8 December 1941. All those assigned to camp duties had to sign an undertaking of secrecy. Nevertheless, word spread about this new form of death-factory and senior officials in the German administration of the Łódz ghetto were keen to visit the facility and see at first hand how it operated.

From what point in time and how much about the true nature of the evacuation measures was known by the chairman of the Jewish Council of Łódz, Chaim Rumkowski, is something about which we have no evidence. But in a speech he made on 25 January 1942 he hinted at his suspicions: 'The Jews of the ghetto criticise me because I did not foresee the catastrophe. Deportation on its own is not the worst that can happen. . . . Openly I cannot say more.'

Yet there is no doubt that he was aware of the cruel dilemma the German ghetto bosses plunged him into when, in December 1941, they ordered him to select 20,000 Jews from the ghetto for 'resettlement'. Rumkowski acceded to their demands by establishing a 'resettlement committee' consisting of the heads of the 'statistical department' of the Jewish police and criminal department, of the law court and the ghetto prison.

Once again the murderers left it to the victims to nominate the shortlist for slaughter. The Germans saw it as the 'cleanest' way of fulfilling their prescribed liquidation quota. They could delegate the selection and delivery of the candidates for death to those who had in any case no hope of escape themselves. And they also knew by what means they could bring the men they had appointed as representatives of the Jewish population of the ghetto to hand over their fellow-sufferers voluntarily to the mercy of the thugs. There always remained a glimmer of hope that at least those left behind might be protected, that their lives could be bought as useful labour for their German masters, by weeding out the 'unproductive' inmates of the ghetto.

It was explained to us that – with certain exceptions – the Jews were to be resettled in the east, without regard to sex or age. By 4 o'clock this afternoon 6,000 people have to be made ready for deportation. And this is to happen (for at least as many) every day.

Note by Adam Czerniakow, chairman of the Jewish Council in the Warsaw ghetto, 22 July 1942

Leon Rosenblatt, head of the Jewish ghetto police, described to a German counterpart, who relayed the conversation, the impossible moral pressure which this collaboration put on him: 'If I refuse an order, I get shot. So for me that's the simplest answer. But then what happens? The SS has already said: they will seek them out. That's to say, the ones whose spirit has not been broken, pregnant women, Rabbis, scholars, professors, poets – they will be first for the ovens. But if I stay alive, then I can take the volunteers. They're often queuing up to go. And sometimes I collect as many as required. But sometimes it's fewer. In that case I can take the dying, whose names I get from the Jewish doctors, and if there aren't enough, I take the very sick.

'But what if even those aren't enough? Well, I can take the criminals: but for God's sake, who doesn't turn to crime here? A loaf of bread in ghetto-money, which we have to print and convert to German, costs 300 to 500 marks. I know of mothers who just for a slice of bread to prevent their child starving, will denounce their neighbour. Who's to judge them for that? And yet, if I can't reach my full number any other way . . . ? I can often get by without criminals. But not always. And sometimes even *with* criminals there aren't enough. Then you can take the very old. But what age-limit do you apply? . . . In the name of the God you believe in: do you know a better method than the one I use? If you can tell me one, I will bless you day and night. And if you don't know a better way, then tell me: should I stay or should I get myself shot?'

On 22 July *Sturmbannführer* Höfle arrived with his men to liquidate the Warsaw Jews. It was called 'Operation Reinhard'. He called a formal meeting and I was told to take the minutes. He dictated to me what were called the 'arrangements and conditions' for the Jewish Council in Warsaw. These were the instructions about the deportation, though the term was never used. It was called the 'Resettlement of the Warsaw Jews in the East'. Initially the instructions made it sound as though only those Jews considered by the Germans as superfluous would be deported and that anyone who could work would be allowed to stay. That was all nonsense. In fact all the Jews were being removed. The Jews in the Warsaw ghetto began to wonder whether perhaps a large German defensive line was being built in the east. Then they might need 50–100,000 workers. That was just an illusion, as was soon clear from the terrible way people were being transported – in cattle-trucks. Many died in the trains before they ever reached their destination – namely Treblinka. You don't transport people like that if they are intended as a labour force. Transports to Treblinka were much worse than those to Auschwitz. The great difference was this: more people died in Auschwitz than in Treblinka, but in Auschwitz there was also a camp, a concentration camp. Not everyone was gassed straight away; some were sent to the camp, where they were put to work and suffered in other ways. That did not happen in Treblinka. All who arrived went straight to the gas-chambers.

Marcel Reich-Ranicki, Polish-born Jew from Berlin, deported in 1940 to the Warsaw ghetto where he joined the Jewish underground movement. Now an eminent author and critic

The victims were never told how the decision on the life or death of thousands was made under the pressure of fixed quotas, how lists of names were drawn up, some of them crossed off, replaced with others, how human lives were reduced to numbers in a grim arithmetic. They were presented with the result, picked up conflicting rumours, read posters which peremptorily announced the date of the next 'resettlement' and saw the long columns shuffling towards the Radegast railway station in Łódz.

'Today is Tuesday. As if that mattered', noted Oskar Rosenfeld in his diary. 'More important, more disturbing is the news, to our great consternation, that preparations are being made for the resettlement of initially 10,000 of the original inhabitants of the ghetto. Who will be next? The answer: those with a criminal record, those needing care, those unwilling to work and other "burdens". On the "criminal" list are mainly people who have spent a few weeks in prison for selling the food rations allocated to them. . . . The police forced their way into the homes of the Jews to be evacuated. They frequently found starving children and aged people dying of cold. Terror had seized the ghetto. We were only allowed to take 12.5 kilos of luggage with us and 10 Reichsmarks in cash. Hence the order to the ghetto to hand over all Reichsmarks. People were selling their belongings for a pittance, so as to buy food, especially bread. The temperature dropped to 20 degrees below zero. Keys froze in their locks. In the middle of the room mice lay frozen beside shoes and rags which (like the humans) they were too weak to chew through. . . . In terrible driving snowstorms people – children and old people included – were herded along to the station.'

> Hitherto, I admit, I was prepared to take your property from you, but now that they are demanding Jewish lives, I no longer wish to live. I will give myself up to the Germans, so that they can kill me. I had thought I could use your wealth to purchase your lives.
>
> *Mine Tobias, deputy-chairman of the Jewish Council of Bursztyn, addressing the inmates of the ghetto*

Most of those condemned to the death transports knew neither the reason nor the purpose of their removal. In the benumbed atmosphere of the disease-ridden Łódz ghetto there was no organised protest or resistance. A few asked for mercy and for exceptions to be made, particularly for their children. Anyone who had a friend in the ghetto administration stood a better chance. The majority went on clinging to the myth of resettlement in agricultural labour camps.

Among those who were left behind the ceaseless dangers of their ghetto existence created a climate of resignation and despair. 'We put a figure on those deported for labour', we read in an unposted letter, 'but the very next day another thousand are added, and all the lonely ones left behind, many of whom have good specialist skills, lose all desire to work, since they have absolutely no certainty that the next day they will still be able to follow their occupation. The continual fear that someone will come for them in the night, drag them out of bed and deport them – that is what wears them down. Not everyone has been taken away. The ones who could pay were not touched. Even so, those remaining behind have lost all status and have to start a new life; they are left with no alternative. It may seem funny, or perhaps not, to see a doctor of chemistry pulling a cartload of faeces – but it won't help him. The round of deportations has started again. First they took away the old inhabitants, then incomers as well.'

I was brought up with Germans and in normal times I could find no fault with them. They were cultivated people. How they could do such things later on I cannot understand to this day.

Estera Frenkiel, Jew from Danzig,
on her life in the Łódz ghetto

Not all the candidates for deportation accepted their marching orders as pre-ordained, particularly as the dark forebodings grew at an increasing pace. The greater the exodus became, the more hesitant were the nominees to report to the assembly-points. Many tried to escape from the ghetto – an almost hopeless undertaking in view of the prison-like conditions – others went underground, hiding in whatever seemed to offer a refuge, in dungeons, holes in the ground, sewers, cupboards, chimneys, behind wooden lean-tos, even in cess-pits. The tone of the announcements took on a threatening quality: 'I hereby require those nominated for resettlement to report at the assembly-point with *absolute punctuality* at the time to be announced. Those who do not report voluntarily will be *fetched by force*, even if they are not in their own homes, since they will be found wherever they are', warned the chairman of the Council of Elders, Chaim Rumkowski, in a poster put up on 14 January 1942. 'Should those nominated for resettlement be staying with other families in order to avoid resettlement, then not only the nominated persons but also the families who have taken them in, as well as the watchmen of the houses in question, will be forcibly resettled. This is my *final warning*!'

From time to time there were selections. Roll-calls were held, which we all had to attend. Women, children and old people were picked out. They were all sent back home but had to report a few days later. They had been grouped together for a transport and we were told they were all being taken off to work in a jam-factory. The transport went away, and some friends of mine were on it. Of course we never heard from them again. Today we know that all those people were killed.

Erza Jurman, German Jew,
then in the Riga ghetto

The machinery of selection operated ineluctably. True, every departing transport left, in those remaining behind, both grief and a feeling of relief that they had been spared for a little longer. In the streets, as one chronicler described it, they greeted each other 'like the survivors of an earthquake'. Yet it was scarcely imaginable that they might ultimately escape. Even someone who with a great deal of luck, with adroitness or bribery, often by sacrificing every last possession, survived one clearance, might be caught again the next day, or in a week or a month. The quota had to be filled, no matter who was affected.

'The chairman must nominate the quota', noted Oscar Singer on 13 May 1942. 'There have to be a thousand in each transport. The people have to be fetched. By day and night they are dragged out of their homes, out of bed. Many still have petitions being processed. It is bitterly unjust. The medical committee ought at least to check the patient's state of health. But in Fischgasse [the address of the 'Office for Resettlement'] they are getting nervous about the unfilled quota. The police have been instructed to be tough. And they are tough enough as it is.'

During all that time there was a constant deterioration in living conditions. The percentage of those who survived it, who maintained a normal appearance, who could dress normally and keep themselves tidy, became smaller as time passed. After about six months you could say that a third of people could live a respectable life, still had money and so would survive for a while longer. A further third could only adapt to the conditions with difficulty, hardly able to maintain the appearance of normality. The final third were facing death by starvation or were already dying of hunger. They could no longer walk, or even move; their bodies were bloated.

Professor Israel Gutman, Polish Jew,
then in the Warsaw ghetto

The Jewish ghetto police, reinforced by German policemen, combed the houses and hiding-places. They attacked the terrified occupants with the utmost brutality – often literally in a state of intoxication. Every Gestapo official assigned to this task received a special ration of a quarter-litre of schnapps, since it was 'irresponsible', as the ghetto administration wrote in a request, to send men out on that duty without a shot of spirits. These squads would indiscriminately grab as their victims anyone who seemed to them clearly 'unproductive'. It was enough that they should have grey hair or still be too young to work. Anyone who resisted risked being shot on the spot. When one of the pursuers tore a young woman's child from her arms, she screamed, as the ghetto chronicle relates: 'Leave me my child, or else shoot me!' Whereupon the man dressed in field-grey challenged her three times to tell him whether he should shoot her. Three times the mother answered yes. Then he gunned her down.

'Last night there was a lot of commotion. They went through many of the houses from top to bottom. This manhunt is dreadful', Oskar Singer went on in his diary. 'The police make raids. Tormented with fear, the people sit in their houses hardly daring to breathe. Is it possible we will be spared that ordeal? It is only a matter of hours. Today, 13 May, is the last day of the round-up, and anyone who gets through this day will probably be safe. We write petitions, we plead with the medical committees, again and again the office in the Fischgasse gets swamped with paper. The system still functions there, although clear signs of panic are becoming noticeable. People race from one *Protektor* to the next, from department to department, because somewhere there is a straw to clutch at. The frantic day is drawing wearily to its close. What will tomorrow bring?'

It merely brought a new wave of deportations, as Singer recorded in his diary on 15 May. By the end of May 1942 over 55,000 Jews from the Łódz ghetto, roughly a third of those interned there, had been forced to embark on their final journey.

> Every day there was a selection. We had to line up outside and they weeded out anyone whose face didn't fit. We heard shots fired in the forest every day. And we knew people who were shot there.
>
> *Tobi Biber, Jewish woman from Poland,*
> *then in the Cracow ghetto*
>
> We lived our lives from minute to minute, not even from hour to hour, and the sword of Damocles didn't just hang over us, it struck us.
>
> *Ben Helfgott, Polish Jew,*
> *then in the ghetto of Piotrkov*

However, this was still not enough to meet the target figures of the murder plan. On the evening of 31 August 1942 the Germans demanded that fifty Jewish policemen should hold themselves in readiness at 5 the next morning. As dawn broke, their orders were made clear, as seventeen-year-old David Sierakowiak recorded in his diary: 'The (fourth) anniversary of the outbreak of the war brought us the terrible news in the morning that the Germans were clearing all the hospitals in the ghetto. In the early hours the whole area around the hospitals was sealed off and all the sick were, without exception, loaded on to trucks and taken out of the ghetto. Since by now we knew from the reports of people brought in from the provinces, how the Germans "processed" such deportees, a massive panic arose in the city. As the sick were put on to the trucks, we witnessed appalling scenes. The people knew they were going to their death! They even tried to resist the Germans and had to be forced on to the vehicles. The hospitals were later occupied by the Germans, but some of the patients escaped in lots of different ways.'

The mother of Ester Brunstein and her brother was one of those lying in the hospital, her body bloated with hunger. When her two children heard about the clearance, they immediately rushed to the hospital, only to find it sealed off by police barricades: 'There were literally hundreds of people who, like me, were screaming and weeping: "My mum, my dad, my child, my brother." Then something happened which I later had trouble convincing myself I had actually seen. There were trucks standing there, on to which bundle-like things were thrown. In fact they were new-born babies. At the time, I think all we could do was blot out those images – but today they keep returning to torment me.'

Within two hours the five ghetto hospitals had been completely cleared. Two thousand patients, four hundred of them children, were dragged from their beds. Any who resisted were shot. After the sick-lists had been examined, the search began for missing people, as we learn from Sierakowiak's diary for 2 September: 'The tragedy of the sick being dragged off from the ghetto had not yet ended. Yesterday the Germans, having heard that some of the sick had escaped from several hopsitals, demanded that they be brought to book. Using the hospitals' sick-lists, the Jewish police began to search the homes of relatives and to recapture the escapees. In doing so they were guilty of a crime that up till then had not been committed in the ghetto. The Germans demanded the handing over of all those whose names were on the sick-list, but since the police, following directives from various influential people, wanted to protect the families of those same people (who had also fled), different methods were employed. They went into the homes of various sick people who had already been deported and, as if nothing had happened, asked where they were. When the unfortunate relatives replied that apparently they had already been taken away, because no-one had come home, the police took hostages and held them until the alleged escapee, who had long since been transported from the ghetto, might be handed over. And to round things off, when the Germans sent trucks for the rest of the sick, the police despatched some of the hostages with them, in order to make up the required numbers . . .'

A similar danger threatened Ester Brunstein and her brother. In the turmoil of the hospital clearance their mother had managed to elude her pursuers by jumping through a broken window. Soon a Jewish policeman came up to them and demanded they go with him until their mother gave herself up. While her brother accompanied the policeman, fourteen-year-old Ester ran to where her mother was hiding and told her about the blackmail. 'Then my mother said: "I can't let a healthy child go in my place. I must give myself up!" I flung myself on the floor, beat my head on the boards, cried and screamed: "I could just about live without a brother, but I can't live without my mother. If you go, then I'm going too!" Fortunately her brother managed to escape, and for the moment at least the family was out of danger.

> When the hunt began, Jews began to gather in their thousands, silently, like lambs being led to the slaughter. . . . Where were they going? Not one of them knew. That's how the Nazi did things. He committed his atrocities in the dark.
> *Chaim A. Kaplan, inmate of the Warsaw ghetto, describing in his diary the deportations from the Lublin ghetto, 17 April 1942*

Scarcely had the trains left the ghetto, laden with sick, wounded and other sufferers, than the chairman of the council of Jewish elders, Chaim Rumkowski, was faced with a new demand to deliver up his people. This one was too much even for the most hardened survivalists. The Jewish Council had to hand over 20,000 people, and this time not only would all those over sixty-five be affected, but also children under ten years old.

'Even when one is hardened by the experiences of wartime', wrote the father of a family in an unposted letter, 'one cannot ignore the bitter tears of one's nearest and dearest or be unmoved by the terrible cries of the people living through the most heartrending experiences of their lives. If I am truthful, I must confess it is hard for me to pick up my pen and write.'

Not even the members of the 'resettlement committee' could bring themselves to consign the very youngest in their community to a certain death. For by this time even the credulous could no longer believe that the children might be granted any kind of future. And yet Rumkowski bowed once more to this inhuman demand.

'The ghetto has been smitten with a deep anguish', the community leader said in a speech on 4 September. 'What is demanded of us is the best that we possess – our children and old people. I was not blessed with a child of my own, and that is why I have devoted the best years of my life to children. I lived and breathed with children. Never did I imagine I would have to bring them with my own hands to the sacrificial altar. Now, as an old man, I must stretch out my hands and beseech you: brothers and sisters, give them to me! Fathers and mothers, give me your children!'

In order to obtain any support at all for the handing over of small children, Rumkowski had made a dispensation whereby the sons and daughters of administrative employees, police and firemen were to be spared from transportation. Each house in turn was searched for children. Hidden in the attic, with other members of the household, Ester Brunstein saw the fear of a neighbour for her child as the raid was carried out. This mother had been unable to bring her 2½-year-old daughter Eljunia with her, because it would have woken her up, and her crying would have betrayed their hiding-place. So she was left in the house, hidden in a large basket, in the hope that she would sleep through the search undiscovered. After the clearance-squad had driven the other occupants into the street, Ester Brunstein heard a German voice telling a Jewish policeman to search the loft: 'He came up, saw us, went down again and said: "No-one up there." But suddenly, when it was nearly all over, we heard the baby downstairs start crying for her Mummy. They took the child with them. Her parents were up in the loft with us and couldn't do a thing, because any noise would have given us all away.'

> We were standing like sardines in a can, with hardly enough air to breathe. It was if we were going through a long, dark tunnel, from which there was no escape. We didn't know where we were heading or when or how the end would come.
> *Valeria Wache, a Jewish woman from Hungary,*
> *deported to Auschwitz*
>
> We were all loaded into cattle-trucks and then they locked the doors with a big iron bolt. There was one small window, but you couldn't see a thing. We had nothing to eat and it was very hot. We were all together – old and sick people and little children – and the train went on like that for three days and three nights, until we got to Sobibor.
> *Selma Engel, a Jewish woman from Holland*

In this way were families torn apart. Even for the children all hope of a future was destroyed. Rumkowski, the Jewish leader, had no more consolation to offer: 'Mothers,' he went on in his speech, 'I understand you, and see too well your tears. I feel, too, the pain in the hearts of the fathers who, tomorrow morning when they have taken away your children, will have to go to work. Only yesterday you were playing with your dear children. I know all this and have felt it since 4 o'clock yesterday when I received the order, and was utterly distraught. I live with your pain, your woe torments me, and I do not know what strength I will have to live through it. They demanded 24,000 children from me, 3,000 a day for the next eight days. Yet I succeeded in bringing the figure down to 20,000, perhaps even less, though on condition that the children are not more than ten years old. Children over ten are safe. Since the number of children and old people together only amounts to about 13,000, the remaining quantity will have to be made up of sick. It is hard for me to speak these words, I lack the strength. All I can pronounce is my plea to you: help me carry out

1. German *Ordnungspolizei* (civilian police) round up men in a Lithuanian village in summer 1941. Police battalions from Germany took an active part in the murders carried out by the *Einsatzgruppen* in the conquered territories.

2. German armoured units were engaged in heavy fighting. This is why, to begin with, soldiers in the front line noticed little of the killing of civilians in the conquered territories.

3. An SS man shooting civilians. Wehrmacht soldiers are among those looking on.

4. Abuse of a Jewish girl in Lvov. Following the withdrawal of the Soviet army in early July, the Ukrainian inhabitants of the city unleashed pogroms against the Jewish population. Some 4,000 Jews were killed.

5. Lithuanians beat Jewish fellow-citizens to death at a filling-station in Kaunas. German soldiers look on; June/July 1941.

6. Prisoners in Buchenwald have their heads shaved and are immersed in baths of disinfectant. For some years the SS had been trying out means of humiliating the inmates of concentration camps and were developing the camp system to a cruel 'perfection'.

7. In the conquered territories Jews were rounded up and identified, and the men were ordered to forced-labour units. The systematic registration of the Jews facilitated their systematic murder later on.

8. In August 1941 *Feldmarschall* Walter von Reichenau, commander of the 6th Army in the southern sector of the Eastern Front, gave express orders for the execution of Jewish children in August 1941.

9. Reinhard Heydrich (right), head of the Central Office of Reich Security, was responsible for imposing the Nazi regime of terror by the police in occupied Europe. In this early photograph from 1934, he is seen talking to his colleague, Alfred Naujoks.

10. A Jewish family in the streets of Berlin in 1941. After September 1941 German Jews, who had already suffered discrimination for a long time, were obliged to wear a yellow star.

11. An entrance to the Łódz ghetto – the destination for many Jews deported from western Europe. (The sign reads: Residential area for Jews – entry forbidden.)

12. 'Keep working for the wellbeing of your brethren in the ghetto. It will benefit them.' Such was the recommendation from Heinrich Himmler (sitting in car, on the left) to Chaim Rumkowski, leader of the Jewish elders. On 15 June 1941 Himmler inspected the Łódz ghetto.

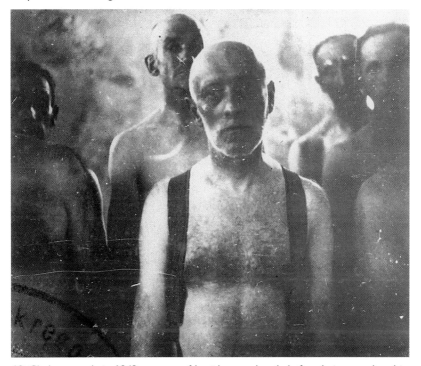

13. Chelmno, early in 1942: a group of Jewish men shortly before being murdered in a gassing-vehicle.

14. About two miles from the original Auschwitz camp, the real 'death-factory' – Auschwitz–Birkenau – was erected.

15. SS guards in front of the camp commandant's house at Belzec. Auschwitz was not the Nazis' only extermination camp – in Belzec, Majdanek, Chelmno, Treblinka and Sobibor, human beings were also slaughtered on an industrial scale.

16. Death on the transports: at a stop in Roumania dead bodies are unloaded from railway wagons on to a truck. Many deportees died in the overcrowded wagons, on to which they had been loaded like cattle.

17. When all the crematoria were ready for operation, corpses could be disposed of in industrial quantities.

18. The machinery of murder functioned almost without a hitch: a transport arrives at Auschwitz.

19. The boy from Warsaw – there is scarcely another picture which symbolises so poignantly how defenceless the Jews of the Polish capital were at the hands of their SS persecutors.

20. The Riegner telegram: on 8 August 1942 the German emigré and representative of the World Jewish Congress in Geneva told the head of the World Congress in the USA that he had learned from an informant that in the east the Jews of Europe were to be 'exterminated at a stroke'.

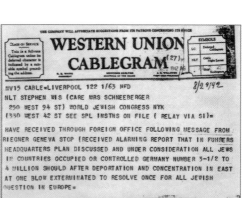

21. Oskar Schindler (standing second from right) in Munich with Jews who, thanks to his courage, did not die in Nazi camps.

22. Escaping from the Germans: Hungarian Jews, who have been issued with Swedish visas by Raoul Wallenberg, leave Budapest in December 1944.

23. Raoul Wallenberg, a Swedish diplomat in Hungary, rescued large numbers of Hungarian Jews about to be deported to German camps in 1944. After the occupation of Budapest by the Russians he was never seen alive again.

24. Only the names on the suitcases remain: the gassed and cremated victims of Auschwitz left their luggage and belongings at the scene of their destruction.

25. We are the shoes, we are the last witnesses.
We are the shoes of grandfathers and grandchildren.
From Prague, Paris and Amsterdam.
And because we are only made of fabric and leather
And not from flesh and blood, each of us has been spared the fire of hell.
(From the poem 'I saw a hill' by Moses Schulstein.)

26. The means of industrialised annihilation: after being taken prisoner by Soviet troops, guards from Auschwitz show the photographer cans containing Zyklon B.

27. The shock: Majdanek was the first extermination camp to be liberated by the Russians. It was in late July 1944 that they stumbled across this crematorium.

28. The perpetrators and their victims – guards in Bergen-Belsen had to bury the corpses after the camp had been liberated.

29. Fields of corpses, mountains of corpses: countless inmates died shortly before the war ended – maltreated on death-marches and transports, weakened by hunger and disease.

30. The Americans seemed like people from another world – Corporal Larry Mutinsk hands out cigarettes in Allach camp, a satellite of Dachau.

31. One perpetrator who did not escape: Rudolf Höss, commandant of Auschwitz, was handed over to the Poles by the United States on 25 May 1946. In Poland he would be condemned to death and executed.

this action! I tremble with fear at the thought that – God forbid – others will take the operation into their hands . . .'

Like a drowning man he clung to the notion that by sacrificing the weakest he would at least be able to rescue those fit for work and finally satisfy the bloodlust of his tormentors. His speech to the inhabitants of the ghetto illustrates the whole tragedy of the hostage condemned to be executioner under the violent pressure of a treacherous and calculating German occupying power: 'Before you stands a Jew destroyed. Do not envy me! This is the hardest order I have ever had to carry out. I stretch out my trembling, defeated hands to you and implore you: place your sacrificial victims in my hands so that I can prevent further sacrifice, so that I may save as many as a hundred thousand Jews.'

This hope was to remain a vain one. In an agonising process, the ghetto bled to death. The group of the chosen, those who were still useful because they were producing goods for the German war-machine, grew ever smaller. Anyone whose strength to work failed him, saw himself under sentence of death. One house after another was subjected to raids in which Jewish policemen, doctors and nurses had to pick out from the occupants those who were 'weak and unfit for work'.

The full effect of this on those who suffered it is shown in David Sierakowiak's diary entry for 6 September 1942. During a house-search a Jewish doctor had diagnosed his mother as having a weak heart and sent her to hospital. In this way she had forfeited her life under the selection criteria of the manhunters. 'Sometimes my heart is so constricted and convulsed that I feel as though I am about to sink into madness or delirium. And yet inwardly I cannot turn away from Mum, and suddenly it is as if I am split in two, in her brain and her body. The hour of her deportation approaches and no rescue comes from anywhere. True, there was some thunder and lightning in the evening, and it even rained, but that brought no relief in our pain. Not even the heaviest rain in the world can soothe a totally broken heart, nothing can fill that infinite emptiness of the soul, the mind, the heart and the senses, that overcomes you when you have lost the one you love most, the one who loves their own life as . . .'

Here the diary breaks off. It is the last testimony of its author.

Most of the thousands of deportees left the ghetto entirely without trace, without a farewell, leaving nothing behind them. Although of all the ghettos in occupied Poland Łódz existed the longest, in the end it offered no refuge even to those who had escaped selection over the years. The initial destination of the death-trains was Kolo, whose German name was Warthbrücken. From there they were taken by narrow-gauge railway and finally on trucks to the incongruous castle complex in Chelmno (Kulmhof), whose true purpose was hidden from public gaze by a high fence.

The new arrivals were greeted in the castle courtyard with a friendly and reassuring talk by a member of the *Sonderkommando*, generally even wearing a doctor's white coat. He assured them they would now be put on to labour duties and all the misery of the ghetto would soon be forgotten – a fatal deception dressed up as humanitarian care. Afterwards the victims had an opportunity to send postcards to their relatives, telling them they had arrived safely. Finally they were told that, before being put to work, they were just to take a shower while their clothing was being disinfected. They had to undress in a large hall and hand in their valuables – all with the comforting assurance that their property would be returned to them afterwards.

Polish workmen accompanied the unsuspecting victims to the cellars of the castle where their suspicions were allayed by signs reading 'To the baths' or 'To the doctor'. At the end of the vaulted cellar they had to go up a ramp which was blocked off on either side by boards. The only exit led through open double doors into the cargo-space of one of three large vans. Now they realised they had been tricked into a deadly trap. But there was no escape. Roughly and violently they were now driven, shoved, beaten and kicked until 100 or as many as 150 people had been squeezed into the truck. Then the double doors were brutally locked. The diesel engine howled into life and its exhaust fumes streamed into the van's interior.

Even as the people in the back were suffocating in agony, the truck drove to a 'forest camp' about 2 miles away. There, members of Jewish labour squads had to drag the corpses out of the vehicle, search them for hidden valuables and pull out their gold teeth. If anyone was found still alive among the bodies they were shot by the guards. To begin with, the bodies were dumped in large pits. From the spring of 1942 the mass graves were replaced by incinerators. Prisoners had to exhume the mortal remains and burn them. So as to wipe out all traces, the bones of the cremated bodies were ground up in a bone-mill.

The thirty to forty Jewish gravediggers, who were given a brief reprieve from the process of annihilation, had to wear shackles all the time and were kept incarcerated in the castle cellars. When one of them had no energy left for this inhuman labour, he had to 'go to the doctor' and never came back again.

Members of the German administration of the Łódz ghetto were also engaged in the 'special operation'. They handled the book-keeping aspects of the mass murder. They balanced the 'operating costs' of the *Sonderkommando* against the proceeds from the death-factory, as was explained in matter-of-fact commercial terms: '. . . all moneys arising from the evacuation of the Jews from rural districts are, by order of the Reich town governor, to be assigned to the ghetto administration, since all the costs of resettlement, tax-arrears of the Jews, invoices for supplies and the financing of the *Sonderkommando* have to be met from our funds.' As a reward for their cooperation in this trade, office-holders were granted a special ration of alcohol and cigarettes.

Chelmno was the killing-plant for the Łódz ghetto, which acted as a human 'buffer-stock'. And the plant operated with appalling thoroughness. Anyone who was shipped in here met their death, almost without exception: in total, over 150,000 people, among them most of the Jews who had been deported to Łódz in the autumn of 1941, from Prague, Vienna, Luxembourg and the big German cities.

Millions of other European Jews would come to the same fate by other routes, though their deportation followed a similar pattern. Between 8 November 1941 and 6 February 1942, in a second wave of deportations, thirty further transports, generally with 1,000 people in each, left German cities bound for the ghettos of Riga, Kovno and Minsk. The cities they came from were in the main those considered to be targets for enemy bombing. In this way, the displacements were intended to appear like reprisals against the Jews, whom the propaganda branded as accomplices of the Allies waging war on Germany. Furthermore, in view of the severe housing shortage caused by bomb damage, the populations of those cities were meant to benefit from the vacating of Jewish properties and thus be favourably disposed to the policy for the treatment of Jews.

Nevertheless, for Hitler's paladins, competing with each other in the decimation of the Jewish population in their own fiefdoms, the displacement operation did not go far enough. Thus the propaganda minister, Goebbels, who wore a second hat as *Gauleiter* of the capital city, Berlin, warned in his diary for 28 October 1941: 'A plan has been drawn up for the removal of some 15,000 Jews from Berlin by the end of the year. This means there will still be 50,000 remaining, and that's all wrong. I urge that, if the Jews are evacuated, this process must be completed in the shortest possible time.'

The regime left people in no doubt as to its determination to proceed urgently with the deportation programme in 1942. Admittedly Eichmann, the chief organiser, spoke in a circular to state police offices of 'transport difficulties' and 'limited reception facilities in the east'; however, at the same time he promised 'new reception facilities' with the objective of 'displacing further quotas of Jews'.

As a consequence a third wave of deportations was set in motion, principally from March to June 1942, from southern German cities like Mainz, Würzburg, Munich and Stuttgart, as well as from Vienna and the Czech 'Protectorate'. Their destination was the Warsaw ghetto, the largest internment camp in occupied Poland, as well as ghettos in smaller cities in Lublin province. Just as in Łódz, the living conditions in these 'Jewish residential districts', converted into prisons, were so inhuman that the wretched, vegetating existence of the new arrivals lasted, in most cases, no longer than three weeks. Those who did not die in the ghettos were murdered in the nearest extermination camps: Chelmno, Belzec, Treblinka, Sobibor and finally Auschwitz.

I had the feeling that most of the SS men got a sadistic pleasure from their activities. Their behaviour gave that impression. Without a tendency to sadism no-one could kill like that, no-one could put people into gas-chambers. If they weren't sadists already then they became so during their work.

Stefan Grayek, Polish Jew,
then in the Warsaw ghetto

From registration in the home country through to death in the gas-chamber, the machinery of death ran with increasing efficiency along the lines described. With time it crystallised into a system: the original Jewish inhabitants of the ghettos in Poland and the former Soviet regions were sent to their deaths in train after train, while new human 'supplies' arrived from the west. From time to time, the local town governors received permission to kill 'their' ghetto inhabitants in return for accepting new transports. At first, while this was going on and despite the lethal conditions, the fiction was maintained that the exiles were awaiting some future 'solution', and that the murder operations that had already been set in train were simply the result of 'pressure of events' such as epidemics, food shortage and overpopulation. It still had to look as if Jews from Germany and adjoining regions were being shipped eastwards for labour service. In order to create accommodation and catering capacity for them, the indigenous ghetto-dwellers and the newcomers who were not up to the hard living and working conditions simply had to make way.

With the fourth wave of deportations a new variant in the policy of annihilation became apparent. From May to September 1942 death-trains ran eastward from Vienna, Cologne, Bremen, Königsberg and other German cities, as well as from the 'old people's ghetto' of Theresienstadt, which served as a transit-camp. Most of these ended up in Minsk, the capital of Byelorussia. Yet there the deportees were not even put into the ghetto; their journey led directly to their death.

Once again they were the victims of a deadly deception. 'That was one transport I will never forget', we are told by Helmut Lohn, who on 20 July 1942, as an auxiliary in the Jewish community, was supervising those departing from Cologne. 'All young, strong people, who knew how to look after themselves. This was the only transport in which there was no grief, only hundred per-cent confidence: we will be back! That transport set off in a smooth and orderly way. In spite of everything, they were still singing cheerful songs. This time platform 5 wasn't full of despairing people, but courageous ones, who knowingly accepted whatever was in store for them.'

This time as well, the executioners concealed their true intentions until the last moment. That is why, on 24 July, the day he arrived in Minsk, Oscar Hoffmann from Cologne wrote in good spirits to friends in Germany: 'After an 87-hour journey we have arrived here in Minsk, healthy, cheerful and in good heart. In Wolhonye [he means Wolkowysk] we were transferred from our Cologne train into cattle-trucks. They tell us we have to leave the station with our luggage straight away, to be taken to our camp. We assume that we will be put on to farm work in the area around Minsk. Whether we are staying here for some time is still not certain.'

He wrote that on the day of his death. Yet the reassuring charade was so effective that Hoffmann actually asked for a reference to be sent from Germany, in the hope of being given work. In reality the new arrivals, after handing in their valuables, were not sent off for labour but into a small forest 10 miles south-east of Minsk, where Russian PoWs had dug out huge pits 10 feet deep and 60 yards long. When the capacity of the gas-vehicles was inadequate, the naked victims were shot in the back of the neck with a pistol and thrown into the pits. One of the killers, Johann Paul Rumschewitsch, later described the sequence of events: 'Some of the Jews refused to go up to the pit and ran around the edge of it; others threw themselves straight into the pit without being shot. So the executions became disrupted. I could see that some already lying in the pit were still moving. This necessitated, after firing my pistol three or four times, going to the arms issue base to collect an MP [machine-pistol]. With this I went on shooting the ones in the pit who were still moving. . . . At first I aimed the MP and fired single shots. Then I could no longer bear to do this and fired off the rest of my magazine blindly into the pit. I left the pit, went over to Heuser [his superior], who was standing near the undressing area, and said to him: "I can't go on with this." He replied: "Clear off then."'

Close on 26,000 people died in Minsk at the hands of the *Sonderkommandos*. Their deportation had only one purpose: their extermination. 'Resettlement' became the euphemism for murder, without the victims noticing the change.

There was a similar pattern to the human transports which ran, between August and October 1942, from Berlin to Riga and Reval [Tallinn, Estonia], from Theresienstadt to the extermination camps of Treblinka and Auschwitz, and from Vienna and Berlin to Auschwitz.

Marginalisation, ghettoisation, deportation – the merciless machinery of genocide now went into operation everywhere that German troops hoisted the swastika. The wider the radius of the campaign of conquest, the greater was the number of those destined for death who, as the Germans marched in, were exposed without protection to their obsessive racial hatred.

In the German-occupied part of France the deportation of Jews at first served as a substitute for officially imposed reprisals. In reply to the growing number of attacks by the French Resistance on the German military, the leadership in Berlin called for the shooting of French hostages. However, since these terror tactics increasingly got in the way of the policy of collaboration, the military administration replaced the killing of hostages, as a reaction to acts of resistance, by deporting sizeable numbers of Jews, preferably those of foreign extraction, to the east. The strategy worked; the majority of the population were more willing to accept punitive moves against the Jewish population than reprisals against Resistance fighters. In the summer of 1942 five transports with a total of 5,000 people left the Compiègne transit-camp near Paris, bound for Auschwitz.

At the same time the deportation programme for the west was systematised and given specific target quotas. At a meeting in the

Central Office of Reich Security the 'Jewish experts' agreed on these firm figures: 100,000 Jews from the whole of France, 15,000 from the Netherlands and 10,000 from Belgium were to be shipped off to Auschwitz, starting in July. The basic criterion was an age range of sixteen to forty, in which a 10 per cent proportion of Jews 'unfit for work' would be accepted. A little later, Eichmann had one train per day at his disposal, each carrying 1,000 people, and he lowered the target for France to 40,000, at the same time raising the Dutch target also to 40,000.

The fact was that the French authorities were putting unexpected obstacles in the way of the managers of death. It is true that both in the German-occupied north and in the formally independent south, governed by Marshal Pétain's collaborationist regime, there was a willingness to hand over foreign Jews – mainly refugees – and even Jewish orphans. Yet, to begin with, the Germans bought this cooperation by sparing Jews of French nationality. That is why, in 1942, the deportations remained as low as 42,000. It was only as good relations with the collaborators became less important to the German occupiers that more and more French Jews became caught up in the manhunt. Until the time of the liberation in 1944 73,000 Jews were deported from France, roughly a quarter of the Jews living in that country in 1940. Of the rest, 50,000 had escaped to Switzerland or Spain, between 20,000 and 30,000, mostly children, had been taken in by French families and as many as 150,000 had gone to ground in the countryside.

I had a relative who took into his home people who had broken out from the ghetto. He told the people, who had to pay for their stay by the day, that he would arrange forged Aryan papers for them. And then he handed them over to the police and split the stolen money with the policemen.

Roman Frister, Polish Jew

In the Netherlands a section of the population also showed solidarity with the victims of persecution, many of whom initially resisted the order to leave the country. Nevertheless, the occupying power with the support of the Dutch authorities produced close to the required quota of 40,000 deportees – partly by hostage-taking and blackmail, partly by putting pressure on the Jewish Council. In the years that followed, further death-trains rolled out with fateful regularity from the Dutch internment camp at Westerbork, heading for the extermination sites of Auschwitz and Sobibor, until finally 107,000 people had made this journey, of whom some 102,000 never returned.

In Belgium the German occupiers, while scarcely involving the national authorities, exceeded their 1942 target by removing nearly 17,000 Jews – not one of whom was a Belgian citizen. Most of the deportees had vainly sought protection as refugees from persecution. In the next two years the transports to Auschwitz also accounted for 8,000 Jews of Belgian nationality. Nevertheless, in Belgium nearly half the Jewish population managed to evade the threat of arrest by going underground.

In Denmark Hitler's satraps hesitated to strike a blow against the Jewish minority until the autumn of 1943, since they feared unrest in a country which had not allowed itself to become infected with anti-Semitism. Not until the confrontation in domestic policy came to a head was the 'Jewish question' tackled with intensified repression. But the deportation plans did not remain secret. On hearing a report on Swedish radio the Danes responded with an unparalleled rescue operation: the fishing fleet carried more than 6,700 condemned Jews across the straits to safety in Sweden. So when the German police made their raids they found no more than 500 Jews left, who were either too old or too sick to travel or had not been prepared to flee. They were sent to Theresienstadt, the old people's ghetto, where the chances of survival were higher than in other camps.

In Norway, on the other hand, the Nazi occupation force received the active support of the politically sympathetic Quisling regime in their preparations for deportation. From November 1942 until 1944, transport ships took 770 people to the death-trains. But 930 Jews from Norway found refuge in Sweden.

> In Minsk city on 28 and 29 July about 10,000 Jews were liquidated; 6,500 of them were Russian Jews – predominantly old people, women and children – the rest consisted of Jews unfit for work, most of whom had been sent to Minsk from Vienna, Brno, Bremen and Berlin the previous November, on the orders of the Führer.
>
> *Wilhelm Kube, commissioner-general for Ruthenia,*
> *in a report dated 31 July 1942*

The shipment of hundreds of thousands of Jews from the territory under direct German control was not enough to satisfy the Nazi mania for annihilation. In 1942 Hitler's henchmen increased their efforts to bring Jews from allied nations within the scope of their deportation programme. Since these countries were sovereign states under international law the German Foreign Office played an important part in obtaining their compliance. Previously the German diplomats had put pressure on them to hand over those of their countrymen who were already resident in areas within the German grasp. Now attention was turned to the Jews who were still living in the countries concerned.

It began with an 'offer' to the government of Slovakia, that in place of supplying labour for Germany they should hand over 20,000 Slovakian Jews. In the event, between April and June 1942 some 50,000 people were deported – virtually all the Slovakian Jews other than those who had gone underground or who possessed letters of safe-conduct. The only deportees with a slight chance of survival were those in the camps of Majdanek or Auschwitz who were selected for forced labour. The rest were swept into the apparatus of destruction, either directly or with an intermediate stop in occupied Poland.

The government of Croatia proved equally willing to collaborate. In 1941 they had already, without being asked, interned more than half their Jewish citizens in camps run by the Ustasha militia, where most died a slow and miserable death or else were murdered by the pro-Nazi thugs. In the summer of 1942, under German supervision, a further 5,000 or so Croatian

Jews were shipped to Auschwitz, and 2,000 more in May 1943. Nonetheless, many of those persecuted were given asylum in the Italian-occupied part of the country.

In Roumania as well, anti-Semitic extremists had on their own initiative provoked an appalling bloodbath which cost the lives of over 100,000 Roumanian Jews. However, the Roumanian government successfully held out against the German request that the remaining survivors be sent to their death.

In a similar way, Hungary for a long time resisted the German demand for the handing over of the 725,000 Jews who lived in Hungary or had taken refuge there. Not until 1944 was the machinery of murder set in motion, but it was then done with a dreadful thoroughness, especially after the hesitant government of Admiral Horthy had been deposed in a coup d'état instigated by Germany.

In Bulgaria, the Jewish section of the population had been deprived of civil rights early on. But when Bulgaria's German ally insisted that their Jews should be killed, the authorities, backed by protests from parliament and the public, developed a very effective method of non-cooperation. It is true that they sent 11,000 Jews from regions of Greece and Macedonia which were under Bulgarian occupation during the war, to their death in the Treblinka extermination camp, but the Bulgarian Jews were saved.

The Finnish government fended off a request from the *Reichsführer-SS*, Heinrich Himmler, which he made during a visit in July 1942, with the laconic reply that in Finland there was no 'Jewish problem'. And the subject was dropped.

The Jewish children being held in the camps at Pithiviers and Beaune-le-Rolande can be distributed gradually among the planned transports to Auschwitz. However, entire transports of children are *not under any circumstances* to be despatched.

> *Telegram from Central Office of Reich Security to the*
> *Security Police and SD in Paris,*
> *13 August 1942*

> Of the original 140,000 full Jews registered in the Netherlands, the 100,000th Jew has now been removed from the population . . . . Although the Dutch public has a negative attitude towards the deportations, outwardly the great majority appears indifferent.
>
> *Consul-General Otto Bene, representative of the German Foreign Office in the Netherlands, in a report on 25 June 1943*

In 1936, Hitler's principal ally, Italy, had enshrined anti-Jewish discrimination in law as a measure of foreign policy favourable to the German Reich. Italy's internment of Jews and their mobilisation as forced labour also followed the Nazi model. Nevertheless, Mussolini's administration in the territories under Italian occupation did not show any excessive zeal in pursuing further measures of persecution. Despite the desire to encourage emulation, German diplomacy proceeded with caution, in order not to put any strain on the Axis alliance. This changed overnight, following the Italian surrender to the Allies in September 1943, when the Wehrmacht occupied the northern half of Italy and helped Mussolini's Fascists to return to power in a puppet regime. Now the perpetrators of racial vengeance had a free hand to carry out their murderous work in Italy as well. Without delay they shipped more than 5,000 people to the gas-chambers of Auschwitz. Despite this bitter harvest, 80 per cent of the Jews living in Italy managed, with the help of the church, the authorities and the public, to go underground and survive to the end of the war.

In Greece, Croatia, Albania and other Mediterranean areas which Italy had to hand over to the Wehrmacht after the break-up of the Axis, thousands more were placed at the mercy of the Germans. Previously Eichmann's emissaries had already done their worst in the German-occupied part of Greece. In 1943, 45,000 Jews chiefly from Salonika – virtually the entire Jewish community of that city – were sent on the long journey to Auschwitz. Many of them did not survive the rigours of prolonged confinement in overcrowded goods-wagons. Even from the outlying islands those

listed for deportation were sent on complicated routes – despite
the wartime restrictions on transport – to the distant gas-
chambers, nearly 1,000 miles away.

In the country where millionfold murder had been conceived and
organised, the concept of a 'Final Solution to the Jewish Problem'
reached its full significance with a merciless logic. The more the
fortunes of war turned against the Wehrmacht, the harder were
the Jews in Germany hit by this rigorous policy of annihilation.
The 'total war' which Hitler's propagandist Goebbels proclaimed
after the catastrophe of Stalingrad in February 1943 meant an
intensified mobilisation of the German population at home and at
the Front, and for the armies of PoWs, forced labour in
armaments factories; however, for most Jews of working age, for
whom slave labour had up to now been a life insurance, 'total war'
was a death sentence. On 27 February 1943 there was a surprise
wave of arrests aimed at the 'removal of all Jews still engaged in
the labour process' throughout Reich territory. In Berlin alone, in
what was called the 'Factory Operation', Himmler's thugs arrested
about 7,000 people at their workplaces or in their homes. In the
German Reich more than 11,000 were caught up in the wave of
arrests.

As early as the spring of '42 there were rumours in the
Warsaw ghetto that the Germans were experimenting with
gas, and with motor exhaust fumes, and that people – groups
of ten or twenty were mentioned – were being herded into
some kind of shed where gas was piped in, and that was how
they were murdered. Those were the kind of rumours going
around the ghetto, and I was one of the many who didn't
believe them at the time. But the Jewish marshals who
worked in the place the trains left from – in Warsaw we called
it the 'transshipment centre' – noted down the numbers on
the wagons which carried off the human freight – and a
terrible fact emerged: the very same day, only a few hours
later, the same wagons were back again. That meant that

none of the transports were going very far. They couldn't be going more than 150 or maybe 200 kilometres and not the 1,000 kilometres to Minsk or Smolensk, as people thought, because that was where a defensive line was being built. The quick turnround meant that all those people were being taken somewhere relatively close to Warsaw. Then we also found out what was happening to them. Where did this news come from? Some of it came from Polish railwaymen who took the trains there. But it was also the resistance movement that had been formed in the Warsaw ghetto at that time, who made great efforts to find out what was happening to people. Pretty soon it became clear: they were all being murdered. Those people were not being put to work but simply murdered. We knew that.

Marcel Reich-Ranicki, Polish-born Jew from Berlin

One of them was Hans Frankenthal, who up to that time had been forced to work for nothing, building roads for a contractor in the Sauerland. For 14 to 16 hours a day he had to operate a tar-sprayer, wreathed in billowing smoke, until he was often close to total exhaustion. The sixteen-year-old knew, however, that it was only this work that saved him from deportation. On 26 February 1943 the head of the firm told his Jewish forced labourers that the following morning they had to report to the yard of the former Jewish school to have their work documents checked. It all seemed like a transfer to another company. But at Dortmund's central station the unsuspecting men were greeted by the Gestapo. 'When we showed our tickets at the barrier'. Frankenthal recalls today, 'they told us: "You're under arrest. Anyone who tries to escape will be shot!" Then all of us were called up by name; there were about 500 of us, who had been fetched in directly from work. And again they said: "Anyone who tries to escape will be shot!" Then the Gestapo took us in trucks to the Brakel district in Dortmund and herded us into a large hall they had rented in a hotel.

'The next day our families came and brought us some food and clothing. Because we were told we would be going to work in the east and could take 25 kilos of luggage with us. I was very angry with my parents for coming there from their hiding-place. But my father's only reply was: "Well, we can't send under-age children into the world alone." Those were his very words.

'In that hall there were nearly 1,000 people, old, sick people, pregnant women, screaming babies. The marshals from the Jewish community asked the Gestapo to bring mattresses from unoccupied houses, so that the sick and small children could lie down. This was refused; but in the end they let us bring some straw from a farmer's barn nearby. The next day we were taken by tram to the South Station. I stayed behind with a dozen young men, because we had to get the luggage together. But before we had packed everything up, we suddenly heard: "On your feet, you're going!" That should really have told us something.

'At the station we threw the luggage into two empty wagons at the end of the train. My father beckoned us over and I climbed into one of the cattle-trucks with him. At the next stop, in Bielefeld, I saw some other apprentices who I knew. I wanted to jump out and say hello to them, but I was pushed back by the guards. I got back into the cattle-truck and said very quietly to my father: "The two wagons with our luggage aren't attached to the train any longer." Then he answered: "Where we're going, we won't be needing any luggage."'

On 3 March 1943 the train reached its terminus. Through a small slat in the side of the cattle-truck Frankenthal could make out the name on the platform. It was Auschwitz.

A little later, Eichmann came to see me in Auschwitz. He revealed to me the plans for operations in individual countries. Initially, those destined for Auschwitz would be from Upper Silesia and adjacent parts of the *General-gouvernement*. At the same time, and thereafter depending on the situation, the Jews from Germany and Czechoslovakia. Then from the west: France, Belgium, Holland. . . . We went on to discuss the process of extermination . . .

                    Rudolf Höss, commandant of Auschwitz, in notes
                                    he made while in prison

CHAPTER FOUR

DEATH-FACTORY

KNOPP/LIECHTENSTEIN

> It was a blatant fraud that the words over the main entrance, surrounded by electrified barbed wire, were *Arbeit macht frei* (Work is liberation). No-one in Auschwitz was liberated by work; the real system was 'annihilation through work'.
>
> *Frantz Danimann, prisoner in Auschwitz*

Konrad Szweda could not get to sleep. The Catholic priest tossed and turned restlessly on his plank bed in a barrack of the Auschwitz concentration camp. There were too many thoughts running through his head, too many anxieties. Why had the SS men been so busy all that day? What were they up to? Something was brewing that night of 5 September 1941, that was obvious. When a loud whimper suddenly cut through the silence, it seemed to confirm his suspicions. But he could not understand the voices that were getting louder and closer. The priest strained to listen. As his eyes became accustomed to the dark he saw a group of people being herded along towards Block 11. They looked utterly exhausted, scarcely able to put one foot in front of the other. German guards used bull-whips to beat their defenceless charges; they spat on them and kicked them. Those are Russians, Soviet prisoners-of-war, Szweda suddenly realised. What did the SS have in mind for them?

> I just don't know whether I experienced real grief in Auschwitz. All we did in the camp was struggle for our daily bread.
>
> *Chanan Bachrich, Czech Jew, prisoner in Auschwitz*

We knew when the people were dead, because the screaming stopped. We usually waited half an hour before we opened the doors and removed the bodies. After the corpses had been brought out, our *Sonderkommandos* took off their rings and pulled the gold fillings from their teeth.

Rudolf Höss, commandant of Auschwitz, in a statement under oath at Nuremberg, 5 April 1946

A few days previously Szweda had noticed that the cellar windows of Block 11, the cell-block for special prisoners, had been bricked up. The inmates had been moved to another building. What was even more odd was that the guards had brought the prisoners back to camp from their work earlier than normal. They did this twice in fact, for no apparent reason. Rumours about a big transport of 'special prisoners' were circulating. In the evening there was a 'confined to barracks' order. No-one was allowed to leave their building. The guards even took away the prisoners' clothes and blankets; they cowered in the huts, stark naked. It was strictly forbidden to go near a window. This 'dress rehearsal' – for that was what the SS were putting on – was to take place without witnesses.

On 5 September, in the sick-bay, a committee of SS doctors had separated the sick from among the Polish prisoners. It was an arbitrary allocation to life or death – purely on outward appearance; they did not take the time to make a full examination. Suddenly the order came for those selected to parade in the courtyard. A prison doctor named Kasimierz Halgas had been about to issue some food to the sick. Later he recalled: 'I went to the senior man in the sick-bay, the oldest of the "old lags", and asked him what I should do with the food. He tapped his forehead meaningfully and said I should give the food out to the others, because those poor sods would never eat again.'

Those selected for death were instructed to remain in position. Dressed only in shirts and underpants, they shivered in the cold. Not until an hour had passed did the order come: 'Get over to Block 11.' Konrad Szweda was working as an orderly in the sick-bay. He remembers: 'Someone told me that the sick men would be waiting in the punishment company for an overnight transport. That reassured me. We picked up a stretcher with one of the sick and went into the hall of the punishment block. From there we were sent down into the cellar. I felt faint as I found myself in the evil smelling dungeon. We laid the poor wretch on the cold concrete. A second man was immediately placed on top of him, then a third and a fourth. They were being stacked up while they were still alive! In a cell designed for one man, they packed in thirty, forty, as many as fifty people!' When he asked what was going to happen to the sick men he got no answer but was sent back without a word to his own block.

> We were to meant to carry out this extermination in secret, but the foul and nauseating smell coming from the continuous burning of bodies penetrated the whole district, and everyone living in the vicinity knew that extermination was going on in Auschwitz.
>
> *Rudolf Höss, in a sworn statement at Nuremberg, 5 April 1946*

Only a few hours later he observed Russian PoWs being forced to take the same route as their Polish fellow-victims. When they reached Block 11, the guards shoved them into the already crammed cells. Some time after midnight, when the last cell doors were slammed shut, those outside could hear, as if from a great distance, a desperate moaning and screaming. The sounds grew fainter. Soon nothing more could be heard.

> We didn't know that Auschwitz was synonymous with death. We were convinced it really *was* a labour camp.
>
> *Jaacov Gabai, Greek Jew, prisoner in Auschwitz*
>
> I didn't watch the gassing business. Couldn't do it. I'd probably have keeled over.
>
> *Adolf Eichmann describing a visit to Auschwitz*

We knew nothing about Auschwitz. Up till then we thought we could escape death by working in an arms factory – which is where I did work. The fact that there was an extermination camp with murder by gassing, we knew nothing about, although we were living only 30 kilometres from Auschwitz. But at the end of '42 news filtered through.

Arno Lustiger, Polish Jew,
deported in 1944 to the satellite
camp of Auschwitz–Blechhammer

Two days later a number of prisoners were instructed to open the doors again. Jan Wolny was one of them. The picture he was faced with in the cellar of Block 11 is something he has never been able to forget: 'The dead bodies of prisoners and Soviet PoWs were lying wedged across each other. Their eyes were staring, their mouths gaping open. Their eye-sockets were swollen, their fingers and toes, as well as stomachs, were a livid blue in colour.'

For the first time, in the early hours of 6 September 1941, the SS had tested the cyanide preparation known as Zyklon B on human beings. The trial had been 'successful' and the executioners declared themselves satisfied: about 600 Soviet soldiers and nearly 300 sick civilian detainees had been gassed to death. The means of mass murder in Auschwitz had been discovered. The 'advantage' of Zyklon B over the mass shootings, which were already being carried out in the camp, was obvious: not only did it kill faster and more cost-effectively, it was also more 'humane' – for the perpetrators, not for the victims. The camp commandant, Rudolf Höss, later stated in evidence: 'I must say frankly that the gassing had a reassuring effect on me, since in the foreseeable future a start had to be made on the mass extermination of the Jews. I always dreaded the shootings. Now I was assured that we would be spared all those blood-baths.'

The final step towards a crime of historic proportions had been taken. Only a few months after the first gassings, the industrialised killing would begin in Auschwitz, the future centre for the annihilation of the Jews.

When the Auschwitz concentration camp was set up in 1940, not even the German executioners themselves had any idea of the extent of the crime that they would soon be committing there. At the suggestion of the Senior SS and Police Officer in Silesia, Erich von dem Bach-Zelewski, the camp was initially established to hold prisoners. The prisons in his *Gau* were completely overcrowded and he needed more capacity. Since the beginning of the war against Poland the SS thugs had been hunting down members of the Polish elite and 'other unreliable elements', particularly Jews. Those who were not shot during this 'extraordinary pacification exercise' ended up in prison. But now the situation had become untenable and there was no more room for the new batches of detainees arriving every day.

In this situation Bach-Zelewski turned his attention to the former Polish artillery barracks in Zasole, near Auschwitz. The location seemed particularly suitable since the barracks could be occupied immediately. Furthermore, the isolated situation made it possible to expand the complex later on, and thanks to the convenient rail connections prisoners could be transported there from all over the Reich. Even Himmler was enthusiastic. The *Reichsführer-SS* saw in the new camp an opportunity to press ahead with the 'Germanisation of the east'. With the help of prison labour, the boggy terrain was to be turned into a vast area of agriculturally viable land – a large 'model estate' for German settlers. Ethnic Germans were to be resettled here and trained to be efficient breeders of livestock and fish. That at least was the original plan.

> It is hard to explain how we managed to survive Auschwitz. Basically it was pure chance as to who survived and who didn't. But the fact of having a sister there was of course a huge help to both of us. Each of us wanted to survive for the sake of the other. You can understand that, can't you?
> *Anita Lasker Walfisch, Jew from Breslau, member of the Auschwitz women's orchestra*

'Moslems' was what we called the people who had got so thin, they were just skin and bone.

Chanan Bachrich, Czech Jew, prisoner in Auschwitz

By 1940 concentration camps already existed in many places. Not long after the Nazis sneaked into power in 1933, the first camp was opened at Dachau, near Munich. At first the Nazis gave very detailed if flattering reports about how much attention was paid to 'justice and order' there. As time went by, the German name *Konzentrationslager* was abbreviated to KZ and the letters, which quickly entered everyday language, took on a sinister undertone. What went on in these camps no-one knew exactly, but most people lowered their voice as soon as they began talking about KZs. With the establishment of concentration camps the new masters were pursuing one simple objective: the *Volksschädlinge*, or 'pests of the nation', as Nazi jargon termed them, were to be 'concentrated' here. Under this cynical umbrella term they could arbitrarily group together all those who were a thorn in the flesh of the 'master race': communists, socialists, clergy, 'asocial' elements – which included Romany and Sinti gypsies – homosexuals and, above all, Jews.

The Dachau model soon caught on. Under the direction of the Inspector of Concentration Camps, Theodor Eicke, the former commandant of Dachau, all the other camps were structured on the Dachau pattern. From now on guard duties were taken over by the SS 'Death's Head' squadron. For the benefit of the public, the SS boss, Himmler, sought to make the purpose of the camps seem harmless. What was being achieved there was 'hard labour that created new values, and a strict but just regime. Instruction in how to learn to work again and acquire manual craft skills is the method of education. The motto which is written above these camps reads: there is but one road to liberty. Its milestones are obedience, industry, honesty, order, cleanliness, sobriety, truthfulness, self-sacrifice and a love of the Fatherland.' Work and discipline were the necessary means by which the lost sons and daughters of the nation were to be brought back into the

National Socialist community – in the lying words of the *Reichsführer-SS*.

> The senior 'old lag' of the camp, Hans Brun, was one of the most brutal individuals I ever met during my time in the KZs and the ghetto. He was what was known as a 'red stripe' man, because, as a political prisoner, he wore a red chevron on his sleeve. On our 'tour' through the KZs we certainly had a few surprises in store as regards the different stripes. From our point of view, they weren't always what they seemed. So not every 'red striper' was necessarily a friend, and Hans Brun certainly wasn't. But there were 'green stripers', the professional criminals, who behaved very decently, very decently indeed.
>
> *Ezra Jurman, German Jew, Strastenhof concentration camp*

When SS *Hauptsturmführer* Rudolf Höss arrived in Auschwitz at the end of April 1940, he was, by his own account, dead keen to get on with things. He had the task of converting the artillery barracks into a 'proper concentration camp'. Höss, too, had been through the Eicke school. As a memento of the 'good old days' he had the Dachau motto *Arbeit macht frei* put up over the main gate of the camp. But apart from this the newly appointed commandant wanted no more to do with his old mentor: 'From the outset I realised that Auschwitz could only be made into something workable with the tough and tireless work of everyone, from the commandant down to the last inmate. But in order to harness everyone to this task', he recalled later, 'I had to break with all traditions, with everything that had become accepted custom.' As ambitious as he was unscrupulous, Höss wanted to prove himself the ideal commandant for Auschwitz. The very same zeal which at the beginning he displayed in building the prison camp, he applied two years later to the death-factory.

The first inmates who were transported to Auschwitz were thirty criminals from the Sachsenhausen concentration camp. As *Kapos*, or senior men in the camp, block or bunk-room, their job was to supervise the other inmates in the camp and at work. They were given more and better food, wore high leather boots and tailored prison uniforms. 'Divide and rule', was the motto behind this, as Höss arrogantly noted. In plain language that meant that the graded divisions of authority assigned everyone a place in the camp hierarchy and made him part of the system. From the outset the camp administration in Auschwitz employed criminals as *Kapos* and thus gave them the power of life and death over those who had been imprisoned for political or racial reasons.

Under a rain of blows, kicks and loud bawling, the first Polish prisoners were herded into the camp three weeks after the arrival of the criminals in the barrack buildings. They were resistance fighters, politicians, members of the Polish intelligentsia, clergy and Jews. The First Custodial Camp Officer, Karl Fritsch, the right hand of the camp commandant, greeted the arrivals with a speech which, at a stroke, dashed all hope that they would ever leave the place alive: 'You lot haven't come to a sanatorium. This is a German concentration camp, from which there's only one way out – through the chimney. Anyone who doesn't like it can go straight to the electrified wire. If there are any Jews in this batch, they don't have a right to live longer than two weeks. If there are any priests, they can live a month; all the rest have got three months.'

On my first day in Auschwitz one of the older inmates in our hut said to me: 'See that smoke? That's the only way you can get out of Auschwitz.'

Roman Frister, Polish Jew,
member of a Sonderkommando in Auschwitz

People used to say: 'I'm going to the wire.' That meant they would throw themselves on to the electrified barbed-wire fence – the current went straight through their body and they died immediately.

Frantz Danimann,
Austrian resistance fighter in Auschwitz

From noon until evening they made us stand naked. Then the camp *Kapo* came along and picked four of us to carry a gallows. And then with a labour-squad they brought a guy along in chains on a sort of trolley, and they hanged him in front of our eyes. That was our welcome, and so we knew where we were.

Norbert Lopper, Viennese Jew, deported to Auschwitz in 1942, member of the 'Canada' squad

As regards the objective of the sojourn in the camp – the death of the prisoners – all the perpetrators were in agreement. In order to get rid of the inevitably large number of corpses efficiently, the Inspectorate of Concentration Camps had ordered the building of a crematorium. A month after Höss' appointment as commandant the firm of Topf & Sons in Erfurt received an order for the design of an incineration furnace. Two months after that, at the end of June 1940, the furnace was installed in a former ammunition depot and ready for service. The first incinerations went off 'without a hitch'. In the two ovens of the furnace seventy corpses could be burned every day. Not without some pride, the firm named their new model of furnace the 'Auschwitz'. With the installation of two further twin gas-fired furnaces in 1941, it was possible to burn eighteen corpses per hour. In this first crematorium, dead prisoners were incinerated until September 1941.

As the next project the eager conversion team tackled Block 11. Outwardly this building differed at first glance from the rest of the barracks buildings: though like the others it was built of red brick, in contrast to the other blocks in the camp the door to number 11 was always firmly locked. The windows of the upper storeys were almost entirely bricked up. Small slits only let in a little daylight. The basement windows were heavily barred. A high stone wall between Block 11 and Block 10 protected the inner courtyard from unwelcome eyes. On the ground and first floors there were communal cells in which over 100 people were crammed. Anyone caught stealing a potato ended up here. The mere fact of being a Jew or a priest was enough to merit being arbitrarily assigned to the punishment-block. Only a few ever left it alive. The main job of the prisoners was to dig out huge ditches around the grounds of the camp. Nothing and no-one was to be able to leave the camp unnoticed. Auschwitz was planned as a bulwark of extermination. In order to get rid of the soil, the prisoners had to run the gauntlet between rows of guards who hit out at them and kicked them. Anyone who fell to the ground in a faint and could not get back on his feet again was all too often beaten to death by the *Kapos*.

Just as every hour in the camp brought totally unexpected events, so could any step, any decision by a prisoner have good as well as disastrous consequences. For instance, what use was it to be in good physical shape, if you were then trampled to death by a horde of 'numbers' who were being rounded up into the barracks by the SS men, or if you were beaten to death at the main gate for having a badly buttoned jacket?

The camp demanded improvisation from us, which was based more on feeling and intuition than on common-sense assumptions. It also demanded constant vigilance, so that as far as possible you were not taken by surprise. Finally, it demanded an ethical standard, so that however hard they tried to make us into animals, one didn't let go of what it meant to be a human being.

Jadwiga Apostol-Staniszewska, Polish inmate of Auschwitz

In the cellar of Block 11 there were so-called stand-up cells, about the size of a telephone box. Instead of a window they just had an airhole about 2 inches wide. As many as four prisoners were squeezed into them at one time. It was impossible to sit or even squat. The unfortunate prisoners were locked in there for four days and nights, without food or water, unless they were sent out for slave labour during the day and 'only' locked in again at night. Wieslar Kielar was one prisoner who survived the 'stand-up cell': 'If only those damned walls had at least had some recesses or ledges. But there was nothing but a smooth, frozen and slippery surface, covered with frost. I fell asleep. A terrible cold, which seemed to seep into the marrow of my bones, woke me up. There was such a pain in my back, it felt as though someone had thrust a sharp knife between my shoulder-blades. The man on my right was still standing there and leaning against me with all his weight. I shifted my uncomfortable position and at that moment his body slid limply to the floor. I tried to pull him up again, without success. By accident I touched his unshaven face with my hand. It was ice-cold. While I had been asleep, he had died.'

> There were rooms there with three tiers of bunks, iron-framed. We didn't have quilts, only sacks of straw, but the terrible thing was the thousands and thousands of fleas in them. After a few minutes we were black with fleas.
>
> *Dr Margita Schwalbobová, Czech Jew,*
> *deported to Auschwitz in 1942, doctor in the sick-bay*

Most of the inmates of the death-block did not die in the cells but in the yard behind the stone wall between blocks 11 and 10. At weekends the head of the Gestapo's political section in the camp, Max Grabner, used to enjoy going to the block to 'dust it out', as he cynically called it. Here he decided who in the punishment company would be 'allowed' to serve their term and who had to die immediately. So as not to lose track of the living and the dead, he made the victims write their prison-number with a crayon on their torso. In the courtyard of Block 11 they were then forced to stand against a wall made of black insulation-panels and shot. After the war, Perry Broad, a Brazilian-born SS-man under Grabner's command, described the gruesome procedure: 'If one of the men shot was still in his death-throes, one of the SS officers would shout: "He needs another one!" Then a shot in the temple or the eye would put an end to the unfortunate man's life. The body-carriers doubled back and forth with stretchers, loaded the corpses and threw them on to a pile at the other end of the yard. More and more blood-soaked bodies were lying there. Mechanically the executioner loaded his rifle each time and carried out one execution after another. If anything delayed the proceedings, he would put his weapon down, whistle a little tune or talk with the men standing around about deliberately trivial subjects. Often the last moments of the men standing against the black wall are agonisingly prolonged. They can feel the cold, blood-soaked muzzle of the rifle held against their neck, hear the click as it is cocked. . . . The bolt has jammed. Wearily the executioner steps back, fiddles awkwardly with his weapon and talks about how it is time he got himself a new rifle.'

It always annoys me when some of our people claim that even in the SS there were guards who were humane and decent to Jews. I vehemently dispute that. It was only when they knew that the war was finally lost, it was only then that some of them got the idea of 'softening up' and getting friendly with one or two of us, maybe so as to look for a back door to escape through later. But before that they had shown absolutely no feelings. And there were many who remained loyal to the Führer and kept their oath to the bitter end.

Herbert Schrott, Austrian Jew, Auschwitz

The adding-up was done by the prisoners. The SS were too stupid, lazy, drunken and whore-ridden. They weren't capable of counting 500 people at a time.

Hans Frankenthal, German Jew, Auschwitz

On 1 March 1941 there was great excitement in the camp. A high-ranking visitor was on his way. *Reichsführer-SS* Heinrich Himmler wanted to get a picture for himself of how the conversion work was progressing. Apparently, what he saw exceeded his most ambitious expectations. Rudolf Höss was surprised by the orders he received at the end of Himmler's visit. Instead of 10,000, the KZ was now to be expanded to accommodate 30,000 prisoners. Of those, 10,000 were to be

employed on the construction of IG Farben's plant and later in
the production of synthetic rubber there. What Höss did not then
suspect was that the top echelons of the Nazi elite were at that
moment making intensive plans for 'Operation Barbarossa', the
invasion of the Soviet Union.

Under the umbrella of the Commissar Order issued several
months earlier, the head of the Central Office of Reich Security,
Reinhard Heydrich, put into effect Operational Order No. 8 at
the beginning of the assault on the Soviet Union. From the
prisoners-of-war, his men were to sort out and get rid of all Party
functionaries, especially 'professional revolutionaries and People's
Commissars'. There were to be no witnesses to this murderous
exercise, and that is why the concentration camps were chosen as
the scene of the crime. The zeal of the SS men was all he could
wish for. A short time later the first Red Army soldiers were
transferred to Auschwitz and put straight into Block 11, the
death-block. In the last hours of their lives they were forced to
slave for the Third Reich in the gravel-pits behind the block. Most
of them died in the first few days. Those who were 'lucky' were
shot; the rest were beaten to death with picks and shovels by SS
men and *Kapos*.

In all, 10,000 Russians had arrived at Auschwitz by December
1941. Most of them had been sent there from Wehrmacht PoW
camps in which they had lived virtually without food or drink,
in holes in the ground they had dug themselves. They reached
Auschwitz totally exhausted, more dead than alive. Rudolf Höss
described the scene in the following way: 'Physically, the Russians
were simply beyond doing anything. With blank expressions, they
shambled around aimlessly or crept into a sheltered corner
to swallow or force down something edible they had found, or else
to die quietly somewhere. It got really bad during the muddy season
in the winter of '41/42. They were more able to put up with the
cold than with the wetness, the never being dry.' Höss' apparently
sympathetic choice of words is a deceit. Not only did the condition
of the Russians leave him unmoved, but the death of the prisoners-
of-war could not happen fast enough for him and his SS thugs.

In their perverse fantasy the camp officers and their henchmen
dreamed up every possible form of cruelty. One torture

particularly favoured by the SS and their prisoner accomplices was letting the inmates freeze to death in winter. The Polish prisoner Zygmunt Sobolewski describes a typical scene: 'I suddenly heard unusually loud screaming and then saw naked Russians running out of the block. It was at least 30 degrees below zero. A *Kapo* was standing at the door of the block, shouting at them: "You're filthy!" He sprayed the Russians with water in the open air. The Russians huddled together like a herd of cows in winter, so that at least they could get a little warmth from each other.'

I looked over to the other side of the railway tracks and there I saw the older people together with the small children and babies. Then the army trucks arrived, which those people were loaded on to. I considered that a good sign and said: 'You see, we are young and strong, that's why we have to walk. But they're concerned about the old people and children, and so they're picking them up in trucks.' But of course they went to the gas-chambers.

Renée Firestone, Czech Jew,
Auschwitz inmate

Beaten, shot, frozen and worked to death – every month thousands of Russians died in this way. Yet in the long run even these murder methods were too much 'trouble'. And thus it was that in September 1941 the first gassing took place. In the event Block 11, where the first group of victims were murdered with Zyklon B, proved unsuitable for gassing. It took all day to remove the air from the room. This seemed too long for the 'effective' method of killing that they were aiming for. That is why, a little later, the second gas-chamber was moved to the crematorium, where the mortuary could be ventilated or emptied of air. Several holes had been cut in the ceiling, through which to throw the lethal Zyklon B crystals. The engines of trucks were run so that their humming would drown out the cries of the dying. The first gas-chamber in Auschwitz was now in operation – but not yet for Jews.

It was a terrible thing to see people who were prisoners themselves tormenting the others. The *Kapos* could make life hell for a prisoner and even cause his death. By beatings and every possible kind of disciplinary measure they could bring him to the point where he no longer wanted to live.

Arno Lustiger, Polish Jew, deported in 1944 to the satellite camp
of Auschwitz-Blechhammer

While the search went on in Auschwitz for 'more efficient' methods of murder, the German advance on the Eastern Front had lost its impetus. In the autumn supply-lines came to a halt and losses increased steadily. In the winter the thermometer dropped to 50° below zero, yet instead of winter uniforms ammunition was shipped to the Front. The Wehrmacht failed in their attempt to take Moscow. It was the first great strategic defeat of the 'Greatest Military Commander of All Time'. Not even Hitler himself believed in a lightning victory any longer. The dictator had culpably underestimated Stalin's empire. Others would pay dearly for this mistake. More and more frequently Hitler's conversation turned in those weeks to the 'Jewish problem'. The Jews would be made to pay for the toll in German lives at the Front, the dictator threatened darkly. 'That race of criminals has the two million dead in the Great War on its conscience, and now hundreds of thousands more. Don't let anyone tell me we can't send them into the mire', Hitler proclaimed to Himmler and Heydrich in 1941.

What the dictator was planning for the Jews, commandant Rudolf Höss was to learn from Himmler in Berlin. The circumstances themselves pointed clearly to the fact that this was a very special meeting. For contrary to his normal custom, the *Reichsführer-SS* received his guest without the presence of an adjutant. The Führer had ordered the 'Final Solution of the Jewish Problem', Himmler informed the camp commandant. As Höss remembered it, he left no doubt as to what was meant by the 'Final Solution': 'The Jews are the eternal enemy of the German people and must be wiped out. While the war is on, all the Jews we can get access to are now to be exterminated without exception. If we do not succeed in destroying the biological basis of Jewry, then one day the Jews will destroy the German people.' He had selected Auschwitz, Himmler went on, because of its excellent transport links and its remote location.

Höss was well aware of the monstrous nature of this statement. But as a fanatical Nazi he blindly obeyed every order from his Führer. What is more, he may have felt flattered that he had been singled out for the task of resolving this most critical of problems. For while even his immediate superiors were to be kept in the dark, he had been taken into the leaders' confidence. He now wanted to show himself worthy of this confidence. 'For me only one thing mattered: pressing on, driving things forward . . . so as to be able to carry through the measures that had been ordered.' But for the moment he had to be patient. Himmler had not given precise instructions as to how, in fact, the Final Solution was to be carried out. He was not yet in a position to do so; for the plans had not been worked out in every last detail. The only thing certain was the objective – the total annihilation of the Jews of Europe.

2 September 1942: for the first time, outside at 3 o'clock in the morning, present at a 'special operation'. Compared to this, Dante's Inferno seems almost like a comedy to me. Not for nothing is Auschwitz called the camp of annihilation!

5 September 1942: . . . At about 8 o'clock in the evening attended another 'special operation', this time on people from Holland. On account of the special rations issued for this, consisting of 20 cl of schnapps, 5 cigarettes, 100 g of wurst and bread, the men were jostling to join the operation.

9 September 1942: Early this morning I receive from my attorney in Münster . . . the extremely welcome news that as of 1st inst. I am divorced from my wife. I can see things in colour again, a black curtain has been lifted from my life! Later am doctor in attendance at a punishment beating for eight prisoners and at a shooting by small-arms fire. Have been given soap-flakes and two bars of soap. In the evening am present at another special operation (4th time).

20 September 1942: Today, Sunday afternoon, listened in brilliant sunshine to concert from 3–6 p.m. by prison orchestra. The conductor had been conductor of the Warsaw State Opera. Eighty musicians. For lunch we had roast pork and in the evening baked tench.

From the diary of SS doctor, Prof. Dr Johann Paul Kremer, Auschwitz

At the Wannsee Conference on 20 January 1942 the die was cast. In the idyllically situated country house, far away from Auschwitz and its daily horrors, the final preparations for the crime of the century were made. In conjunction with the heads of the state bureaucracy, planning chief Reinhard Heydrich coordinated the extermination of eleven million European Jews. One of the group was Adolf Eichmann, who took the minutes. In all the documents the deed being planned was never once mentioned by name. Things that were discussed openly around the conference table, Eichmann translated into the coded language of the perpetrators. 'Evacuation', 'special treatment', 'Final Solution' – these were the euphemisms for a mass killing of unimaginable proportions. Eichmann the paper-pusher was responsible for organising the death-trains. He drew up the timetables with a pedantic attention to detail. Immediately after the conference he informed all Gestapo offices in the Reich: 'The evacuation of Jews to the east recently carried out in individual areas represents the beginning of the Final Solution of the Jewish problem in the Old Reich, the eastern territories and in the Protectorate of Bohemia and Moravia.'

While his henchmen were already cranking up the machinery of murder, Hitler was preparing the general public for his impending acts: on 30 January 1942, the ninth anniversary of his coming to power, he stated to an audience of arms workers, field-hospital nurses and wounded soldiers: 'This time, for the first time, the good old Jewish law will be applied: An eye for an eye, a tooth for a tooth.' Did his audience understand the full import of this threat? Should the German people have known even then what the second sinister objective of their Führer was: the annihilation of millions of Jews? And if so, why did the population allow it to happen without a word of protest? For years, their Jewish fellow-citizens of the German Reich had been marginalised, deprived of their rights, robbed and persecuted. Jewish neighbours disappeared overnight. Quite often they were herded on to the deportation-trains in full view of the public. The statement by Hitler and his henchmen that the Jews were being sent to labour camps in the east was enough to make people pretend to forget what they had seen, and to salve their conscience. 'Essentially, we knew enough to have really been up in arms about it, but we did not know everything', says Ulrich de Maizière, then a staff officer in the Army High Command (OKH). Most Germans had a suspicion that something terrible was happening to the Jews. But at the beginning of 1942 scarcely a single one of them knew to what a pitch of industrialised murder Hitler's racial madness would lead. 'If anyone had told me then that people were being put to death in an industrialised extermination process of gas-chambers and crematoria, I would not have believed it possible. But at that time it was still something beyond our powers of imagination' – the words of Count Heinrich Einsiedel, then a fighter-pilot on the Eastern Front.

It was a transport of Poles. I can recall a scene with a little boy, maybe five or six years old. Everyone had been loaded on to a truck, but the kid jumped down; he didn't want to stay up there. The SS men kept throwing him back on and he kept jumping off again. He said he wanted to work, he was young, he could work. They knew what Auschwitz meant. The kid just wouldn't let up. The people on the truck were getting restless and now the kid was kneeling at the feet of Aumeier, the commandant, begging him to be allowed to work. He would polish the man's shoes. All he wanted was to work. Aumeier didn't know what to do. He sent the other Jews off in the truck and handed the kid over to us in the camp. The senior prisoner took him under his wing, fitted him out with a blue suit and a blue cap and every day the kid stood at the gate as we went out to work, and he always saluted us.

Norbert Lopper, Viennese Jew, deported to Auschwitz in 1942, member of the 'Canada' squad

On 26 March 1942 the first train organised by Eichmann arrived at Auschwitz, packed to bursting-point with Jewish women from Slovakia. They were quartered in the former barracks of the Russians. By this time only 1,000 of the original 10,000 Soviet soldiers brought to the camp were still alive. The Jewish women not only took over the dead officers' bunks, but were even made to put on their left-over uniforms. The SS men made no effort to conceal from them the fate of the Soviet officers. Helena Gombosova, who arrived in Auschwitz at that time, recalls: 'We were given khaki trousers and blouses. The Soviet star was embossed on the buttons of the blouses. You could still see the bloodstains on them. It was all quite obvious to us.' Their death sentence had been passed, it was just a matter of waiting for the execution. But the machinery of destruction was still short of capacity.

Since October 1941 a new camp had been under construction. Commandant Höss drove the building work ahead with merciless rigour. Russian and Polish prisoners had to tear down the cottages in the little village of Birkenau, not far from Auschwitz. In their place primitive stabling was erected. Originally planned as a PoW camp, Birkenau was later to become the centre for the mass murder – a death-factory for the Jews of Europe.

> I felt that I wouldn't be able to survive the next day. I was utterly exhausted, apathetic, and thought about throwing myself on to the electrified wire. At the morning roll-call, we always heard shots from near the fence. A lot of people went to the wire because they couldn't stand it any longer. And they were then shot by the guards.
> *Norbert Lopper, Viennese Jew, deported to Auschwitz in 1942*
>
> You always had to keep your composure. You were on your last legs with cold and hunger. But you kept your composure.
> *Rachel Knobler, Polish Jew, Auschwitz*

Beyond the grounds of the new camp, at the edge of a wood, stood two attractive and well-maintained farmhouses. Surrounded by fruit-trees, protected from prying eyes by copses and hedges, they appeared harmless enough to deceive the victims to the very last. On the doors the murderers had fixed signs saying 'To the disinfecting area', 'To the wash-room'. Space for undressing was provided by three barrack-huts, which had been erected beside the two houses, from now on known as Bunkers I and II. By the end of June 1942 the two bunkers were 'ready for operation'.

In the same month the war itself offered the Jews a last brief reprieve. Hitler's troops on the Eastern Front had begun to advance again. The Don Offensive had been launched, Charkov captured and Sebastopol and the whole of the Crimea invaded. The Wehrmacht now needed every available train, and consequently transport facilities for the Jews were restricted. The organisers of the mass murder were extremely annoyed, Adolf Eichmann most of all. The 'Expert on Jewish Affairs' had already been busy bringing the deportations from France up to speed. Despite the 'strenuous situation at the Front', Eichmann wanted to increase the weekly transports to 3,000 people. For the partners in crime the extermination could not proceed fast enough. On 14 July Himmler was summed to the Führer in his 'Wolf's Lair' in East Prussia. The dictator expressed the wish that the Final Solution be concluded by the end of the year. Himmler immediately sent a directive to the Reich Ministry of Transport, demanding that 'these transport hold-ups be cleared as rapidly as possible'. After that he headed straight for Auschwitz, to make another tour of inspection.

It was a Sunday afternoon. We actually had the day off. Suddenly we were told: fifty men to the unloading-bay. We went to the bay but there was no transport there, so we waited. All at once we saw the train coming in. There were SS men standing on the wagons and firing into them all the time. Then when they opened the wagons, people fell out in front of us, suffocated and with swollen faces. The seriously injured and children had been trampled to death.

> People had been crammed into the wagons. I reckon the
> temperature was at least 30 or 35°. It seemed like an inferno
> to us. The bodies were heavy – we had to load the dead as
> well as the living and the severely injured on to the trucks. No
> sooner had one transport been emptied than the next one
> came in. It went on like that for two whole days. Nothing but
> dead and seriously injured.
>
> *Norbert Lopper, Viennese Jew, deported to Auschwitz in 1942,*
> *member of the 'Canada' squad*

Just as on the previous occasion the visit of the *Reichsführer* was
awaited with tense expectancy. There was to be absolute quiet in
the camp; cleanliness and order were proclaimed as the First
Commandment. The sick and very weak had been murdered in
the gas-chambers ahead of the visit. The rest were allowed to wash
and were given clean clothing.

Hours before Himmler's arrival the prisoners were rounded up
on the parade ground, and drawn up in rank and file. Sweating
with heat and fear they stood on the dusty square, waiting for what
would come next. 'And then it happened', recounts the Slovakian
Jew, Rudolf Vrba, who had been deported to Auschwitz shortly
before. 'Standing in the tenth rank in front of our block, the senior
prisoner in the block noticed that Jankel Meisel was not displaying
the correct number of buttons on his jacket. It was several seconds
before the enormity of this crime penetrated his consciousness.
Then he floored the man with one blow. An uneasy shuffling ran
through the ranks. I saw the SS guards exchanging angry glances,
and then noticed that the senior prisoner, with two helpers, was
dragging Jankel towards the block. Outside my field of vision, they
acted as men always do when they feel tricked and disgraced. They
beat Jankel and kicked him until he nearly died. The flailed at him
uncontrollably in an attempt to force the life out of him and make
him disappear from the scene and from their memory; and Jankel,
who had forgotten to sew a button on, didn't even have the
decency to die quickly and quietly. He screamed. It was a powerful,
recalcitrant scream. Then this scream changed to a weak and

plaintive moan, not unlike the dying tone of a bagpipe, though it didn't fade as quickly as that. On the contrary: it persisted and filled the void, tugging on our tense nerves. In that moment, I think we all hated Jankel Meisel, the little old Jew, who was ruining everything with his long and lonely rebellion, and storing up nothing but unpleasantness for the rest of us.'

Himmler was present when the crematorium was put into service and he attended the first gassings. He looked through this spy-hole and it made him feel sick. Then he went behind the gas-chamber and vomited.

Hans Frankenthal, German Jew, Auschwitz

When Himmler arrived at Auschwitz in his black Mercedes everything was again in the 'best of order'; Jankel Meisel was dead. He would never know that on that day the future of Auschwitz was finally sealed. The camp would now become that for which, years later, it achieved a grisly notoriety: a death-factory. One of the items on Himmler's 'guided tour' was the gassing of a transport of Jews from Holland. The *Reichsführer* had no cause for complaint. Afterwards he announced to the commandant, as Höss himself recorded: 'Eichmann's programme is going ahead and will be increased month by month. See to it that you get on with the expansion of Birkenau. Be as ruthless as you like in getting rid of Jews who are unfit for work.' That same evening the top SS man sat down for a drink with his thuggish subordinates. Höss described Himmler as 'beaming, in the best of moods'. He even drank a glass of red wine and 'smoked, which he didn't usually do'.

I don't know to this day which is better: going straight from the train to death, without knowing that you are condemned to die, or only later being selected, when you already know that you are being picked out to be killed.

Renée Firestone, Czech Jew, imprisoned in Auschwitz

I think it was in the summer of 1943. A *Kindertransport* of about 200 children came from Theresienstadt. They arrived in a normal passenger train. . . . The children each had a loaf of bread under their arm. They got out and were made to throw the bread into a basket as they went past. And then they marched hand in hand into the gas-chamber.

Norbert Lopper, Viennese Jew, deported to Auschwitz in 1942,
member of the 'Canada' squad

And every day in our camp people marched past with their yellow stars. It never stopped. In ranks of five, children, teenagers, expectant mothers, old men. I called it the one-way street, because not one of them ever came back again.

Karl Stojka, Viennese gypsy, deported in 1943
to Auschwitz–Birkenau

A few days later a factory-owner in Breslau, named Eduard Schulte, who was a passionate opponent of Nazism, found out that in the Führer's headquarters a plan was being discussed, by which all the Jews were to be deported to the east to be killed there with cyanide. Being a conscientious man, Schulte hurriedly boarded a train for Switzerland. In Geneva he secretly passed this information on to two contacts from the Jewish community. Even the representatives of the World Jewish Congress were at first unsure as to what they should make of the news. Gerhart Riegner, then head of the Swiss section, recalls: 'We discussed it for six hours, walking along beside Lake Geneva. Was this possible? Even we, who knew much more about the Nazi persecution of the Jews, and their extermination policy, had to ask ourselves: is it possible that they are killing millions of people? And it was two days before we had convinced ourselves that it was not only possible but probable.' What Riegner himself was at first unable to grasp had for a long time been bitter reality. Chelmno, Belzec, Sobibor, Treblinka, Majdanek and Auschwitz–Birkenau already existed – six extermination camps that were now running at high speed. With pitiless regularity Adolf Eichmann was directing the death-trains from his office desk.

On 8 November 1942 Hitler made this announcement to a selected audience in Munich's Löwenbräu-Keller: 'You will no doubt remember the Reichstag session at which I stated that if Jewry imagined they could bring about the extinction of the European races through an international world war, then the result would not be the extinction of the European races but the extinction of Jewry in Europe. They always laughed at my prophecy. Of those who laughed then, there are countless numbers who are no longer laughing today. Those still laughing may in a short time not be laughing any more either.'

We are receiving alarming reports from camps in Upper Silesia. A deported French worker reports on a large number of Frenchmen, British prisoners-of-war, criminal prisoners and Jews in labour camps. Large factories with sleeping-areas for workers are being erected directly over coal-mines, with a view to producing synthetic rubber. 36,000 men are working on one building-site, 24,000 on another. Among them are several thousand Jewish deportees aged from sixteen to twenty-four years . . .

Telegram from Gerhart Riegner, head of the Geneva office of the World Jewish Congress, to the Czech government-in-exile in London, 2 July 1943

Meanwhile, deportation trains had become a matter of routine in Auschwitz. Thousands of people from all over Europe arrived there every day. Driven from their homes and robbed of their property, they had been crammed into trains and despatched on a journey into the unknown. Men, women and children, the old and the sick, were packed tightly into cattle-trucks. Their bodily functions had to be performed in a single bucket. Another bucket was filled with water. A few gallons were meant to suffice for a journey lasting days. Many deportees died of thirst or exhaustion on the fatal journey. Most of them had no idea of the horrors that awaited them. Others such as the survivor, Herbert Schrott, refused to believe the rumours that came to his ears: 'Were they supposed to have gassed 30,000 people? Were they supposed to have shot 10,000? No-one could conceive that a state-sponsored, industrial-scale murder of human beings was being carried out. . . . Perhaps it is human nature that you don't want to accept it, you suppress it.'

When they opened the doors all we saw were dead bodies, nothing but dead bodies. The space behind was empty, all the corpses were at the front near the door, because I suppose they had all tried to run for the door. One lay on top of the other, one had dropped dead and the next had fallen on top of him. They were piled up in front of the door; that's why it was so hard to bring out the corpses.

A lot of people were employed on the corpses because the work had been split up: some were working on the ovens, then there were all those who fetched the bodies out of the gas-chambers. Then in the crematorium there was a room where we stretched out the corpses. We dragged them across the floor into this room and then two or three of us would go through cutting their hair off or pulling out their gold teeth. After that there was another group who carried them to the ovens, and at the ovens there was yet another group. But most of the people were employed getting the corpses out of the gas-chambers and dragging them across the floor into that room.

Shlomo Dragon, Polish Jew, member of a Sonderkommando *in Auschwitz*

On arrival in Auschwitz after an agonising train-journey, things suddenly began to happen very fast: the doors were flung open, the exhausted victims dragged out and hurried along by loud shouting and the barking of vicious SS dogs. Anyone who was not fast enough was driven along and beaten. Many stumbled, fell in the dust and were trampled over by those behind. The chaos was deliberate, a perfect method of intimidation. Max Garcia, a Dutch Jew, describes his arrival in Auschwitz: 'It was nothing but "Come on, come on! Quick, quick! Move, move!" The Nazis wanted to create a permanent state of confusion. And because you were confused you couldn't think about anything.'

Completely disorientated and demoralised by the stench and misery of the journey, the people could only obey orders. When everyone had been driven out of the wagons, the luggage and the corpses – of those who had not survived the hellish journey – were thrown from the train. This work was done by prisoners; the SS thugs did not want to get their hands dirty. Sometimes the prisoners tried to warn the newcomers. 'Several of the people in striped uniforms went around whispering to the boys and girls like me: "Say you're eighteen or nineteen; don't tell them you're as young as you are"', Ester Brunstein remembers.

> It was always terrible for us when a new transport came in. On the other hand we were happy about it because we knew they would kill us if no new transports arrived and they had no more work for us.
>
> *Selma Engel, Dutch Jew, prisoner in Sobibor*

It was in these few minutes that the fate of the deportees was decided. Husbands and wives were separated from each other, families torn apart in a few seconds. The SS allowed no time for farewells. 'Renzo lingered a moment too long in saying goodbye to his fiancée Francesca; and they laid him out with a punch in the face. It was their daily duty', wrote Primo Levi, the Italian-Jewish author, who had been deported to Auschwitz in February 1944.

After they had been sorted according to sex and age, the prisoners had to line up five deep. Then they had to walk past the camp doctor. With a wordless gesture he motioned them to the right or left. Ester Brunstein was sixteen years old when she stood with her family on the ramp at Auschwitz. 'And then we were all asked: "How old, how old?" I remembered what I had been told and said "Eighteen". My mother was next to me. She said "forty-four". So she went to one side and I went to the other. I wanted to run after her but I was pushed back. That was the last I saw of my mother.' It was only a few steps that in seconds made the difference between life and death. The camp doctor sent to the right those 'fit for work', to the left he sent the old, the weak, children under fifteen and their mothers. If the selecting went on too long and the executioners got tired, then for the remaining victims there was only one direction: to the left, to their death.

What was going through the minds of those doctors? A slight wave of the hand was all that determined the life or death of thousands on the ramp every hour. Some gave themselves Dutch courage or took stimulants which made it easier for them to play the hanging judge. But we can be sure that the most notorious of the Auschwitz doctors always kept a clear head: Dr Josef Mengele made his selection calmly and dispassionately. To the right, to the left, to the right, to the left. . . . Surviving eye-witnesses tell us that he sometimes whistled waltz tunes or themes from operetta while his hand passed the death sentences.

I was seventeen and came from a civilised world, when a German officer looked at the small children and told me they made soap from them. . . . I didn't understand. I didn't think it possible.

Denise Holstein, French Jew, Auschwitz

The people went quietly – that's how it was at the start, in the summer of 1942. They didn't know where they were heading. . . . The ones who were the last to go into the gas-chambers were stabbed in the back with bayonets, because those last ones could already see what was happening inside and didn't want to go in.

Eliahu Rosenberg, survivor and member of a
Sonderkommando *in Treblinka*

Even the victims remained calm for the most part. They had no idea whether it was a good or a bad thing to be sent to the left. The guards lied to the unsuspecting new arrivals, saying that the splitting of families would not last long. 'Madam, you are ill and tired from the long journey; give your child to this lady, and you can pick him up again later in the toddlers' room', Mengele reassured an anxious mother. When transports arrived from Poland the deportees already had a pretty good idea about what lay behind the name 'Auschwitz'. They did not allow themselves to be led off without a word; they screamed and fought back, clinging desperately to the members of their family. Auschwitz inmate Norbert Lopper describes a typical scene: 'I was standing in a wagon when the luggage was being unloaded and saw below me a row of women lined up for selection. And as I'm looking I see a little girl of about three, she's running along the line and crying: "Mummy, Mummy, where are you?" And on the other side I can see the mother hidden from her child. It was a terrible thing to see. Then an older woman took hold of the girl. "Come along now, I'll take you to your mother", she said and then walked into the gas with her.'

I saw a line of deportees walking past a tall, dapper officer who, without a word, like an orchestral conductor, was motioning the prisoners into different groups.
Erszebet Fried, survivor of Auschwitz, describing a selection in which Josef Mengele took part

On the left-hand side those chosen for death were driven straight towards the gas-chambers. Those who could no longer walk were taken off in trucks. It all had to be done quickly; the murderers did not want to waste any time. Until the last moment they tried to lull their victims into a sense of false security: the trucks were marked with the red crosses that promised rescue. Even in the rooms for undressing just before the gas-chambers the fatal deception was carried on. The unsuspecting victims were told they would be given a shower and disinfected. They were urged to hurry up: 'Come on, your food and coffee are getting cold.' As a rule the strategy of reassurance worked as required. If, however, signs of unease were noticed, the 'troublemakers' were discreetly led outside and shot with a small-bore weapon behind the building.

The others had no inkling that any of this was going on. Obediently they noted the number of the hooks on which they hung their clothes, 'so as to find everything as quickly as possible after the disinfecting', as the SS men explained to them.

The presence of prisoners in the *Sonderkommando* also helped to calm anxieties. The *Sonderkommando* consisted of about 200 Jews who were forced to assist in the destruction of their fellow-sufferers – a job which filled them with deep despair themselves. Should they have told the victims what the 'shower-rooms' really concealed? They knew there was no escape, and so it seemed pointless to warn them. In any case their own fate had been sealed long ago. From time to time the prisoners of the *Sonderkommando* were liquidated themselves – they knew too much. Outside the gas-chambers the victims were relieved to find themselves being escorted by Jews. Eliezer Eisenschmidt, a survivor of the *Sonderkommando*, describes their state of mind: 'Here they saw Jews who were alive and therefore believed that they would also stay alive.'

> One of the overseers had a particularly large whip and told the men around him that he could kill a Jew with a certain number of blows. They made jokes about how they could kill someone. They got fun out of it.
>
> *Selma Engel, Dutch Jew, Sobibor camp*

Naked, the victims entered the gas-chamber. The room was clean and painted white. In the ceiling were shower-heads connected to a water-pipe. Nothing out of the ordinary, all quite normal. But from behind, more and more people crowded into the supposed shower-room; batch after batch were pushed through the door by the guards. In the confined space, the first of them began to scream and now those still standing outside began to understand. There was no way out. 'They attacked the people like predators', Eliezer Eisenschmidt remembers. 'The soldiers had rifles, the officers pistols and all of them had truncheons as well. They used them all the time. The sticks were very thick, so that they would last a long time.'

The airtight doors closed with a dull thud; now began the work of the 'trained fumigators', as Höss called the SS orderlies. They were the executioners. From the 'Red Cross' trucks they hurriedly collected the metal drums containing the lethal blue-green crystals. The Zyklon B was then poured into the room through holes in the roof. Through a small viewing-window the murderers could observe the death-throes of their victims.

The members of the *Sonderkommando*, who in the meantime had had to sort through the dying people's belongings, were also witnesses to this bestial drama. 'After a while I heard piercing screams from the gas-chamber, banging on the door and wailing and moaning. The people began to cough and their coughing grew louder. This showed that the gas had begun to take effect. What started was a noise that grew louder and more unmistakable, then died down from minute to minute and soon turned into the rasping of many throats, which now and then was drowned by more coughing. The deadly gas had penetrated people's lungs causing a paralysis of their respiratory system', recalls a former prisoner, Filip Müller.

'*Shema Israel* – Hear me, O Israel!' The lament of the Jews was often the last thing that the few witnesses outside heard from the victims. The SS men mocked the prayers of the dying and shouted: 'Chuck in some more!' After twenty minutes or so, when silence descended again, an SS doctor announced: 'It's over.' The people were dead; the orderlies and doctors had finished their job. They boarded the 'Red Cross' trucks and left the scene of their crime.

Now the real work of the *Sonderkommando* began. Inside the gas-chamber stood the dead, grotesquely intertwined, three or four together, often pressed tightly one against the other. The poison crystals had dropped to the floor from the holes in the roof and turned into a deadly gas, which gradually rose higher and higher. In the struggle to catch the last breath of air the dying had clambered over each other, trying desperately to reach the last remnants of oxygen near the ceiling. In this way they can only have prolonged their life by a few moments.

The Germans said to them: 'Get undressed in this room, you're going to have a hot shower. Tie your shoes together!' The last bit was to make the people believe that after the shower they would find their shoes more easily. That way they didn't suspect they were going into a gas-chamber.

Morris Venezia, Greek Jew,
in the Birkenau Sonderkommando

Four hundred people were forced into the small gas-chamber, so that they could hardly shut the door from outside. After they had shut it, we stayed back on the other side. We just heard the cries '*Shema Israel* – Hear me, O Israel', 'Papa', 'Mama'. After 35 minutes they were dead.

Eliahu Rosenberg, surviving member of a
Sonderkommando *in Treblinka*

Just the one time there was a girl of twelve or thirteen, who hadn't suffocated. She wasn't dead. When we dragged her out, she was unconscious and gasping for breath. Then an SS man came along, drew his revolver, shot her in the head and killed her.

Eliezer Eisenschmidt, Polish Jew, Sonderkommando *in Birkenau*

'Often I saw something white on the lips of the people who had died from the gas. There was a frightful heat in the gas-chamber, you could taste the sickly smell of the gas. Sometimes, when we went into the gas-chamber we still heard groans, especially when we started to drag the corpses out by their arms. Once we found a baby still alive; it had been wrapped in a pillow. The baby's head was actually stuck into the pillow. When we took the pillow away, the baby opened its eyes. It was still alive. We took the bundle to *Oberscharführer* Moll and told him the child was alive. Moll laid it on the ground, trod on its neck and threw it on the fire. I saw him step on the child with my own eyes. It was waving its little arms.' That was the vivid memory that remained with Shlomo Dragon, who was forced to work in the *Sonderkommando*.

Working in pairs, with their bare hands the prisoners pulled the bodies out of the gas-chamber and took them to the crematorium. Before being thown into the fire the corpses were plundered. The thugs robbed them of every last thing. Under the brutal eye of the SS the *Sonderkommando* had to pull out the gold teeth and cut off the women's hair. Washed and combed, the hair was then hung out on lines to dry in the 'hair-drying room'. Then the 'goods' were packed in paper sacks and sent to German factories, to be made into cable insulation, industrial felt and yarns. Firms such as Alex Zink in Roth, near Nuremberg, paid 50 pfennigs a kilo for human hair. After the liberation of Auschwitz the Russians found 7 tonnes of packed hair in the grounds of the camp; obviously the camp staff had not managed to ship the sacks off. The gold teeth were melted down in a foundry installed for the purpose, cast into gold ingots and sent to the Reichsbank.

The machinery of death ran so perfectly that the people responsible for the burning in Crematorium I could not keep up. So the corpses were buried in mass graves. This was not without its consequences. The owners of fish-farms in the Birkenau area complained that their fish were dying off. Experts quickly discovered that poison from the corpses was leaching into the groundwater. SS-man Perry Broad was horrified to see what happened in the pits when the outdoor temperature rose again in the summer of 1942. 'As the summer sun beat down on the ground of Birkenau, the corpses which had not fully decomposed but were rotting, began to stir. The crust of earth cracked and a reddish-black mass bubbled up. It gave off a stench which no words can describe.' Commandant Rudolf Höss paid an official visit to an 'expert', *Standartenführer* Paul Blobel, who knew a lot about covering one's tracks. He had been given the task of removing the numerous mass graves in the east. He was happy to help Höss and recommended burning the corpses in large pits. From September 1942 onward that is exactly what was done. The sickly-sweet odour of burnt flesh could be smelt for miles around.

Around this time Adolf Eichmann also came to Auschwitz to see how things were going. Höss drove him round the camp grounds and proudly showed him the death-factory. 'Then he took me to a large pit, it was very big. . . . In it was a huge grid, an iron grid. There were corpses burning on it. And I felt sick.' At that moment, Eichmann claimed in his memoirs years later, he quietly said the Lord's Prayer to himself. Visiting the true scene of his crimes, the desk-bound perpetrator may well have been shocked. But apart from self-pity, Eichmann showed no emotion. He uttered no word of regret; his conscience remained silent. Following his visit to Auschwitz he went on timetabling the death-trains with the same meticulousness as before.

> There was nothing left there to remind one of life. Everything was dead. The people were dead, the surroundings were dead, the landscape, the timber, the walls. Everything stank of annihilation.
>
> *Rachel Knobler, Polish Jew, Auschwitz*

Like Eichmann, Höss' principal emotion was self-pity: 'In Auschwitz, once the mass extermination had begun, I was never happy again', he complained mawkishly in his memoirs. Whenever his dreadful activities weighed too heavily on him, he would have his horse saddled and go out for a ride 'to blow away the horrible images'.

The pit-burnings were only able to clear the 'bottleneck' in the logistics of Auschwitz for a brief period. And anyway they were far too noticeable. The civilian construction workers in the camp went home and told their families about the appalling things they had seen. The wind carried the stench of the burnings to neighbouring towns and villages.

As early as July 1942 work had started on Crematorium II in Birkenau and three further large furnaces were to follow. In order that the killing process could take place more rapidly, Höss decided to build gas-chambers right beside all the new crematoria. Between 22 March and 25 June 1943 Crematoria II, III, IV and V were completed with adjoining gas-chambers, and the gassing in the converted farmhouses was ended. They had been designed so that air had to be removed and replaced simultaneously. After each gassing the doors of the rooms had to be opened. In winter, however, the removal of air had a big disadvantage: the rooms became ice-cold, but Zyklon B only gasifies at a temperature of 27°C. When building the bunkers the Germans had not considered such details.

By now the perpetrators had become more scientific in their murder. This time, in the new 'bath-houses for special operations', as the criminals cynically named the gas-chambers, nothing was overlooked. The killing-machine was markedly more efficient. Every day 4,756 dead people disappeared into the 52 ovens of the 15 furnaces.

Yet it had to work still faster and 'better'. After all, there was a war on and coke was in short supply. The perpetrators experimented. In collaboration with technicians from the firm of Topf & Sons the camp management came up with the 'express process': the results of their macabre tests showed that three corpses could be burnt at once in a single oven. The burning was particularly effective if one of the three corpses had been tolerably well fed. The body fat helped the two other emaciated corpses to burn better. It also proved highly practical to burn two men's bodies with one woman's. The higher fat ratio in a female body helped to save on furnace-coke. The inventors of the new 'process' were proud of themselves: the 'express' method doubled the capacity of the furnaces. By the end of 1943 as many as 8,000 people could be gassed and then burnt every day. Every operation by the *Sonderkommando* had to be well judged, otherwise the whole cremation process came to a standstill. Shlomo Dragon describes his gruesome labour: 'When we laid the third body on the stretcher, the other two, which were half-way into the oven, had often started to burn already. Because of the heat the arms and legs often curled up and that's why we had to hurry. We had to hurry because the limbs quickly reared up and puckered so that it was difficult to get the third body on to the stretcher. Once the stretcher had been pushed into the oven, one of the prisoners held the bodies with a rake, which he used like a fork while the other two pulled the stretcher out from under the corpses. As soon as the oven was full we closed the door and went on to the next oven.'

The remains of bones which had not burned up had to be broken down separately. Using large hammers the prisoners crushed the bones to dust. In order to remove all traces, the ashes were later tipped into the river.

After the first two large crematoria had been completed in 1942 (the two others were finished six months later), the mass transports began to arrive from France, Belgium, Holland and Greece. Here we used the following procedure: the transports arrived in a specially built bay with three platforms, which was located directly between the crematoria, the personal effects store and Birkenau camp. The separating of those fit for work and the storing of the luggage took place in the arrival-bay itself. The able-bodied were taken directly to the camps and those to be exterminated to one of the new crematoria.

. . . Those on the transports from Belzec, especially, since they mostly originated in the east, knew when the trains had arrived in Upper Silesia that in all probability they were being taken to be exterminated. On the transports from Belzec security measures were strengthened and the transport was divided up into small groups. These groups were then allotted to different crematoria in order to avoid pandemonium. SS men formed a tight chain and violently forced the ones who resisted into the gassing-rooms. However, this seldom happened as the methods of calming them down made the process easier.

Rudolf Höss, commandant of Auschwitz, writing in prison after the war

However, what happened to those who, on the unloading-bay, were condemned to live? Condemned to a life that was nothing more than death by instalments?

Even the prisoners who were detailed off for work were first robbed of their belongings: anything of use ended up in the camp stores, known by the prisoners as 'Canada'. 'Maybe because

Canada is a rich country, a Promised Land', the Auschwitz survivor, Fania Fenelon, supposed. Watches were sent to soldiers at the Front, money found its way to the Reichsbank, and the clothes would keep the troops warm in the Russian winter. Hundreds of prisoners were occupied in sorting the contents of suitcases. However, before the desirable goods left the camp the more adept prisoners sometimes managed to steal articles from the store. They smuggled out the valuables in order to exchange them among the inmates for the necessities of life. 'In that abyss of misery you could get a cup of water in exchange for the finest French perfume, or swap a jewelled ring for a slice of white bread, a bottle of champagne for some tablets. Because the wealth of all Europe came to Auschwitz', recalls the Auschwitz inmate Margitta Schwalbova. In principle the SS guards were strictly banned from helping themselves in 'Canada' – but only a few kept to that. Of course, they dealt summarily with any prisoner caught stealing: 'The SS man came along, stopped by him, took a stick, lifted the blanket with it and saw the can. Then he said: "You know damn well that jam is for the SS canteen." He drew his pistol, pointed it at his temple and fired. The man fell over like a piece of wood', relates Norbert Lopper of the 'Canada' *Kommando*.

> I was particularly pleased to hear the news that for the last 14 days one train has been running to Treblinka every day, each carrying 5,000 members of the Chosen People.
> *SS-Obergruppenführer Karl Wolf, Himmler's adjutant, writing on 13 August 1942 to Theodor Ganzenmüller, Under-secretary in the Reich Transport Ministry*

From the unloading-bay the first stage of the calvary for the new arrivals took them along an apparently endless barbed-wire fence. Signs painted with skulls indicated that it was charged with high-voltage electricity. At intervals the fence was broken by watch-towers from which the barrels of machine-guns could clearly be seen pointing. Beyond stretched a vast camp of huts laid out symmetrically and crisscrossed by streets. This was another world, with its own terrible laws – something that the newcomers now realised, if they had not done so before. 'There wasn't a single blade of grass. There was only hard-trodden mud. Not a single tree, let alone a flower. There weren't even birds flying. It was a ghastly desert.' Thus Anna Palarczyk describes her first impression of the concentration camp.

Having arrived in the camp the people first had to stand around for hours in a state of confused uncertainty. At a given moment, depending on the mood of the SS men, the registration began. Name, date and place of birth were neatly entered in a card-index. Even in this inhuman hell nothing mattered more to the executioners than tidiness. From now on they were merely numbers, which were tattooed in blue on their forearms. Like cattle they had been transported to Auschwitz and now like cattle they were branded. 'From then on we ceased to be human beings,' says Helena Gombosovà.

> When I worked in the crematorium there was one man – I'd never in my life come across such a sadist. He usually turned up when new transports arrived, and picked himself the prettiest girls. He was a very good shot and he shot at the girls, at their breasts. Never in my life have I seen such a thing.
> *Dario Gabbai, Greek Jew, in the Birkenau* Sonderkommando

Next they went to the 'sauna'. Here the prisoners had to undress in order to be shaved all over. 'Young soldiers stood around while we were being shaved and made nasty, insinuating remarks about our bodies', Ester Brunstein remembers. After that they were all plunged into a tub of disinfectant. Then, freezing cold, they waited endlessly to be issued with new clothing: coarse, striped prison uniforms, consisting of a thin shirt, light trousers, a cap and uncomfortable wooden clogs. Even when issued the kit was dirty, torn and louse-ridden; no attention was paid to whether it fitted. During the bitterly cold winters the ragged garments afforded no protection against snow and ice: freezing to death was a common occurrence.

It was usually in the first few days that newcomers learned of the fate of the relatives they had been separated from; but this was seldom from the perpetrators themselves. More often, as with Zdenka Ehrlich, it was from other prisoners: '"Isn't your mother with you?" I say: "No, no. She went to the left." Instead of answering me he opened the door. I could see flames coming from a chimney and leaping into the sky. Quite without feeling he said: "That's where she went, up the chimney." I thought: Whatever is he talking about? What nonsense. The poor fellow has lost his mind.' But even those who could not or would not accept that human beings could do such things to other human beings, realised sooner or later that there was a connection between the continuously arriving transports and the smoking chimneys.

And then I arrived at the camp, went into the hut with its tiers of bunks and suddenly I hear: 'Hey, Lustiger, get down to the fence.' Apparently one of the women there wanted to speak to me. I was amazed. Who knows me here? I go down to the fence and who do I see? A girl from my class in high-school. She's got her hands behind her back and is looking very shy. At school she was always so cheerful, always laughing. We were in the same class together. Then she says: 'Oh, I'm so happy to see you, I've brought you something.' What was it? A little cake made of grated carrot with a dollop of jam on top. It looked like a real cake. I ask her: 'Why are you doing this?' So she says: 'It's your birthday today.' It was the 7th of May. I'd quite forgotten it was my birthday, but she'd remembered. That was a wonderful day in my life, I can tell you that today.

Arno Lustiger, Polish Jew,
deported in 1944 to the satellite camp of Auschwitz-Blechhammer

The new prisoners spent the first weeks in quarantine. As they had not yet been given a work assignment they had to spend the whole day doing agonising drill and fitness exercises. Harassed and hunted as if in a rabbit-shoot, they ran and crawled, driven on by blows from the overseers. One command brusquely followed another: 'Caps off, caps on!' In these exercises the prisoners tore the caps off their shaven heads hundreds of times and slapped them with the palm of their hand against their thighs. Anyone who lost the rhythm, and thus upset the drill, was summarily beaten. Threats from the old lags, such as: 'You've all come here to die and I'll do my best to see you do', were meant in all seriousness.

Since the autumn of 1942 the majority of deportees had been going straight to Birkenau. Only the prisoners who were required to work in the administrative offices stayed in the main Auschwitz camp. In comparison to the original camp, Birkenau represented a higher level of horror. Whereas the brick-built barracks in Auschwitz were halfway clean, Birkenau consisted of nothing but filth and misery. 'There was a huge mound', recalls Dagmar Ostermann, who had been deported to Birkenau from Vienna. 'In the semi-darkness I took it to be a heap of twigs and branches, although there wasn't a tree or bush for miles around. It was October, when most of the autumn pruning is done. As it got lighter I saw that they weren't twigs and branches; it was a mountain of corpses. Bare skeletons. The way the arms and legs stuck out from the heap on which they had been thrown indiscriminately, they had looked in the half-light just like branches and twigs.'

The sanitary conditions were very bad – awful washing facilities. We were crammed very close together, sometimes three in one bed. The food was just enough to keep us alive.

Frantz Danimann, Austrian resistance fighter, Auschwitz

We were allowed to shower and then we were shaved. I had beautiful hair and now thought I looked hideous. Then we stood naked in front of these German officers who stared at us and laughed.

Denise Holstein, French Jew, Auschwitz

In the primitive wooden barrack-huts, originally designed to accommodate 52 horses, as many as 800 people were crammed. In close-packed rows stood three-tiered bunks. In each set slept five or six people, sometimes as many as eight. Apart from rotting blankets and filthy straw-sacks which served as mattresses, the huts were empty. Lying so close together, the body-warmth of the nearest person provided the only protection against the icy winter nights. In winter the muddy ground became a quagmire which flooded the lower bunks. But even the other beds were dirtied with the diarrhoea which nearly all the starving prisoners suffered from. They had to relieve themselves in holes in the ground outside. There was no lighting and virtually no running water. From rusty taps in the wash-huts there was no more than a thin trickle each day. 'Not until three months after my arrival in Birkenau did I wash for the first time. And then I could only wash because my girl-friend worked in the kitchens, where there was water. So in the evening she brought a bucket of water out for me.' Such was the nightmare that Anna Palarczyk had to live through for two-and-a-half years.

The place was crawling with rats and lice. Soon after their arrival the newcomers were completely covered with parasites. 'One louse – one death' was the cynical warning on notices posted everywhere. For the bite of a louse could carry typhoid and in Auschwitz that meant certain death. Every inmate who showed signs of the disease was immediately put to death. In this way, entire blocks were wiped out from one day to the next. Since the guards had a great fear of being infected with the disease themselves, extensive delousing operations were carried out again and again.

In a camp where there was scarcely any water and even less soap, the unwashed were treated like murderers. Any louse that was discovered by a *Kapo* during a shirt-check or bunk-room clear-out, could have the direst consequences. This was a result of 'Auschwitz justice'. For a prisoner on whom a single louse was found after a delousing had been ordered, had failed to follow the order. That made him a refuser of orders and as such he was condemned to death. It happened every day in Auschwitz.

After one roll-call a Gestapo man came and said to me: 'You're a singer. Sing us a song.' I sang a Hebrew song. 'Not Hebrew, another language.' I learned Italian, Greek and Neapolitan songs, and from that day I was known as 'The Singer of Auschwitz'; I had to sing every day at roll-call. Fine, I got a bit more soup, a bit more bread, and so I could live.

Estrongo Nachama, Greek Jew, Auschwitz

They took a prisoner's cap off, threw it over the row of guards and shouted at him: 'Go fetch your cap back!' and as soon as he had dodged the row of guards he was shot in the back. That meant three days special leave for the SS man, 20 cigarettes and a quarter-litre of schnapps. And every day we heard a few shots being fired as we marched out.

Hans Frankenthal, German Jew, Auschwitz

The daily routine for the maltreated victims began before day-break, after a few hours of fitful dozing. The night had been filled with the groans and cries of the dying. 'Some whimper and talk to themselves', wrote the Italian Jew, Primo Levi. 'Many others smack their lips and grind their jaws. They dream that they are eating. A pitiless dream. One only sees the food, one feels it with one's hands; one absorbs its rich, penetrating smell; someone brings it close to our lips and then some circumstance or other, which is different every time, prevents the act from being completed. At that moment the dream dissolves, breaks down into its component parts; yet it immediately reassembles itself and begins once more in a similar but unfamiliar form. All this goes on incessantly, in each one of us, every night and for the whole duration of our sleep.'

The morning began with the *Appell* or roll-call. At the shrill ringing of the camp bells all the prisoners ran out from the blocks. They had to line up in five ranks outside their huts. Now it was a matter of waiting again. The dead bodies from the previous night were thrown out of the block and then began the wearisome business of counting heads. Standing rigidly to attention the senior prisoners in each block reported the number of prisoners fit for work, of the sick remaining in the block and of those who had died. The SS compared the figures with their lists. 'There was invariably some discrepancy. The people were so terrified and desperate. Many thought that if they hid under their straw mattresses or somewhere, nothing would be done to them. There was always someone missing at the *Appell*', Anna Palarczyk recalls. Whenever one of the 'numbers' was missing, a search began. For the prisoners on parade this meant hours of waiting in their ranks, in all weathers, even if the snow lay thick on the ground or it was raining in torrents. When the missing person was finally found, 'breakfast' was served. There was tea or 'coffee', a hot brownish concoction of indeterminate ingredients.

After that the whistle blew for work. In long columns the labour-squads headed out from the camp. To help them along an orchestra of prisoners played march music or folk-songs. 'It was an edelweiss . . .' still rang in the prisoners' ears as they left the camp behind them. For miles the procession wended its way through the countryside. Wearing their coarse clogs, the prisoners' feet soon began bleeding. The road led to gravel-pits, quarries, large farms and arms factories in the district. In the course of time a total of 15 satellite camps grew up.

> There was a lot of infection; people got so bitten by lice and fleas, they had inflammations all over their bodies. At the same time they got nothing to eat, so they had no resistance.
>
> *Hans Frankenthal,*
> *German Jew, Auschwitz*

Auschwitz' 'sphere of interest' from which the Germans had expelled the indigenous population, extended over about 16 square miles, in which 34 German companies made their profits at the expense of the prisoners. The camp management received 4 Reichsmarks per day for a skilled worker, 3 Reichsmarks for an unskilled one. Working people to death was a profitable business for the Germans.

The prisoners themselves built the factories in which they were expected to work. Breaking stones, digging ditches, levelling roads – the sweated labour on the construction sites would have taxed even a strong, healthy man to the limit. But for those weakened by hunger and disease, it was fatal. On the construction of a plant to make synthetic rubber for the arms industry, the life-expectancy of the workers was particularly short. Rudolf Vrba, himself a worker on the building site of death, describes the scene: 'Men were running about and stumbling; they were kicked and shot. Wild-eyed *Kapos* cut a blood-soaked swathe through the hordes of prisoners, while SS men, like cowboys on TV who inadvertently found themselves in a grotesque and unending horror-film, fired from the hip.'

For lunch the workers were given a litre of 'soup' – usually a watery, foul-smelling liquid in which potato-peelings or bits of rotten carrot floated. The starvation rations were carefully worked out: enough to prevent immediate death, too little for long-term survival. Then work went on at the same pace until the evening. Filthy and encrusted with blood, the procession of half-dead men trailed back to the camp. The living were obliged to drag the dead with them, since even the corpses had to be counted again. Once the dead had been laid out on the parade-ground, another *Appell* began and lasted for hours.

'Supper' consisted of about 10 ounces of bread. If the guards were feeling charitable, they would also dish out a little rancid margarine or a slice of stale wurst. From time to time, when a prisoner could bear the torment no longer, he or she would 'go to the wire' as it was called in camp parlance. Death on the electrically charged barbed-wire fence was the only discernible way out of the hell endured by these tortured souls.

Other prisoners tried to escape. But only a handful succeeded in getting through Auschwitz' high-security perimeter. Usually the escapers were recaptured within hours, or at most a few days. The bodies of those shot while trying to escape were displayed on the parade-ground as a deterrent. The SS men hung signs round their necks which said: *Hurra, hurra – wir sind wieder da* (Hooray, we're back again). The ones caught alive were hanged on the parade-ground in front of all the prisoners.

There was a woman lying on the ground, dying. Beside her stood a wardress, kicking and beating her and shouting: 'Give me your number! Give me your number!' She needed the number, otherwise there would be another 'unknown corpse'.

Anna Palarczyk, Polish inmate of Auschwitz

It was January and one truck after another drove through the camp, loaded with naked women. They drove through the camp and turned off towards the crematorium.

Anna Palarczyk

As we leave the camp we march in ranks of five past the band and the SS sentries counting heads. Cap in hand, arms hanging down limply, necks stiff; we aren't allowed to talk. Then we re-form in threes and, against the clatter of ten thousand pairs of clogs, we attempt to exchange a few words with one another.

Primo Levi, Italian Jew, prisoner in Auschwitz

Those sent to the sick-bay with dysentery or typhus did not have to go out on forced labour every morning. But they had no hope of being cured. Scarcely a single prisoner sent to the sick-bay ever emerged alive. There were no medicines, no dressings, no antiseptics. The doctors and nurses, also prisoners, had no choice but to stand helplessly and watch their fellow-inmates die. Even there the rooms were filled to overflowing, with every bunk occupied by more than one person. Often the new arrivals had to wait until someone had died before they could take over a bed-space that was smeared with blood and excrement. Every night one could hear the dull thud of bodies falling to the floor. In the desperate struggle for a little space, those alive were shoving them out of the beds.

Sick people who under normal circumstances would get well again, were regularly weeded out by the SS doctors. It was particularly those suffering from typhus who, instead of medication, were given a 'flush-out'. This meant a deadly injection of phenol. The Viennese doctor Ella Lingens who, as a prisoner, did service in the sick-bay, once challenged the SS doctor Fritz Klein on how he could reconcile his murderous activities with the Hippocratic Oath. Klein's answer was: 'Because I have sworn the Hippocratic Oath, I can cut the appendix out of a human body, and the Jews are the festering appendix in the body of the world. That is why they have to be excised.'

In the eyes of the German doctors, this contempt for humanity legitimised not only killing but also pseudo-medical experiments. The most notorious camp doctor, Josef Mengele, usually looked for his victims as soon as they reached the unloading-bay – for preference he chose twins. As Yitzhak Taub recalls: 'My twin brother and I were on our way to the gas-chamber with our mother, when suddenly she said: "Children, run over to the Germans. Run back to where they're looking for twins!"' Together with his brother Zerah he arrived in Dr Mengele's experimental laboratory. 'My little guinea-pigs', the death-doctor called the children contemptuously. He was bent on immortalising his name in the medical textbooks with his own theory on twins. Mengele compared the two boys in every detail; every day they had to give a blood-sample. Often this would be drawn from both arms simultaneously. Yitzhak Taub relates how blood went on being taken from them until 'the children fell to the floor like empty plastic bags'. For the purposes of 'research' he injected chemicals into the children's eyes, to see whether brown eyes could be permanently altered to blue. Others he killed with injections of evipan or phenol, and removed their organs. Moshe Offer, another Auschwitz twin, tells us: 'I was injected with poison. To this day I don't know what it was. As a result of the experiments I am two-thirds disabled. I have tremors. I get epileptic fits. What kind of a life is that!'

In the sick-bay we first had to pull the dead bodies down from their palliasses. They were horribly smeared with blood, filthy and covered with shit. Then two of us would get into the bed and lie there. There was nothing to drink and one bucket to go in.

Anna Palarczyk, Polish woman in Auschwitz

Mengele took women from there for gynaecological operations without anaesthetic. Young women who were quite nice-looking came back in a terrible condition.

Ruth Elias, Czech Jew, Auschwitz

After every injection the women got a high temperature, ovaritis, severe pains and cramps which often ended in unconsciousness. All the woman had one or both ovaries removed, which were sent to Berlin. The women also had parts of their sexual organs removed and those were also sent to Berlin.

Sylvia Friedmann, Slovakian prisoner in Auschwitz and medical assistant on an experiment involving 350 young Jewish women from Holland and Greece

Undersized people and pregnant women were also of particular interest to the uniformed doctor. Ruth Elias was eight months pregnant when she was deported for the second time, this time to Auschwitz. Mengele decided not to send her to the gas-chamber. When, in spite of everything, she gave birth to her baby, on the doctor's orders her breasts were bound up to prevent her feeding it. Every day Mengele turned up to check that the baby really was going without nourishment. 'Slowly, gradually, my child faded away', Ruth Elias recounts. 'It hardly cried at all, just whimpered.' After eight days the baby was scarcely showing any signs of life, and a prisoner-nurse secretly helped her give it a morphine injection. 'I killed my own baby and when I had done it, I just wanted to die myself', Ruth Elias confesses.

Today the name of Josef Mengele stands for all the inhuman experiments carried out at Auschwitz. Yet this man from Günzburg, a pretty Bavarian town on the Danube, was far from being the only doctor who placed himself unquestioningly at the service of the Nazi murderers. The gynaecologists, Carl Clauberg and Horst Schumann, to name but two, experimented with perverted methods of sterilising both women and men. Jews were to be deprived of their fertility through injections or high doses of

X-ray radiation, but at the same time would retain their ability to work. The orders for this came from the highest authority. *Reichsführer-SS* Heinrich Himmler kept himself personally informed on the progress of the project. In June 1943 Professor Clauberg reported with satisfaction that, with his methods, 'it is highly probable that several hundred if not a thousand' women could be sterilised every day.

In the beds of the sick-bay the unscrupulous doctors found more and more prisoners with 'interesting' symptoms, who then had to die to meet the endless pressure for experimentation. Whenever the medics needed fresh organs for their tests, prisoners died in the process of donating them. In the camp there was no shortage of 'recently living material', as the doctors called their victims' organs.

> Our camp alone provides a workforce of 10,000, drawn from every nation. We are the slaves of slaves, whom anyone can order about; our names are the numbers tattooed on our arm and sewn on to our chest.
>
> *Primo Levi, Italian Jew in Auschwitz*
>
> We all got a number tattooed on our arm. This was done with a knife and a needle, and the arm was swollen for a long time afterwards. We no longer had names, we were just numbers.
>
> *Dario Gabbai, Greek Jew, Auschwitz*

In this apocalyptic world of evil the thoughts of those prisoners whose will to live was not yet broken focused on naked survival. Their whole being centred on getting through the next few minutes and hours at least, in the hope that perhaps they might still make it, that perhaps there was some way of escaping. For anyone who wanted to survive it was imperative not to stand out from the mass of prisoners, not to attract attention to themselves. The first and most important rule to be learned was: 'Always stay in the middle. Don't stand at one side, because at the side you're sure to be beaten up', Andrej Lepkowski tell us. Punishment beatings were part of the daily routine. There were endless variants. The sadistic imagination of the torturers knew no limit. At interrogations in the main camp, the 'swing' was particularly notorious. The prisoner was made to grasp his hands in front of his drawn-up knees. His wrists were then handcuffed in front of his legs. Then a solid iron bar was thrust between the victim's knees and elbows. The torturers then lifted the iron bar on to two wooden blocks so that the prisoner was hanging with his head downwards. Then they beat him with a bull-whip on the buttocks and genitals and on the bare soles of his feet. The blows were so violent that the victim turned complete somersaults. If his screams became too loud, a gas-mask was placed over his face. Many died in Birkenau, not because they had been guilty of some trivial 'offence' but simply to amuse the 'VIPs' in the camp. Sometimes the selection of a victim was entirely arbitrary. Then they forced the unfortunate man to stretch out on the floor. They placed a truncheon across the back of his neck and jumped on it with full force, thus breaking his neck.

Selections were also part of everyday life in the camp. Anywhere and everywhere the prisoners ran the risk of being picked out. Whenever the block curfew was imposed again, the prisoners knew what was in store for them: the SS were searching for new victims for the gas. The murderers were especially looking out for 'Moslems': men and women who were so weakened that they were no more than skin and bone. More dead than alive, they were scarcely able to take in their surroundings. Their sunken eyes staring straight ahead, they shambled aimlessly around the camp. Dagmar Ostermann describes their feelings: 'The fear becomes acute when selections are taking place. Once a selection is over, there's a distinct sigh of relief. You've come through! And life goes on. I suppose we had a certain fatalism about it.'

No sooner was life back to 'normal' than the survivor's thoughts turned to one subject above all others: food. Everyone tried, somehow or other, to get hold of something edible, in order to avoid becoming 'Moslems' themselves. For prisoners who were right at the bottom of the camp hierarchy or who had no links with the workers in the 'Canada' Kommando, the search was largely in vain. 'When the snow melted, the first green weeds sprouted out of the ground and we went looking for them every day', Ruth Elias remembers. 'How happy we were when we caught sight of one, picked it and were able to keep it in our mouth for hours. The little leaves from weeds gave us the feeling that we could at least imagine having something in our mouth, which could drive away our hunger.' Every night, in their desperation, starving people stole from those who had saved up part of their meagre bread ration for the next day. If prisoners caught someone stealing, they would not infrequently kill him.

Having access to bread meant power over the other prisoners. Arpad Bacsi was one of those who used this power in a terrible manner for his own ends. Bacsi was one of the VIP prisoners because he had a particular gift: he could fashion artistic sculptures from bread. The SS, who ordered figures from him, supplied him with ample raw material. Roman Frister, one of Bacsi's victims, describes his unscrupulousness: 'My bunk-sharer kept his mouth shut when Arpad Bacsi chased him out of his place and lay down next to me. Even before he touched me I knew what was coming. I wanted to scream. At the same instant, as if he had expected my reaction, he clamped his other hand over my mouth. In his palm he had a slice of bread. I stifled my scream. I ate from his hand. No sooner had I eaten the first slice than he stuffed another into my mouth. Where rape was concerned, Arpad Bacsi was a professional as well. But it was only as he let go of me and I had gulped down the last breadcrumb that I was overcome by a feeling of humiliation, because he had attacked me so crudely, and a wave of shame that hunger had got the better of my self-respect.' Frist was left on his bunk, lonely and degraded. Suddenly he noticed that Bacsi had taken more from him than his pride. 'He had stolen my cap. A prisoner at morning *Appell* without a cap was a dead prisoner. Obviously that man didn't want any witnesses to what he had done. He knew that at the morning *Appell* I would be shot. But I wanted to stay alive. I nicked a cap from another prisoner. I'd never seen him in my life. I didn't know his name, or whether he was young or old. The next morning that prisoner was shot. I survived. It is a terrible thing to have done. Do I feel guilty? In my head, yes. In my heart, no.'

In the daily struggle for bare existence, the moral values of civilised life often got in the way: 'We were like animals in the jungle', is how Zygmunt Sobolewski attempts to describe the situation then. The treacherous camp system with its continual degradations made many prisoners doubt not only their own values but even their own identity. In the words of a survivor, Samuel Pisar:' After a while I said to myself: this is the world as it's supposed to be, and perhaps it's true, perhaps I *am* an *Untermensch*. Perhaps they're right, perhaps they *are* the master race.'

I cut the flesh from the bodies of healthy girls for Dr Mengele's bacterial cultures. I bathed the corpses of cripples and dwarfs in a solution of calcium chloride and boiled them in tubs, so that the properly prepared skeletons could be sent to museums in the Third Reich, where they would serve as proof to future generations of the necessity to exterminate 'inferior breeds'.

Miklos Nyiszli, Hungarian Jew and prisoner-doctor, performing autopsies for Josef Mengele

When we were strapped on to Mengele's operating-table, we never knew what would be done to us next. We felt a cold hand on our back, a stethoscope and then a hypodermic which hurt horribly. We were utterly terrified.

Kalman Braun, twin and Mengele victim in Auschwitz

When I awoke, I was lying on my bunk again and my abdomen was covered in blood. Then I had such terrible pains that I twisted and turned like a snake. The pain was so bad I dug my finger-nails into my flesh.

Rosa Finkelstein, victim of the sterilisation experiments of SS doctor Prof. Carl Clauberg

---

How could humans commit such inconceivable atrocities on other human beings? To Heinrich Himmler humanity was merely a sign of 'the over-refinement of a decadent civilisation'.

According to his doctrine, the German people had to be protected by every possible means from the 'Jewish pestilence'. The victims of Nazi racial hysteria were not only Jews but also the allegedly 'inferior' Romany and Sinti gypsies. From February 1943 there was a 'gypsy family camp' at Birkenau. In Auschwitz alone, 13,000 German and Austrian 'gypsies' were murdered, and 5,000 more were gassed in Chelmno. During the Nazi occupation, 25,000 Polish Sinti and Romany met their deaths, and 16,000 to 18,000 French *gitans* died in the camps.

The Nazi elite established their own morality. The perpetrators were persuaded that they were 'killers with clean hands' who were carrying out a 'great task'. 'Most of you will know what it means when a hundred corpses are lying side by side, or five hundred are lying there, or a thousand. To have gone through this and at the same time – apart from some exceptional cases of human weakness – to have remained decent people, has made us tough. This is a proud page in our history, but one which never has been and never must be written', Himmler declared with mawkish emotion to a gathering of senior SS officers on 4 October 1943.

Remaining decent people – that was how Adolf Eichmann and Rudolf Höss saw it as well. For them it was important to remain 'honourable' SS men, ever loyal to the Führer. Their maxim was the same as that of the other Nazi thugs: 'Führer, command! We will follow!' Like them, all the other perpetrators later claimed they had been obliged to obey orders. Hitler alone bore responsibility for the mass murder. But it was not as simple as that. The bulk of henchmen and accomplices were recruited from perfectly ordinary citizens – 'the man next door'. A career in the hierarchy of murder seemed to offer them a chance of amounting to something at last. 'When I took Schwarzhuber's boots and jacket off to clean them, and he was standing there in his underwear he looked like a nobody. All of them without their uniforms were nothing. But when I had put the jacket back on him, and he had put on his boots and cap, suddenly there was a monster.' That is how the prisoner Helmuth Szprycer remembers SS *Untersturmführer* Johann Schwarzhuber.

Friendship in the camp was possible perhaps, but not practical. We knew that selections took place every day, and that tomorrow you yourself or a girl-friend might disappear. We tried not to form any close friendships.

Renée Firestone, Czech Jew in Auschwitz

Auschwitz was the incarnation of death and destruction.

Rachel Knobler, Polish Jew in Auschwitz

When Auschwitz was put into operation, the German population had no inkling of the dreadful crimes in the east. Yet the longer the murder machinery went on running, the more rumours filtered through to them. Germans who had been travelling on business in the vicinity of Auschwitz came home with horrifying reports. Workers in the twelve civilian firms involved in the construction of the crematoria also told of the appalling things they had seen, when they went home on holiday. We have no means of knowing how many people actually learned the truth about Auschwitz in this way. But what is certain is that several companies knew precisely that the crematoria they had helped to build were intended for functions other than the burning of corpses of people who had died of natural causes. For example, Kurt Prüfer, Chief Engineer of the furnace company Topf & Sons, had known since August 1942 that the rooms originally planned as mortuaries were to be converted into gas-chambers. It was open to him or his firm to refuse the order. By accepting it the firm made itself an accomplice to the murders. The directors of the suppliers of Zyklon B, the firms of Tesch & Stabenow and Degesch were fully informed about what went on in Auschwitz.

Even the factory workers must have had their suspicions about the enormous quantities of Zyklon B delivered to Auschwitz: in 1942 and 1943 the camp management ordered nearly 20 tonnes of the poison. No-one could imagine that such huge quantities were being used solely to attack lice. If one added to that the persistent rumours that were circulating, a fairly complete picture emerged. Companies like IG Farben, Topf & Sons, or Tesch &

Stabenow were making their profits from the annihilation of the Jews, either by employing slave labour or selling their products and thus the means to mass murder.

For the period from 15.12.1942 to 10.1.1943, due to the increased home-leave traffic of the Wehrmacht, the Reichsbahn is no longer in a position to make special trains available for evacuation.

From a telegram from the Security Police and SD to Heinrich Himmler, 16 December 1942

In 1944, during the big transports from Hungary and Holland, gassings took place every day of course. But for normal running, everything was shifted to night-time. There was only gassing at night.

Dr Hans Wilhelm Münch, hygiene specialist at Auschwitz

It was too dreadful to describe. Words cannot describe it. We went into hell and came back.

Tobi Biber, Jewish woman from Poland, prisoner in Auschwitz

By the beginning of the year 1943, if not earlier, the war was irrevocably lost for the Third Reich. Stalingrad had fallen, the Allies had decided to make a landing in Italy and demanded 'unconditional surrender'. From now on the German troops were no longing fighting for a Final Victory but in reality for the continuation of the Holocaust. Did they know this? For many of the foot-soldiers on the Eastern Front the suspicion about the murder of the Jews was becoming more and more of a certainty: 'We knew then, from various conversations, that in addition to so-called "normal" concentration camps, other camps had been set up principally for the killing of Jews. That was vague knowledge, with no real evidence', as Hubert Pfoch, then a pioneer with the 9th Panzer Division, puts it. This vague knowledge was repeatedly confirmed by new horror-stories about the SS. Yet what could those soldiers who were concerned have done about it? What is more, in spite of information that had filtered through to them, many others would still not accept it. They closed their eyes and ears to what had been seen and heard.

Until the end of the war Germany and the world lacked the imaginative power to grasp the monstrous extent of the crime. 'One simply could not believe that a civilised nation in the twentieth century was in any way capable of such acts', says the Auschwitz survivor, Rachel Knobler, about her thoughts before being deported. A total of six million Jews were murdered in a bestial manner by the thugs of the 'civilised nation': one million of them in the largest death-factory of all – Auschwitz.

I lived in one room with five other women doctors, one of whom was Jewish. She said: 'You know, we had a selection today and again they took my patients away.' She did something which I thought was clever: the patients who were really quite hopeless she had put to the front, and the healthy ones she had hidden in beds at the back, assuming quite rightly that he had decided, whatever happened, to take one-third of the women away, that is, to select them, since none of them were in very good shape. The seriously ill ones were dying anyway, and those who might in fact have been able to survive their illness would be sent to the gas-chamber. So, she thought, if I put those patients at the front, I will have twice as many deaths. I'd rather put at the front the ones I know will die anyway, and that way I'll only have half the number of deaths. But somehow she was accused of collaborating in the selection. I heard later, after the liberation, that she was put on trial in Prague for collaboration.

Dr Ella Lingens, a half-Jewish woman from Vienna,
deported to Auschwitz in 1943, worked as a
prisoner-doctor in Birkenau

CHAPTER FIVE

RESISTANCE

KNOPP/DIECK

Whenever Alfons Zündler knocked on a front door, he struck dread into people's hearts. Aided by two Dutch 'police auxiliaries' it was the job of the *SS-Unterscharführer* to arrest Dutch Jews in Amsterdam and take them to the Hollandsche Schouwburg, a former theatre that now served as a collection centre. From there the transports were put together which departed from the central Dutch transit camp at Westerbork, bound for the east. Admittedly, *Unterscharführer* Zündler did not know the exact details of what then awaited the Jews, yet within his unit it was an open secret that propaganda terms such as 'eradication' and 'extermination' were to be taken literally.

> The deaths, of which we are thinking today, are so utterly useless, squalid and unspeakably cruel. . . . Only victory will put an end to it all. But meantime let no-one say: 'We are not responsible.' We are responsible if a single man, woman or child perishes whom we could and should have saved. Too many lives, too much time has been lost already. Do not lose any more.
>
> *Eleanor Rathbone, independent British Member of Parliament, in a House of Commons debate, 19 May 1943*

One evening in the late summer of 1942 it was the turn of the Gobitz family who lived in Vegastraat. When the front door was opened, Zündler found that only the mother was at home with her four children. As usual, his two Dutch colleagues from the *zwarte politie*, the 'black police', immediately set about searching the house for valuables. Throughout the Netherlands collaborators like these helped the occupiers in their hunt for Jews. In return, the SS allowed the auxiliaries to join in the looting. When Mr Gobitz returned home, the German officer ought to have arrested him immediately. But he was in luck. Zündler did what he had often done before: he put a spoke in the monstrous machinery of death. He had only become a part of it when Heinrich Himmler ordered all the Danzig police to be integrated into an SS police division.

The SS man leapt at Gobitz, tore the jacket with its Jewish star from his body and sent the astonished man, complaining bitterly, back into the street: 'Clear off. We don't need any gawping Christians here.' Then he stuffed the jacket with the yellow star into a dustbin. One life had been saved. However, he had to take the rest of the family to the Schouwburg. When they arrived there, the four children, Carla, Hennie, Chellie and Jaap, were separated from their mother and put into a room that was already crowded with thirty other Jewish children aged from three to twelve. The Germans designated the room as a crèche. Carla Gobitz, then eleven, has never forgotten the way the incarcerated children cried for their mothers. For two nights and a day they had to lie on the floor of the crèche, while their mother, with several hundred other women due for deportation, waited in the stalls of the large auditorium. Then *Unterscharführer* Zündler appeared, called out the name Gobitz and told them they could go home. He had secretly got rid of the identity documents that Mrs Gobitz had brought with her. Without papers no-one was registered, and the Gobitz family survived through the war in their own home. Because Alfons Zündler had reported the house in Vegastraat 'Jew-free', no other grab-squads made an appearance there.

Several hundred Dutch Jews have Zündler to thank for their lives. Sometimes he 'miscounted' at a roll-call, sometimes he looked the other way when activists from the Jewish resistance smuggled people out of the Schouwburg. He knew he was risking his life, but he heeded his conscience. 'I was so sorry for those people, especially the children', he explained. True, the policeman from Danzig was no reclusive angel of mercy. He enjoyed the delights of an occupier's life to the full. Among other things he embarked on numerous affaires with attractive Jewish girls, a fact which after the war earned him the accusation that he had traded freedom for sex. There was certainly no proof of that. On the contrary, those he rescued described him with gratitude as being humane and naïve in equal measure. 'He had such kindly eyes', says Carla Gobitz.

> While governments prepare memoranda and exchange notes and hold conferences, week after week and month after month the Nazis go on killing men, women and children. . . . There is still in this country, however, a rigid refusal to grant visas for any persons who are still in enemy-occupied territory.
> *Lord Samuel, British peer, in a House of Lords debate,*
> *23 March 1943*

In May 1943 the SD arrested a Jewish family whom Zündler had earlier allowed to flee. Under torture the parents gave away the name of their benefactor, who was immediately condemned to death for 'favouring Jews'. It was only because of a severe war-wound that clemency was granted and his sentence commuted to imprisonment in a concentration camp. Thus Zündler survived the war. His modesty and simplicity contributed to the fact that his acts of humanity remained largely unknown. In 1948 he was found by a de-Nazification tribunal in Munich to have a 'clean record'. But he had missed the closing date by which to make a claim for state compensation for the time he had spent in the concentration camp. He did not regard himself as a hero. He had to help, he said, 'because I am a human being and I do have a good heart'. In 1994 Alfons Zündler was the subject of a heated debate in the Netherlands. When it was announced that the now aged and bedridden man was to receive the Yad Vashem medal, the highest Jewish decoration for non-Jews, there was an outcry, especially from orthodox Jews. They argued against giving the award to a man who had been 'part of the Nazi machine' which had put to death '100,000 people in the Netherlands'. It was a complex case. For of course Alfons Zündler had indeed deported families whom he was no longer able to help. The saviour was simultaneously a perpetrator.

> . . . the most bestial, the most squalid and the most senseless of all their offences, namely the mass deportation of Jews from France. . . . This tragedy fills one with astonishment as well as with indignation; and it illustrates as nothing else can the utter degradation of Nazi nature . . .
> *Winston Churchill in a speech to the House of Commons,*
> *8 September 1942*
>
> Alarming reports received that a plan is being discussed and considered in the Führer's headquarters, by which all Jews in countries occupied or controlled by Germany, numbering 3.5 to 4 million, after deportation and concentration in the east, are to be annihilated at a stroke, so that the Jewish question in Europe is resolved once and for all. . . . The start of the operation is said to be planned for this autumn.
> *Telegram from Gerhart Riegner, German Jew and Director of the Geneva office of the World Jewish Congress, to the US Vice-Consul and the British Consul in Geneva*
>
> When the hour of liberation strikes in Europe, as strike it will, it will also be the hour of retribution.
> *Winston Churchill in a speech to the House of Commons,*
> *8 September 1942*

Resistance against a terrorist state, revolt against the crime of the century – the Zündler case shows how difficult it can be to evaluate such things. Under what circumstances was resistance possible? Who dared to resist? How many were they? What did they achieve? Hannah Arendt, the Jewish philosopher, defined resistance in political terms, seeing it only in acts aimed at 'the overthrow of the Hitler regime'. But that yardstick is perhaps too strict. If we apply it to most of the rescuers, who are honoured with their own trees in Jerusalem's Avenue of the Righteous, then what they did was not 'resistance'. And that includes Alfons Zündler. Nonetheless, the

'Righteous' have sent a message to posterity, which in moral terms carries every bit as much weight as the attempts to bring Hitler's tyranny to an end: and that message is that in the darkest days of terror, humane instincts can survive. The Nazi system was bent on removing every trace of compassion and humanity – particularly where Jews were concerned. But all those courageous rescuers – men and women – made sure it did not succeed. Theirs was resistance in the best sense of the word: against inhumanity, crime and unpardonable opportunism. 'He who saves a single life, saves the whole world.' This saying from the Talmud, which introduced Spielberg's film about Oskar Schindler, is true for all the rescuers.

The great expulsion from Warsaw began on 22 July 1942. Tens of thousands were being dragged off to Treblinka and put into the gas-chambers. We knew this because a few people managed to escape; they came back to Warsaw and told us what was happening. We immediately founded combat groups. We were all young and hadn't been in the army. We had to have weapon-training exercises for the groups who were going to fight – not with rifles but pistols. In Warsaw we succeeded in training 500 young people, male and female, so they could take up arms in an uprising. We realised we might die in the attempt, but we would die with honour and not be shipped off to Auschwitz or Majdanaek or to some other camp. We did all this in secret. The only ones to know about it were those we talked to and who belonged to a combat group themselves. There were 22 such groups.

When we started the revolt, not one of us believed we would survive. Our intention was not to stay alive – we had only survived by chance, because the Germans hadn't managed to wipe us all out. We had a different aim: not to save our own lives but to react against the killing and get even with them.

It was our last chance to get our revenge on the SS men for the murders they had committed in earlier years. No-one thought they would survive.

Stefan Grayek, Polish Jew, in the Warsaw ghetto at that time

On 18 January 1943 there began one of the most moving chapters in the Jewish resistance against the Holocaust. Just as it had done dozens of times before, the SS had informed the 'Jewish Council' of the Warsaw ghetto of the date for a new deportation. Eight thousand people were to make themselves available for 'evacuation'. The order came from the very top: SS chief Heinrich Himmler had visited Warsaw on 9 January and issued instructions for the early liquidation of the entire 'Jewish residential district', the Nazis' cynical euphemism for the ghetto. However, on that January day there were unusually small numbers of Jews at the assembly-points. Even the Jewish police, who could normally be relied on to help in organising the transports, now refused to give assistance – although they knew that their own families would be the next to be deported if they did not each hand over at least five people to the Germans. Not until several hours later had the SS men rounded up a column of scarcely 1,000 people from the tenements of the ghetto. But as the death-train arrived at the assembly-point, a handful of men suddenly jumped out from the ranks and opened fire on the SS guards.

It was a dramatic turning-point in the history of the Warsaw ghetto. For the first time Germans had died at the hands of Jewish resistance fighters. Led by the young commander of the Jewish Combat Organisation, Mordechai Anielewicz, the victims had risen up against their murderers. The reaction of the Germans was confused. Despite deploying massive strength, the SS took a whole week to collect up 6,500 Jews for a transport to Treblinka. Then the deportations had to be stopped temporarily – a first victory for those confined to the ghetto.

Ringed by a wall 11 miles long, the ghetto was regarded by the Germans as 'enemy territory'. When 'combing' the tenements the SS squads began to stay clear of the attics and basements. An eerie tension hung over the city of the dead. Of the original Jewish population of 400,000, scarcely 60,000 were now left. All the others had been murdered in the gas-chambers or had died from disease or starvation.

Gradually the realisation had spread through the ghetto that the Germans were blatantly lying when they claimed that the transports were going to labour camps. 'There were of course a few who had escaped from the extermination camps of Chelmno and Sobibor'. recalls Marek Edelmann, one of the resistance leaders, 'and what they reported was published in precise detail in the underground press. But for far too long people simply refused to believe it. How can it be possible? Surely they won't kill hundreds of thousands!'

> After the first few days it was clear that the Jews had absolutely no intention of being resettled voluntarily, but were determined to use all their resources and the weapons at their disposal to make a stand.
>
> *SS General Jürgen Stroop on the beginning of the*
> *Warsaw ghetto revolt*

The decision to mount organised resistance only gradually gained acceptance in the Warsaw ghetto. 'The religious Jews were against it', says Edelmann. 'They kept saying, it is God's will and this is how it must be.' But others, especially politically minded men and women, thought otherwise. On 1 January 1942 the Jewish Youth Pioneer Association sent out a call which summed up their creed: 'Jewish youth! Hitler plans to destroy all the Jews of Europe. Let us not go like lambs to the slaughter. Yes, we are weak and defenceless. But there is only one answer to give the enemy – resistance! Brothers! It is better to die as a free fighter than to live at the mercy of the murderers.' It was the courage of desperate people who knew that they stood no chance.

Led by Anielewicz, several hundred fighters now began feverishly to build bunkers, prepare hideouts and reconnoitre escape routes. The hardest thing was getting hold of weapons. Apart from some captured German machine-guns, all that could be obtained by devious means outside the ghetto and smuggled in through the sewers, were old shotguns, pistols and a few German uniforms. Calls for help to the Polish national 'Home Army', well armed by the Allies and waiting in hiding for their big moment, fell on deaf ears. General Stefan Rowecki, the commanding officer of the Home Army, sent them precisely ten ancient revolvers.

Jews from several groups, even including communists, recently appealed to us, asking for weapons, as if our stores were filled with them. As a trial I offered them a few pistols. I am not sure that they will be able to make any use of these weapons at all. I will not give them any further weapons because, as you know, we have none ourselves.

General Stefan Rowecki, commander-in-chief of underground forces in Poland, in a message to the government-in-exile in London, 4 January 1943

On 19 April 1943 the Battle of the Ghetto began. Himmler had put SS General of Police Jürgen Stroop in charge of the German troops; 1,300 men, SS and Wehrmacht, stood at the ready with several tanks and some light artillery. Stroop had already earned himself a dubious reputation for exceptional brutality in the war against the partisans and when commanding mobile murder-squads behind the Eastern Front. As his SS units advanced they were met by an eerie sight. On the streets where a few months before thousands of starving people had been seen – and zealously filmed by German propaganda units – total silence now reigned. The Jewish civilians had hidden in cellars and bunkers. Filled with fear, without adequate food and water, they waited for the end.

In Muranowski Square, in the centre of the ghetto, the tense silence was suddenly shattered by machine-gun fire. From well-concealed positions in large buildings the Jewish fighters inflicted painful losses on their opponents. Ryszard Walewski recalls: 'While a troop of German soldiers crowded into a doorway to take cover, a German officer in SS uniform suddenly appeared from nowhere, drew a pistol and rushed towards the door of No. 7, shouting "Death to Judah!" With astonishing speed the officer raced ahead of his subordinates, disappeared into the entrance, climbed up the staircase to the first-floor apartment and threw a hand-grenade out of the window – straight into the group of soldiers who had not yet reached the entrance. Exhausted from his exertions the "SS officer" took off his helmet and wiped the sweat from his brow. It was the deputy commander of our combat organisation, Abraham Rodal.'

The Germans retreated, leaving behind their dead, as well as a disabled armoured-car, in the streets around Muranowski Square. Hitler's representative in Poland, *Generalgouverneur* Hans Frank, described the situation to Berlin in lurid terms: 'Since yesterday in Warsaw we have had a well-organised uprising in the ghetto, which has necessitated retaliation with armed infantry. The murder of Germans is increasing in the most appalling fashion.' Whether one should take seriously this grotesque indignation on the part of someone who shared responsibility for mass murder, it is hard to say.

A comprehensive plan is to be submitted for the levelling of the Ghetto. At all events we must ensure that the accommodation previously available for 500,000 sub-humans disappears from the scene.

Secret order from Himmler to SS General Krüger,
16 February 1943

The dream of my life has come true. The self-defence of the ghetto has become a reality. The armed Jewish resistance and revenge are facts. I have witnessed the unprecedented struggle of the powerful and courageous Jewish fighters.

Mordechai Anielewicz, Jewish ghetto fighter, in a letter,
23 April 1943

The streets of the ghetto were filled with dense, acrid smoke. . . . In the houses thousands of women and children were burning alive. Terrible screams and cries for help could be heard from the blazing buildings. People appeared at the windows of many houses, engulfed in flames like living torches.

From a report by the ZOB
(Jewish Combat Organisation), Warsaw

The joy of the brave rebels at their success was short-lived. Stroop changed his tactics and now started setting fire to one tenement after another. Soon the whole ghetto resembled a flickering torch. The fire gradually deprived the rebels of all their hiding-places and positions. The SS troops now began systematically blowing up the ruins that were left standing. Several thousand fighters and others in hiding – as the murderous Stroop later calculated in his official report – then suffocated in cellars or were crushed by collapsing buildings.

On 8 May the command-bunker of the Jewish combat groups fell. Anielewicz and his staff were killed. In his last letter dated 23 April the leader of the revolt had written to a friend: 'I lack the words to describe to you the conditions under which the Jews are living. Only a few chosen ones will survive; sooner or later all the rest will perish. The die is cast. In the bunkers where our comrades are hiding you can no longer light a candle – due to the lack of air. But the important thing is that my life's dream has come true; I have lived to see Jewish resistance in the ghetto in all its greatness and glory.'

Once the last nests of resistance had been crushed, some 7,000 Jews were deported to Treblinka. How many were able to escape through the sewers of the Polish capital is not certain. According to some estimates, as many as 20,000 managed to go to ground in 'Christian' districts or make their way to the forests of eastern Poland. Several hundred took part a year later in the Warsaw Uprising of the Home Army and there lost their lives. However, in the final days of the battle the ghetto was 'razed to the ground'. On 16 May Stroop announced: 'The former Jewish residential district of Warsaw no longer exists.' As a symbol of his triumph he gave a further order for the great synagogue that lay outside the ghetto to be blown up and flattened. Jürgen Stroop immortalised his 'achievement' in a concluding report to Himmler, which he illustrated with 53 sardonically captioned photographs. They are images of chilling cruelty. One of them leaves a particularly vivid impression. It shows a small Jewish boy who, with other victims, is being rounded up for deportation by SS toughs. The boy, wearing a cap several sizes too large, holds up his hands in fear. The rifle-barrels of his pursuers are aimed at him. The picture symbolises the suffering of the Jewish people. Stroop's caption reads: 'Dragged out from bunkers by force.'

> For eight days now we have been in a life-or-death struggle. . . . The number of casualties . . . is huge. But for as long as we are able to hold our weapons, we will go on fighting and resisting. We refuse to accept the German ultimatum for surrender. Since we can see our final days approaching, we ask this of you: do not forget us!
>
> *From the report by the ZOB (Jewish Combat Organisation),*
> *Warsaw, 26 April 1943*
>
> *24 April 1943.* . . . Not until the block and all the tenements on both sides were ablaze did the Jews emerge from the buildings, some with their clothes on fire, or try to escape by jumping from windows and balconies on to the street, into which they had first thrown beds, blankets and suchlike.
>
> *Daily report by SS General Jürgen Stroop*
>
> *16 May 1943.* The former Jewish residential district of Warsaw no longer exists. The main operation ended at 20.15 hours with the blowing up of the Warsaw Synagogue. . . . The total number of Jews captured or known to have been killed comes to 56,065.
>
> *Daily report by SS General Jürgen Stroop*

The heroic courage of the Warsaw rebels is just one example of how the European Jews did not allow themselves to be led 'like lambs to the slaughter', to quote a widespread misconception. There is evidence of resistance in over a hundred ghettos. True, it often arose only when the final destruction of the 'residential district' was imminent – as was the case in Warsaw. Not once did it end in victory; indeed it could not have done so. Yet it remained as a symbolic warning.

Not infrequently the death of many saved the lives of a few: for example on 15 August 1943 in Bialystok, north-eastern Poland, when the 45,000 Jews still living in the ghetto were about to be 'evacuated'. The Jewish underground, encouraged by the news of the Warsaw revolt, decided to mount a frontal attack on the barbed-wire fence around the ghetto. Under fire from the automatic weapons of the guards, hundreds fell dead before they reached the fence. One of the leaders of the uprising, a woman named Chaika Grosmann, risked her life travelling incognito from ghetto to ghetto, as an emissary of the various Jewish combat groups. 'We knew we would be the first to be killed. But behind us were the masses. Once the barriers were open, thousands would run and get away. If dozens died – hundreds would make it. If hundreds died, thousands would make it. And as for us? We would be the bridge. Our bodies would form a bridge to life for those masses.' In the end, only a few dozen managed to escape into the forests around Bialystok. But the courageous Chaika Grosmann was among them.

Admittedly, those who tried to join non-Jewish partisan groups were likely to risk their lives yet again. Right-wing factions of the Polish 'Home Army', who sometimes collaborated with the Germans in fighting communist partisans, shot any Jews who made themselves known as such. Samuel Willenberg, who succeeded in escaping into the forests, makes this accusation: 'Everyone who joined the partisans in the mountains of southern Poland was shot – and what is more, shot by Poles in the "National Combat Group". Naturally, I didn't know that at the time. Otherwise I would have been able to warn the others.'

One must have a certain attitude to resistance, and our hatred towards the Germans was enormous. This hatred was due to the fact that they had treated people so inhumanly.

Marek Edelmann, former Jewish resistance fighter
in the Warsaw ghetto

The Jews showed a capacity to resist and a strong and effective resilience, both physical and mental. No people in the world would have held out so long and so toughly. The best proof of this is the low number of suicides among the Warsaw Jews. This is why the Germans are taking it out on Poland's Jews.

Emanuel Ringelbaum, occupant of the Warsaw ghetto, in his notes

> The rebels didn't ever stand a chance of winning. Their sole
> aim was to die with dignity.
>
> *Arno Lustiger, Polish Jew in the resistance,*
> *deported in May 1944 to a satellite camp of Auschwitz*

Measured against the total Jewish population of Poland, the
20,000 or 30,000 underground fighters in the forests and ghettos
were certainly a small minority. Successful operations, such as the
grenade attack on the Zyganeria club for SS officers in Cracow, in
which more than a dozen Germans were killed, were isolated
exceptions. After the war, critical voices, especially from Zionist
circles in Israel, complained of the small number of Jews joining
the resistance. It was chiefly the behaviour of people in the death
camps that met with incomprehension. How was it possible that
millions of victims could have been murdered by just a few
thousand perpetrators – and virtually without resistance? As the
argument ran – and not just in Israel – could not a surprise mass
attack have overwhelmed the small number of guards?

Questions like these arose, of course, more from the military
self-assurance of the young state of Israel than from the reality of
the death camps. For the perpetrators did in fact make every
effort, up to the last moment, to conceal the deadly reality from
their victims. The shower fixtures in the gas-chambers, the well-
tended flower-beds in Sobibor, the fake railway station at Treblinka,
which was even fitted with ticket-windows for the return journey –
all this camouflage reinforced the diabolical lies of the murderers as
they sent their victims 'into the showers'. Furthermore, the
victims were for the most part no longer in a fit state, either
physically or mentally, even to think about offering resistance.
Shlomo Dragon, a member of the Jewish *Sonderkommando* in
Auschwitz, says: 'They just had no strength left. By the time they
finally arrived at Auschwitz, the victims had been on the train
for three or four days. When they did arrive, sometimes three-
quarters of the people were dead. You see, they'd been locked in
cattle-trucks with nothing to drink and nowhere to relieve
themselves.'

Nevertheless, there were outbreaks of resistance even in the midst of the death-factories. Much of it was never known about because those involved nearly always paid for their courage with their life. Yet there must have been many cases like that of the spirited actress in Auschwitz, about whom we are told both by the camp commandant Rudolf Höss and by members of the *Sonderkommando*. On 23 October 1943 a transport of Polish Jews, 1,700 men and women, arrived in Birkenau and were immediately led off in the direction of the crematorium. Two-thirds of them were already in the gas-chamber when an incident occurred in the undressing-room. Shlomo Dragon tells the story: 'Two women, a mother and her daughter, who was an actress or a dancer, refused to undress completely. The daughter kept on her brassière and panties and the mother kept her petticoat on. The notorious overseer, Schillinger, went in and shouted: "Get undressed, the lot of you!" He fumbled with his pistol. And do you know what the young woman did? She took off her bra and knocked the revolver out of his hand with it. Then she grabbed the weapon and shot him.'

What happened next was described by Höss to his judges after the war: 'The wire to the lights in the room was torn out. The SS men were attacked, one was stabbed and all had their weapons taken from them. As the room was now in total darkness, a chaotic shoot-out took place between the guards at the entrance and the prisoners inside. When I arrived I had the doors shut, completed the process of gassing the first two-thirds, and then went into the undressing-room with the guards, carrying torches. We forced the prisoners into a corner and took them out one by one to a room next to the crematorium where they were shot on my orders.' The courageous actress was among the victims.

On 2 August at about 4 a.m., our guys began handing out weapons in the camp. It was a Sunday and some of the Ukrainian guards had driven off for a bathe in the River Bug. So only a small group of sentries were left in the camp. . . . Suddenly there was an explosion near the German barracks and we knew the revolt had begun. So we started shooting at the Ukrainians who were guarding the main gate, and we moved towards the camp, fighting the Ukrainians. At that moment a mass of prisoners came out towards us, towards the gate. Then they began to storm the gate. Immediately behind the first fence there were defensive structures camouflaged with barbed wire, which you could get your legs caught in. The first wave of people to reach this barrier were shot by machine-guns. The Ukrainians were firing from the watch-tower. The next wave climbed over the bodies, and I did the same. I simply jumped on to the heap of corpses and leaped across the ditch. At that moment I got a bullet in the leg and started running and limping; I ran with a group of other prisoners across the railway track, then along an asphalt road, and soon we were deep in the forest. And suddenly a village rose up before our eyes, we were approaching a village.

Samuel Willenberg, Polish Jew, deported
to Treblinka in 1942

Those camp inmates who had temporarily been allowed to stay alive so that they could work had more scope for resistance. In several camps members of the *Sonderkommandos*, who worked under indescribably distressing conditions at the gas-chambers and furnaces, rose up in revolt. On 7 October 1944 they succeeded in blowing up a crematorium in Auschwitz. All the rebels either died in the gun-battle that followed or were executed – including the legendary Rosa Robota and her band of brave women who smuggled the explosives into Birkenau from the factories in Monowitz. The horrors of life in the *Sonderkommando*, whose tasks included the removal of mountains of corpses, are described in diaries which were buried in the grounds of the camp before the uprising.

In the Sobibor extermination camp it was again the *Sonder-kommando* who took action against the perpetrators. But an escape tunnel which had been miscalculated triggered an explosion in a minefield that the SS had laid around the camp. All 150 members of the *Sonderkommando* were immediately shot. But then the running of the Sobibor underground was taken over by Soviet prisoners-of-war of Jewish extraction. On 14 October 1943, through a cleverly worked-out plan, they succeeded in taking the guards by surprise. Eleven SS men were killed, and more than 300 prisoners managed to escape through the minefield into the surrounding forest. Although the SS as well as farmers in the neighbourhood went in pursuit of them, fifty of the escapees survived to the end of the war.

The extent of the fear felt by the murderers for the wrath of their victims is demonstrated by Himmler's reaction to the news from Sobibor. On 3 and 4 November 1943 he ordered 'Operation Harvest Festival', the murder of all Jews still engaged in forced labour in the Lublin district – more than 40,000 were shot. At the site of the Sobibor camp the SS erased all traces of its existence. After the buildings had been flattened and the fences torn down, trees and shrubs were planted. In the place where a quarter of a million people had met their death a former prison guard now managed a farm.

Another dramatic outbreak of the Jewish spirit of resistance took place in the third big Polish extermination camp, Treblinka. Here no fewer than 870,000 people had been murdered. In February 1943, on Himmler's orders, the *Sonderkommandos* began to reopen Treblinka's mass graves and burn the corpses. It was work which drove those involved to insanity. The tall, black columns of smoke could be seen and the pungent stench of burning corpses smelt from miles away. The men of the *Sonderkommando* had to crush the bones that remained and mix them with ashes under the earth.

> It's very difficult to plan conspiracies in a camp. That's because one man doesn't know the next man. One person is a stranger to the other. The fear of being betrayed by someone is great. You don't know his mentality, you don't know what sort of a person he is.
>
> *Samuel Willenberg, Polish Jew, deported to Treblinka in 1942*

When it became clear to the *Sonderkommando* that their gruesome work would soon end and thus their liquidation was approaching, they decided on rebellion. Some prisoners succeeded in making a duplicate key to the armoury. On 2 August 1943 the revolt broke out. 'At exactly 4 o'clock in the afternoon the news came that we were immediately to go to the shed where the weapons were', Stanislaw Kons, one of the rebels, remembers. 'Everyone who comes to collect a gun must give the password: "death". Then the reply was "life". "Death" – "Life"; "Death" – "Life". The words were called out repeatedly in quick succession and hands reached out to receive the longed-for rifles, pistols and hand-grenades. Then we attacked the murderers.' The Ukrainian auxiliaries in the watch-tower opened fire with their machine-guns. The prisoners did not succeed in putting the watch-towers out of action. Hundreds died in the hail of bullets. Samuel Willenberg recalls: 'Suddenly my friend the Rabbi was hit in the leg. I dragged him behind a pile of wood. He begged me to kill him. I looked at him and thought: what shall I do? Then I said: "Look over there, towards the camp. Your wife is there, and your children too." Then I shot him in the head.'

Stanislaw Kons describes the progress of the battle: 'We have 200 armed men. The rest attack the Germans with axes, picks and spades. They set fire to the gas-chambers. They burn the phoney station with the signs saying "Bialystok-Wolkowysk", the "ticket-office" and "waiting-room". The flames and the shots echoing around bring the Germans running from all directions. We try to break through to the nearby woods. Most of us get killed, but Germans are killed as well.'

Six hundred men and women escaped to the forest but scarcely seventy of them survived to the liberation by the Red Army, 18 months later. In Treblinka, as in Sobibor, the SS made the last prisoners plough up the ground and remove all traces of the camp. Then they were shot.

People awake and fight for your life! Let every mother become a lioness defending her young! Let no father again look on calmly as his children die! The shame of the first act of our destruction must never again be repeated. Let every house become a fortress! People awake and fight! In fighting lies your salvation!
From the call to arms of the ZZW (Jewish Military Union)
in Warsaw, 22 January 1943

After the war, the survivors of the uprisings felt their fortune as a heavy burden. Many reproached themselves and were haunted by the memory. They certainly did not regard themselves as heroes. But most gave detailed evidence about their experiences. It is to them that we owe much of what we know today about how the camps functioned. Yet the hopelessness of their resistance, the knowledge that for the great majority of them no rescue had been possible, drove many to the depths of self-doubt. Marek Edelmann from the Warsaw ghetto describes his experiences very sceptically: 'Humanity agrees that dying with a gun in your hand is better than dying without one. So we followed that convention. But can it really be called a rebellion? It was simply a matter of not letting ourselves be slaughtered when our turn came.' The attitude of the great majority, who died without resisting, commands more respect from Marek Edelmann than does his own: 'Those people were quiet and composed, and they died decently. It is terrible when someone goes to their death so calmly. That is far harder than all the shooting; it is actually much easier to die shooting. How much easier dying seemed to us than to the people climbing into a cattle-truck, making that journey, digging their own grave, having to strip stark naked.' The heroic hyperbole of the struggle against their oppressors is corrected by the hero himself. According to him, Jewish resistance was one thing above all: a cry of despair in a time of limitless atrocity.

We have received a great many indications that Jews from all over Europe are being deported and concentrated in the [Polish] *Generalgouvernement*, and further that the Jews are being so badly treated there that a large number of them have perished. . . . Indeed such reports provide the basis for Herr Riegner's report, but of course they are not proof of 'annihilation at a stroke'. German policy seems rather to extend to the elimination of 'useless mouths' than to the use of able-bodied Jews for slave-labour.

Note on the Riegner telegram by David Allen, of the British Foreign Office, 10 September 1942

How clearly did the west hear that cry? For decades there has been a debate about whether the Allies did too little to bring the killing to an end. The eminent Washington historian, Richard Breitman, gave a subtitle to his book *State Secrets*: it was 'The crimes of the Nazis tolerated by the Allies'. Is this serious accusation justified? Did Hitler's wartime opponents share in the guilt of the Holocaust? In a historical perspective, did the behaviour of the Allies amount to assistance by default? The first thing to remember is this: the mass murder was brought to an end by Soviet, British and American soldiers. It was only their complete victory over Hitler's Germany that put an end to the Nazis' murderous frenzy. Because the SS pursued Hitler's planned annihilation to the very last minute – even after his death – every day's delay in the Allied advance would have cost the lives of thousands more victims.

The crime was known about in the west – at least within an exclusive circle – much earlier than had for a long time been assumed. In Germany the Holocaust was admittedly a matter of 'Reich secrecy', but from the outset it was no secret. As early as the summer of 1941 British code-breakers had monitored the radio traffic of the *Einsatzgruppen*, from which it was possible to judge the extent of the genocide behind the German front in the east. Winston Churchill knew about it – and at first remained silent. Any public denunciation would have betrayed to the Germans that their coded radio messages were an open book to the British.

Yet a few months later, in November 1941, the prime minister sent an article to the *Jewish Chronicle* in which he made specific reference to the crime: 'The Jews have taken the full weight of the Nazi assault on the bastions of freedom and human dignity. Their suffering and their part in the struggle will certainly not be forgotten on the day of victory. It will be shown that, while the mills of God grind slow, they grind exceeding small.' The last sentence was a reference to the announcement by the US president, F.D. Roosevelt, that after the war all those guilty of war-crimes would be severely punished.

From now on the British and Americans would use this lever again and again. In 1944 they even arranged for a list of the names of fifteen guilty SS officers in Auschwitz to be broadcast by the

BBC. Yet for the moment the threat of the 'mills of God' appeared to have little effect on those it was addressed to, since in autumn 1941 it was still by no means certain who would win the war.

Again in 1942 German radio transcripts reached the desk of the British prime minister. Himmler had admittedly given orders that all messages relating to the Final Solution were to be carried by courier, but references to 'natural deaths' in the camps were excepted from this. At a place called Auschwitz, Churchill now read in the reports from his code-breaking centre, no less than 6,829 men and 1,525 women had died of typhus in a single month.

> The things that were reported were so cruel and so horrific that they were not believed; people refused to accept them because they could not live with the idea of absolute evil.
> *Gerhart Riegner, German Jew, emigrated to Switzerland in 1933*

In May 1942 Jewish trade union officials passed on to the British press information about the illegal underground movement in Poland. The BBC reported it in detail and on 7 June the *Daily Telegraph* wrote: 'More than 700,000 Polish Jews have been slaughtered in the greatest massacre in world history.' The article also mentioned special trucks which the Nazis were using as mobile gas-chambers. In the west the general public learned more and more about the Holocaust. But the figures seemed to be so high that, privately, both the experts in the Foreign Office and the responsible newspaper editors believed they were 'Jewish exaggerations'. For those living at the time, the crime of the century was, in the most real sense, unbelievable. In fact, by that time, the number of victims in Poland was about twice as high.

> Those helpless unfortunates cannot be helped except by a landing in Europe, by a victory over German arms and a crushing of German might. There is no other way.
> *A.A. Berle, US Assistant Secretary of State, at a protest meeting in Boston, 2 May 1943*

In summer 1942 the sum total of information about Hitler's programme of murder grew considerably. In July, a German army officer, *Oberstleutnant* Arthur Sommer of the Wehrmacht High Command, told a confidant in Switzerland that 'camps were being prepared in the east, for the annihilation of all Europe's Jews'. A few days later the Silesian industrialist Eduard Schulte also sent reports about the extermination camps to Switzerland. There they came to the attention of a German-Jewish emigrant working for the World Jewish Congress. Gerhart Riegner, a young lawyer, immediately sent identical telegrams to London and Washington: 'Have received alarming report that in Führer's headquarters plan discussed and under consideration all Jews in countries occupied or controlled Germany number 3½ to 4 million should after deportation and concentration in east at one blow [be] exterminated to resolve once for all the Jewish question in Europe – stop.'

Then in November 1942 an eye-witness to the terror arrived in London. Jan Karski had spent three years travelling around occupied Poland on behalf of the Polish government-in-exile. He had been imprisoned and interrogated but had escaped. He had seen the Warsaw ghetto from the inside, as well as a camp near Lublin, into which members of the Jewish underground had smuggled him, dressed as a Ukrainian SS man. In the course of this his cover was nearly blown because, at the sight of a mountain of naked corpses, he had suffered a complete nervous breakdown. The fact that Karski was not a Jew apparently increased his credibility in the eyes of his interlocutors in the west. The message he brought from the underground groups in Poland was unambiguous. The west must elevate the rescue of the threatened Jewish population of eastern Europe to a war aim, and use leaflets and radio propaganda to reveal to the Germans the mass murder that was being committed in their name.

Karski made a gallant effort to complete his mission. He spoke to diplomats and politicians and even succeeded in obtaining a personal interview with President Roosevelt. The President certainly listened to the reports with rapt attention but his only response was that now America 'must win the war all the more quickly'.

The undersigned Dutch churches, already deeply disturbed by the measures against the Jews in the Netherlands, which exclude them from participation in the normal life of the people, have noted with horror the new measures by which men, women and children and entire families are being taken away to German Reich territory and subject territories. The suffering brought by this upon tens of thousands, the awareness that these measures conflict with the most profound moral consciousness of the Dutch people, and the infringement which these measures contain against everything that is our right and just duty in the sight of God, compel the churches to make the urgent request to you not to put these measures into effect.

Announcement from the pulpit in all Dutch churches on 26 July 1942, and telegram from all Dutch churches to the German Reich Commissioner in the Netherlands, 11 July 1942

Since the Catholic bishops – with no direct interest in the matter – have interfered in it, all Catholics of Jewish race will now be deported this very week. Any interventions are to be disregarded.

Reaction of the German occupation authorities to the statement by the Dutch churches

On 17 December 1942, at the very time when the German Sixth Army was being decimated in Stalingrad, Hitler's military opponents finally made a public statement about the Holocaust. Americans, British, Soviets and eight governments-in-exile from countries occupied by Germany condemned 'in the severest terms Germany's bestial methods of extermination'. The statement, which was repeatedly broadcast by the German-language service of the BBC, left no doubt as to the seriousness of the message: 'Not one of the deportees has ever been heard of again. The able-bodied are forced in camps to do arduous work until they die of exhaustion or are cold-bloodedly slaughtered in vast numbers. No-one responsible for these crimes will escape his punishment.'

After this statement had been read out in the British House of Commons, all the members of Parliament stood in silence as a mark of respect. Three months later, on 9 March 1943, a mass demonstration was held in New York, organised by the American Jewish Congress. Their slogan was: 'Stop Hitler now!' Addressing an audience of 750,000 the organisers demanded immediate measures 'to rescue the European Jews'.

The fact that the non-Aryan or half-Aryan Catholics, who are children of the Church like any others, now in the collapse of their worldly existence and in their spiritual need, require our paternal love and paternal care, is something we do not even need to assure them of. In the present situation as it is, we unfortunately cannot send them any effective assistance other than our prayers.

Pope Pius XII, in a 1943 letter to the Bishop of Berlin,
Konrad von Preysing

In 1944, at the request of Jews in Budapest and Bratislava, we raised the question of bombing Auschwitz. And we were told it couldn't be done, it was too far, the planes wouldn't get back. That was all lies. We know that throughout 1944 the Allies had absolute control of the air, all over Europe. We know that at the same time as we were asking them to drop a few bombs on Auschwitz, the IG Farben synthetic-rubber plant, just 5 kilometres from Auschwitz, was bombed three or four times.

Gerhart Riegner, German Jew, official of the World
Jewish Congress in Switzerland

The New York demonstration thus brought the fact of the Holocaust clearly to the public's attention. What credence people in the west gave to the figures of deaths that were published is hard to say – but in most cases the figures were actually lower than the true toll of killings. Yet the governments as well as the people of the western nations knew for certain that the Germans were committing genocide in Europe, on a scale that had not been thought possible. But what was to be done to prevent the perpetrators from continuing their crimes? The German dictator and his accomplices were not in the least impressed by appeals or threats, and a military victory over the Wehrmacht was clearly still a long way off.

It was the representatives of Jewish organisations who made the most desperate efforts to procure help from outside – usually in vain. For example, various attempts to persuade the Pope in Rome to send a clear message to the German Catholics and to excommunicate the perpetrators, all fell on deaf ears. The pro-German Pius XII was too much a prisoner of his anti-communist sentiments to have been prepared openly to take a stand against Hitler. Furthermore, like most of his predecessors, the Holy Father was not free from the Church's traditional anti-Semitism. Even in the summer of 1942, long after the Curia had been informed about the mass murders, he expounded to his College of Cardinals the theological reasoning behind the deep gulf between Christians and Jews: 'Jerusalem has responded to His call and to His grace with the same rigid blindness and stubborn ingratitude that has led it along the path of guilt to the murder of God.' Such a comment was utterly incomprehensible at a time when 'Jerusalem' was being murdered by the million. Even so, in his Christmas Address for 1942, the same Pope Pius remembered those hundreds of thousands 'who without any blame, sometimes merely on account of their nationality or race, have been delivered up to death or a slow wasting away'. Certainly he failed to pronounce the hoped-for declaration of war against the mass murderers. Pius was no Peter. His great moment did not come until 1944 when he played a significant part in saving the Jews of Budapest.

The legal department confirms that that if we grant our protection in any form to stateless Jews anywhere in the world, word of this will soon get round and we will then have the greatest difficulty explaining why we grant such protection in some cases and not in others.

Statement by J.R.M. Pink, British Foreign Office staff, April 1943

If it had not been for the restrictions placed on immigration to Palestine in pre-war years . . . partly for economic reasons and partly to please the Arabs, tens of thousands of men, women and children who now lie in bloody graves, would long ago have been among their kindred in Palestine.
Eleanor Rathbone, independent British Member of Parliament, in a House of Commons debate, 14 December 1943

There was another institution which carried moral weight in Germany but failed to respond to all appeals that it should intervene against the Holocaust: that was the Red Cross. To place any hope in its German offshoot proved illusory. To all intents and purposes the German Red Cross was part of the Nazi system. It was headed by a certain Dr Ernst Grawitz MD, who was an *Obergruppenführer* in the SS and an SS 'Reich Doctor' who, in the context of the euthanasia programme, had personally offered to carry out the killing of mental patients. So his support could hardly be counted on. But what would be the reaction of the International Red Cross (IRC), whose headquarters was in Geneva? Gerhart Riegner, the tireless advocate of the interests of his threatened fellow-Jews, recalls having sought the Red Cross's assistance 'dozens and dozens of times' – without success. Carl Jakob Burckhardt and Max Huber, the two academics at the head of the IRC, argued for the same reticence as the Pope: it would be undesirable to put at risk the Red Cross's access to German prisoner-of-war camps, and in any case the status of the imprisoned Jews under international law was as 'civilian internees' and as such beyond the remit of the IRC. Privately delegates in individual countries were instructed 'only with the greatest discretion and caution to show concern for the Jews'. Not until 1944 – when the outcome of the war was assured – did the Red Cross start despatching aid-parcels to concentration camps.

The indefatigable Cassandras like Gerhart Riegner were in despair. 'We were utterly powerless', Riegner says today, still flushed with rage at the memory. 'Never were we more powerless than at the moment of greatest need. And the Allies knew that perfectly well. Of course we couldn't simply switch sides, because that's where Hitler was.' Indeed, it seemed that once London and Washington had made a clear public condemnation of the mass murder, the 'problem' of the European Jews was pushed into the background. When the war was won, they said, the killing would stop as well. This was the standard answer given to all pleas and appeals at least to increase the diplomatic pressure on Hitler's Axis allies or to facilitate the intake of refugees.

In America the 'Jewish question' posed particular problems in domestic policy. Roosevelt knew that American Jews mainly voted for him and his Democratic Party. But from the Republican side the accusation grew louder that the President was placing Jewish interests above American ones. This was far from being comparable with Hitler's hatred of Jews, but it was anti-Semitism nonetheless. Roosevelt therefore had to take care to placate Jewish calls for help, but at the same time avoid providing the opposition with further ammunition. The refugee question became a particularly tricky test for him. In the mass unemployment of the 1930s the USA had – like many other countries suffering from the Slump – severely limited its immigration quota and now kept rigidly to an annual intake of 30,000. In the years leading up to Himmler's 1941 ban on emigration, this upper limit – combined with the closed frontiers of other countries – became a matter of life and death for tens of thousands of European Jews who wanted to leave their homelands. Those who did not obtain a visa had to remain under Hitler's tyranny, and those who did get one were often forced to flee again from the host country once the visa had expired. The unwillingness of the 'free world' to take in those who were threatened by Hitler is not a proud page in its history. The greatest tragedy of all was the fate of the refugee ships, roaming across the oceans of the world without ever finding a port that would accept them. True, the tragedy was initiated by Hitler and his henchmen, but it was only made possible by the half-heartedness of the rest of the world.

On 19 April 1943 a conference opened in Bermuda, at which the British and Americans wanted to tackle the 'refugee question'. The sub-tropical warmth of the venue was balanced by cold calculations. Here, far from the great newspaper offices, the press were easier to control. For both sides agreed that the real objective of the conference was to influence public opinion. Nothing had changed in either London's or Washington's attitude to questions of immigration. But a few headlines about an international meeting were intended to remove the pressure of public opinion for a while.

As was predicted, the Bermuda Conference ended with no concrete results. The Americans did not raise their upper limit of 30,000 immigrants per year, nor did Britain abandon its restrictive policy on immigration into Palestine – out of consideration for Arab interests. Even if President Roosevelt, at least, felt otherwise in his heart, he had to be satisfied with the results of the conference. In the coming year he was going to stand for the presidency once again, and wanted to win it for the fourth time in succession. His prospects were not good and he did not want the dispute about the number of Jewish immigrants to stand in his way. Roosevelt could still remember well that in an opinion poll on accepting Jewish refugees, 67 per cent of Americans had answered: 'We ought to keep them out.'

> Many times we saw the silver vapour-trails in the sky. All the SS men used to run into the shelters, but we came out of our huts and prayed for a bomb to drop or for soldiers and weapons to come floating down on parachutes – but in vain.
>
> *Erich Kulka, prisoner in Birkenau*

31 May 1944: in harbours along the south coast of England the greatest invasion fleet of all time was being equipped for the assault on Europe. The end of the war now seemed to be in sight at last. British and American air armadas controlled the skies above Hitler's crumbling empire. On that day a US reconnaissance plane was flying over Upper Silesia. Its assignment was to photograph the large plants for producing synthetic petrol around Oswiecim, or Auschwitz. One of the aerial photographs taken from a height of 30,000 feet showed a large camp, laid out on a rectangular grid, with a railway platform and other installations that were not

identifiable at first. It was the first aerial photo of the biggest German extermination camp: Auschwitz–Birkenau, the factory of death. On the same day, down below in the camp, the SS were drawing up a list, from which it emerged that in the two previous weeks gold teeth and fillings with a total weight of 40 kilograms had been taken from the corpses of Hungarian Jews who had been gassed.

The fact that, following the Anglo-American advance through Italy, Allied aircraft had since February been in a position to reach the death camps in the east, gave rise to bold plans. It finally seemed possible, by military means, at least to slow down the Holocaust. In April and May four prisoners in all managed to escape from Auschwitz into Slovakia. The stories they told urgently warned the world of the start of the deportation of the Hungarian Jews – about 750,000 people, whom Hitler and Eichmann had long had in their sights. Up to that point, the Hungarian head of state, Admiral Horthy, had certainly persecuted the Jews in his country, but had not consigned them to their death. However, after the Germans invaded Hungary in March 1944, preparations began for the murder of the last big Jewish population in Europe. Eichmann led the operation in person. Since mid-May the transport trains had been rolling. The escaped Auschwitz prisoners, Rudolf Vrba, Alfred Wetzler, Czeslaw Mordowicz and Arnost Rosin, reported that 12,000 people were now being killed every day in the gas-chambers of Birkenau. Since that meant that the capacity of the crematoria was exceeded, the SS arranged for the mountains of corpses to be burnt in large pits.

On 18 June 1944 the War Refugee Committee set up in Washington at the beginning of the year received a message from the Slovakian Rabbi Weissmandel. In it he urgently asked for the stretch of railway track between Kaschau and Preschau to be bombed, since it was the only rail route for deportations from eastern Hungary. Weissmandel explained in detail that this 'short and uninterrupted route' carried transports of 15,000 people a day. His telegram ended with a desperate appeal: 'There is not a day to lose. For God's sake, help.' On the same day the BBC broadcast a summary of the 'Auschwitz Protocols', the shocking reports provided by the four escaped prisoners. All at once the largest of all the extermination camps became famous in the west. Six days later, as a spellbound world watched the Allies advancing from their Normandy beachhead, Gerhart Riegner appealed to the US ambassador to Switzerland, Roswell McLelland. Riegner also called for the immediate bombing of the railways from Hungary to Auschwitz and was the first person to ask for the bombing of the camp itself, 'especially the buildings which house the gas-chambers and crematoria, and which can be recognised by the tall chimney. Also the sentry-posts on the fence around the camp, the watch-towers and industrial installations.'

> A bombing raid would give the Germans a welcome excuse to claim that their Jewish victims were not being massacred by German murderers, but killed by Allied bombing.
> *Leon Kubowitzki, head of the rescue section*
> *of the World Jewish Congress,*
> *June 1944*

In Washington a member of the War Refugee Committee, the Riga-born Benjamin Akzin, strongly supported the plan to bomb Auschwitz. On 29 June he urged the Pentagon to act quickly, since an air attack could 'possibly lead to a noticeable, if only temporary, slowdown in the systematic mass murder'. Furthermore, he wrote, the bombing 'would represent the most tangible – and perhaps the only tangible – sign of the outrage which the existence of these charnel-houses has unleashed'. Yet Benjamin Akzin's heartfelt appeal, like all those before it, fizzled out with no effect. On his letter, which has been preserved in Washington's National Archive, there is a hand-written comment by one of the staff of the Assistant Secretary of War, John McLoy. It reads: 'Shut him up!' The official reply was that the US Air Force did not currently possess the operational capability to attack targets so deep in enemy territory – a barefaced lie. A few days earlier, on 16 June 1944, seventy-one American B17 heavy bombers with a fighter escort bombed the synthetic fuel plants in the operational area of Upper Silesia. In doing so they actually flew over three stretches of track used for bringing deportees into Auschwitz. By that point in time more than 300,000 men, women and children from Hungary had been murdered in the death-camp.

On 7 July 1944 the proposal to bomb Auschwitz finally reached the highest reaches of government. In an annotation to a document, Winston Churchill urged his Foreign Secretary, Anthony Eden, to expedite the matter with the Royal Air Force: 'Get what you can out of the RAF, and involve me if necessary.' On the very same day Eden got to work. In the name of the British prime minister he instructed the Royal Air Force to look without delay at the possibility of a bombing raid, and sent a note to Stalin in which he asked the Soviet ally for assistance in rescuing the Hungarian Jews.

What the British leaders could not know and did not know for almost another two weeks was that the previous day the Hungarian head of state, Admiral Horthy, had stopped the deportations. One of the reasons for this was a moving appeal from his own family, but chiefly it was international pressure, which increased as the end of the German domination of Europe came in sight. Horthy revealed to Hitler's emissary, Veesenmayer, that he was being 'bombarded with telegrams day after day'. They had been sent by such figures as the king of Sweden, the head of the World Jewish Congress and – at last – even the Pope and the Red Cross. The Papal Nuncio had telephoned him 'several times a day', and neutral countries like Turkey, Switzerland and Spain had also demanded an end to the transports. On 2 July a particularly heavy US air raid on targets in Budapest had lent weight to these appeals. It was the only occasion when diplomatic intervention was able to hinder the Holocaust. Even so, it was only possible because Hitler's might was no longer great enough to force the Hungarians to cooperate with Eichmann – and because a brave Hungarian general, commanding an armoured brigade in the capital, kept the militia penned up in their barracks, thus preventing them from continuing their murder. For a while at least, over 200,000 Budapest Jews were saved.

> We hoped and prayed they would bomb us so that we would be spared a helpless death in the gas-chambers. Being bombed meant there was a chance that Germans would be killed as well. That's why we were deeply disappointed and saddened when they flew over us without dropping a single bomb.
>
> *Shalom Lindenbaum, prisoner in Auschwitz*

Horthy's intervention was nullified by the cynical proposal whereby Himmler and Eichmann wanted to sound out the possibility of making a separate peace with the Western Powers. Their offer, passed on by a middleman named Joel Brand, provided for the release of one million Jews in exchange for war materials, including 10,000 trucks which were to be used on the Eastern Front. Unlike the British, and the war-hardened Soviets, the Americans were initially willing to negotiate in the hope of perhaps saving lives. However, once the BBC made the German offer public on 19 July, the 'blood for goods' deal was morally discredited. The very next day, just as *Oberst* Stauffenberg's bomb exploded in the Führer's East Prussian headquarters, an outraged British press commented that Himmler's 'monstrous offer' to trade in human lives was a scandalous attempt to split the Allies.

This certainly did not mean the question of bombing Auschwitz was off the agenda. On 11 July 1944 the Jewish Agency had appealed to President Roosevelt and once again stressed the importance of such an attack. While it was clear, the note explained, that bombs were 'scarcely able to make a significant contribution to saving the victims', an air raid was 'worthwhile in itself and would have a manifest and far-reaching effect on morale'. The message went on to state: 'Firstly it would mean that the Allies have declared immediate war on the annihilation of the victims of Nazi tyranny – today the Jews, tomorrow the Poles, Czechs or some other nation. Secondly this would put paid to the oft-repeated lies from Nazi mouthpieces, that in reality the Allies had no particular objection to the Nazis ridding Europe of the Jews. Thirdly it would contribute greatly to dispelling the doubts which, on the part of the Allies, are still being shed on the reports of mass annihilation by the Nazis. And fourthly it would lend weight to the threat of retaliatory measures against the murderers.' Yet even this impassioned appeal ran into the sand – because the military were now playing for time. US Air Force General Spaatz claimed to be 'extremely well-disposed' towards the plan, which was expressly supported by Churchill and more tentatively by Roosevelt, but Spaatz first required better information about the 'location, extent and functioning' of the installations in Auschwitz.

On 7 August US aircraft bombed the oil refineries at Trzebinia, a mere 12 miles from Birkenau. Prisoners in the camp saw the columns of smoke rising from the blazing tanks. Many of them wished the Americans would finally attack the hated SS and their death-factory. Hugo Gryn, then fifteen years old, remembered: 'The most painful thing about life in the camp was the feeling of being totally forgotten.' His fellow-inmate Andras Lorenczi adds: 'I simply cannot understand why they didn't help us. Later I realised that they didn't bomb the camp for fear of hitting us. But at least the crematorium, the railway tracks – surely that would have been possible. Perhaps then a few thousand would have been killed. But we were doomed to die anyway.'

You wrote to me on 7 July to ask whether the murder of the Jews in Hungary could somehow be stopped by sending in bombers. . . . I have therefore examined the following options:

(a) Destruction of railway tracks
(b) Destruction of installations
(c) Other disruption of the operation of the camps

I was assured that (a) is beyond our capabilities. Even to destroy transport links in Normandy we required an enormous concentration of bombers; the great distance of Silesia from our bases completely rules out an operation of this kind.

The bombing of the installations themselves is beyond the capabilities of our bomber fleet, because the distance is too great for a night attack. The Americans could perhaps fly a daylight sortie, but that would be a costly and reckless operation. It might be a fiasco, and even if the installations were destroyed, I am not at all sure it would really help the victims. There only remains one possibility, and that is to bomb the camps and if possible also drop weapons at the same time, in the hope that some of the victims manage to escape. . . . Even if the attack on the camp were to succeed, the chances of escaping would admittedly be small.

Nevertheless, I would like to suggest we present the project with all the facts to the Americans, to see whether they are willing to try it. I certainly doubt very much whether, after examining the project, the Americans will consider it feasible, and would not wish to raise any hopes.

Sir Archibald Sinclair, British Minister of Aviation, in a memorandum to Anthony Eden, 15 July 1944

On 20 August the US 15th Bomber Squadron attacked the petrol refineries in Monowitz which lay only 5 miles from the gas-chambers of Birkenau. Arie Hassenberg, a prisoner on forced labour in Monowitz, experienced the air raid at first hand: 'We were really glad about the bombs. We wanted just once to see a German get killed. Then we could sleep easier.'

For three years now I have been giving lectures to the troops . . . . They do not believe in the concentration camps . . . you can convince them for an hour or so, then they shake themselves, the spiritual defence-mechanism begins to operate, and after a week the shrug of disbelief takes over again, like a reflex that has been temporarily impaired through shock.

Arthur Koestler, author and journalist, in the New York Times *magazine, January 1944*

In October 1944, when still no bombs had been dropped on Auschwitz, Nahum Goldmann of the World Jewish Congress made a last attempt to change the minds of the military. Having been fobbed off with misleading information by McLoy, the US Assistant Secretary of War, to the effect that it was only the British who decided on bombing targets in Europe, Goldmann came up against Britain's burly Air Marshal Dill. As Goldmann describes it, Dill stated baldly that 'the British had to conserve their bombs for military targets, and that the only salvation for the Jews lay in the Allies winning the war'.

That is where the matter rested. Until the camps were liberated or abandoned, the obstructive attitude of the top military brass, both British and American, prevented the bombing of the extermination camps. It was not the fault of the political leaders – although, of course, more pressure from Churchill or Roosevelt would have helped. The recalcitrance of the generals arose not from a moral deficiency, which many historians accuse them of, but from sheer timidity in the face of imponderable factors. Internal discussions had simply left too many questions unanswered. How would the world react if US carpet-bombing reduced dozens of prison-huts to ashes, instead of hitting the crematoria? Goebbels would gleefully release photographs of charred corpses to the press. What would be the verdict of posterity if, out of fear of further attacks, the SS were to shoot all the inmates straight away? The hesitancy of the armed forces is understandable: bombing Auschwitz was an incalculable risk. David Ben Gurion, who later headed the new state of Israel, had urgently advised against it. He feared that Allied attacks 'would kill a large number of Jews and expose the survivors to the brutal revenge of the Nazis'. The accusations levelled today at the Allies, that by their passivity they tolerated the killing, are misleading. All the calculations of how many Jews might have been saved – or killed – by bombing, are based on false premises. While there is no doubt that in the matter of accepting refugees the Western Powers can be held guilty – their conduct of the war brought an end to the Holocaust; they did not 'allow it to happen'.

However, the verdict has to be different on Stalin, the problematic ally in the anti-Hitler coalition. It is true that the notion of 'race' had no place in Marxist–Leninist ideology, yet by 1942 the Soviet Union had begun systematically to free government departments and institutions from 'Jewish dominance'. The fact that 'Hitler's Fascists' were making the Jewish population the chief victims of their terror did not fit this image. Therefore reality had to be adapted to suit the ideology. When the Red Army liberated Kiev in November 1943, a fully documented investigation of the German massacre at Babi Yar took place. It was there, two years earlier, that Himmler's *Einsatzgruppe* C had shot more than 33,000 Kiev Jews in a few days. In the first draft by the Soviet committee of enquiry we read: 'The Hitler bandits carried out a massive and bestial slaughter of the Jewish population.' However, when the report was finally submitted to the Central Committee of the Soviet Communist Party, having been through several stages of editing, it stated that the 'Hitler bandits' had killed 'thousands of peaceable Soviet citizens'. Stalin had simply had a different slant put on the Holocaust. Similarly, in the report on the liberation of Auschwitz by the Red Army in 1945, there is no explicit mention of the Jews – even though they formed by far the largest group of victims.

Stalin waged the 'Great Patriotic War' solely for the purpose of increasing Soviet power. His objective was to end Hitler's domination and extend his own as far west as possible. In all this the fate of the European Jews interested him not at all. The moral outrage of the west certainly meant nothing to the Red tyrant, who himself had the deaths of millions of his own countrymen on his conscience. Whether someone was a Jew or a non-Jew was immaterial – what mattered was their usefulness to the Soviet Union. The many tens of thousands of Jews who fought in the ranks of the communist partisans were extremely welcome. But a man like Raoul Wallenberg, who saved the lives of Jews, was not. Something which remained a riddle for a long time is today known for a fact: the courageous Swede died in July 1947 in Moscow's Lubyanka gaol – in all probability from an injection of poison. For the KGB, the vague suspicion of espionage and Wallenberg's refusal to become a Soviet agent, were reasons enough to liquidate one of the most admirable campaigners against the Holocaust – a man to whom the American Congress awarded honorary US citizenship, who is also honoured in Jerusalem's 'Avenue of the Righteous', and after whom streets and squares in countless cities are named.

Wallenberg's memorable campaign had begun on 15 October 1944, when the Hungarian Fascists, known as the Arrow Cross, seized power in Hungary and plunged the country into a maelstrom of violence. Armed with submachine-guns, Arrow Cross gangs burst into Jewish homes, SS style, forced the occupants to strip naked, divided their victims' possessions between them and shot men, women and children indiscriminately. At the same time, Eichmann began his deportations again. But because the rail traffic had been disrupted, his men, aided by the Arrow Cross, forced thousands to march to their death.

As an attaché at the Swedish Embassy in Budapest, Wallenberg did everything in his power to stem the great surge of bloodlust that Hitler had released. He distributed thousands of Swedish 'safe-conduct' documents – some of which were produced in the workshops of the OSS, the American secret service – placed numerous 'Jew-houses' in Budapest under the protection of the Swedish crown, bribed Hungarian and German officers, dined with SS men and begged influential Hungarians to intercede on behalf of the Jews. Whenever a new deportation column was being assembled, Wallenberg in his large American limousine was not far away. Eichmann called him the 'Jew-hound', with something akin to respect. In return, Wallenberg described him in a letter to his mother as 'quite a nice man'. Per Anger, who at that time was helping Wallenberg to turn the Swedish Embassy into a rescue centre, describes with what bravura Wallenberg went about his work: 'I was there when a group of fifty students, Jewish students, were to be handed over to the Eichmann squad. It was at the frontier, and Raoul Wallenberg went up and asked if there was anyone there with a safe-conduct. There were only two who had them, so he said to the others: "Well, as I'm sure you remember, the authorities recently confiscated your safe-conduct documents. All of you must have had safe-conducts." They cottoned on quickly. Fifty students stepped forward and were simply taken back to Budapest in a big truck. Once again he had saved lives simply by bluff and ingenuity.'

Tens of thousands of Hungarian Jews have Wallenberg to thank for their lives, as they do another diplomat with heart, Carl Lutz from Switzerland. In doing what they did, the two rescuers placed themselves in mortal danger. However, the many attempts by the Arrow Cross to kill Wallenberg all failed, thanks to his good connections with the secret services. The embassy attaché whose family back in neutral Sweden was making good money from business deals with the Germans as well as the Allies, cultivated contacts simultaneously with the US Secret Service and with the SS, as is revealed in documents dating from December 1944, now held in Washington's National Archive. According to these papers, Wallenberg was a double agent entrusted with a 'secret mission' on President Roosevelt's behalf, but who had simultaneously 'placed himself under the protection of the German Waffen-SS'. His friend Per Anger confirms this: 'Yes, it looks as if the Germans turned a blind eye to everything he did. Perhaps they just thought, well, we have already killed millions of Jews, what are a few thousand more or less?'

Even in the final days before the liberation of Budapest by the Red Army, Raoul Wallenberg was instrumental in foiling a plan by the SS and the Arrow Cross to blow up the entire Budapest ghetto – where 100,000 Jews were still living. After the Red Army marched in, he was summoned to their headquarters in Debrecen. He relied on his diplomatic immunity and on the fact that the Swedish Embassy had also represented Soviet interests in Budapest. On 17 January he returned to Budapest escorted by two Red Army soldiers. He secretly told friends that he did not know whether he was a prisoner of the Soviets or their guest. After that, all trace of him was lost – until the publication of KGB papers more than 50 years later finally shed light on the bitter fate of this 'righteous man among nations'.

Raoul Wallenberg was one of the 'points of light' in a time of darkness, as the German philosopher Karl Jaspers put it – one of those people whose actions give hope to others. For such people, resistance against inhumanity was as selfless as it was natural – and nearly always involved risk to their own life. They deserve that their names should be rescued from oblivion: people like Dimitar

Pesev who, as Deputy Speaker of the Bulgarian parliament in 1943 prevented the deportation of 48,000 Bulgarian Jews at the very last minute. It was thanks to his intervention that the families waiting with their bags packed on station platforms, all over the country, were able to return home only three hours before their scheduled departure. As an old man Pesev said that he had only acted 'as a normal human being'.

Another of the 'points of light' is the Dutch woman, Miep Gies, even though in the end her deed was not rewarded with success. For two long years she fed and looked after the Frank family, who were Jewish, in an attic hiding-place in her house on Amsterdam's Prinsengracht. She knew that she herself could be sent to a concentration camp for 'favouring Jews'. In August 1944 the hiding-place was discovered and the Frank family deported. Only the head of the family, Otto Frank, survived his time in the camp. The diary of his youngest daughter Anne is one of the most moving testimonies of the Holocaust. The brave Miep Gies rescued it from a mountain of papers which the SS bloodhounds had left behind after the arrest. Anne Frank died in Bergen–Belsen.

> The only country which offered to let Jews in was the Dominican Republic; they wanted to take 5,000 Jews and re-train them as farmers.
> *Gerhart Riegner, senior official of the World Jewish Congress*
> *and participant in the Evian Conference*

Almost the entire Danish nation broke ranks from the rest of impotent Europe and stood up for their threatened countrymen. King Christian X protested publicly; the churches called on the people to help. Even the universities closed for a week in protest. Meanwhile the Danish resistance was organising an escape route into neutral Sweden, whose government had signalled that it was willing to accept refugees from Denmark. In this, the greatest risk was of course taken by the individual boat skippers. 'The Gestapo had to let the boats leave harbour to go fishing', Captain Ib Børgensen tells us, 'but they became suspicious when the trawlers came back next morning with no catch.' Swedish shipmates helped out and gave them a few nets full of fish, to keep up the pretence.

A particular example of the willingness to save human lives is provided by the Danish fishermen of the Øresund Straits. In Denmark the Germans did not begin preparing for deportations until October 1943. For over three years the 7,200 or so Danish Jews remained untouched by the Holocaust, because the German authorities did not want to put at risk the smoothly functioning pattern of cooperation between the occupying power and the Danish administration. But the good relationship foundered on the 'Jewish problem'. Unlike many countries occupied by the Wehrmacht, Denmark had no significant anti-Semitism on which the Germans could place hope of assistance with the 'Final Solution'.

My mother had resigned herself completely and said she didn't believe that anyone would help us now. She almost spoke as though the Germans might just as well grab us. By some strange coincidence there was a lady who had got up early that morning and was cleaning her windows. And she saw our family of four walking along in the early hours, and because of the way we were dressed and the way we were walking, she thought, there's something wrong there, that's not an ordinary family; perhaps they're Jews trying to escape. She immediately beckoned to us and said: 'You oughtn't to be out on the streets; you're welcome to come into my house, and I'll try to help you.' It sounded wonderful that there were people willing to help us in that situation. We went into her house and she said we were to stay there for a while, and later on she would bicycle over to see an acquaintance, a man who, as it later turned out, had helped many Jews escape to Sweden. She was a great comfort to us and said: 'Now you'll be able to get away, because I know a man you can trust.' And that is just what happened.

Aaron Skop, Danish Jew, hidden by Danes and taken by boat to safety in Sweden

'They were very confused, they had fear in their eyes', recalls Christian Algreen-Petersen, who organised escapes from the little fishing-village of Søndermarksvej, from his brief encounter with the refugees, 'and because it had to be done so quickly and unobtrusively, there was no time for gratitude.' Admittedly, the actions of the fisherman on the Danish coast were not entirely altruistic. They demanded large sums for the crossing, which sometimes had to be raised by Jewish organisations. 'Of course, the price was very high. They collected a formidable amount of money', Algreen-Petersen confirms, and adds that after the war quite a number of fishermen preferred to keep quiet about their heroism, rather than draw the attention of the Danish tax collectors to the wealth they had accumulated. Nevertheless, the relationship between rescuers and rescued remained unaffected. Year after year refugees from those days still come to the coast of Denmark to give thanks and remember.

The Danish people, Christians, helped their Jewish fellow-citizens to escape. The fact that they succeeded in saving nearly all of them – only 500 out of 7,000 Jews were picked up – is a unique achievement.

> We went on to the deck of the fishing-boat and it was a fantastic sight to see all the lights on the Swedish side. We had never seen them so clearly as we did from the fishing-boat, and we silently thought to ourselves: 'Yes, now we're very near to safety.'
>
> *Aaron Skop, Danish Jew*

Of course, there were some Germans among the 'points of light', who stood out against the Holocaust. The one who became most famous was Oskar Schindler, who with daring and commitment protected the employees in his Cracow porcelain factory from being sent to the gas-chamber. Another of the selfless saviours was Berthold Beitz, who later became chairman of the supervisory board of the Krupp corporation. In 1942, as a representative of the Reich Ministry of Economy in the town of

Borislaw, in eastern Galicia, he witnessed brutal pogroms and decided to try and help the victims. In August of that year he succeeded in rescuing 250 Borislaw Jews from being sent to the Belzec extermination camp – just as they were being loaded on to the train. His pretext was that he needed the people as skilled workers for the oil industry. From then on he did everything in his power to hinder the SS, issued forged work-permits and warned of planned house-raids. In the event of his arrest he had worked out a plan with a Jewish resistance group, who were to free him by force. After the war Beitz explained his conduct: 'From morning till night we saw at close quarters what was being done to the Jews in Borislaw. When you see a woman with a child in her arms being shot, and you have a child of your own, then there's only one way you can react.'

Many of those who used their position to save human lives were members of the military resistance movement against Hitler: men like Hans von Dohnanyi and Hans Oster, the most active resistance members in the foreign section of the Abwehr, the secret service of the Wehrmacht. In autumn 1942 they succeeded in getting fifteen Berlin Jews into Switzerland by declaring them to be German agents. Their chief, the legendary Admiral Canaris, knew about the rescue operation and covered up for them. Nevertheless, it is difficult to accept him too as one of the 'points of light'. This opponent of Hitler was too deeply mired in wrongdoing. As head of the secret service, Canaris was in charge of the 'Secret Field Police', a Wehrmacht unit which had been deployed as a mobile death-squad in the east, alongside Himmler's *Einsatzgruppen*. It was Canaris who signed off the reports of the Secret Field Police. He bore the military responsibility for their activities and we know how greatly this practising Christian suffered under the burden. True, his ambiguous attitude only becomes explicable in the light of the deep-rooted anti-Semitism which this naval officer from the industrial upper crust carried with him. In 1935 he had recommended to the new men in power that the German Jews should be resettled in the 'plundered' German colonies, which the victorious powers of the First World War should immediately hand back. Only by a strict physical separation could the nettle of the 'Jewish problem' be grasped.

Canaris is not an exceptional case among the plotters of 20 July 1944. For many of those officers and politicians from aristocratic or upper-class backgrounds, the focal point of their political thinking was the November Revolution of 1918, which they regarded as a catastrophe. And quite a number of them blamed the collapse of the Kaiser's empire on precisely those 'Jewish-Bolshevist' forces, which ex-corporal Hitler, in the same vague conceptualising, had also made out to be the guilty parties. For this reason, not a few conservatives greeted Hitler's 'seizure of power' with delight. Their latent anti-Semitism was a common denominator with the new wielders of power, whom they otherwise looked on with repugnance.

Generaloberst von Fritsch, whom Hitler had dismissed in 1938 for criticising his war plans, stood for most of the rest of his class, when after being fired he spoke of being engaged in a 'battle against the Jews' which had to be won in order to make Germany 'mighty' once again. Another of the anti-Hitler conspirators, Carl Goerdeler, who was to replace Hitler as Reich Chancellor but was later condemned to death by Judge Roland Freisler in the 'People's Court', as early as 1941 advocated a Jewish state overseas, as far away as possible, and urged people not to forget 'the great guilt of the Jews, who have invaded our public life in ways which lack all customary reticence'.

In 1938, another martyr of 20 July, Fritz Dietlof von der Schulenburg, vehemently called for the exclusion of Jews from all important functions in state and society. Even in early writings of Henning von Tresckow, perhaps the most able intellect in the rebellion, we find the notion that 'the Anglo-American idea, which can also be called the Jewish idea, of democratic capitalism . . . does the dirty work, albeit with the best intentions, for the communist or Marxist idea'. Even the otherwise unimpeachable Pastor Martin Niemöller identified himself with the underlying anti-Jewish sentiment when he said in a sermon in 1935: 'We speak of the "Eternal Jew" and picture a restless wanderer who has no home and finds no peace. And we picture a highly gifted race of people who produce one idea after another with which to delight the world, but whatever they embark on, transforms itself into poison. And what they reap again and again is contempt and hatred, because again and again the deceived world notices the deception and avenges itself in the only way it knows.' It is painful to acknowledge that most of the middle-class anti-Nazis were guilty of a fundamental anti-Semitism. The strong identification of the postwar Federal Republic with the uprising against Hitler has for a long time prevented people from coming to grips with this unpalatable fact.

> Of course, Stauffenberg and I spent many evenings in discussion. There were two things that disturbed us. One was Adolf Hitler's lack of military professionalism, and the other was being implicated in infamous acts which were committed in the rearward areas of the Russian Front.
>
> *Ulrich de Maizière, then an officer on the Wehrmacht General Staff*
>
> The persecution of the Jews, which has been carried out in the most inhuman, deeply shaming and irreparable ways, is to cease.
>
> *From Carl Goerdeler's Government Declaration No. 2, in the event of the successful assassination of Hitler*

In the search for truth, blanket judgements serve no purpose. The brave men and women of 20 July deserve neither beatification nor condemnation. The anti-Semitic statements quoted here date from a time before the murder of millions of Jews began. With the spread of knowledge about the Holocaust a radical rethinking began to take place among the plotters against Hitler. While most of them had welcomed the marginalising of the Jews and their exclusion from public life, very few could countenance mass murder.

Admittedly, one of those few, the Reich Director of Criminal Police, Arthur Nebe, is proof of how imprecise the frontiers could be. As early as 1938 Nebe was in contact with the resistance and in his capacity as an SS *Gruppenführer* was an important source of information for the conspirators. After 20 July he went to ground but was caught and executed. For a long time he was considered a 'moderate SS officer' and was honoured in the same breath as men like Stauffenberg and Oster. Only later were voices raised in protest against this. For Nebe, as leader of SS *Einsatzgruppe* B, which he joined voluntarily, had by his own reckoning been responsible for the murder of 45,467 people up to the end of October 1941. Later, in the deportation of gypsies from Berlin he had been notable for his murderous ingenuity and punctilious cooperation with Eichmann. Arthur Nebe was thus a highly active perpetrator in the Holocaust, personally guilty of tens of thousands of deaths. From the conspirators' standpoint, it may perhaps have been convenient to seek the cooperation of a leading SS man holding the levers of Nazi power, and to postpone dealing with his crimes until after a coup d'état – but in the eyes of posterity this evil man has no place on the roll of honour of anti-Hitler resistance. Not every Saul has his Road to Damascus.

What was the attitude of the other conspirators to the Holocaust? The sources are unambiguous on this: horror and repugnance were predominant. Even in 1941 Augustin Rösch of the anti-Nazi Kreisau Circle was lamenting 'the horrifying plight of the Jews'. Father Alfred Delp spoke of a 'loathsome capital crime'. In 1944 Goerdeler recorded that Hitler had 'bestially destroyed millions of Jews'. Oster and Dohnanyi were almost in despair at the appalling news of the mass murder. The government declaration, prepared for the event of a successful coup, expressly ordered an immediate halt to all forms of 'persecution of the Jews'.

If one compares this determined attitude with the anti-Jewish tone from the years prior to 1941, then it is clear what kind of learning process the majority of the conspirators had been through. Their anti-Semitism was not the 'murderous' kind, of which the American sociologist Daniel Goldhagen accuses even the resisters themselves, but was aimed more at marginalisation. That they were anti-Semitic at all must, from today's viewpoint, be a matter for criticism and regret. Even the reproach that it was this kind of 'moderate' anti-Semitism which first prepared the ground for the Holocaust, must be taken seriously. Yet the anti-Hitler group do not deserve to be ranked alongside the murderers. On the contrary: beside the saving of the Reich, putting an end to the Holocaust was the main motive for the resistance.

One very revealing source for this is found in the transcript of interrogations which the head of the Central Office of Reich Security, Ernst Kaltenbrunner, compiled after the revenge campaign against the plotters. One can only assume that one or more of the accused under interrogation chose their words very carefully, in the hope of saving their heads from the noose. Nevertheless Kaltenbrunner comes to the clear conclusion that the men of the resistance 'while basically approving of anti-Semitism, rejected the methods by which it was put into practice. In some cases humanitarian motives were emphasised, rather on the lines that the procedures had not been humane enough and went against the German nature. At other times questions of political expediency were raised, on the grounds that the swift and rigorous removal of Jewry has provoked great tension with the rest of the world.' A remarkable summary and one which must have a disturbing effect on all those who have held up the 20 July plot as a shining example for modern democracy. Berthold von Stauffenberg, the brother of the leading conspirator, makes this statement: 'As regards domestic policy we largely approved of the fundamental ideas of National Socialism. Their racial thinking seemed to us sound and progressive.' It was only its implementation that the plotters thought had been, as Stauffenberg puts it, 'taken much too far'.

It is especially tricky to portray the military figures at the head of the resistance movement who, in the line of duty, came into direct contact with the mass killing. *General der Infanterie* Carl Heinrich von Stülpnagel, the army commander in France, by disarming and arresting SD and SS officers in Paris on 20 July 1944, had played a courageous and successful part in the planned revolt against Hitler. Stülpnagel was firmly convinced that peace negotiations had to be opened with the Western Allies immediately. However, when it emerged that Hitler had survived Stauffenberg's bomb, Stülpnagel's superior, *Feldmarschall* Kluge, put an end to the putsch in France. After attempting unsuccessfully to commit suicide, Stülpnagel was executed in Berlin's Plötzensee prison on 30 August 1944.

After the war, the general was accepted as having been one of the leading lights of the resistance. In 1998, no less a figure than

Germany's Minister of Defence, Volker Rühe, called him 'exemplary in his attitude and the performance of his duty'. But was he? In the summer of 1941 that same Stülpnagel, then commander-in-chief of the 17th Army when it invaded Galicia, was a noted advocate of the war of racial annihilation. On 30 July 1941 he ordered the closest cooperation between his soldiers and the murderous thugs of *Einsatzgruppe* C. At the same time, in reprisal actions he specified that 'first and foremost Jewish and communist inhabitants' were to be shot. On 12 August he again decreed in military orders 'an intensified battle against Bolshevism and its principal supporter, international Jewry'. A good example of the consequences of such orders can be found in the occupation by the 295th Infantry Division, part of Stülpnagel's 17th Army, of the small town of Zloczow, whose population was predominantly Jewish. Lipa Tennenbaum, who owned a printing firm there, saw a German army vehicle stop in a busy square: 'Two NCOs jumped out and without warning drew pistols and began firing into the crowd.' A report by *Einsatzgruppe* C on incidents in and around Zloczow, noted tersely: 'Wehrmacht has right kind of attitude towards Jews.'

The instructions issued by Carl Heinrich von Stülpnagel were, of course, part of a chain of command whose supreme inspirer was Hitler himself. But there was no urgent necessity to pass on these incitements to crime. Many other officers, also prominent members of the resistance, gave impressive proof of this. One of the men who openly resisted orders to commit atrocities was Helmuth Groscurth, a staff officer with the same 295th Infantry Division and later a member of the anti-Nazi group around Admiral Canaris. In early July Groscurth was already complaining about 'mass shootings and murders in the open street', though admittedly he achieved nothing by this. Some weeks later he intervened with Army Group South against the killing of ninety Jewish children in Byelaya-Tserkov. They were locked up without food or water after their parents had been shot by *Sonderkommando* 4a. After a good deal of dithering, *Feldmarschall* von Reichenau reached a decision and announced that he 'recognised the necessity of removing the children and wished to know when it had been done'. The children were shot and Groscurth was officially reprimanded.

In the case of other members of the 20 July plot the evidence is more ambivalent. We know that by reason of their military position Stauffenberg and Tresckow were intensively involved in 'combating partisans', an operation which implicated the Wehrmacht in the Holocaust. Yet on the basis of available documents it is impossible to estimate the extent to which they themselves supported the war of annihilation or, conversely, how much they contributed to the will to resist it. In Tresckow's defence, it has been proved that in the operational area of his Army Group Centre he played a significant part in amending the 'Martial Law Decree', whereby German soldiers were to be exempt from prosecution for crimes against the civilian population. Thus, administratively at least, by 1941 he was opposing the wrongdoing. The notes which Stauffenberg was carrying with him on the day of the attempted coup condemned in unmistakable terms 'allowing prisoners-of-war to starve' and 'carrying out manhunts'.

What importance was ultimately given to the murder of the Jews, among the many different motives of the 1944 plotters, is shown by their attempts to involve the most senior ranks of the armed forces in the rebellion. Yet field marshals such as Kluge and Manstein cannot be exonerated simply by their pointing out the intolerability of the 'Jewish horrors'. It was only the plotters themselves who, after a long process of rethinking, recognised the moral dubiousness of their earlier behaviour. Their decision nevertheless to go to their death in order to achieve the moral restoration of their country, deserves the highest respect. In honouring the memory of those men, a historical reappraisal of their long path to resistance can do nothing but good. A clear awareness of history does not require heroic legends but rather an explanation of the circumstances at that time.

This is a scandal, and a stain on the honour of the German people. We will all have to pay dearly for it one day, and may the Lord forgive us for the terrible things that are going on.
Major Claus Schenck, Count von Stauffenberg, writing in May 1942 to Hans Herwarth von Bittenfeld on the subject of Jewish persecution

At lunch yesterday it was rather interesting because the man I was lunching with had just come from the *Gouvernement* and gave us genuine information about the SS furnaces. Up to now I hadn't believed it, but he assured me it is true. In these furnaces 6,000 people are dealt with every day.

Count Helmuth James von Moltke, member of the anti-Hitler resistance, in a letter to his wife, 10 October 1942

How misleading crude stereotypes can be is exemplified by a man who used his close family relationship with a top Nazi to throw sand in the works of the Holocaust. In September 1945 two men named Göring sat in the cells of the Nuremberg war-crimes tribunal. In court one of them, Hermann, the chief defendant and once Hitler's designated successor, played the part of a defiant victim of the victors' justice and had just one year to live. The other, his brother Albert, faced the arrogance of his interrogators undaunted. 'I was never in any way a Party member', he wrote in his justification. 'I neither persecuted nor mistreated any Jews, but on the contrary helped dozens of them. A list of the 34 most important people whose lives I saved at risk to myself, can be found in the papers that were taken from me.' His plea did no good. By now the interrogation officers had questioned hundreds of Nazis, each one of whom had claimed to have secretly rescued Jews. And now, of all people, the brother of the *Reichsmarschall*!

In fact, in this case the American officers were completely wrong. Albert was what in Yiddish is called a 'mentsh', a real human being. Though a bon viveur and ladies' man, Albert was always willing to use his name, his money and his documents to help those in need. He once persuaded Heydrich to release some Czech resistance fighters from the cellars of the Gestapo. On another occasion he set up an account at the Orelli Bank in the Swiss capital, Bern, which provided funds for Jews to escape via Lisbon. In the autumn of 1943 he signed passports with his own hand for a Jewish family he had befriended – no Gestapo official dared challenge papers signed with the name 'Göring'. Albert even helped the famous composer Franz Lehár by approaching his eminent brother and getting him to guarantee the safety of Lehár's Jewish wife. But after the war no-one would at first believe that the brother of Hermann Göring had been an anti-Nazi. Albert had to spend more than two years in gaol before the truth finally came to light.

The story of Albert Göring illustrates the problem that the victorious Allies, and others too, had in assessing the attitude of the Germans after the war. Who had been perpetrators, who just went along with things, and who were victims? What was the position of the average German vis-à-vis the Holocaust? This is the crucial question for a whole generation. And it was this question that triggered off the student revolution of 1968. An American scholar named Goldhagen discovered what an explosive subject it is, when he claimed that the majority of Germans had advocated the policy of mass murder. His thesis has generally been rejected by other historians. But the debate over his book about the 'willing executioners' has once again brought to the fore the still controversial judgement on the guilty knowledge and active participation of the Germans.

> The whole Jewish business, as far as one heard or read anything about it at all, was something we simply put out of our minds. There was nothing we could do about it. That should not be forgotten. There was nothing we could do about it. The only way to change it was by coups d'état and assassination.
>
> *Count Johann Adolf von Kielmansegg, former staff officer in the Army High Command and 20 July conspirator*

The usual postwar claim, that one 'knew nothing', is today seen as a cover-up. The Germans not only knew that their Jewish neighbours were suddenly disappearing – and quite a few acquired the vacated homes or enriched themselves from the property of the persecuted victims – they also suspected, as the war dragged on, that in the east the Jews were meeting a dreadful fate. Since 1942 the BBC had been regularly reporting on the Holocaust. At the beginning of that year, when the novelist Thomas Mann spoke on the air about 'mass killings by poison gas', he was probably heard by one million Germans, in spite of the ban on listening to 'enemy' broadcasts.

British aircraft dropped millions of leaflets containing facts about the crime – one of these, which originated from the 'White Rose' resistance group in Munich, spoke of 'a most terrible crime, to which nothing in the whole of human history can be compared'.

> If you said you were prepared to join the resistance, you first had to overcome your cowardice. That's not so easy. And I must say I had to get a grip on myself time and again, to stifle the fear that rose up inside me. So as to be ready to do something that was out of the ordinary.
>
> *Ulrich Gunzert, former Wehrmacht officer, who distributed 'White Rose' leaflets*

Of course, leaflets and BBC broadcasts were suspected – in many ways quite rightly – of spreading propaganda. Quite a number of Germans still preserved memories of the 'enemy propaganda' of the First World War, which had claimed that German soldiers cut Belgian babies into pieces. However, what could not be dismissed as propaganda were the surreptitious reports of mass shootings behind the front line, which many husbands, brothers and sons brought home with them on leave. Soon hundreds of rumours were in circulation. Had not Hitler himself repeatedly threatened the 'annihilation of the Jewish race in Europe'? Martin Bormann, the dictator's cabinet secretary, noted in 1942 in a circular to all *Gauleiter* that 'within the population in various parts of the Reich' there were 'discussions about the "very severe measures" against the Jews, especially in the eastern territories'. Another observation from the viewpoint of the perpetrators provides proof that their activities were widely known about: when, in the spring of 1943, Goebbels launched a propaganda campaign about the mass murder of Polish officers by the Red Army at Katyn, it proved surprisingly counterproductive. Reports by the Security Service on the public reaction stated that 'a large part of the population' considered the fuss about Katyn to be 'hypocritical, because on the German side, Poles and Jews have been done away with in much larger numbers'.

Precise figures about the degree of public knowledge of the crimes simply do not exist. Despite all the suspicion and rumour, it was probably at most a small minority who were really able to assess the monstrous dimensions of the murder. The resistance member, Helmuth James von Moltke, an accurate observer of the situation in Hitler's Germany, wrote to a friend on 25 March 1943: 'At least nine-tenths of the population do not know that we have killed hundreds of thousands of Jews. People go on believing they have merely been segregated and are living roughly the same kind of life as before, only farther east; perhaps rather more meagrely, but away from air raids.' Ironically, the very scale of the Holocaust made it easier to disguise – the systematic murder of millions was for most people at the time simply not conceivable. 'We could not and would not believe it', is how German-Jewish Inge Deutschkron describes the moment in late 1942, when she received news of the gassings. And according to an opinion poll in the USA, even at the end of 1944, the majority of Americans believed that fewer than 100,000 Jews had been killed by the Germans.

What kind of resistance was there to the ostracism that was visible to everyone? Who dared to offer their help to the persecuted? The courageous people who, despite the threat of severe penalties, risked their life to help others were of course the exception. Even so, the 6,000 Jews who survived illegally in Berlin as 'submarines', had at least the same number of 'Aryan' helpers, who provided them with food, made hiding-places available to them and shielded them from denunciation. One of those who were rescued in this way was the popular German quizmaster, Hans Rosenthal, who as an adolescent was hidden in a summerhouse by an old lady in the Berlin suburb of Lichtenberg, for the last two years of the war.

We couldn't have survived if it hadn't been for Germans who supported us with food and lodgings. There was a woman we knew who kept a brothel – Alexanderplatz was that sort of area – and she hid people in her annexe.

Miriam Rosenberg from Berlin, defined by the Nazis as a 'half-Jew'

There was no lack of smaller gestures of sympathy. The persecuted Jews noticed that particularly after the compulsory wearing of the Star of David had been introduced. Jewish children were slipped apples by total strangers. Victor Klemperer, the brilliant chronicler of Jewish survival, recounted after the war how people he did not know would suddenly shake him by the hand. He also describes a characteristic incident in a Dresden tram: a young man brusquely ordered an elderly Jewish woman to give up her seat for him, whereupon two other 'Aryan' men jumped up and offered their seats to the woman.

On the other hand, it is true that there was that section of the population which remained morally indifferent or openly hostile. These were the Germans who made the Holocaust possible in the first place: as denouncers on whom the Gestapo could rely right to the end of the war; as accomplices, whether in the guise of *Blockwart*, a kind of Nazi concierge, or as policemen or railway employees; or simply as the silent majority. Yet at what point does a lack of courage turn into guilt? Hitler's Reich was ruled by terror. From 24 October 1941, public demonstrations of solidarity with the Jews were made punishable by three months in a concentration camp. A house-painter named Louis Birk, who had spoken about Jews dying in gas-chambers, was executed. According to Nazi figures, between 1933 and 1945 three million Germans spent time in prison or a concentration camp, of whom 800,000 were there because of their resistance activities. The Nazis ruled in a climate of fear. Anyone who showed resistance was in the greatest danger. Thus virtually all activities by Germans against the regime and its crimes took place under cover. Secrecy meant survival.

Yet there is only one single example of a successful protest against the Holocaust: in the last days of February 1943, under the code-name 'Factory Operation', the Gestapo mounted the last big wave of deportations in Berlin. Their victims were the 15,000 Jews remaining in the capital, who up to that time were mainly employed as forced labour in factories. As *Gauleiter* of Berlin, Goebbels planned, on Hitler's birthday, to report the city 'clear of Jews'. But his seizure of 1,500 Jews living in 'mixed marriages' misfired, because the 'Aryan' partners staged a spontaneous mass protest in the streets.

> It wasn't resistance in the sense that fighters like Bonhöfer would have understood it, but it was a purely civil resistance based on love, affection and the desire to have one's relatives back again.
>
> *Gisela Meissner, 'half-Jew' by Nazi definition, one of the Rosenstrasse demonstrators*

> They shouted 'give us our children, give us our husbands'. It was like the chorus in a Greek drama. For that time it was something tremendous.
>
> *Gad Beck, half-Jew by Nazi definition, prisoner in the Rosenstrasse collection-centre*

The event took place in Rosenstrasse, a little side-street not far from Alexanderplatz, where a building formerly belonging to the Jewish community had been converted into a collection centre. Under appalling conditions with more than twenty people to a room, the partners of those 'mixed marriages' had been waiting more than a week for deportation. Meanwhile, their partners, children and relatives had gathered in the street outside the building. There were a few hundred of them – mostly women – waiting there in silent reproach, from early morning until dusk. Now and then they shouted: 'Give us back our husbands!' Only after several days had passed did the atmosphere become explosive. Charlotte Israel, who was demonstrating on behalf of her husband, remembers: 'The SS aimed machine-guns at us, "If you don't leave, we'll shoot." The crowd instinctively drew back, but then for the first time we really began to bellow. We didn't care any more. We shouted: "You murderers!"'

On 6 March Goebbels gave in – with Hitler's approval. 'I gave instructions that the Jewish evacuation was not to be continued at such a critical time as this,' Goebbels wrote in his diary, and was referring to the Stalingrad disaster that had just been announced, as well as the first heavy air raids on Berlin, on 1 and 2 March. The Jewish partners of the Berlin mixed marriages were released – and survived to the end of the war. Twenty-four other husbands were even allowed to return from Auschwitz, though until the end of the war the SS kept them in 'protective custody' near Berlin, in fear of what they knew about the death-camp. Massive protest had thus – in this solitary instance – been successful. Hitler and his henchmen feared nothing so much as a reversal in the 'mood of the people', as had been shown by the termination of the programme for killing the mentally and physically disabled. Once the people became restive the Holocaust was under threat.

Sometimes – as my mother told me later – there were so many people in Rosenstrasse that the traffic had to be diverted. It was simply closed off. Sometimes there really were nearly a thousand people milling around. At times it was quiet and at times they shouted: give us back our children, or our husbands . . . that sort of thing. It was pure protest, passive resistance, and it worked. In the centre of the capital too. Today it is simply incomprehensible. One of the women there was Frau Friedenthal, an embodiment of the Nordic type, which almost none of the Nazis were. Tall, blonde, blue-eyed; she had two little granddaughters or nieces, little fair-haired girls with plaits, proper little German kids. She went up to the SS guards standing outside the building with machine-guns and shouted at them: 'You bloody swine. You're shooting at German women and children here' – she showed them her little girls – 'instead of protecting us from the Russians on the Eastern Front. Aren't you ashamed of yourselves, you swine?' What were the little SS men supposed to do? They were totally flabbergasted, and of course they had no answer. Three or four hours later the two machine-guns were dismantled and then taken inside the building. After that there was only an ordinary sentry at the entrance.

Hans-Oskar Löwenstein de Witt, prisoner in the
Rosenstrasse collection-centre

On the evening of 3 March 1943, when the situation in Rosenstrasse was beginning to force those in authority to retreat, a goods-train with open cattle-trucks left the station in Berlin's Quitzowstrasse, bound for Auschwitz. Its cargo consisted of 1,763 Berlin Jews – women separated from their husbands, mothers from their children. SS men had rounded up these people and transported them to the station in full view of the public. As the train pulled out, there was no-one on the platform to protest.

CHAPTER SIX

LIBERATION

KNOPP/DREYKLUFT

Sometimes there are those particularly clear, blue-skied spring days, when it is almost impossible not to feel on top of the world. One such day was 16 April 1945. Chatting excitedly, a group of people from Weimar were walking up Ettersberg hill, not far from the historic city. Although the path was steep, they strode out briskly. 'There was something of a spring excursion about it all', one of the walkers later recalled. They were not short of things to talk about. The Americans had occupied the city and people were already saying that 'the Hitler business' would soon be over now, thank God. The previous day General George Patton, commander-in-chief of the US 3rd Army, had summoned the burgomaster of Weimar. A representative group from the city were to assemble on the path up the hill. 'I want at least a thousand', Patton specified, 'half of them men and half women. And make it one-third ordinary workers, one-third affluent members of society and as many party members as you can find.' From Weimar today, if you look carefully, you can see there the sombre memorial to the Buchenwald concentration camp rising among the trees. It is only a few miles as the crow flies, from Goethe's summer-house to the scene of horror.

'On the way back, no-one spoke at all', recalls Gisela Hemmann from Weimar, who was present on that April day. When they reached Buchenwald they were received in silence by a group of GIs and led into the camp. As they entered they could read the cynical words wrought in iron over the gateway: 'To each his own.' Without a word, the soldiers divided the crowd into columns of 150 people each and conducted them into the interior of the camp. And then the men and women of Weimar saw why they had been sent on this strange expedition.

Through the open doors of some of the furnaces parts of half-burnt human bodies could be glimpsed. They saw the room in which people, supposedly undergoing a medical examination, had been shot through a crack in the wall. They saw the chambers in which prisoners had been hanged on butchers' hooks. Once outside again they stood aghast in front of mountains of piled-up corpses, countless pallid bodies, grotesquely intertwined, reduced by starvation to a mass of skin and bone scarcely recognisable as human. And they saw those who had survived the hell that was Buchenwald: in the barrack-huts emaciated, lemur-like figures were crammed, three, four or five together, on the bare boards of wooden bunks. With bony hands they tightly gripped the mess-tins which seemed to be their most important possession. All her life Gisela Hemmann has never been able to forget the moment she entered the first hut. 'They didn't say a word, but their eyes followed us as we walked through the room. Those eyes were so big, so reproachful, and filled with such immense suffering.'

The photographs which the Allies took of the liberated concentration camps in April and May 1945 came as an appalling shock to the general public abroad – and in Germany as well. Reproduced and displayed a thousand times since then, they have become synonymous with the horror of Nazi tyranny: vast heaps of corpses, bulldozers pushing the pale bodies into mass graves, half-dead survivors standing apathetically in front of the cameras. The days following the end of the war, the oft-quoted 'Hour Zero', were for the German population also days of confrontation with the horror and the beginning of a hesitant examination of the past, one which has not yet been completed.

> Without doubt we are dealing here with what must be the worst and most repulsive crime that has ever been committed in the entire history of the world, committed with the use of scientific equipment by nominally civilised people in the name of a great nation and of one of the foremost peoples of Europe.
>
> *Winston Churchill writing on 11 July 1944 to his Foreign Secretary, Anthony Eden*

> We in Europe thought we had achieved the highest stage of civilisation. But beneath this veneer of civilisation a savage and diabolical brutality had gained control. This must never be allowed to happen again anywhere.
>
> *John Dobai,*
> *Hungarian Jew*

The pictures from the liberated camps have today become the symbolic 'Image of the Holocaust'. And yet they only present a very incomplete view, the devastating finale of a development that had begun years before. Buchenwald, like Dachau and some others, was not in fact intended as a camp for Jews. It was only towards the end of the war that the survivors of the death-marches from camps in the east had found themselves there. The millions of victims who, in Treblinka, Majdanek, Belzec, Chelmno, Sobibor and Auschwitz, were mechanically and systematically slaughtered, went to an anonymous death. Their suffering can only be described by the witnesses who saw with their own eyes things which words can scarcely encompass. What the world at large saw was the outcome of the last year of the war, the final act in a dreadful theatre of horror. In the last twelve months of its existence the system of annihilation achieved the final stage of 'perfection', when the Jews of Hungary were deported and destroyed with pitiless speed and precision. A few weeks later it broke apart between the advancing fronts and dragged its victims into the abyss. It was in this period that the 'victims of the last hour' died in overcrowded railway wagons and on death-marches – precisely the people whom those in charge of the liberation wanted to rescue from the racial frenzy. As many as half the 700,000 prisoners who, in January 1945, were still dying a slow death in the camps, did not live to see the arrival of the Allies. This final catastrophe coincided with the end of the Reich – as the man behind the annihilation had intended.

> In reality, no wrong is being done to the Jews. They are being allowed to live according to their own racial and ethnic laws . . . . I have given instructions that their personal safety is to be carefully respected.
>
> *Lázló Endré, of the Hungarian Ministry of the Interior, writing in the magazine of the Arrow Cross, the Hungarian Fascist movement, on 15 May 1944*

> Satellite governments who expel citizens to destinations named by Berlin must know that such actions are tantamount to assisting in inhuman persecution or slaughter. This will not be forgotten when the inevitable defeat of the arch-enemy of Europe comes about.
>
> *Anthony Eden, British Foreign Secretary, in a statement to the House of Commons on the threatened deportations from Hungary, 30 March 1944*

Back in the spring of 1944 a change was about to take place in the extermination camp of Auschwitz–Birkenau. A number of prisoners who, like the Slovakian Jew Rudolf Vrba, had been in the camp for some time, sensed that a new evil was in the offing. For several weeks he had observed suspicious activities. Prisoners were detailed to lay new track leading to the road which connected the two sections of the camp, Birkenau I and Birkenau II. This brought the sidings ever closer to the gas-chambers. The new arrivals would be sent directly from the wagons to the gas. He had seen other activity at the old pits in which the SS had burned the corpses of the murder victims, before the crematoria had been built. Apparently the pits were being prepared for renewed use. This could only lead to one conclusion: Auschwitz was being prepared for 'capacity operation', at a level never seen before. Was it in fact possible to increase the horror to a yet higher pitch? And whom would it strike? 'The SS made jokes about Hungarian salami', Vrba recalls. Of course, Hungary! Now the axe would also fall on the Jews in one of the few countries in Europe that had remained as yet largely untouched by Hitler's racial vengeance.

By this time several million people had already been done to death. Only in Hungary did there still exist a Jewish community of 750,000 – the largest in Europe. Under the leadership of the ageing 'Regent', Admiral Miklós Horthy, Hungary had leaned heavily towards Nazi Germany. Backed by the Third Reich the country had been able to extend its frontiers substantially, but now, in the fifth year of the war, the Hungarian leadership sensed that it had manoeuvred itself into a hopeless situation. In the war against the Soviet Union its own troops had suffered devastating defeats; and by now the Wehrmacht was in retreat on all fronts. The days of the 'Thousand Year Reich' were numbered and the once-powerful ally would be the loser of the future. With little attempt at concealment, the government in Budapest put out peace feelers to the Allies. If Hungary really were to change sides, as Hitler and his generals well knew, the south-eastern flank of the Reich would be exposed, virtually unprotected, to the assault of the Red Army. It was vital to use every means to prevent Hungary from breaking ranks. Yet the considerations which were keeping Hitler's interest in Hungary alive were not exclusively military.

On 17 April 1943 the dictator had invited Admiral Horthy to Klessheim castle near Salzburg. The 'Jewish problem' had still not been solved, Hitler reprimanded the elderly head of state. 'What am I supposed to do?' replied Horthy helplessly. 'I can't strike the Jews dead.' But that is just where he would be proved wrong in the most horrific way. Less than a year later, on 18 March 1944, the head of state again had to report to Klessheim. And this time Hitler's aim was sharper. Still nothing had been done about the pressing 'Jewish problem', he warned, and furthermore he had precise information about the treachery which was leading Hungary in the direction of the Western Allies. Hour after hour the Führer blustered, accused and threatened. From time to time he sent Horthy and his delegation back to their rooms like a bunch of schoolboys. Hitler had 'orders to issue', was the cryptic reply to their enquiries. The play-acting achieved its purpose: the Hungarian leadership, cut off from the outside world, was thoroughly intimidated. Late that evening Hitler dismissed the exhausted Horthy and his entourage. The dictator's parting message was brief and to the point: by midnight at the latest the Wehrmacht would march into Hungary. The trap had been sprung.

The following morning eleven divisions crossed Hungary's borders from every direction. Neither the civil population nor the Hungarian army offered any resistance to the invaders. 'Instead of gunfire and hostilities we were plied with wine, bread, meat and cigarettes by cheering Hungarian villagers', was the later recollection of a man who celebrated his 38th birthday that same day – Adolf Eichmann. For him the Holocaust of the Hungarian Jews represented the climax of his 'career'. In the Hotel Majestic, high above Budapest, he set up his annihilation headquarters. He was assisted by a group of proven 'specialists', men like Siegried Seidl, former commandant of the Theresienstadt concentration camp, Theodor Dannecker, who had already gained notoriety in the deportation of Jews from France, Bulgaria and Italy, and Dieter Wisliceny, head of deportation in Slovakia and Greece. In total the *Sonderkommando Eichmann* consisted of less than 200 men. Two hundred – to round up three-quarters of a million people, lock them up in ghettos and then deport them? Eichmann knew that his team would be adequate, because he was sure of active support from the Hungarians.

'Over the years I have learnt from experience which hooks to use for which fish', the executioner boasted. In plain language this meant that the Hungarians were to solve their 'Jewish problem' themselves; Eichmann's staff would merely lay down the guidelines. And with tragic consequences the method proved highly effective. The new prime minister, Döme Sztojay, was more than willing to go along with his plans, while the Ministry of the Interior harboured two fanatical anti-Semites, Lásló Endré and Lásló Baky. Their sphere of operations was defined as 'all matters affecting the Jews'. They baldly announced that 'the Royal Hungarian government will soon have cleansed the country of Jews'. That was the Hungarian way of describing the German objectives which Eichmann's team had sketched out at a conference at the Mauthausen concentration camp in Austria on 10 March.

What the Nazis are setting out to do in Hungary today is of course only the continuation of what, on a larger scale, they have already done in Poland. We know that breed of men to which those who order and carry out such policies belong. But let them be warned. Everyone who takes part in this killing will be called to account and subjected to the full penalty for his crimes.

Warning broadcast in the German-language service of the BBC, 11 July 1944

Without those anti-Semitic traditions, it would not have been so easy for the Germans, for the SS and the Nazis, to induce the Hungarian administration to exterminate nearly half a million people in the space of weeks. And without any compulsion at all.

Paul Lendvai, Hungarian-Jewish journalist and historian

When the Germans marched into Hungary I had a non-Jewish boyfriend. He was the only one who cared about what would happen to us. Our neighbours wanted nothing more to do with us. We were completely isolated from the non-Jewish community.

Renée Firestone, Czech Jew in Hungary

The devious plan looked like an extract from the timetable of the state railways. Hungary was to be divided up into zones and then 'cleansed' in stages. The annihilation campaign was to begin in the Carpathians and the Siebenbürgen region and finish – with bureaucratic neatness – in the capital, Budapest. How long would this take? The targets looked ambitious. In roughly three months, or probably rather less, Hungary would be 'clear of Jews'; after all the routine was familiar enough by now.

It had already been used in Germany, France, Belgium, Holland, Poland and other countries. But here in Hungary the executioners wanted to present their 'masterpiece'. Marginalisation, segregation, deportation, annihilation – the usual story. It was a replay of the Holocaust, but this time speeded up.

The first to be hit were Hungary's Jewish intellectuals. On the day after the German occupation, patrols swarmed out and indiscriminately seized doctors and lawyers whose names they had jotted down from the telephone book. In the country secret police knocked on doors and searched Jewish homes for valuables. The men assured the enraged householders that they would not be troubled further. The Jews merely had to hand over everything they possessed. This was an utter lie, like everything else the Jews were led to believe, in order to keep them calm before the impending deportations.

In the Budapest synagogue well-fed men in uniform suddenly appeared, who readily gave accounts of their wonderful life as 'Jewish labour' in 'German arms factories'. More and more frequently Jewish families received mysterious mail through their letter-box. 'It's lovely here in Waldsee', wrote 'relatives' who had supposedly left their home-towns and moved to a 'labour camp'. The sinister system of lies and deception was successful because it exploited to diabolical perfection the fears of those affected. The Hungarian Jews were not living on an island of ignorance in the midst of the terror which was being played out in the rest of Europe. As early as the summer of 1942 the BBC's Hungarian Service had reported the mass murder of Jews. Many Hungarians, both Jews and non-Jews, listened to that station.

There had been frequent rumours and even detailed accounts of atrocities committed against Jews. But was it possible to believe things that were literally 'incredible'?

On 7 April 1944 the Auschwitz inmate Rudolf Vrba, together with his friend Alfred Wetzler, succeeded in escaping from Auschwitz–Birkenau. They made their way unrecognised over the Beskyd mountains into Slovakia. There, in the town of Zilina they made contact with leaders of the Jewish community, but their reception was not what they had expected. With exaggerated politeness the officials sat them down, asked for an account of their experiences – and refused to believe them. 'And why should they? How could they? Human consciousness first had to be educated merely to take in the concept of mass murder on the scale of Auschwitz', Rudolf Vrba recalls. Separated from each other, the refugees were intensively questioned and more and more of the details stood up to examination. 'Gradually the fairy-story of resettlement areas fell apart in their minds. It was an appalling blow for them.'

Vrba and Wetzler dictated their descriptions of the Auschwitz hell in a report which came to be known by the name of the 'Auschwitz Protocols'. The document which listed with astonishing accuracy how many Jews had met their death in Auschwitz, and in what manner, was copied to the Jewish leaders in Hungary, to the Vatican, Switzerland and the Western Allies. To this day Vrba is deeply disappointed that the report which he had brought over at the risk of his life did not produce more effect. He has called the Protocols an 'unheeded warning'. 'I had thought it would make a substantial difference, if I were to succeed in breaking out of Auschwitz and broadcast the truth to the outside world. The secret was out and thus the essential precondition for the uninterrupted progress of the mass murder was removed.' It is certainly true that in its detail and precision the 'Protocols' exceeded anything that had gone before. By spring 1944 Auschwitz was no longer a secret. Yet the tragedy of the Hungarian Jews took place in broad daylight.

Anyone who had a rifle, a pistol, a whip or merely the certainty that he was not one of the persecuted, could blackmail other people and force them to do unbelievable things.

Paul Lendvai, Hungarian-Jewish journalist and historian

It was an outburst of hatred made manifest. People were given complete liberty to decide the life or death of others. I didn't see many German soldiers doing it. There were some SS men involved, whom we recognised by their uniforms, but it was the Hungarians who were particularly zealous in their work. They felt they were conducting a cleansing operation in their country.

John Dobai, Hungarian Jew, describing the killing of Jews in Budapest in late 1944

In Siebenbürgen, the Carpathians and other rural areas of Hungary the Jews packed up their belongings and boarded trains which initially shipped them to transit-camps. The calmness with which they accepted their fate only appears incomprehensible at first glance. Even though many may have been filled with dark foreboding, for the past few years most of them had been protected by the Hungarian government. Why should things suddenly be different? 'Good Lord, it was already March 1944 and we were sure that Hitler's war was over.' That is how Renée Weinfeld, from the little town of Uzhorod in north-eastern Hungary, attempts to explain this fatal mistake. The Red Army had already reached the Polish frontier, the British and Americans were in Italy. What more could the Germans do to the Jews at this eleventh hour?

Even the Jewish leadership called for calm. The message they sent out was that, for 'reasons of safety', Jews living near the battle-front were to be evacuated. It sounded perfectly plausible, especially from the mouths of their own top people.

As before in other countries, in Hungary too Eichmann knew how to make his victims assist him, with tragic consequences. Following the tried and tested pattern he had ordered the setting up of a Central Jewish Council for the country, which in future would act as a mouthpiece, passing on the occupiers' instructions to the Jewish population. Having been betrayed all along the line by the Hungarian government, the Jewish officials saw no alternative but to do as the Germans told them. On 19 May – when the Auschwitz trains had already been running for four days – the Jewish leaders appealed to their community to trust them. Any doubts, they said, were based on 'vague rumours' spread by 'dubious sources'. Eichmann had pulled out all the stops to convince the leading Jews that by cooperating with the enemy they could prevent the worst from happening. Sceptics were given the executioner's personal attention. He certainly understood how they felt, Eichmann said with feigned sympathy, sitting at his desk in the Hotel Majestic, to which he invited Jewish leaders for frequent discussions. Of course, the situation of the Jews in Hungary was 'extremely difficult', smirked the man who had personally brought about that very situation.

On 5 April the tactics of the annihilator reached a new height of perfidy. Rudolf Kasztner, head of the Jewish-Zionist Rescue Committee, made him a tempting offer: what price, he asked, would Eichmann demand to abandon the deportations. Kasztner was no dreamer; he knew that deals of this kind had already been successfully struck. As he hoped, Eichmann proved pliable. After referring back to Heinrich Himmler, he summoned the Zionist leader again. 'I am prepared to sell you one million Jews', Eichmann declared. 'Goods for blood – blood for goods. You can take that million from any countries in which there are still Jews. You can take them from Hungary, Poland, from the eastern territories, from Theresienstadt, from Auschwitz, wherever you want. Who do you want to rescue? Women of child-bearing age? Fertile men? Old people? Children? Take a seat. Let's talk!'

Kasztner grasped at the straw which Eichmann held out to him. Every day without deportations was a day gained in the race between annihilation and the end of the war. In return for the promise of shipments of coffee, tea, soap and tungsten by the ton he would stop the deportation, Eichmann promised. In addition he demanded 10,000 army trucks for the Eastern Front. In order to drum up the ransom money, Kasztner sent an emissary, Joel Brand, to Istanbul, to negotiate with the Allies. Eichmann was happy to let him go. He was sure he would come back, since as a guarantee he was holding Brand's children and his wife, Hansi, who had to report daily to the Hotel Majestic. Today Hansi Brand energetically defends the actions of her husband and Rudolf Kasztner. 'It wasn't a pact with the Devil, it was a rescue attempt.' Many survivors of the Holocaust have reached a different verdict on this. After the war Kastner was publicly accused in Israel of corruption and betrayal of the Jewish cause. He sued for libel and in 1958 Israel's Supreme Court largely upheld his claim. But Kasztner himself did not live to hear the judgment. A year earlier he had been murdered by an extremist in the open street.

The 'blood for goods' deal never went through. On 20 July the BBC reported that the offer had been rejected. In the end the Allies refused to get involved. Whether behind Himmler's and Eichmann's offer there lay more than merely an attempt to keep the Jewish officials occupied, while the deportations continued behind their back with undiminished speed, is something that will never be known with certainty. But one thing was revealed by this macabre cat-and-mouse game: Heinrich Himmler, *Reichsführer-SS* and supreme executor of the genocide, was putting out cautious feelers, offering to act himself as a 'negotiating partner' with the Western Allies.

> They told us we would be taken to Germany to work for the German Reich. Perhaps we would be helping with the harvest or working in the munitions industry. It seemed to make sense. I think, when you're in danger, you don't want to see the danger, only the way out. And the way out for us was that we would work hard, and soon the war would be over and we could go home again.
>
> *Renée Firestone,*
> *Czech Jew living in Hungary*

'Do let's go,' the nineteen-year-old Renée Weinfeld begged her father. 'It surely can't be worse than it is here.' Within a few days the Hungarian Jews in their home towns would have to suffer the complete programme of marginalisation and segregation of the Jewish population: the yellow star, the cutting off of post and telephone, the ban on using public transport, the withdrawal of employment, and finally being corralled into an enclosed area of town. The conditions there were scarcely to be endured, or so it seemed to those who did not yet know what was awaiting them in their next 'residence'. The trains would take the Jews to a 'labour camp', they were told again and again. Renée's father was sceptical, but he really had no other choice. On 15 May the Weinfelds left Hungary on one of the first deportation trains.

For the final destruction of the Hungarian Jews Rudolf Höss, one of the most 'experienced' of the mass murderers, had returned to Auschwitz, where he now made sure that the death-mills were grinding with pitiless precision and at an unprecedented speed. Day after day the trains rolled in – as many as 14,000 Hungarian

Jews were being expelled from their homeland every day. For most of them the route ran without a stopover straight to the gas-chambers of Birkenau. 'The trains had not even been emptied before another lot came in', recalls Dagmar Ostermann, a woman who was in Auschwitz when the 'efficiency' of the death-factory broke all previous records. 'There was no more time for pulling out gold teeth or cutting off hair; it just had to be done wham-bam. Wham-bam.' Since the crematoria could no longer keep up with the flow of corpses, the bodies of the gas-victims had to be burned in open pits. Day and night the stench of charred flesh hung over the camp. Auschwitz inmate Norbert Lopper describes the horror: 'In the dark we always had this glow from the fire-pits before our eyes. The blokes in the *Sonderkommando* told us that sometimes the gas wasn't strong enough to kill everyone. So not all of them were even dead when they were burned.'

At such a tempo even the seasoned team of Eichmann and his henchmen ran up against their limits. Chiefly, they lacked enough trains to deliver the 'freight' on schedule. For these were now needed to keep on top of the precarious military situation. Eichmann appealed to Himmler, who always proved cooperative in such cases, and was given the trains he asked for. The 'war against the Jews' had this time taken precedence over the war on the front line. While the Western Allies had landed in Normandy on 6 June and the Red Army was now only a couple of hundred miles from Budapest, the lackeys of the annihilation had managed – by the application of faultless logistics – to deport 435,000 Hungarian Jews in just twelve weeks.

Eichmann was of course just a cog in the machinery. . . . As I once described him, he was certainly not the mass murderer, he was the 'supplier of death'. He herded people into the extermination camps; and the largest numbers were from Hungary. . . . Despite his poor education, which dogged him terribly, Eichmann was an organisational genius.
  Wilhelm Höttl, SS Sturmbannführer, *and a senior member of the foreign secret service in the Central Office of Reich Security*

By 9 July 1944 more than half of those were dead. It was on that day that the Hungarian 'Regent', Miklós Horthy, finally put a stop to all further deportations. Was this due to a belated realisation of the truth? Hardly. Horthy had stood idly by and watched his countrymen being sent to their death by the thousand. 'No-one who has played a part in this act of barbarism will go unpunished', President Roosevelt had proclaimed on 24 March. On 2 July the Americans bombed Budapest. Horthy knew that the long arm of retribution was knocking on his own door. Assailed with protest notes even from the Vatican, and by belated appeals to his conscience from his own family, the head of state finally gave in.

Eichmann was apoplectic when he heard about Horthy's stop order. Someone had drawn a line under his figures, just before he had been able to complete his work. He did not intend to give in meekly. On 14 July he attempted to have a group of 1,500 Jews deported from the Kistarcza camp. But Horthy, alerted by the Jewish Council, immediately had the transport halted. A few days later Eichmann tried again. This time he 'invited' the Jewish Council for 'consultations' and kept the men in his office until the trains had departed.

The Hungarians were simply unaware of what was going on here. They said: 'See that chimney? That's where my relatives are working, the ones who were segregated.' And I couldn't tell them that those were crematoria, because they would have gone to the nearest SS man and said: 'She told me that people are being gassed here.' It was a terrible situation.

Margita Schwalbová, Czech Jew, deported to Auschwitz in 1942, worked as a doctor in the sick-bay

There were people being shot on the bank of Danube, but not by Germans. By the Hungarian Arrow Cross men. They were chained together. One of them was shot and so they all got pulled into the river.

Paul Lendvai, Hungarian-Jewish journalist and historian

In August Himmler put a ban on all further deportations from Hungary to Auschwitz. Was this the end of the Final Solution? It was the end of the mechanical annihilation; a few months later the gas-chambers of Birkenau were closed down. This was not an abandonment of their objectives by the annihilators, but the result of sober calculations: the days of the death-factory were numbered. The Red Army was already on the River Vistula, scarcely 120 miles from Auschwitz – and who knew how long it would be before Stalin's men advanced into southern Poland? What is more, the economic planners had sounded the alarm. The German Reich was short of labour. On their own, prisoners-of-war would no longer be enough to plug the gap that the war had left in the ranks of the conveyor-belt operatives. The reserve of 'Jewish labour' would have to clear the bottleneck.

Reluctantly the paper-pusher in the Hotel Majestic found his hands were tied, yet the Jews from Kistarcza were not to be his last victims. On 14 October 1944 the Hungarian Fascists, the Arrow Cross, staged a coup d'état and overthrew the aged head of state, Horthy. Two days later Eichmann returned to Budapest and greeted the Jewish leaders maliciously: 'You see, I'm back again.' Three months had passed, during which the remaining Jews in Hungary might have hoped that the end of the war would lift the threat to their lives. There had been no more deportation trains for a long time. By now the Soviets were only 60 miles from Budapest. Then Eichmann despatched 40,000 Hungarian Jews on foot towards the Austrian border. The marches began on 6 November and cost thousands of lives. Yet they were only the beginning of the countdown to insanity for which the concentration camps in the east were bracing themselves.

The provincial ghettos are like sanatoria. The Jews have at last begun to live in the fresh air and to exchange their old lifestyle for a healthier one.

Adolf Eichmann, writing to the Hungarian leader,
Miklós Horthy, in 1944

In the early days of January 1945 the wind blew glowing scraps of paper between the blocks of huts in Auschwitz. For days now the stench from the crematoria had been overlaid by smoke from other fires which had been lit between the barracks. SS squads were hastily trying to burn the documents, lists and files in which, with typical German thoroughness, they had kept a tally of the millions of deaths. On the horizon the dull rumble of artillery could already be heard. It would probably only be a matter of days before the Red Army arrived.

That this day would come had been obvious for a long time to those in charge. As early as the spring of 1944 *Reichsführer* SS Heinrich Himmler had given instructions on the spot to the executioners for what was known as 'Situation A'. Should the opposition arrive at the gates of the concentration camps, absolute authority of command would be transferred directly to the camp officers. By then there would anyway be nothing left to control from Berlin; and Himmler knew that. He and the other leaders of the Third Reich knew exactly what would face them, should the scale of their atrocities become public. There could be no doubt that on the day of their military defeat the full might of the law would descend on Hitler's henchmen.

But how could they ensure their tracks were erased? In the death-camps numerous victims of the Nazis' racist frenzy were still alive – just. Every one of them could give an account of what had happened there. The plan which Himmler and his thugs devised sealed the fate of hundreds of thousands: all prisoners left in the eastern camps were to be 'evacuated', as it was euphemistically termed. In simple language this meant that the inmates of the death camps close to the front line were to be taken back to the heart of the Reich, at whatever cost. No witness to the horror was to fall into enemy hands alive.

On 10 January 1945 we were told we were going on a march and had to pack our things. Under my prison clothes I put on a pair of blue trousers and a jacket, which I had secretly purloined from a shipment of clothing. My plan was, on the way, to take off my prison uniform and escape. We marched in a column through the town. An old man took my arm and asked: 'Can I hold on to you? I can't walk too well.' So for the time being I couldn't break away from the column. I walked along with him for a while, until he and other old people who could no longer walk were loaded on to a horse-drawn wagon. We came to a crossroads and turned on to the road towards Auschwitz, where we came across a woman selling roses; and people asked her if they could buy some. It was grotesque to see a transaction like that in the face of death, but the German guards were tired and let them buy the roses. I seized the opportunity, stripped off my prison garb and, as the rose-seller turned to go, I took her arm and walked with her. 'What are you up to?' she asked, and I said: 'I'm escaping from a concentration camp.' The woman took me home with her and showed me the way to the town, which was liberated by the Russians a few days later.

Karl Horowitz, Polish Jew, who was on the march from Plaszov concentration camp to Auschwitz

Of the 130,000 people listed as being in the Auschwitz camp in August, over half had left by the end of the year, the majority being Polish and Russian prisoners who the Germans feared would rise up against them. However, the most important witnesses were silenced on the spot: the prisoners in the *Sonderkommando* had been forced to burn the corpses of their fellow-victims after gassing. Now, many of them had to take the same route along which they had escorted so many others before. Clothing, jewellery and other valuables – the loot from a state-organised grave-robbery – left the camp in an endless convoy of vehicles. Then bricks, timber, lime and cement were loaded and sent back to the Reich for 'further use'.

In autumn 1944 the convoys were still setting off at a fairly leisurely speed, but in January, when the Red Army's Vistula–Oder offensive caused the German Eastern Front to collapse like a house of cards, panic suddenly broke out. There were still countless thousands of prisoners left in Auschwitz and there was little time left to 'evacuate' them.

As the Russians approached, the Germans became nervous, they got panicky. They began to destroy the crematoria, and one day they drove us out from our huts. We walked with thousands of other prisoners, first of all to Auschwitz. It was 18 January 1945 and very cold, 23° below zero celsius.

Dario Gabbai, Greek Jew, in the Birkenau
Sonderkommando

That march was a nightmare. Each of us had been given a large loaf of bread to eat on the way. But we threw them away as we marched. We hadn't the strength left to carry them. The SS men gave the prisoners their rifles to carry.

Norbert Lopper, Viennese Jew, who took part
in the death-march

And so it was that the pitiful remnant of those millions who, in the previous months, had been shipped eastwards in cattle-trucks and goods-wagons from all over Europe, were sent on another journey – this time in the opposite direction. And this time under conditions that even the inmates of Auschwitz, who had already seen hell, could not have pictured.

In mid-January the mass evacuation began from the camps at Auschwitz, Gross-Rosen and Stutthof, on the Bay of Danzig, which were under the greatest 'threat' of capture by the Red Army. On the evening of 18 January the hour of departure for the Auschwitz inmates had come. 'For the first time I noticed that they weren't counting heads in Auschwitz', the German Jew, Hans Frankenthal, tells us. 'Everyone was running around in chaos. The SS men were in a terrible panic and were firing in the air.'

Like many of his fellow-prisoners, for the past hours he had been thinking feverishly about the options open to him. Those unfit to march would be left behind, the guards had announced impassively. Hans Frankenthal's knee had a suppurating infection.

In fact he could not put one foot in front of the other. But what would happen to the ones left behind? There was no shortage of rumours going round. 'The SS will shoot everyone', some were saying. Others thought they had heard that the camp had already been mined with explosives, so that it could be blown up as soon as the marchers had gone. Frankenthal and his brother decided to join the march. That night, they and 58,000 others staggered out from the gates of Auschwitz.

The only ones left behind were some 9,000 invalids, ignored by the few remaining SS guards who continued working frantically to remove all tell-tale traces. Lacking even minimal medical care and nourishment hundreds of prisoners died in the last days before liberation. The Italian Jew, Primo Levi, who had been left behind, seriously ill, in the Buna satellite-camp of Auschwitz, later recalled the days of waiting which dragged on, between the departure of his fellow-victims and the arrival of the Red Army. 'We lay in a world of the dead and of maggots. All around us the last trace of civilisation had disappeared.'

We only marched at night. Presumably because the population were not meant to see us, like skeletons dressed in rags.
Arno Lustiger, Polish Jew from Bedzin, describing the death-march to Gross-Rosen and on to Buchenwald

You were afraid and so you walked faster. Fear and marching faster; that was the feeling that dominated all others, the naked fear of death.
Paul Lendvai, Hungarian-Jewish journalist and historian, who escaped from a death-column heading for Austria

We were no longer human beings in the accepted sense. Not even animals, but decomposing corpses, moving on two legs. . . . The dead didn't trouble us. We still wanted to survive.
Reska Weiss, Jewish woman from Czechoslovakia who took part in the death-march

On 27 January soldiers of the 1st Ukrainian Front trod through knee-deep snow towards the main gate of the Auschwitz–Birkenau camp. They were unable to understand the cynical inscription, *Arbeit macht frei*, above the barrier. And no-one had prepared them for the scene that confronted them. Huge crematoria lay in rubble and ashes; the last of them had been blown up by the SS only 24 hours earlier. The dense network of watchtowers had been abandoned. The searchlights which had probed along the high-tension electric fence were now dead. In neatly arranged storerooms the Red Army troops found: 836,525 women's dresses, 348,820 men's suits, seven tons of women's hair – collected for the manufacture of mattresses – spectacles, shoes and dentures in piles the height of a man. And behind the barbed-wire fence grey figures were standing, lying or crawling. Men, women and children, clad in stinking rags from which bony yellow limbs protruded: the 'Moslems' of Auschwitz stared out at their liberators with expressionless eyes.

> We didn't know how long that march would last. As I walked I saw the telephone-poles along the road and said to myself: Roman, you'll walk to the next telephone-pole, and then to the next one, and the next. I think that enabled me to survive. Had I known I still had 5,000 or 10,000 telephone-poles ahead of me, who knows whether I'd have made it.
>
> *Roman Frister,*
> *Polish Jew*

> The worst thing on a death-march was death, of course. Death was there all the time, because people who could no longer walk – and there were many – were told by the soldiers: 'Sit down by the roadside, please; you can't walk any further.' The rest of us carried on, then we heard shots; they were dealt with, they were shot.
>
> *Jules Schelvis, Dutch Jew, describing the death-march*
> *to Tomaszow*

Auschwitz inmate Anita Lasker Walfisch was one of those to whom liberation had been denied. She recalls today that she almost felt a feeling of relief as she passed through the gates of Auschwitz. After all, what could be worse than that hell? 'The fact that we were getting out of there at all was incredible for us. We had long resigned ourselves to the idea that we would only leave Auschwitz as smoke. This gave us a spark of hope.' However, most of her fellow-victims knew that the 'evacuation' did not mean rescue. Hard as the guards tried to keep the inmates in the dark about the military situation, the marchers nevertheless suspected that the Russians were only a few miles away as the crow flies. Hans Frankenthal was seized by a profound despair as he watched the camp dwindling behind him. 'As we marched, we felt we were going in the wrong direction. We were actually walking away from liberation.'

For most of the Auschwitz prisoners the road led initially to Gross-Rosen in Silesia – after a few days or weeks there they would be taken back to one of the camps in Germany or Austria, to Buchenwald, Bergen–Belsen, Flossenbürg, Mittelbau-Dora, Dachau or Mauthausen. Those who survived have called the evacuation measures 'death-marches'. They remember them as the most dreadful part of their martyrdom. Like gigantic grey caterpillars the endless columns crawled through Poland, East Prussia or Silesia. The paper-thin prison clothes afforded no protection at all against the cutting winter wind. 'We dragged ourselves in bitter cold through snow that was 30 or 40 centimetres deep', Hans Frankenthal recalls. 'Icicles hung from our eyebrows, we were trembling with cold but were so exhausted that we couldn't even carry our blankets.' Along the route, the marches left a trail of death; stragglers were shot on the spot. The instructions for the 'evacuation' of the Stutthof concentration camp were unambiguous: 'Escape attempts and mutinies must be ruthlessly broken up by the use of weapons.' The guards decided arbitrarily what constituted an 'escape attempt'. It was significant that these instructions were headed 'sentry and shooting duties'. After only a few miles the edges of the road along which the tormented victims dragged themselves were littered with corpses. The prisoners desperately tried to encourage and urge one another on. Zdenka Ehrlich, who was made to march from Auschwitz towards Silesia, describes the struggle to stay alive: 'We marched in ranks of five. Those in the middle slept and the others led them. It is actually possible to fall asleep while your feet keep going automatically – one, two, one, two. . . .'

Like Zdenka Ehrlich, most of the other prisoners were completely exhausted even before they left the camps. The result of months of undernourishment and brutal forced labour had already used up their last reserves of strength. The forced march was now too much for them. Every yard was a hellish torment. The prisoners had no goal in sight, and no concept of one; it was a matter of surviving the next few steps. If the marchers were given anything to eat at all, it was hardly enough to quell their agonising hunger for more than a few moments. Most of the marches lacked any kind of coordination, since the roads were clogged with military vehicles and with the hordes of refugees fleeing westward ahead of the Red Army. Shelter was only available if the prisoners happened to come across a barn or farmhouse along the way. At the end of the day they simply dropped exhausted on the ground where they stood. When the ragged army got moving again the next day, they left behind the corpses of those who had died of cold or starvation during the night.

What torment can a human being endure? Many prisoners lost that last spark of will to survive, the spark they had been able to preserve through all their time in the concentration camp. In the certain knowledge that they were signing their own death-warrant, they let themselves drop behind. Soon afterwards the echo of shots at the rear of the column announced to those at the front the fate that had befallen their companions. Elie Wiesel, whose memoir entitled *Night* is one of the most moving testimonies in the history of the Holocaust, found himself quite simply longing for a bullet from a guard's gun: 'Death enveloped me to the point of suffocation. It clung to me. It was as though I could touch it. The thought of dying, of being no more, began to entice me. To feel nothing more, neither cold nor fatigue, nothing. To jump out from the ranks and let myself sink down on the edge of the road. . . .' One prisoner in every four who left Auschwitz in January 1945 died on a death-march. And for those who reached their goal after long weeks of marching, the horror was not over. It merely took a different form.

> On all the roads and tracks in Upper Silesia, west of the River Oder, I now found columns of prisoners struggling through the deep snow. The guards in charge of these shuffling processions of corpses generally had no idea where they were supposed to be going.
>
> *Rudolf Höss, former commandant of Auschwitz, describing the death-marches from Auschwitz to Gross-Rosen*

> Instead of staging a comprehensive massacre in a certain spot, the method they applied was to despatch potential victims, who were already half starved, on long marches or to transport them in overcrowded trains, with no other objective in view than their annihilation.
>
> *Report by the Department of Civil Affairs of the US XIIth Corps, 27 April 1945*

In the remaining camps within Germany the situation of the inmates had dramatically worsened in the first weeks of the new year. Thousands upon thousands of captives from the east were flooding into camp complexes which had only been designed for a few hundred or a thousand prisoners. One of the needle's eyes through which the proverbial camel had to be pushed was a camp in Lower Saxony, not far from the town of Celle.

The name Bergen–Belsen has horrifying resonances. Yet if the war had come to an end six months earlier, Bergen–Belsen would probably be known only to local historians as just one place among many, too many, where Jews were held captive under inhuman conditions.

But during the spring of 1945 the camp was transformed into an ante-room of Hell. Built in 1943, Bergen–Belsen was originally intended to accommodate what were known as 'exchange Jews'. Himmler planned to hold a group of 'privileged' prisoners here, with whom he wanted to blackmail foreign countries into releasing Germans who were interned there.

In autumn 1944 the first transports arrived there from Auschwitz–Birkenau. What awaited them was a few extra makeshift tents erected in the mud. Many of the prisoners were ill, usually with tuberculosis. In the camp which had cynically been given the title 'Recovery Camp', their fate was not recuperation but death through neglect. Deprived of all medical attention, the life-expectancy of the patients, who included a higher than average proportion of women, was often only a few days or weeks.

In spring there began what has in retrospect been called the 'Inferno of Bergen–Belsen'. Ever more columns of half-dead, sick and starving prisoners dragged themselves in through the gates of the camp. Despite the enormously high mortality in the camp, in the end 60,000 people were crammed into tents, huts and barracks.

In Bergen–Belsen only a few prisoners died as result of violence by the guards. There was no further need here for gassing or shooting. 'In Auschwitz they murdered people', says Anita Lasker Walfisch, whose road of suffering brought her here from Auschwitz. 'In Bergen–Belsen they just left them to peg out.'

The sanitation in the camp beggared description. 'The whole of the camp was like one big cess-pit', is the way the prisoner-doctor, Dr Leo, describes it. He was waging a hopeless war against typhus, tuberculosis, dysentery, and cholera which spread like wildfire in this swamp of mud, excrement and insects. The emaciated inmates could put up no resistance against the plagues. Most of them suffered from digestive ailments, which meant they could no longer control their bowel movements. Those who could not get up relieved themselves in their bunks; and the filth dropped from the upper tiers on to those lying underneath. In Camp II, where the guards had crammed 10,000 prisoners, there was neither a water-tap nor a single latrine. A large number of the inmates had completed an odyssey through many different kinds of camp but the survivors are unanimous in condemning Bergen–Belsen as the most nauseating place they had ever seen.

The guards made no effort to control the hellish scenes that were being played out before their eyes. How little would have been needed was demonstrated by the improvised rescue-squad from the British army, a few weeks later. The neglected inmates were denied even minimal nourishment. Two slices of bread and a pint of watery soup per day – by March, in many parts of the camp, nothing at all was issued for days on end. In their desperation, many could not help themselves and were reduced to eating parts of the corpses of their companions. Such was the level of dehumanisation to which they had been reduced by the callousness of the guards. According to a statement by Dr Leo, after the war, there were at least 200 cases of cannibalism in Bergen–Belsen.

As the final month in the apocalyptic history of the camp began, the clearing squads had abandoned the hopeless battle against the daily increase in the mountains of corpses. 'This half-existence that is all I am left with', noted the Bergen–Belsen inmate, Hanna Levy-Hass, in her secret diary, 'I spend it in the company of other ghosts, living or dead. The corpses, the real ones, are still here with us, in our beds.' The bodies lay on the bunks, or between the huts and in the streets – turning a greenish colour in the spring sunshine, in every stage of decomposition. The repugnant stench of the camp could be smelt for miles around. 'There is no way of describing that smell', says Anita Lasker Walfisch. 'Bergen–Belsen was one great pile of corpses, nothing but corpses, rotting corpses.'

> There seems to be no limit to what humans can suffer, or perhaps those who survived were the confirmation of a miracle. . . . A strong will-power had possessed me, a demand to go on living, and an inexplicable conviction that I had a right to life.
>
> *Reska Weiss, Czech Jew who took part in a death-march*

It was in the hell of Bergen–Belsen that Anne Frank died too, the Dutch girl whose name often stands for all those victims who went anonymously to their deaths. 'Surely, one day this terrible war will be over, one day we will be people again and not just Jews', she confided to her now-famous diary. Like so many of her fellow-sufferers she would not live to see the day of liberation.

The end of Bergen–Belsen is among the most bizarre episodes in the final weeks of the war. On 12 April 1945, Himmler's recently appointed 'Special Reich Commissioner' for the camps, SS *Standartenführer* Kurt Becker, reached agreement with the British that the camp would be handed over 'peacefully'. The agreement was chiefly based on the fear on both sides that in the event of fighting in the grounds of the camp an unstoppable outbreak of disease would sweep through the opposing troops. But unlike what happened in other camps, Himmler made no attempt to drive the prisoners onward and out of the reach of the liberators. On 13 April most of the SS guards retreated, though not before staging a macabre dance of death that seemed to spring from some medieval depiction of Hell: 2,000 prisoners were detailed to remove the corpses from the camp streets. Working in fours they dragged the corpses by their arms and legs, using straps of leather or cloth, to the mass graves. All the while the camp orchestra was playing dance-music. 'To cheer people up', as the camp commandant, Kramer, said in his orders.

On the afternoon of 15 April – a Sunday – a group of British officers entered the grounds of Bergen–Belsen. 'Until we went through the gate, it looked like an ordinary camp. . . .' recalls Captain William Roach, who arrived with the first British units. 'I imagined we would come into the camp, the German flag would be hauled down, we would shake hands with the German guards, and they would go on looking after things until our reinforcements arrived. Of course it was nothing like that.'

What did the prisoners think and feel when their liberators were finally standing before them? When they realised that the horror had finally ended? Questions like this have been put to the survivors of the Holocaust time and again. Many of them know that the questioners have a very definite scenario in their mind's eye. Images of the final exchange of fire between SS men and Allied troops, fighting their way into the camp yard by yard knowing that every minute counts. The gates open, the tormentors throw down their weapons and a chorus of cheering rises from a thousand throats. The liberated prisoners stream out of their barracks and fall on the necks of the soldiers, beaming with joy. But there was hardly a single case where it happened like that.

And then when the first British trucks arrived – it's impossible to describe what we felt. But people shouldn't imagine that we jumped about for joy like Red Indians, as is sometimes shown in films nowadays. No, there was absolute quiet in the camp. First of all, few people had the strength to jump about. And anyway it was completely incredible that we were still alive.

Anita Lasker Walfisch, a Jew from Breslau, prisoner both in Auschwitz and Bergen–Belsen

Zdenka Ehrlich was lying in a barrack-hut with about 300 other women. She estimates that at least two-thirds of them were already dead. As she was on a bunk at the back of the hut she could hardly see the door to their miserable quarters. 'Someone said: "They're here",' she recalls. '"Who?" asked someone else. "The British." "Oh", I said. That was the only reaction.' The prisoners lay, apathetic and feverish, in the barracks or on the streets of the camp. In buildings that normally would have provided room for a hundred people at the most, as many as a thousand were packed. The listless inmates lay on bare planks, some with rags thrown over them instead of a blanket. Only a few could raise themselves unaided, let alone walk. In the midst of a terrible chaos of faeces, mud and decomposing corpses the living could only with difficulty be distinguished from the dead.

Captain Roach finds it hard to put into words his first impression of the camp. 'There was no shouting and no waving. The prisoners didn't even smile. They simply stood there, staring at us. And most of us just stared back.'

At first hesitantly and then more quickly, those prisoners who still had some strength left began to realise that their martyrdom had come to an end. The ones who could muster a few words of English spoke to the liberators; some prisoners touched the soldiers in disbelief and stammered out their names. The relief produced in many an energy which they did not realise they possessed. One after another they tried to crawl out of the dilapidated huts and beg the soldiers for food and water. Their delight, anxious at first, finally escalated into a wild frenzy of elation. Only by armed force could the starving people be prevented from looting the field-kitchens and storerooms. In the afternoon Russian and Polish PoWs broke open the locks of the SS stables and pigsties. That evening the aroma of roast pork drifted over the camp. The glow of the fires between the barracks cast a flickering light on the corpses of those for whom liberation came too late.

There were two kinds of guards in the camp; one kind were troops who prevented anyone from leaving the camp and spreading disease. Oddly enough, they were Hungarians. They must have been a Hungarian regiment serving with the Germans. Then, of course, there were the SS, who had been running the camp.

William Roach, former British officer
and liberator of Bergen–Belsen

When we reached Buchenwald, a lot of SS people had already fled. There were helmets and jackets with the SS insignia scattered along the road. The men didn't want to be recognised as SS.

Roy Wolfe, formerly in the US army, liberator of Buchenwald

They didn't say hello, they didn't smile; they seemed embarrassed, not so much out of pity as from a kind of inhibition which locked their mouths and kept their eyes riveted to the grim scene. It was the same familiar shame that came over us after the selections and whenever we witnessed maltreatment, or had to endure it ourselves: that shame which the Germans did not know, but which the righteous man feels for a blame which another has taken on his own shoulders.

Primo Levi, Italian survivor of Auschwitz,
on the reaction of his Soviet liberators

In the first months of 1945, around 35,000 people had perished in Bergen–Belsen. Rescue came too late for another 14,000; they died within weeks of the camp being captured.

Himmler's 'flexibility' in the case of Bergen–Belsen did not come as a surprise. For months the *Reichsführer* had been playing a treacherous double game. In October 1944 he had officially declared the Final Solution at an end. The mass murderer even gave orders that henceforth no Jew in a concentration camp should have 'anything inflicted on him'. But what this meant for the victims was no more than a stay of execution.

Over many years the 'faithful Heinrich' had shared his Führer's racial obsession and put it into effect with eager obedience. But once he recognised the hopelessness of Germany's military position, the executioner turned traitor. For some time he had been secretly putting out feelers towards the USA and Britain. His goal was a separate peace with the West. In the crass thought processes of the SS chief, he would then, as the 'sensible negotiating partner' of the Western Allies, definitely be the right man to step into Hitler's shoes in postwar Germany. 'Himmler the Führer' was an enticing idea for this insignificant man.

Yet for all his dreaming, Himmler's calculations were shrewd. How attractive might it be for the Allies to extend a conciliatory hand to Germany, the enemy whose final defeat was only a matter of time? Himmler still had an ace up his sleeve: the hundreds of thousands of Jews still in the concentration camps were to become the lever with which he proposed to exert pressure on the inexorably advancing Allies. 'They are my best investment', he had told the *Gauleiter* of Vienna, Baldur von Schirach, as the latter later recalled. The executor of genocide believed in all seriousness that this last-minute conversion would be able to save his head from the noose. As a 'pragmatic politician', he told himself, he would once again return to the ranks of civilised mankind. The road to crime had been easy enough. Why should he not return from it with equal facility?

It is terrifying to realise that Himmler's reflections, as crazy as they may seem in retrospect, were at that particular time not entirely unrealistic. Treblinka had been razed to the ground long ago. In Sobibor, lupins were blooming on the ashes of his murdered victims. The SS had succeeded in driving hundreds of thousands of prisoners back into Germany before they were discovered. And perhaps just a small part of the Reich would remain unoccupied. Perhaps he would be able to remove every last trace of his atrocities.

What is more, Himmler knew how to exploit the rift that was more and more clearly opening up between the Western Allies and Stalin's armies. The Red Army had overrun Majdanek and had liberated Auschwitz. Western correspondents were given permission to report at first hand on the things they found there, yet in spite of this, the stubborn belief persisted that they were being duped by 'Russian horror propaganda'. It would be possible to haggle over the price of the lives of the remaining Jews; of that Himmler was certain.

At first his plan seemed to be working out. Time and again Himmler proved open to offers whenever the question of individual groups of prisoners came up. In late 1944 1,684 prisoners were allowed to leave Bergen–Belsen for Switzerland; in early February 1945 1,210 Jews were released from Theresienstadt. Like a Roman emperor he turned his thumb up or down. Salvation or damnation, both rested in his hands. Hitler's hangman still had his favourites. It was chiefly the 'privileged' prisoners, especially from Scandinavia, about whom he allowed himself to be swayed. Nonetheless it was a dangerous game.

Sometimes I tell people, they see before them today a man who was born twice. The first time on my real birthday and the second time on 27 January 1945, when I was liberated from Auschwitz.

Frantz Danimann, survivor of Auschwitz

I'll never forget the day we were liberated. In the morning we no longer heard whistles summoning us to the head-count muster. We were afraid to go out because we thought they might be waiting for us with machine-guns. We waited till noon, then one of the women could stand it no longer. She raced out on to the parade-ground, turned round and ran back to us shrieking: '*Nazi kaputt, Nazi kaputt!*'

Renée Firestone, survivor of Auschwitz

People were shouting, 'It's over, it's over. We're free, it's all over!' I couldn't understand, couldn't grasp it. Then I saw four pieces of black bread and some tins of condensed milk. That alerted my brain. That's bread there and it's telling me we've been liberated!

Ester Brunstein, Polish Jew, survivor of Auschwitz

The Reichsführer vacillated between obedience and treason, between naked fear for his own life and awestruck terror of his Führer. Hitler knew that the war on the Front was lost but he never abandoned the 'war against the Jews', even with his dying breath.

On 8 February the Swiss newspaper, *Neue Zürcher Zeitung*, reported that the release of over 1,000 Jews from Theresienstadt had been obtained 'with Himmler's authorisation'. Hitler went berserk. 'Any German who assists a Jewish, British or American prisoner to escape', he ranted, was to be executed forthwith. Once again, Himmler did manage to elude this fate, but he was teetering on an ever smaller knife-edge. In strict secrecy he pursued his negotiations with contacts which his personal physician and masseur, Felix Kersten, was chiefly instrumental in setting up. Count Folke Bernadotte, the president of the Swedish Red Cross, succeeded in saving 21,000 prisoners, including 6,500 Jews, and bringing them to safety in Sweden before the end of the war. And that was not all: in mid-March Himmler announced to his Swedish interlocutors: 'At the approach of the Allies the concentration camps are to be surrendered in an orderly manner by showing a white flag.' Yet even as they were issued, Himmler's assurances were not worth the paper they were written on. At the beginning of April the Dora–Mittelbau and Buchenwald camps were evacuated. On 19 April the prisoners in Flossenbürg had to move out – on foot to Dachau, 120 miles away. On 20 April the order was issued for the evacuation of Ravensbrück and Sachsenhausen.

On the same day the 'faithful Heinrich' once more paid a dutiful courtesy call at his Führer's birthday 'celebrations' in

Berlin. Together with the other paladins he found himself joining in a macabre chorus of congratulation in the bunker beneath the Chancellery. Once more they shook the hand of the man whom they had followed unquestioningly for the past twelve years, and with whom they bore the joint guilt for one of the worst crimes in human history – and then they departed hurriedly in every direction. Göring muttered something about 'pressing duties', the top brass of the Wehrmacht High Command headed back to their headquarters. Only Joseph Goebbels, the firebrand, remained, with the stoic loyalty of a Nibelung, by his master's side.

Heinrich Himmler set off for Mecklenburg on the Baltic. At 2 o'clock in the morning he arrived at the country property of Felix Kersten, where a negotiator was already waiting for him. He was Norbert Masur, an envoy of the World Jewish Congress. In the night hours an eerie conversation unfolded. It had been necessary to build crematoria, the *Reichsführer* blustered, because such large numbers of inmates of the camps had died in epidemics. The pictures from Bergen–Belsen, which the British had published, had been nothing but scaremongering. It was a 'poor reward' for his work on behalf of the Jews. Norbert Masur could not believe what he was hearing. 'It's time for you Jews and us National Socialists to bury the hatchet', Himmler suggested generously. Bury the hatchet? Masur queried. Come on, we must let bygones be bygones, insisted Himmler. After all, it wasn't so bad, was it? Only with the greatest effort could the Jewish representative maintain his self-control. He produced a list of names. These people, at least, should be released, among whom were 1,000 Jewish women in Ravensbrück and the Dutch Jews in Theresienstadt. Heinrich Himmler seemed amenable. Of course, all the prisoners on the list would be freed. No, from now on no more prisoners would be 'evacuated' from one camp to another.

Even as the *Reichsführer* continued making these cordial promises, only a few miles away a death-march column was shuffling along the road from Sachsenhausen concentration camp.

The evacuations from the camps in the east were intended to remove the prisoners from the hands of the Red Army. As the processions arrived on German territory, the Western Allies were already at the gates of the German camps. On 16 April the armies of the anti-Hitler coalition split the remnants of the 'Greater German Reich' into a northern and a southern half. In these two enclaves of horror the suffering of the prisoners still did not come to an end. In a mindless odyssey, death-march after death-march plodded along country roads, across fields, through the middle of villages and towns – often only a mile or two from the approaching battle-front. The victims wandered back and forth in a crazy cat's-cradle across the diminishing strip of land between the Red Army and the Allies. The rumble of artillery – for the prisoners a long-awaited sound of liberation – was often no more than a signal to change direction once again.

The escorting guards had long since lost their orientation. Who knew whether the camp originally named as their destination still existed at all? Many roads were blocked by a flood of retreating troops, others were taken up by convoys of refugees. Where were they going? How much longer would it take? What was it all for anyway? Drawn on a map, the routes taken by the death-marchers in the last days of the war look like a pattern drawn by a lunatic. One column, which left Flossenbürg concentration camp on 27 March, ended three weeks later in Regensburg, only 50 miles away – after the victims had covered nearly 250 miles in every known direction.

What motivated the guards to keep driving their charges on? Roman Frister, who was with a death-column in April 1945, still asks himself this question today. 'Although the Red Army was breathing down our necks, the guards acted towards us as though the Wehrmacht were at the gates of Moscow. Didn't they see it was the end of the "Thousand Year Reich" that Hitler had promised them?'

Germany lay in ruins and surrender was only days away. But still the guards bludgeoned their victims forward yard by yard. Many were afraid of being shot themselves for 'disobedience', others may have been concerned at the thought that the Allies might catch them with the dreadful 'evidence' and call them to account. But why did they not simply allow the victims to run away and then go to ground themselves? The oft-cited compulsion to obey orders, which so many of Hitler's greater and lesser accomplices pleaded after the war, had long ceased to have any hold on them. There *were* no more orders. The seamless hierarchy of the Nazi extermination system had already broken down. No-one forced the guards to prolong the suffering of their victims by a single day. No-one was checking whether they were continuing to follow the insane orders of the Führer, to 'exterminate Jewry root and branch'.

At the time I felt I had been cheated of something which I should have been entitled to all those years. Each of us had a dream and I remember that my dream was to be sitting at a table laden with food, and to be allowed to eat and eat until I burst.

Ester Brunstein, Polish Jew, survivor of Auschwitz

On the day of the liberation a Soviet officer rode into the camp and told us we were free and could go home. But I remembered that my mother would never come back, I suspected my sister was dead and I didn't know what had happened to my father and brother. I didn't know where to go. What kind of freedom was that?

Renée Firestone, survivor of Auschwitz

On 26 April a group of prisoners from Mühldorf, a satellite of Dachau concentration camp, were bundled on to a train and despatched 'southward'. Two days later the doors were flung open and the guards curtly informed them they were now free to escape as best they could. The helpless victims dragged themselves off towards the little village of Poing, 12 miles east of Munich, in a desperate search for something to eat. They had no inkling that their first steps in freedom were leading them straight into the gun-barrels of a renegade Waffen-SS unit. With brutish violence the SS men drove the prisoners back into the railway trucks, shot those trying to escape and bayoneted people who fell down. In the words of one of the few survivors: 'All along the road from Poing to the station lay our dead and wounded companions, who had been left behind in this manhunt. Some were rolling in their own blood, groaning, pleading for help, but none of us could pay any attention to them. Everyone ran for his life. If you didn't move fast enough you were shot or bayoneted.' The last days of the Third Reich are a terrifying testimony to how much the racial frenzy and fanatical last-ditch resistance had taken on an impetus of their own. The things that happened on those death-marches were the work of lower-ranking SS who had no further need of instructions.

When people in the neighbourhood tried to bring out coffee, the sentries threatened to shoot them. On a street corner nearby another prisoner was being kicked, and passers-by protested. One of the guards was particularly brutal. . . . He threatened the women that if they didn't shut up they would have to join the march.

Liesel Oppermann, a villager in Gauting, near Munich, describing attempts to help the death-marchers

And what about the civilian population? The perfectly ordinary inhabitants of the villages in Bavaria, Lower Saxony or Franconia, through which the death-columns marched, were now being confronted with the reality of the Nazi Reich. The trainloads of deportees were no longer rumbling eastward, no longer heading for some unknown town with an unpronounceable name. The victims of the racial frenzy were now dragging themselves through their own towns and villages, were being beaten up and shot in front of their eyes. Fritz Kunstwald who, as a child, saw a death-march passing through his home village in Bavaria, has to this day never forgotten the horrifying sight: 'Those striped uniforms, those legs sticking out from under the woollen blankets. The feet were wrapped in rags, or stuck into clogs which clattered on the tarmac. I have never heard another sound like it. Nothing makes the same dull, hollow thudding, that clumping noise on the road as those dragging, drumming wooden shoes.'

On the fourth night I escaped. We were marching through a village. It was a very dark night, which helped me. I didn't really want to escape, because I saw no chance of ever finding a place to hide. I was afraid of being denounced, if anyone found me. But before I died, I wanted to eat something one last time. You see we hadn't been fed on the march. During the day we bivouacked in wet fields. Somewhere on the ground we might find a half-rotten cabbage or beetroot or something. We ate them raw.

Towards dawn I heard a dog barking, and was soon dragged out by two men with *Deutsche Volkssturm* [militia] armbands. With them were eight other prisoners, friends of mine, who had escaped the same night, in the same village, and had been recaptured. We were taken to our camp which was in the next village. I knew that this was the last hour or the last kilometre of my life. And I ran away again without caring that I would probably be shot. The bullets didn't hit me. I will never know whether those men were poor shots, or whether, in the last hours or days of the war, they simply didn't want to have another death on their conscience.

Arno Lustiger, Polish Jew, describing the death-march
to Gross-Rosen and Buchenwald

Is it possible to close one's eyes when the terrible truth comes knocking at one's own front door? Roman Frister was being herded along in a wretched procession when, without warning, the column came to a halt beside a tanker-truck from which civilians were drawing water. The scene which was played out here is etched in his memory. 'A prisoner marching in front of me broke away from the ranks, went up to the man at the water-tap and held out his tin bowl with a mute plea for some drinking-water. The civilian was roused from his apathy and kicked the bowl out of the man's hand. It rolled on to the cobblestones and as the prisoner stepped over to pick it up, one of the guards fired. No-one in the queue showed any reaction. As we marched off again, the prisoner was still writhing in his death-agony.'

It is obvious that these skeletons scarcely have more than a few days to live. Their worn-out skin is no more than a grey envelope. It clings tightly to their bony frames. . . . The men relieve themselves unconcernedly on the ground before our eyes. If they still have the strength to utter a few sounds, their gibberish is incomprehensible.

Edmond Michelet, French prisoner, describing the arrival of death-marchers in Dachau

The exception or the rule? There are no historical sources, no validated surveys about the behaviour of the civilian population towards the death-marchers. In the recollection of the prisoners, the 'spectators' seemed transfixed by the horrific scenes that were taking place before their eyes. It required moral courage to protest – especially against the pitiless intransigence of the guards, who were often brutal in preventing any offers of assistance. Women who were herded along on a death-march from the Helmbrecht camp recalled later that a few civilians had been very happy to offer them food and water. 'When a woman tried to hand out bread, a guard threatened to shoot her if she gave any more food away to the prisoners.' A few, like the young Fritz Kunstwald, did display courage. As he stared aghast at the pitiful column coming along the village street, a man suddenly broke away from the ranks. The boy could scarcely recognise the man's face. He had wrapped rags around his head as a protection against the incessant rain. 'Gimme some bread, boy', he implored in a breaking voice. Fritz Kunstwald reacted instinctively: 'At that moment it was as if the whole Hitler Youth business and all the talk about a "nation of Aryan elite" were swept away. I just saw this man, this poor sod who didn't even have a bit of bread.' He ran back into the house and fetched a loaf, which the prisoner fell upon as if possessed. Evidence of humanity was rare in those days, and yet many survivors of the Holocaust interpreted even small gestures as signs that people felt for them and shared in their suffering.

Rachel Knobler, who was taken away from Auschwitz by train, describes the following scene: 'By the railway station at Halle an oldish woman was standing at a window with a baby in her arms. And when she saw us sitting there and shivering, the tears ran down her face. All that time we had never cried, but at that moment we cried with her. The strain of it all melted away and we cried and cried.'

Our tanks slowed down but they didn't stop; they blew straight at and through the barbed wire. . . . When we broke through the first of those fences we got a clue, the first clue, as to what we had come upon, but we had no real comprehension at all of what was to assault our senses for the next hours, the next days. . . . I was an assistant bazooka man, and I had a sack with ten bazooka rounds hung over my shoulder; I had an M1 Garand, and some bandoliers of ammo for that; some grenades hanging one place and another; a fully loaded cartridge-belt. . . . We were fully expecting a fire fight with German troops, whose camp we had just stormed and taken, and we thought they would be angry at us. It turned out there were no Germans present. . . . The prisoners came out of the buildings and just stood there, making me feel foolish with all of that firepower hanging on me. I certainly wouldn't be needing it with these folks. . . . Our platoon sergeant had us form up some and relax, then signalled that horde of human beings to stand fast; he just held both hands up, palms out, and motioned them backwards slowly. Everything was very quiet. The tank motors were just idling slowly.

Harry Herder, former private in the US Army, describing the liberation of Buchenwald on 11 April 1945

In April 1945 moments of liberation were closely accompanied by moments of terror. While medical teams were looking after the prisoners in most of the camps, and many death-columns were taken in charge by Allied forces as they marched, in Dachau 15,000 inmates were still awaiting liberation. The first concentration camp ever to be established in Germany was also one of the last to remain operational. Yet the prisoners sensed that it could not be for much longer. A strange kind of anarchy was spreading through the camp. On 27 April, when the whistle blew for the head-count muster, many simply stayed in their huts. Between the buildings where the SS were quartered rose dark clouds of smoke. The perpetrators were setting fire to their account-books of death. At the very last minute quite a number of the guards attempted to ingratiate themselves with the inmates. In a few hours their victims would be standing at the side of the victors. With the day of reckoning looming, the guards wanted to earn a few 'Brownie points', to be remembered by their charges as being 'not all that bad'. Many of them miraculously found extra food rations and even had a friendly word for everyone.

> Well, the faces were just bone. There was skin on them but that's all. And the fingers, they were dreadfully long. And the arms were so thin. And if you touched them they just fell apart. If you touched them, they just snapped, and that was it.
>
> *Herta Bothe (née Lange),*
> *German wardress in Bergen–Belsen,*
> *forced to bury the corpses after liberation*
>
> It took people to cross the ocean, to free us at the last minute from the murderous clutches of our own 'countrymen'.
>
> *Heinrich Pakullis,*
> *prisoner in Dachau*

But what did the last hours of Dachau still have in store? The guards were getting more and more nervous. On 25 April a Dachau prisoner, Edgar Kupfer-Koberwitz, noted in his diary: 'If something doesn't happen very quickly, it will get more dangerous for us by the hour.' Suddenly people were saying that an order from Himmler had been found. No prisoner was to fall into enemy hands alive! Liberation or apocalypse? The next hours would decide the fate of the prisoners. 'Then they would be shot by machine-gun and the camp was to be set on fire with flame-throwers', a Dachau camp officer named Böttger testified after his arrest. He could even remember the precise time at which the operation was to take place: on the night of 29/30 April 1945.

It was on that night that Adolf Hitler called in his secretary, Traudl Junge, to take some dictation. Weeks earlier he had gone to ground in the warren of bunkers beneath the Reich Chancellery in Berlin. The delusion of a world empire had shrunk to a few square yards for Hitler, his mistress, Eva Braun, and the remnants of his entourage. Yet a venomous hatred of the Jews still burned within him, as his political testament makes clear: '. . . those who really bear the guilt for this murderous struggle: Jewry. Furthermore, I have left no-one in any doubt that this time the millions of children of the Aryan races of Europe who have starved, the millions of adult men who have met their death, and the hundreds of thousands of women and children who have burned to death in bombed cities, will not have died without those who are actually guilty having atoned for their guilt, albeit by more humane methods.' And then at the very end of this macabre document comes the final evil appeal: 'Above all I make it binding upon my successors as leaders of the nation, to uphold meticulously the racial laws and to resist mercilessly that poisoner of all peoples of the world, international Jewry.'

Traudl Junge put down her pencil. She had been able to note down the words without listening to them. Hitler had sworn his hatred of the Jews countless times before, in private conversations with his henchmen, and in public speeches. From the beginning of his career to the end he had clung to this delusion with a manic obsessiveness. Right up to 1945 his words had never altered. But by now they had become deeds.

A few hours later a single shot echoed through the corridors of the Führer-bunker. Adjutants rushed in to find Hitler and Eva Braun dead. The dictator had evaded responsibility for his hideous acts. He had never set foot in those places where his worst crimes had been committed.

In the morning we went through the camp, where people were showing tentative signs of life again. The crematorium had been swept out but the ovens were still full of ash and bones and in one of them lay a charred, twisted skeleton. Outside the crematorium the ashes and bones had been piled into sizeable mountains, beside which stood countless small urns, in which the mortal remains were sent back to the relatives on payment of a fee. . . . The huts stank infernally of decomposition and excrement. Piles of ordure were drying in the air. . . . Every day, between 15 and 20 people were dying in Buchenwald. There was no way of saving them. Our army doctors tried intravenous injections, but many of the living skeletons no longer reacted. They lay on the ground and tried to smile, but their wide-eyed faces were just skin and bone. Those creatures, who stretched their skeletal hands out to us imploringly, had ceased to be human beings. I felt sick.

Saul K. Padover, interrogation officer in the US Army's
Department of Psychological Warfare,
in a 1945 report on Buchenwald

History is very fond of symbols. The very camp which, for the Americans, summed up the Nazi terror, was liberated on the day which proved to be the last in the life of Adolf Hitler. The rescue of the Dachau inmates took place literally just in time, only a few hours before the guards could put into effect the planned elimination of the camp. Built as early as 1933, the year the Nazis took power, Dachau was notorious in Germany and abroad as a 'detention centre for political prisoners'. But what had been going on there in the last few weeks was largely unknown to the liberators. As with most of the other camps, the liberation of Dachau was basically a sideshow. The concentration camps were at no time an operational objective for the Allies, even in the final days of the war. In February 1944 the War Department in Washington had decided: 'It is not our intention to call upon units of the armed services to rescue the victims of enemy oppression, unless such rescues are the direct result of military operations, carried out with the aim of crushing hostile forces.' The Allies wanted to end the war. The extent of the horror which had remained hidden in its shadow came as a great shock to the units, which often found themselves by pure chance at the gates of a camp.

Before we reached the main gate, we came across a railroad siding where freight-cars were standing. Some of the doors were open and as we got nearer I saw that the cars were loaded with piles of emaciated corpses.
Glenn E. Belcher, former US soldier, who saw Dachau
after it was liberated

Near the building was a monster of a chimney, a monster both in diameter and height. Black smoke was pouring out of it. It was blowing away from us but we could still smell it. It was an ugly, horrible smell. A vicious smell.
Harry Herder, former private in the US Army,
describing the liberation of Buchenwald on 11 April 1945

Since all the many corpses were in various stages of decomposition, the stench of death was overpowering.
Felix L.Sparks, then a colonel in the US Army, whose unit was
the first to enter Dachau

'The sight stopped me in my tracks. Dante's Inferno paled in comparison with the Hell of Dachau.' Colonel Felix Sparks, who later described his impressions in those words, had only found out a few days earlier that the notorious camp was situated in the battle sector which his battalion was to capture. In fact, he had already been on the way into Munich with the men of the 157th Infantry Regiment.

The first thing the soldiers saw as they entered the grounds of Dachau was a goods-train, negligently parked in a siding. As an appalled liberator later described it: 'At first glance the freight-cars appeared to be laden with dirty clothes. Then we saw feet, heads, bony fingers. More than half the cars were full of bodies, hundreds of bodies. The neck of one man was so thin and shrunken that it scarcely seemed capable of carrying a head, but the man was still alive.'

I did not learn the full extent of the so-called Final Solution until after the war. In the camp we were so cut off from the outside world that only people who had escaped and then been recaptured could tell us anything. What is more, it was of great help to the Nazis that we considered the things they were said to have done as quite implausible.

Simon Wiesenthal

Quite without warning, the battalion had stumbled on the remains of a death-transport of several thousand prisoners who had been brought from Buchenwald several days beforehand, and which the guards had simply left standing there. Without food or water the prisoners had perished in the confined space of the wagons. The dreadful sight was too much for the American soldiers. Many burst into tears or vomited. 'Once we had seen the freight-train we moved on, boiling with rage and half out of our minds', one GI recalls. 'We're taking no prisoners', the soldiers are said to have muttered to each other. The battalion approached the camp fence. By now the inmates realised that the longed-for liberators were here at last. Colonel Sparks describes the scene: 'They streamed out of the overcrowded huts in their hundreds and were soon pressing against the confining barbed wire fence. They began to shout in unison, which soon became a chilling roar.'

Suddenly people were coming at us from all directions – filthy, starved skeletons with torn rags on their bodies, shouting, screaming and weeping. They ran up to us and grabbed us. Then a terrible thing happened. Some of the prisoners went wild and ran on to the barbed-wire fence to embrace us and touch us. They were immediately killed by the high-voltage current in the wire. I myself saw three people die like that.

From a letter written by Lieutenant William Cowling of the US 222nd Infantry Regiment, which was assigned to Dachau

Having reached the gates, Sparks' men ran into another American unit, the 222nd Infantry Regiment, part of the 42nd Division. Neither of the regiments wanted to miss out on the honour of going down in history as the 'Liberators of Dachau', and so a ludicrous quarrel ensued at the gates of Dachau, about who should take the leading role. The question of who really was 'first', has never been satisfactorily settled. At that moment nothing could have mattered less to the inmates.

No heroic battle for the Dachau camp took place. The few guards who remained were put out of action in brief skirmishes. The shooting certainly did not last long, as numerous inmates can remember. And nearly all the firing was from the American side. 'They were all shot. The Americans did not allow any SS men who fell into their hands to live', noted Edgar Kupfer-Koberwitz in his diaries. There are several photographs in existence which clearly show SS men being executed against a wall by the Americans. Just how many were executed is still difficult to establish. The figures provided by eye-witnesses vary from a few dozen to nearly five hundred.

Most of the guards in Dachau were youths, who had only been posted to the camp a short time before. They were certainly perpetrators. But today there is no longer any disputing the fact that the lynch-law meted out to the Dachau guards was in itself a war-crime. The investigations into the soldiers who took part were discontinued on the personal order of General Patton.

As I watched, about fifty German troops were brought in from various directions. A machine-gun squad from Company 'I' was guarding the prisoners. After watching for a few minutes, I started for the confinement area. After I had walked away for a short distance, I heard the machine-gun guarding the prisoners open fire. I immediately ran back to the gun and kicked the gunner off the gun with my boot. I then grabbed him by the collar and said: 'What the hell are you doing?' He was a young private about nineteen years old and was crying hysterically. His reply to me was: 'Colonel, they were trying to get away.' I doubt that they were, but in any event he killed about twelve of the prisoners and wounded several more. I placed a non-com on the gun. . . .

> Within about an hour of our entry, events were under control. Guard posts were set up, and communications were established with the inmates. We informed them that we could not release them immediately but that food and medical assistance would arrive soon. The dead, numbering about nine thousand, were later buried with the forced assistance of the good citizens of the town of Dachau.
>
> *Felix L. Sparks, then a colonel in the US Army,*
> *whose unit was the first to enter Dachau*

By the afternoon the elation of the freed prisoners of Dachau welled up into wild anarchy. At last it was over! In a frenzy of rage the inmates fell upon their tormentors, beating them in the face with cudgels, stones or their bare fists. Shortly before the arrival of the Americans, several of the guards had disguised themselves in prison clothing or hidden themselves in the grounds of the camp. Here and there cries of triumph could now be heard as a perpetrator was unmasked and lynched on the spot. A US Army Rabbi, Eli Bohnen, who reached Dachau shortly after its liberation, takes up the story: 'To this day I can still picture the emaciated figure of a prisoner urinating in the face of a guard, who was lying there stone dead.' For a long time Bohnen's colleague, Max Eichhorn, felt guilty for not having intervened to stop these excesses: 'We stood aside as the guards were bludgeoned to death, beaten so violently that their bodies burst open and their entrails came out. We watched with less feeling than if it were a dog being beaten. To tell the truth, we felt nothing at all.'

> A US Army major, who was a prisoner in the camp, as well a British naval officer, a Canadian and a Belgian officer, volunteered their services to set up a prisoners' committee, which would restore order in the camp and prepare the prisoners for release. With their help we succeeded in calming the prisoners down.
>
> *Operational report of the 42nd US Infantry Division,*
> *assigned to Dachau in April 1945*

> We had to restrain many of our surviving fellow-inmates who had the strength to walk, because they simply wanted to kill the German soldiers. I must confess that at that moment all of us, even I, harboured the desire to kill. But I thought, please let me not be consumed with hatred, otherwise all this will have been worth nothing.
>
> *Ester Brunstein, Polish Jew and survivor of Auschwitz,*
> *writing after her liberation*

Who has the heart to condemn the vengeance of the freed prisoners, which broke out in Dachau and elsewhere? There were certainly similar excesses in other camps. But they were the exception. Many Holocaust survivors stress how important it was for themselves to have retained their feeling of humanity – even towards their tormentors. After being freed from the Mauthausen concentration camp in Austria, Roman Frister collapsed into a deep coma. When he awoke he saw an SS officer hanging from a beam with his hands tied. Several prisoners-of-war took turns to stab the defenceless man with a kitchen knife. As Frister recalls: 'Someone thrust the knife into my hand and said: "Make him bleed, lad." I could have ended the life of that Nazi, but I couldn't see any sense in it. My clenched fist went limp and the knife dropped from my hand.'

> Americans stand in a semi-circle and shoot at the SS as they surrender. . . . Americans are liquidating SS men who had crawled into lofts, barracks and sewers.
>
> *Frantizek Kadlec, Czech prisoner, in a diary entry*
> *for 29 April 1945*

In Nuremberg in 1946 twelve of those most responsible for the state-organised terror of National Socialism died by hanging. Many others had already disappeared into the faceless masses from which they had emerged decades earlier. Several died by their own hand. In the final days of the war, *Reichsführer* Heinrich Himmler had disposed of the uniform which for all those years had given a menacing demeanour to his paltry figure. Dressed as an ordinary soldier, he attempted to make his way from northern Germany down to Bavaria. His name was 'Heinrich Hitziger' the executioner lied when – quite by chance – on 20 May he fell into the hands of a British army patrol. Rank? Corporal! In accordance with his supposed rank, the British treated him with only moderate interest. Himmler may have put aside his uniform, but not his vanity. He requested a 'personal interview' with the CO of the interrogation camp and lifted his incognito. On 23 May he was called in for further questioning. When a doctor began a routine physical examination, Himmler bit on a cyanide capsule that he had concealed in his mouth. After a brief death-agony, the most feared man in the Third Reich was no more. On 26 May his body was buried by British soldiers in a shallow grave. Today his bones still lie, anonymous and unconsecrated, in a copse on the Lüneburg Heath. Thus the office-bound executioner met the same end that he had decreed for his millions of victims.

Adolf Eichmann succeeded in escaping to South America. There he lived undisturbed until the Israeli secret service tracked him down in 1960 and abducted him to Jerusalem. The perpetrator now gained the attention of world opinion, which had for so long been denied to his victims. In a sensational trial held in front of the international press, he was condemned to death. His body was cremated and the ashes scattered over the Mediterranean. Nothing was to be left as a reminder that he ever existed.

Josef Mengele, the death-doctor of Birkenau, was never caught. On 7 February 1979 – 34 years after Auschwitz – he drowned while bathing in Sao Paolo, Brazil.

Rudolf Höss, the commandant of Auschwitz, was executed at the scene of his crimes. In 1947 he was tried by the Polish authorities and hanged in the grounds of Auschwitz. In the years after the war other thugs of the annihilation system met the same fate. Other leading offenders who survived Allied justice were for the most part pursued by their own consciences – as far as they had any.

In the first years after my liberation I could not sleep at all. My thoughts were always returning to those people I had lost. I had made no new friendships; my only friends were former KZ prisoners. The whole past was alive before my eyes, filled with the dead. For me the war was not over, because I told myself: they are all under the earth, but the ones who put them there are still living untouched, in every part of the world. There are people who were with me in the KZ and for whom those events were like water off a duck's back. But not me. There may no longer be an open wound, but there is a visible scar. I have a wounded soul, and I know that this wound can never heal. It is something I will carry around with me as long as I live.

Simon Wiesenthal

For the prisoners in the camps the day of their liberation did not bring the end to their suffering that they had longed for. 'The end of the camp was not the end of the dying', wrote Buchenwald inmate Jorge Semprun in his diary. The consequences of months of brutal under-nourishment could not be removed from one day to the next. The first thing that freedom meant for the prisoners was food. 'We had nothing else on our minds except eating. I have survived and now I want to eat. People didn't talk about the camp, didn't talk about the war or about freedom, only about food', recalls the liberated prisoner, Herbert Schrott.

For the survivors the end of hunger represented the greatest relief but also the greatest danger to their life. In the Sachsenhausen camp the prisoners had prepared a celebration meal of rabbit, accompanied by rivers of champagne from the SS stores. Sometimes the prisoners had to be forcibly restrained from stuffing themselves full of food indiscriminately. 'Even people seriously ill with high temperatures were running around with ham and wurst, and taking it to bed with them', the freed Sachsenhausen prisoner, Hans Hers, tells us. Well-meaning GIs often handed out tins of jam, corned beef or bars of chocolate, in fact whatever food they happened to have with them. But the prisoners' completely dehydrated bodies were unable to cope with the massive intake of calories. Hundreds died of food-poisoning in their first days of freedom.

He [the American] stood in the middle of the bunk-room, very embarrassed and awkward, only hiding his emotion with difficulty and scarcely able to hold back his tears. Then, with a determined gesture, he laid his sub-machine-gun on the table and went from bed to bed, embracing each of the sick men in turn. He did it very gently and cautiously, as though he might crush those fragile bodies with his strong arms.

Nico Rost, prisoner in Dachau, in a diary entry for 29 April 1945

These people are amputees, but it isn't a leg or an eye they have lost. It is the will to live and the zest for living. . . . They are no longer normal human beings.

Elie Wiesel

Typhus, dysentery, cholera and other epidemics continued to rage among the prisoners with undiminished virulence. There was the risk of fatal infection from the countless rotting corpses which took several days to remove. In Bergen–Belsen, army medical units rushed to evacuate the survivors from the camp area. On 21 May the hopelessly contaminated camp was ceremoniously set alight with flame-throwers and burned to the ground.

In many other camps the gates closed again soon after liberation. Like a medieval city where plague was raging, the camp complexes were hermetically sealed off, in order to prevent the spread of epidemics, but also to discourage looting by the starving prisoners. Many camp inmates were outraged when limits were once again imposed on their freedom with armed force. 'The gates had been opened, but we weren't allowed out', says Chanan Bachrich, who had been liberated by the Americans from a satellite-camp of Dachau. He no longer understood the world. 'I was still wearing my prison clothing, and I just wanted to get some normal clothes on.' Unnoticed by the American soldiers, he managed to sneak off to a neighbouring village. The horrified villagers rapidly handed over a suit, with which Bachrich proudly returned to the camp. For many of the prisoners it was precisely these small gestures that first made them realise their time in the concentration camp was over. But what was to come?

Liberation could not turn the clock back, could not undo what had been done. Why me? Why have I survived? For quite a number of survivors the thought that they had been spared was an agonising burden; they felt guilty towards the millions who had been murdered. Often the only motivation for them to summon the strength to go back to the everyday world was the hope of finding friends or family again, something to cling on to and on which to build a new life. However, for the few children who had survived the Holocaust, liberation represented above all a bewildering change in their world, which at first they could not fathom.

Eva Mozes and her sister Miriam were twins who were used, and abused, by Josef Mengele for his medical experiments in Auschwitz, and so they were spared from being 'selected' for the gas-chamber. They had spent long years in the concentration camp and could scarcely remember a time when they were free. Eva Mozes recalls how, after the SS had abandoned the camp, she went to the river to fetch water. 'Suddenly I saw a little girl of about my age. Her hair glistened, she was wearing a dress with a little coat over it. A school satchel bounced on her back.' Eva Mozes thought her eyes were deceiving her. 'I simply couldn't believe it. There's another world outside. A world where people are clean, where children wear nice clothes and go to school. That's when I first realised that not everyone lived in a concentration camp.'

We saw an uncertain future ahead of us. There was nowhere we could go back to. There was no home anywhere. Where our forefathers had once lived for generations, there was no family waiting for us any more. Only stones, to which clung the stench of indignity and humiliation. This was no happy ending. It was the beginning of something unknown and disturbing. A hollow victory.

Sigmund Strochlitz, Jewish inmate of Auschwitz, who marched to Bergen–Belsen and was liberated there

> After my homecoming it was months before I lost the habit of fixing my eyes on the ground as I walked, as though I was always on the lookout for something edible, or for things which I could quickly pocket and then exchange for bread.
>
> *Primo Levi, survivor of Auschwitz*

About 50,000 Jewish prisoners were liberated by the Allies from camps on German soil. They called themselves 'the rescued remnant'. Yet they were only a small minority among the total of 8 million 'Displaced Persons', or DPs, as those made homeless by the Second World War were called. For them the watchword was 'repatriation'; they were to return to their homelands as quickly as possible. But what did that mean for the liberated Jews? Most of them came from Eastern Europe. The long shadow of Stalin had long since fallen across their native countries. In many cases their long and genuinely involuntary sojourn in Germany was interpreted as collaboration with the enemy. Not many Jews, even from Hungary, would be anxious to return to their home towns, where neighbours had watched or actively helped in their deportation. And from Poland, only a few months after the truth about the greatest crime in human history had been broadcast, there were once again reports of pogroms against the Jewish population.

> I am incapable of hating in the abstract. I can only hate people who I know have done me some wrong. And even then, I can only *feel* the hate. There have been many emotional *acts* of hatred on the part of people liberated from concentration camps. I was never in that situation. I would have been incapable of committing murder, or anything like it. I had the opportunity. I was actually called in to question prisoners-of-war, German PoWs. I could have acted viciously – but I didn't. I valued myself as a human being. I was very grateful that I survived, and I never dreamt of doing to others the sort of things that were done to me.
>
> *Arno Lustiger, Polish Jew, survivor of the death-march to Buchenwald*

For numerous survivors there was only one destination: Palestine, the Promised Land. Until this dream came true, most of the survivors were faced with months of waiting, penned up behind barbed wire. They had been liberated – but they were not free to go where they wanted. It was the British, not surprisingly, who were anything but happy about a mass exodus of survivors to Palestine, since it would create a situation which anticipated the founding of the state of Israel. The period of waiting became an agony of uncertainty for many survivors – left behind in a no-man's-land and not really welcome anywhere.

Long-standing tensions between groups of prisoners, such as between Jews and Poles, were not brought to an end by liberation. In Dachau the liberated Poles threatened to use violence to break up the Jewish celebration of the Sabbath, if they held it in the main square of the camp. A football match between Jewish and Polish teams ended abruptly when the Jewish team seemed likely to win.

Even the relationship between liberators and liberated was far from being as problem-free as it was portrayed in the western and especially the American media shortly after the liberation. The soldiers who were now administering the liberated camps had been trained for armed combat. No-one had prepared them to deal with the profound physical and psychological damage suffered by these human beings. It was particularly the troops who had not themselves taken part in the liberation, but only arrived some weeks later, who seemed baffled and sometimes downright irritated by the strange behaviour of their charges. Why on earth did these people hoard food like that, when there was more than enough available? Why didn't they keep themselves clean when there were ample washing facilities? Why did they steal from each other, eyeing up someone's bread or clothing, whenever he wasn't looking?

Some Americans had great difficulty explaining to the prisoners, who came from all sorts of different countries, that they would have to remain in the camp until the Americans had set up orderly release procedures. In one or two cases officers had to order their men to fire over the prisoners' heads, in order to get their attention and push them back within the perimeter.
Operational report of the US 42nd Infantry Division, April 1945

Approximately two or three months after the liberation, when I crawled from my sick-bed, I opened the window and saw the people in the village – the children, the women – and I knew that I now had to take the second step, from the window out into the world. But I was afraid: my parents' house no longer existed; the world I lived in as a child no longer existed. It was not easy for a boy of seventeen to go out into that world without really knowing what life was.

The worst thing for me was, and is, that the life my parents had planned for me, and the life I imagined for myself, did not exist. I had to lead a quite different life. Perhaps better, perhaps worse, but quite different. A life which in the true sense of the word was not my own. . . . The worst thing also is that, as a victim, I was made by the Nazis to do things which I would never in my life have done as a normal human being. Acts which, even if I say that in my heart I feel innocent, were objectively – purely objectively – pretty terrible things to have done. And it is not easy to go through life with this load on my back.

I believe that, even if we do not admit it aloud, something of those Holocaust years has remained deeply imprinted on our souls. My wife sometimes tells me that I am always under control. I control myself; everything is controlled. And she says to me: 'Roman, the KZ is over, it's in the past.' But it is because in the camp every step, every movement had to be under control, self-control. Because any wrong movement, any wrong step, could end in death.

I was robbed of my life. I am living the life of someone else – a person whose character was forged in a totally different situation. If it had not been for the Holocaust, I would be a completely different man today. I do not know exactly what it is I have lost, but my soul has been gravely wounded. And to wound a soul is no less a crime than to kill a body.

Roman Frister, Polish Jew,
survivor of Auschwitz

The deep traumas which the horror had left these people with were scarcely comprehensible to those who had not experienced it themselves, particularly as a superficial normality established itself in the DP camps with astonishing rapidity. Even before the war had ended Jewish newspapers were being published in some camps. In the Upper Palatinate football league, in 1945, clubs with names like 'Maccabi Marktredwitz' or 'Hakaoch Schwandorf' were playing again, bringing together prisoners who appeared to have made a pretty full recovery.

The survivors found to their dismay that the story of their martyrdom fell on deaf ears. 'Auschwitz, where's that then?' asked a neighbour in Hans Frankenthal's home village, when he truthfully answered the question as to where he had been during the war. Others were greeted on their return with a curt 'Oh, so you're back'. Hardly anyone really wanted to listen.

Quite a number of victims remained silent, often for decades. Not even their children knew what sufferings their father or mother had been through. Only today, at the end of their lives, do many find the courage to speak about their torments, to give a testimony for posterity. The road back to the past is a painful one, but a great number find in it the hope that they are doing something to ensure that what happened then is never repeated. To this day the survivors bear the scars of the Holocaust on their bodies and in their souls. Liberation has not been able to free them from Auschwitz.

In telling the story of their suffering, for many survivors it is not the moment of their liberation that moves them to tears. It is the point when they returned home, the day when – just like the citizens of Weimar – they had to come to terms with what had happened. But unlike most Weimarers, their lives would never again be as they once had been. 'In the autumn of 1945 my sister and I were sent home from a Catholic orphanage', Eva Mozes remembers. 'After getting out of the train at Porz, we walked through the streets of our home town. When I saw my parents' house, I knew that they hadn't come back. They would never have let the grass grow so high in the front garden. As we opened the door, we were greeted by my mother's red dachshund, Lili, wagging her tail. I remember wondering why Jewish dogs hadn't been deported as well. I went from room to room, looking for anything that would remind me of the former occupants. The only thing I found was a crumpled family photograph, which someone had carelessly thrown on the floor. It was then I suddenly realised that no-one from the Mozes family had survived. There was no-one left. No Father, no Mother, Edith was dead, Aliz was dead. We were completely alone.'

SELECT BIBLIOGRAPHY

Bauer, Yehuda and Keren, Nili, *History of the Holocaust*, New York, 1982

Berenbaum, Michael, *The World Must Know, The story of the Holocaust as told in the United States Holocaust Memorial Museum*, Washington DC, 1993

Braha, Randolph L., *The Politics of Genocide: The Holocaust in Hungary*, New York, 1994

Browning, Christopher, *The Path to Genocide*, Cambridge University Press, 1995

Fleming, Gerald, *Hitler and the Final Solution*, University of California Press, 1992

Frank, Anne, *The Diary of Anne Frank*, Puffin Books, 1997

Frister, Roman, *The Cap, or the Price of Life*, London, Weidenfeld, 1999

Gilbert, Martin, *Auschwitz and the Allies*, Michael Joseph, 1981

Goldhagen, Daniel J., *Hitler's Willing Executioners*, Little, Brown, 1996

Johnson, Frank, *The Nazi Terror*, London, John Murray, 1999

Kershaw, Ian, *Hitler* Vol. I 1889–1936, Vol. II 1937–1945, London, 1998, 2000

Klemperer, Victor, *Diaries, 1933–1945*, Berlin, 1995. Weidenfeld, 1998–2000

Lebor, Adam and Boyes, Roger, *Surviving Hitler – Choices, Corruption and Compromise in the Third Reich*, Simon & Schuster, New York and London, 2000

Levi, Primo, *Is This a Man?* Abacus, 1987

Mommsen, Hans, *Alternatives to Hitler*, London, I.B. Tauris, forthcoming, 2002

Pick, Hella, *Simon Wiesenthal: A Biography*, Weidenfeld, 1996

Reich-Ranicki, Marcel, *The Author of Himself*, London, Weidenfeld, 2001

Sierakowiak, David, *The Diary of David Sierakowiak*, London, Bloomsbury, 1996

Spielberg, Steven and Survivors of the Shoal Visual History Foundation, *The Last Days (or the Final Days)* Pub'd in German in Cologne 1999

Vrba, Rudolf, *When Canada was in Auschwitz. My escape from the extermination camp*, Munich, 1999

INDEX

References in **bold**, prefixed by the letter 'p' refer to numbered photographs
eg. Kaunas **p5**